Taking Sides: Clashing Views in Adolescence, 4/e

Scott Brandhorst

http://create.mheducation.com

ISBN-10: 1259176622   ISBN-13: 9781259176623

2-LKV-20

Contents

Detailed Table of Contents

Unit 1: Adolescent Health

David R. Camenisch and Robert J. Hilt provide information related to the treatment and side effects associated with SSRIs in the treatment of depression and anxiety. They discuss the importance of monitoring and describe how to manage the reported SSRI risk for suicidality in adolescents. Regina Taurines, Manfred Gerlach, Andreas Warnke, Johannes Thome, and Christoph Wewetzer provide a general framework, therapeutic strategies, and the issues of antidepressant pharmacotherapy for the treatment of depression in childhood and adolescence.

Cynthia Dailard, a senior public policy associate at the Guttmacher Institute, argues that making universal vaccination against HPV mandatory for school attendance is a necessary step in preventing cervical cancer and other HPV related problems. Rebuttals to the issues of the high cost as well as the suitability for the vaccination in schools are presented, and she marks universal vaccination as a key step in future vaccination policy reform. Gail Javitt, Deena Berkowitz, and Lawrence O. Gostin argue that while the risks of contracting HPV are high, and its demonstrated link to cervical cancer has proven strong, it is both unwarranted and unwise to force mandatory vaccination on minor females. They discuss the potential adverse health effects, both long- and short-term risks, the lack of support for the HPV vaccine within the justifications for state-mandated vaccination, the consequences of a vaccination targeted solely at females, as well as the economic impact that would result from making the HPV vaccination mandatory.

Jo Cavallo in his conversation with Chris Feudtner discusses the importance of including adolescents and young adults in advance care planning and potential ethical dilemmas posed by these conversations. Dr. Feudtner argues that taking part in this helps them gain some sense of independence and control and provides them with a chance to write their legacy and feel less alone or isolated. Lainie Friedman Ross debates different scenarios that are possible in treating adolescents with life-threatening illnesses and states that courts and state legislatures are mistaken in their polices to respect family refusals of treatments aimed at treating these illnesses. Dr. Ross concludes that mature minor laws that permit refusals of effective life-saving treatments by adolescents alone or in conjunction with their parents are morally unjustified.

Cynthia I. Joiner, MPH, RN and nurse research manager at the University of Alabama, views having body mass index (BMI) report cards in the schools as an extension of what schools are already managing to highlight the important role they play in helping to address childhood obesity. Betsy Di Benedetto Gulledge, an instructor of nursing at Jacksonville State University, highlights what she sees as the disadvantages of having body mass index (BMI) report cards in the schools; she challenges the accuracy of BMI measures and notes the risks of labeling on children's psychological well-being.

Unit 2: Sex, Sexuality, and Gender

Issue: Is There Cause for Concern About an "Oral-Sex Crisis" for Teens?
YES: Sharlene Azam, from *Oral Sex Is the New Goodnight Kiss: The Sexual Bullying of Teenage Girls* (2008)
NO: SIECCAN (The Sex Information and Education Council of Canada), from "Do You Think 'Oral Sex' Is 'Having Sex'? Does the Answer Matter?" *The Canadian Journal of Human Sexuality* (2011)

Journalist Sharlene Azam, in a book about teen prostitution, discusses the cavalier attitude toward oral sex that some girls report. As well, she discusses a famous Canadian case of oral sex with under-aged girls that had major press coverage. The Research Coordinator of the Sex Information and Education Council of Canada reviews the academic research regarding oral-sex practices and their associated meaning for youth. Their take-home message is that oral sex among teens is not at "epidemic" levels and that many youth feel that oral sex is an intimate sexual behavior.

Issue: Is "Coming Out" As a Sexual Minority Earlier in Adolescence Detrimental to Psychological Well-Being?
YES: Justin Jager and Pamela E. Davis-Kean, from "Same-Sex Sexuality and Adolescent Psychological Well-Being: The Influence of Sexual Orientation, Early Reports of Same-Sex Attraction, and Gender," *Self and Identity* (2011)
NO: Margaret Rosario, Eric Schrimshaw, and Joyce R. Hunter, from "Different Patterns of Sexual Identity Development over Time: Implications for the Psychological Adjustment of Lesbian, Gay, and Bisexual Youths," *Journal of Sex Research* (2010)

Using the ADD Health longitudinal dataset, researchers Justin Jager and Pamela E. Davis-Kean investigated the association of early same-sex attraction on mental health outcomes of depressive affect and self-esteem. Those who had early (12–15 years) same-sex attractions and whose attraction remained stable throughout adolescence had the most negative psychological well-being. However, this group of adolescents gained or "recovered" the most, in terms of psychological well-being, over time. In a longitudinal study, Professor Margaret Rosario and colleagues found that early versus later acknowledgment of one's minority sexual orientation was not related to psychological distress; thus, sexual-minority identity formation was unrelated to psychological distress. Rather, identity integration—how well one accepts and integrates that sexual-minority status into one's life—was predictive of psychological well-being. Those who had a well- integrated sexual-minority identity had the most favorable measure of psychological well-being, while those with lower sexual-minority identity integration had the poorest measures of psychological well-being.

Issue: Does a Strong and Costly Sexual Double Standard Still Exist Among Adolescents?
YES: Derek A. Kreager and Jeremy Staff, from "The Sexual Double Standard and Adolescent Peer Acceptance," *Social Psychology Quarterly* (2009)
NO: Heidi Lyons, et al., from "Identity, Peer Relationships, and Adolescent Girls' Sexual Behavior: An Exploration of the Contemporary Double Standard," *Journal of Sex Research* (2011)

Derek A. Kreager and Jeremy Staff, both associate professors of sociology and crime, law, and justice at Pennsylvania State University, used data from the National Longitudinal Study of Adolescent Health to examine the existence of a contemporary double standard among adolescents. They found significant differences in peer acceptance among sexually experienced males and females, with higher numbers of sexual partners associated with significantly greater peer acceptance for boys than for girls. Heidi Lyons, assistant professor of sociology and anthropology at Oakland University, and her colleagues, Peggy C. Giordano, Wendy D. Manning, and Monica A. Longmore, all of Bowling Green State University's Department of Sociology, examined the sexual double standard in a longitudinal, mixed-method study of adolescent girls' popularity and lifetime number of sexual partners. The results paint a nuanced picture of the contemporary sexual double standard. Number of sexual partners was not associated with negative peer regard, and whereas young women acknowledged the existence of a sexual double standard, violating it did not seem to be associated with significant social costs. In fact, these authors highlight the buffering role of friendships against possible negative outcomes.

Issue: Do Reality TV Shows Portray Responsible Messages about Teen Pregnancy?
YES: Amy Kramer, from "The REAL Real World: How MTV's '*16 and Pregnant*' and '*Teen Mom*' Motivate Young People to Prevent Teen Pregnancy," an original essay for this edition (2011)
NO: Mary Jo Podgurski, from "Till Human Voices Wake Us: The High Personal Cost of Reality Teen Pregnancy Shows," an original essay for this edition (2011)

Amy Kramer argues that reality television shows engage teens in considering the consequences of pregnancy before they are ready for it and motivate them to want to prevent it. She discusses some of the other possible influences on the decline of the teen pregnancy rate (e.g., affordable contraception), but also supports her ideas with research that shows a decline in teen pregnancy rates as a result of these shows (e.g., Kearney & Levine, 2014). Mary Jo Podgurski, founder of the Academy for Adolescent Health, Inc., argues that although such television shows have potential benefits, they inadequately address the issue and may even have a negative impact on those who participate in them.

Issue: Is the Pressure to Have a Muscular Physique Recognized Equally Between Male and Female Adolescents?
YES: Marla E. Eisenberg, Melanie Wall, and Dianne Neumark-Sztainer, from "Muscle-enhancing Behaviors Among Adolescent Girls and Boys," *Pediatrics* (2012)
NO: Larry D. Burlew and W. Matthew Shurts, from "Men and Body Image: Current Issues and Counseling Implications," *Journal of Counseling & Development* (2013)

Marla E. Eisenberg, Melanie Wall, and Dianne Neumark-Sztainer looked at how the emphasis of muscularity has increased in recent decades and found muscle-enhancing behaviors were common for both boys and girls. In addition, the rates of engaging in muscle-enhancing behavior were higher than reported previously. The study also suggested that muscularity is an important component of body satisfaction for both genders. Larry D. Burlew and W. Matthew Shurts examined male adolescents and their body image dissatisfaction. More importantly, they looked at how this dissatisfaction is portrayed, and oftentimes missed by the experts in the field. The study examined reasons this occurs and discusses some interventions strategies.

Unit 3: Peer and Family Relationships

Issue: Does Having Same-Sex Parents Negatively Impact Children?
YES: Michelle Cretella, from "Homosexual Parenting: Is It Time For Change?" *American College of Pediatricians* (2012)
NO: Simon R. Crouch et al., from "Parent-Reported Measures of Child Health and Wellbeing in Same-Sex Parent Families: A Cross-Sectional Survey," *BMC Public Health*, (2014)

Michelle Cretella, a physician writing a position statement for The American College of Pediatricians, argues that having biological, heterosexual parents is the best situation for the development of children. She criticizes the same-sex parenting outcome literature as being fraught with design flaws and she argues that homosexual lifestyles pose dangers to children. Dr. Crouch and colleagues examined the physical, mental, and social well-being of children with same-sex attracted parents. They conducted a cross-sectional survey that included 315 parents and 500 children, which included both female and male index parents. The researchers found children with same-sex attracted parents are faring well on most measures of child health and well-being, and demonstrate higher levels of family cohesion than population samples. However, the researchers found a negative impact on the child's development due to the "stigma" associated with being raised by a same-sex attracted parent. So any negative impact is not a result of the sexual orientation of the parent, but due to the social stigma associated with the parent's sexual orientation.

Issue: Does Dating in Early Adolescence Impede Developmental Adjustments?
YES: Diann M. Ackard, Marla E. Eisenberg, and Dianne Neumark-Sztainer, from "Associations Between Dating Violence and High-Risk Sexual Behaviors Among Male and Female Older Adolescents," *Journal of Child & Adolescent Trauma* (2012)
NO: K. Paige Harden and Jane Mendle, from "Adolescent Sexual Activity and the Development of Delinquent Behavior: The Role of Relationship Context," *Journal of Youth and Adolescence* (2011)

Diann M. Ackard, Marla E. Eisenberg, and Dianne Neumark-Sztainer examine dating relationships among adolescent males and females and the possible correlations between dating violence and high-risk sexual behaviors. The researchers note a strong positive correlation between dating violence and high-risk sexual behaviors. They discuss the potential impact on development and health of the adolescent and the need to provide resources and opportunities to talk to adolescents who are dating. K. Paige Harden and Jane Mendle, assistant professors of psychology at the University of Texas and the University of Oregon, respectively, examined the associations between adolescent dating, sexual activity, and delinquency, after controlling for genetic influences. They found evidence for genetic influences on sexual behavior and for a link between these genetic predispositions and an increased likelihood to engage in delinquent behavior. They argue that early dating and/or early sexual activity do not cause delinquent behavior; in fact, this study suggests that sex in romantic relationships is related to lower levels of delinquency in both adolescence and later life.

Issue: Should Parents Supervise Alcohol Use by or Provide Alcohol to Adolescents?
YES: Mark A. Bellis, et al., from "Teenage Drinking, Alcohol Availability and Pricing: A Cross-Sectional Study of Risk and Protective Factors for Alcohol-Related Harms in School Children," *BMC Public Health* (2009)
NO: Barbara J. McMorris, et al., from "Influence of Family Factors and Supervised Alcohol Use on Adolescent Alcohol Use and Harms: Similarities between Youth in Different Alcohol Policy Contexts," *Journal of Studies on Alcohol and Drugs* (2011)

Mark A. Bellis, a professor at Liverpool John Moores University in the UK, and colleagues suggest that potential harms to youth can be reduced by having them drink in the safety of their own home where they can be supervised by their parents. Barbara J. McMorris, a senior research associate in the Healthy Youth Development Prevention Research Center within the medical school at the University of Minnesota, and colleagues argue that early alcohol use coupled with adult supervision of alcohol consumption leads to increased alcohol-related problems.

Issue: Should Parental Consent Be Required for Adolescents Seeking Abortion?
YES: Teresa Stanton Collett, from Testimony Before the United States House of Representatives Committee on the Judiciary, Subcommittee on the Constitution. H.R. 2299 the "Child Interstate Abortion Notification Act," (2012)
NO: Advocates for Youth, "Abortion and Parental Involvement Laws: A Threat to Young Women's Health and Safety," *Policy Brief: Abortion and Parental Involvement Laws*

Teresa Stanton Collett, law professor at the University of St. Thomas School of Law in Minnesota, testified about the "Child Interstate Abortion Notification Act" before a U.S. House of Representatives subcommittee that minors would benefit greatly from parental involvement in youth abortion decisions. She argues a federal law is needed to protect girls from exploitation and improve medical care. *Advocates for Youth* reviews the differences between parental consent and parental notification and provides data in relation to what different states require in relation to these concepts. The authors put forth the position that parental involvement laws do more harm than good in relation to the well-being of adolescent females.

Unit 4: Technology, Mass Media, and Criminal Justice

Issue: Does Playing Violent Video Games Harm Adolescents?
YES: Benedict Carey, from "Shooting in the Dark," *The New York Times* (2013)
NO: Christopher J. Ferguson and Cheryl K. Olson, from "Video Game Violence Use Among "Vulnerable" Populations: The Impact of Violent Games on Delinquency and Bullying Among Children with Clinically Elevated Depression or Attention Deficit Symptoms," *Journal of Youth and Adolescence* (2014)

Benedict Carey provides an article examining the relationship between violent video games and violent behavior. In reviewing the relevant research, he states that there is evidence of short-term increases in hostile urges and mildly aggressive behavior. However, upon reviewing the long-term effects, the results are more mixed, and he notes that it is hard to control for all possible variables within the studies that examine this relationship. Some research looks at the socialization effect video games have on adolescents over the long-term, leading to imitation of behaviors seen within the video games and questions the kinds of values and social skills the child is learning. Christopher J. Ferguson and Cheryl K. Olson examine the impact of violent video games on children with clinically elevated depression or attention deficit symptoms. They state that there is a need to examine the impact of video games on vulnerable populations. The researchers found no evidence for increased bullying or delinquent behaviors among youth with clinically elevated mental health symptoms who also played violent video games.

Issue: Should Juvenile Offenders Be Tried and Convicted as Adults?
YES: Charles D. Stimson and Andrew M. Grossman, from "Adult Time for Adult Crime. Life Without Parole for Juvenile Killers and Violent Teens," *The Heritage Foundation* (2009)
NO: Laurence Steinberg, from "Adolescent Development and Juvenile Justice," *Annual Review of Clinical Psychology* (2009)

Charles D. Stimson, senior legal fellow and Andrew M. Grossman, past senior legal policy analyst, Center for Legal and Justice Studies, The Heritage Foundation, argue that for serious offenses, trying juveniles in adult court and imposing adult sentences—such as life without parole—is effective and appropriate because youth who commit adult crimes should be treated as adults. Laurence Steinberg, Distinguished University Professor, Department of Psychology at Temple University, argues that adolescents often lack the cognitive, social, and emotional maturity to make mature judgments and therefore should not be sanctioned in the same way as adults. He supports a separate juvenile justice system where adolescents should be judged, tried, and sanctioned in ways that do not adversely affect development.

Preface

Adolescence is a critical developmental period in everyone's life. In order for us to become adults, we have to "survive" adolescence. For some, this stage of life is characterized by "storm-and-stress," while others glide through the transition unscathed. Most of us have some fond memories of pleasant and exciting experiences coupled with recollections of embarrassing and awkward experiences. Some events that occur during adolescence are universal—such as puberty, physical growth, and psychological maturation—whereas other phenomena are a function of environmental forces—such as cultural context, family structure, school organization, and peer group practices.

How do these different forces and context influence the development of adolescents in western society today? The purpose of this book is to examine some of the issues that may have any impact on adolescents in a didactic, dialectic fashion. To this end, *Taking Sides: Clashing Views in Adolescence* has been developed to foster critical and incisive thinking about issues that may have a significant impact on adolescent development in the twenty-first century. I have included interdisciplinary writings (e.g., from psychology, sociology, medicine, law, and religious studies domains) representing issues relevant to the period of adolescence in developed "western" societies (e.g., Australia, Canada, and the United States). *Taking Sides: Clashing Views in Adolescence* presents YES/NO perspectives in response to 15 questions. Consequently, 30 lively selections written by opponents who sit on different sides of the various topics under consideration are included. Each issue involves:

- A *question* that attempts to capture the essence of the debate.
- An *introduction* whereby information is presented that can be used by the reader as a background to the issue. Also available is some information about the selection authors of the debate as this may help to explain the perspective from which the writer comes.
- Two *selections* where one supports the yes side of the controversy while the other speaks to the no side of the question.
- An *Exploring the Issue* section that presents additional information, which may help to elucidate the issue further, raises additional and thought-provoking questions, and synthesizes the two author's perspectives.

It is important to note that no issue is truly binary. There are always "gray" areas that fall in between the YES and NO perspectives. The *Recommended Readings* section provides more references for the interested individual; some readers will wish to delve into particular topics in greater detail. This section was included to give some additional direction for that purpose. At the end of the book, the *Contributors to This Volume* provides information about each selection author. A person's training, career track, and life situation colors her/his perspective on any issue; no one is completely objective. Also, the *Internet References* present some useful website addresses (URLs) that are relevant to the issues directed in each part. As you read the different perspectives, you may find that you disagree with one side or both viewpoints. Regardless, it is important to read each selection carefully and critically and respect the opinions of others. The format of this textbook necessarily challenges the reader to face his or her own biases, beliefs, and values about the controversial topics presented. Two of the most important tools that a student can develop in his or her scholarly pursuits are (1) to be able to keep an open mind such that you may consider dissenting views while respecting the opinions of those who disagree with your perspective and (2) to become a critical thinker and evaluate arguments from many different angles and viewpoints. I encourage you to challenge your own perspective so that you can develop these crucial skills.

Editor of This Volume

SCOTT BRANDHORST is an Instructor in the Psychology Department at Southeast Missouri State University. He received his PsyD in Clinical Psychology from the Forest Institute of Professional Psychology and MA in Counseling from Webster University. He teaches courses in abnormal psychology, introduction to clinical psychology, psychotherapy, and adolescent development. He has over 18 years of clinical expertise, with the last 11 years as a licensed clinical psychologist. He currently maintains a successful private practice and focuses mainly in the areas of adolescent issues, clinical assessments, and disability issues. His research has focused on sexual experiences within college students and environmental sustainability. He helps facilitate student research and serves as the co-chair of the annual Student Research Conference at Southeast Missouri State University. He is active in the Society of the Teaching of Psychology (APA Division 2) and serves as a reviewer for various publications and journals within the field of psychology. His writings have appeared within journals such as *North American Journal of Psychology* and *Psi Chi Journal of Psychological Research*.

Acknowledgments

I would like to thank my family, friends, and colleagues whose help and support helped make this project possible. I would especially like to thank my wife, Gretchen, for all of her patience, encouragement, support, guidance, and love that allowed me to complete this work. Without her, I would have never been able to finish this project.

I would like to thank Mary Foust at McGraw-Hill for her professional guidance and support, which has been valuable in the completion of this project.

Academic Advisory Board Members

Members of the Academic Advisory Board are instrumental in the final selection of articles for each edition of TAKING SIDES. Their review of articles for content, level, and appropriateness provides critical direction to the editor and staff. We think that you will find their careful consideration well reflected in this volume.

Leilani M. Brown
University of Hawaii, Manoa

Maria Carla Chiarella
University of North Carolina, Charlotte

Joan E. Dolamore
Wentworth Institute of Technology

Deborah Ellermeyer
Clarion University of Pennsylvania

William M. Gray
University of Toledo

Aleesha Grier
Yale University School of Medicine

Jennifer Holleran
Community College of Allegheny County

Jeffrey Kaplan
University of Central Florida

James Kuterbach
Pennsylvania State University

Terry M. Salem
Lake Land College

Claudia Whitley
Stephen F Austin State University

Introduction

Adolescence is a period of development marked by a transition spanning the second decade of life. Developmentally, adolescence begins at approximately age 10 and lasts into the early twenties, although from 18 or 19 onwards, the period is referred to as "emerging adulthood" (Arnett, 2013). Adolescence is a period of time when individuals leave the security of childhood to meet the demands of the adult world. They pull away from the structure of family in search of independence. This involves finding an identity, making commitments, and carving out a responsible place in society. Although the transition is very individualistic (i.e., occurring in different ways and at different rates), it involves dealing with different sets of developmental challenges or tasks. The challenges involve the biological, psychological, and social changes occurring during this crucial period of development. The biological changes are the most visible with puberty and hormones driving changes in body appearance. Adolescents must learn to cope and accept these changes. The psychological changes involve advance in cognitions and enhanced emotional development leading to stronger decision-making, mature judgment, better planning, and advanced perspective taking. The task here is to cope with these new characteristics and to use them to adapt to the transition and find a place in the world. The last challenge is to find a responsible role in society and commit to a revised sense of self. The social changes (i.e., relationships, newfound independence) taking place during this time permit the adolescent to explore different roles. Taken together, the challenges and changes result in children becoming adults.

History of Adolescence

Historically, the period between childhood and adulthood has always been recognized as distinct; however, it was not researched or given a specific name until the twentieth century. In Ancient Greek times, Plato, Socrates, and Aristotle had specific views of adolescence. Plato, for example, recognizing the advances in thinking and judgment during the second decade of life, believed that formal education should only start at this time. Socrates, also aware of the advances in cognitions, believed the stronger thinking skills allowed youth to become better at arguing. In addition he recognized the down side to this developmental advancement, stating youth were inclined to contradict their parents and tyrannize their teachers. Aristotle believed the most important aspect of this period of development was the ability to choose. He believed that human beings became capable of making rational choices and good decisions during the second decade. Aristotle also recognized that, although youth exhibited gains in thinking, they were still immature and different from adults. His strong opinion and knowledge about youth is clearly stated in the following passage:

The young are in character prone to desire and read to carry any desire they may have formed into action. Of bodily desires it is the sexual to which they are most disposed to give away, and in regard to sexual desire they exercise no self-restraint. They are changeful, too, and fickle in their desires, which are as transitory as they are vehement; for their wishes are keen without being permanent, like a sick man's fits of hunger and thirst. They are passionate, irascible, and apt to be carried away by their impulses. They are the slaves, too, of their passion, as their ambition prevents their ever brooking a slight and renders them indignant at the mere idea of enduring an injury. They are charitable rather than the reverse, as they have never ever yet been witness of many villainies; and they are trustful, as they have not yet been often deceived. They are sanguine, too, for the young are heated by nature as drunken men by wine, not to say that they have not yet experienced frequent failures. Their lives are lived principally in hope. They have high aspirations; for they have never yet been humiliated by the experience of life, but are unacquainted with the limiting force of circumstances. Youth is the age when people are most devoted to their friends, as they are then extremely fond of social intercourse. If the young commit a fault, it is always on the side of excess and exaggeration, for they carry everything too far, whether it is their love or hatred of anything else. (Aristotle, fourth century B.C.)

The early philosophical views such as those mentioned above went unchallenged for many centuries. However, by the late nineteenth century/early twentieth century, this changed and the age of adolescence was recognized. It was argued that children and youth were not miniature adults and, therefore, should not be treated in the same way as adults, especially with respect to labor and family responsibility. As a result, child labor laws were implemented, followed by mandatory schooling until age 16. These laws provided that children were being protected and not permitted to work; however, they could not be left unsupervised. With these changes in the early 1900s, the concept of adolescence became more defined. Adolescents were not children and were not yet adults, resulting in the recognition that they were unique in their development and, as such, deserved special attention.

At this time (i.e., circa 1900), G. Stanley Hall began studying adolescence in terms of their behaviors, their emotions, and their relationships. Hall, also known as the father of adolescent research, concluded children went through turmoil and upheaval during their second decade of life and as such were in a state of constant *storm-and-stress*, a term he coined from the German "*sturm und drang*" movement. Hall identified three key aspects of adolescent storm-and-stress: risky behaviors, mood disruptions, and conflict with parents. Hall argued that the physical changes occurring during this period of the lifespan (e.g., growth spurts, sexual maturation, and hormonal changes) resulted in psychological turbulence. He further argued the turmoil was both universal and biologically based. In other words, it was inevitable regardless of other factors. To disseminate these arguments, Hall published *Adolescence* (1904), the first text on adolescent development, making the study of adolescence both scientific and scholarly. Since the time of Hall's book, research on adolescence has attracted attention from many disciplines, including psychology, sociology, anthropology, and medicine.

Soon after Hall's view of adolescence, Margaret Mead published *Coming of Age in Samoa* (1928), which challenged Hall's view of universal adolescent storm-and-stress. After conducting observational research in Samoa (a distinctly different culture than western society), Mead explained how Samoan adolescents experienced a gradual and smooth transition to adulthood because of the meaningful connections made between their roles during adolescence and the roles they would perform as adults. She argued the transition through adolescence was not simply biological, but rather sociocultural, and the turmoil identified by Hall was environmentally and culturally specific and certainly not universal. Some cultures, she stated, provided a smooth, gradual transition that allowed adolescents to experience minimal, if any, storm-and-stress.

For many years, Mead was alone in arguing against Hall's view. Most social scientists based their research on what Richard Lerner and colleagues (2005) called Hall's deficit model of adolescence where developmental deficits caused turmoil resulting in problem behaviors such as alcohol and drug use, school failure, teen pregnancy, crime, and depression. Essentially, Hall's deficit model and view of storm-and-stress as universal was not disputed or challenged until the 1960s when it was realized that not all adolescents had a turbulent time during the transition from childhood to adulthood. Research in the 1960s began providing evidence to support Mead's perspective, arguing that many adolescents had good relationships and strong core values with few, if any, problem behaviors. Researchers, in supporting Mead, were not necessarily disputing Hall. They recognized that, while some adolescents did in fact experience an intense period of storm-and-stress, many had a smooth and uneventful transition. This led to the more recent view of a *modified storm-and-stress* period of development. From this perspective, conflict with parents, mood disruptions, and risky behaviors are on a continuum, dependent on many psychological, sociological, cultural, and environmental factors.

Theories of Adolescent Development

During the twentieth century, many theories have been proposed to explain human development. A simple overview of a few of the key theories is provided, with a particular emphasis on the period of adolescence.

Psychoanalytic theory states that development is unconscious and dependent on early experiences with parents. It is predicated on the premise that personality comprises three mostly unconscious psychological constructs: the Id, where raw desires, urges, and drives are housed (e.g., sexual desires, hunger, thirst); the ego, which "manages" the desires and tries to appease or satisfy the wants of the Id while working within the constraints of the real world (e.g., satisfying unacceptable sexual desires with fantasies or substituted behaviors); and the superego, which is the social conscience of the personality (e.g., where parental and societal values reside). Within the framework of psychoanalytic theory, these three hypothesized constructs must work in harmony in order for the person to be well adjusted and function effectively within society. The development of these structures arises out of different psychosexual states—which are a series of sexual obstacles the child must overcome in order to proceed to the next stage of development. Sigmund Freud (1938) and daughter Anna Freud (1958) argued that the balance previously achieved between the Id, the ego, and the superego is destroyed during adolescence because of the new pressures on the ego. As a result, the sexual drives brought on by puberty and hormonal changes affect an adolescent's sense of reality and subsequent behavior. From a psychoanalytic point of view, a positive sense of self, prosocial behavior, and overall healthy development can only occur if psychosexual development was not restricted in earlier years. Essentially, the sexual reawakening during adolescence (i.e., the genital stage) leads to healthy adult sexuality and overall well-being if children are not restricted during any of the previous psychosexual stages (i.e., oral, anal, phallic, and latency).

From a *cognitive perspective*, human development is a bidirectional process, explained in terms of an individual's action on the environment and the action of the environment on the individual. As a child matures, he or she becomes more active in his or her environment and more advanced cognitively. Jean Piaget (1972), a pioneer of cognitive developmental theory, proposed that children proceed through a sequence of distinct developmental stages: the sensorimotor stage (birth to age 2), the preoperational stage (ages 2–5), the concrete operational stage (age 6 to early adolescence), and the formal operational stage (early adolescence to adulthood). Piaget argued that, between the ages of 11 and 15, adolescents enter the formal operational stage. Abstract and hypothetical thinking emerges during this stage, and as a result, children attain the ability to see that reality (e.g., how others treat them) and their thoughts about reality (e.g., how others "should" treat them) are different. They gain the ability to generate and recognize hypotheses about reality. The ability to think abstractly also allows adolescents to project themselves into the future, distinguish present reality from possibility, and think about what might be. Once in the formal operational stage, Piaget also argued that adolescents gain competence in formal reasoning, which is marked by a transition from inductive reasoning (e.g., "Jane had unprotected sex and did not get pregnant, therefore if I have unprotected sex, I will not get pregnant") to deductive reasoning (e.g., "there are risks involved when having unprotected sex and because Jane did not get pregnant, does not mean that I will not get pregnant"). This transition means that adolescents are not only able to systemize their ideas and critically deal with their own thinking to construct theories, but they are also able to test their theories logically, and scientifically discover truth. They can devise many interpretations of an observed outcome (e.g., pregnancy may be the result of unprotected sex, failed contraception, or invitro fertilization), and they can anticipate many possibilities prior to an actual event (e.g., unprotected sex may lead to pregnancy, an STI, or HIV/AIDS).

Currently, there is debate as to whether Piaget was correct in saying that adolescents gain the competencies cited above by age 15. Neuroscientists argue that the adolescent brain may not be fully developed until late adolescence or early adulthood. Neuroimaging indicates that the prefrontal cortex, the "home of the executive functions," is the last part of the human brain to develop, not reaching full maturity until the early twenties or later. This would mean that, until the brain has reached maturity, adolescents would not be competent in planning, setting priorities, organizing thoughts, suppressing impulses, weighing out consequences, and formal reasoning. Without these competencies in place, adolescents may have a difficult time with decision-making. Neuroscientists, therefore, tend to attribute bad decisions to an underdeveloped brain.

Social cognitive theory (Bandura, 2005) is another approach to understanding adolescent development and behavior. From this perspective, adolescent development is understood in terms of how adolescents reason about themselves, others, and the social world around them. Theorists such as David Elkind (1967, 1978) describe adolescent reasoning and thinking in terms of the advances in metacognition. With the ability to "think about their own thinking" (metacognition), adolescents spend most of their time focused on themselves. They daydream more and, as they become preoccupied with their own thoughts, they come to believe that others are or should be as preoccupied with them as they are with themselves. As a result, they think everyone notices them. A typical example is the adolescent who cannot possibly go to school because of a facial blemish. To the distraught adolescent, everyone will notice and criticize them. David Elkind uses the term adolescent egocentrism to describe these changes in behavior and thought.

Moving toward a more social perspective is Erik Erikson's (1959) *psychosocial theory* of ego development, which encompasses the entire life span. He describes development from birth to old age as occurring in eight stages, with each stage characterized by a crisis, between two opposing forces (e.g., trust versus mistrust), which must be resolved successfully. According to Erikson, the resolution of a crisis is dependent on the successful resolution of all previous crises. For example, the adolescent crisis, of *identity formation* versus *role confusion*, can only be resolved if adolescents were successful in resolving the previous four crises of childhood (e.g., having a sense of trust versus mistrust, autonomy versus shame and doubt, initiative versus guilt, and industry versus inferiority). In addition, the resolution of the adolescent identity crisis will affect the resolution of future crises. Resolving the identity crisis means

showing commitment toward a role—personal, sexual, occupational, and ideological (i.e., a concept about human life that involves a set of beliefs and values). Once complete, the established identity is a distinctive combination of personality characteristics and social style by which the adolescent defines himself/herself and by which he or she is recognized by others.

The final theory presented is Urie Bronfenbrenner's *ecological systems theory* (1979), which examines the role of five different environments in an individual's development and well-being. Imagine the adolescent at the center of a large circle with each system radiating outward. The first system immediately surrounding the adolescent is the microsystem. This is the setting in which a person lives and includes one's family, peers, school, and neighborhood. The second system, called the mesosystem, consists of the relationships between the different microsystems. An example is the relationship between an adolescent's family and school.

According to Bronfenbrenner, the relationship between these two microsystems has a different effect on the individual than each microsystem separately. The third system is the exosystem, which comprises the linkages between different settings that indirectly involves the adolescent. An example is the relation between the home and a parent's workplace. Outside the exosystem is the macrosystem. This is essentially the cultural and social influence on an individual, such as belief systems, material resources, customs, and lifestyles, which are embedded in each of the previous inner systems. Finally, there is the chronosystem, which involves environmental events and transitions over time. For example, adolescents who were directly involved in a major trauma such as one of the recent school shootings or other mass shooting will have different life experiences affecting their development than adolescents who were not directly involved.

The theories presented above provide only an introduction to understanding human behavior and, in particular, adolescent behavior. Other theories exist and contribute to the interdisciplinary approach currently used to enhance our understanding of adolescence. For a more comprehensive discussion of these theories, refer to the suggested readings list at the end of this introduction.

Adolescence in the Twentieth Century

Adolescence in and of itself is a period of human development marked by many changes, transitions, and both positive and negative behaviors. Adolescents are the individuals going through this particular period of development.

Since the study of adolescence first began in the early twentieth century, researchers have examined how particular events and issues affected adolescent attitudes and behaviors. In this section, I provide an overview of how events shaped the way adolescents behaved, and how they dealt with particular issues. For example, in the 1920s, when the period of adolescence was officially recognized, North American youth responded with a sense of newfound freedom. They were essentially given permission to stay young and have fun while they could. The decade became known as the Roaring Twenties, with increased autonomy and freedom. An interesting effect was that many adults responded to the behaviors of the young by adopting a similar appealing lifestyle with more music, dancing, and partying. This was short-lived, however, with the Great Depression of the 1930s followed by World War II in the 1940s. Irresponsibility and the age of adolescence were put on hold during these difficult times. Many young people were forced to seek employment or to serve their country in the war. The exposure to poverty, family struggles, war, violence, and death resulted in a drive for stability and security following the war. The 1950s were a time when adults focused on ensuring this security and stability for their families. During this time, adolescents were considered to be the "silent generation" because life seemed perfect. They had only their futures upon which to focus. In North America society, gaining a college degree, finding a good job, getting married, and raising a family were the goals for the adolescents of the 1950s.

In the 1960s, there was once again disruption to stability and security with the Vietnam War and the assassinations of North American politicians and leaders. Many adolescents reacted with anger and frustration. They did not trust politicians or decision makers because they were seen as disrupting their perceived ideal world and sense of security. They held political protests to voice their views of idealism. They challenged authority and promoted peace, love, and freedom with drug use, loosening of sexual behavior, and cohabitation. This peace movement of the 1960s is remembered with phases such as "make love not war" and "reject authority." For most, there was no focus on working hard and establishing a stable career. Attending college was as much about fun and freedom from parents as it was about studying.

The sexual revolution of the 1960s lasted into the 1970s, with adolescents becoming more focused on their own needs and goals but not without further struggles. Adolescent girls and young women, aware of the opportunity differential and stereotyped careers for men and women, began the long and difficult fight for equality. The previous argument that women would be homemakers was no longer valid. When the contraceptive pill was introduced in the 1960s, women gained further control over their reproduction, which led to freedom to choose and/or engage in family planning. Gender inequality was no longer an issue of biology. The success of the Women's Movement in the 1970s and 1980s resulted in many more young women attending college—eventually bridging the gender gap in many professions such as medicine, law, and engineering. With more women attending to their careers, and postponing childbearing or deciding to be childless, two-income families became more popular. Small families, large homes, travel, and material possessions such as the "best" home computers became the goals. This way of life has had a profound effect on children born since 1980. For example, carry-over effect from the 1960s and 1970s is the notion that if you want

something badly enough, you can get it. Parents have become so involved in their children's lives, providing material possession upon material possession, that kids have come to expect it. Large screen televisions, personal computers, electronic devices, cell phones, and disposable income are common expectations among many of today's youth. The adolescents of the twenty-first century, known as Generation Z, are unique and different from adolescents of the past.

Adolescence in the Twenty-First Century

Today's adolescents have unique experiences and issues not encountered by previous generations. There are many factors contributing to this. For instance, the advances in technology have been influential in shaping the lives of adolescents today. Many carry a cell phone, a personal tablet, and have their own personal computer, enabling them to communicate with anyone—regardless of where they are. These devices also give them instant access to music, computer games, and information. Essentially, we have technology savvy adolescents who spend much of their time alone with inanimate objects

A second factor contributing to the uniqueness of today's adolescents is their perceived sense of entitlement. Parents have protected and provided so much for their children that, once they leave home for college or work, they come to expect the same. Having had to fight for rights in the 1960s and 1970s, parents have taught their children "if you want something, it's your right to have it." As a university educator, I have seen first-hand the effect this has had. For example, Generation Z students are often more persistent in their demands compared to previous cohorts of the 1980s, 1990s, and 2000s. A typical example is demanding an exam be rescheduled because of personal travel plans. Generation Z are also more likely to have their parents involved in their postsecondary education, making calls to professors and administrators requesting information or favors for their adolescent.

A third unique factor contributing to the novel experiences of the youth of the Generation Z age involves sexual freedom. That is, youth of today experience a more open sexual discourse because of significant social events including the Sexual Revolution and Women's Movement of the 1960s and 1970s, the Gay Rights Movement of the 1970s and 1980s, as well as the HIV/AIDS crisis of the 1980s and onward. Different forms of media have also played a large role in opening up knowledge and discussion about sexuality; for example, the Internet has made many sexually oriented websites accessible to youth despite efforts to provide filters. Some of these websites are informational, while others would be characterized as obscene or pornographic. Television, films, as well as magazines and books tend to involve more overt sexuality, as regulations regarding these media have been relaxed over recent decades. These changes have had an impact on social programs including more explicit and precise sexual health education in the school system—although this has involved considerable controversy. All of this cumulates in a more sexually savvy adolescent than perhaps was the case in previous generations.

The Generation Z cohort is probably more aware of pregnancy and STI prevention as well as issues surrounding sexual violence—more so than previous generations. According to a recent report published by the Centers for Disease Control and Prevention (Martinez & Abma, 2015), the teenage pregnancy rate has dropped 57% from its peak in 1991. Between 2011 and 2013 teen intercourse has decreased by 14% for females and 22% for male teenagers over the past 25 years. Also between 2011 and 2013, 79% of female teenagers and 84% of male teenagers used a contraceptive method at first sexual intercourse. All of these changes might be positive side-effects of the increased openness and more positive attitudes toward the sexuality of adolescents.

Not only have sexual behaviors of adolescents changed across the generations, but gender roles have also changed significantly. This involves the roles of girls and boys in relation to "feminine" and "masculine" traits. Gender rigidity has declined and greater tolerance for gender variation has increased, although early adolescence is known as a time when youth are less understanding of violations of gender rules. Regardless, this has made the youth of the twenty-first century more accepting of lesbian, gay, bisexual, and transgender people (Ponton & Judice, 2004). In sum, sexual behaviors, attitudes, and roles have changed dramatically for Generation Z and, while always an important aspect of adolescent development, these topics have become more central in adolescent research.

The introduction thus far has provided an overview of adolescence from when the term was first coined to the present. Through the twentieth century, adolescents were faced with many hurdles and issues that affected their development and overall transition from childhood to adulthood. The goal of this book is to present issues facing adolescents in the first and second decades of the twenty-first century. We address controversies such as adolescent use of antidepressants and sucidiality, end-of-life decision-making rights, and youth justice. We debate mandatory HPV vaccination, the impact of same-sex parenting on adolescents, as well as consent for abortions and parentally supervised alcohol use by teens. We also cover body image, gender roles, sexuality, dating in early adolescence, obesity, and the impact of reality TV on teenage pregnancy. Finally, we examine behaviors such as cyberbullying, oral sex, and playing violent video games.

These issues will shape the behaviors of tomorrow's adolescents and guide future research. As is evident from the issues listed above, this book presents adolescence as in interdisciplinary topic. I have selected issues that can be used in a variety of disciplines and courses. These issues are addressed and analyzed from multiple perspectives, not limited to psychological analysis. Articles were chosen from a variety of disciplines in order to capture not only the empirical debates around these issues, but also the social spin placed on adolescent concerns. The public discourse around adolescent issues is not necessarily informed by empirical evidence; however, it often holds more power than empiricism in shaping people's views and behaviors. It is in this spirit that the controversies in this book are examined.

References and Suggested Readings

Arnett, J. J. (2013). *Adolescence and Emerging Adulthood: A Cultural Approach* (5th ed.). Upper Saddle River, NJ: Prentice Hall.

Bandura, A. (2005). The evolution of social cognitive theory. In Ken G. Smith & Michael A. Hitt (Eds.), *Great Minds in Management: The Process of Theory Development* (pp. 9–35). New York: Oxford University Press.

Bronfenbrenner, U. (1979). *The Ecology of Human Development.* Cambridge, MA: Harvard University Press.

Elkind, D. (1967). Egocentrism in adolescence. *Child Development, 38,* 1025–1034.

Elkind, D. (1978). Understanding the young adolescent. *Adolescence, 13,* 127–134.

Erikson, E. (1959). Identity and the life cycle. *Psychological Issues, 1,* 1–171.

Freud, A. (1958). Adolescence. *Psychoanalytic Study of the Child, 13,* 255–278.

Freud, S. (1938). *An Outline of Psychoanalysis.* London: Hogarth Press.

Hall, G. S. (1904). *Adolescence.* New York: Appleton.

Lerner, R., Brown, J., & Kier, C. (2005). *Adolescence: Development, Diversity, Context, and Application.* Toronto: Prentice Hall.

Martinez, G. M. & Abma, J. C. (2015). Sexual activity, contraceptive use, and childbearing of teenagers aged 15-19 in the United States. NCHS data brief, no 209. Hyattsville, MD: National Center for Health Statistics.

Mead, M. (1928). *Coming of Age in Samoa.* New York: Morrow.

Piaget, J. (1972). Intellectual evolution from adolescence to adulthood. *Human Development, 15,* 1–12.

Ponton, L. E. & Judice, S. (2004). Typical adolescent sexual development. *Child & Adolescent Psychiatric Clinics of North America, 13*(3), 497–511.

Santrock, J. (2016). *Adolescence* (16th ed.). New York: McGraw-Hill.

Steinberg. L. (2017). *Adolescence* (11th ed.). New York: McGraw-Hill.

Unit 1

UNIT

Adolescent Health

*A*dolescent psychical and psychological health has important implications for future well-being. An adolescent who is both mentally and physically fit has a better chance to develop into a strong, productive, and happy adult. There are a multitude of adolescent health-related issues that could have an influence on the healthy development of a teen. In the following part, issues that relate to different aspects of adolescent health are examined.

Selected, Edited, and with Issue Framing Material by:
Scott R. Brandhorst, *Southeast Missouri State University*

ISSUE

Do Selective Serotonin Reuptake Inhibitors (SSRIs) Increase Adolescent Suicide Risk?

YES: David R. Camenisch and Robert J. Hilt, from "SSRIs for Anxiety and Depression in Children and Adolescents," *Pediatric Annals* (2013)

NO: Regina Taurines et al., from "Pharmacotherapy in Depressed Children and Adolescents," *World Journal of Biological Psychiatry* (2011)

Learning Outcomes

After reading this issue, you will be able to:

- Outline and describe the benefits for treating depression and anxiety with SSRIs.
- Outline and describe the risk associated with using SSRIs to treat adolescent depression and anxiety.
- Evaluate the research methodologies from the studies examining SSRI efficacy.
- Understand effective treatment options for adolescent depression and anxiety.

ISSUE SUMMARY

YES: David R. Camenisch and Robert J. Hilt provide information related to the treatment and side effects associated with SSRIs in the treatment of depression and anxiety. They discuss the importance of monitoring and describe how to manage the reported SSRI risk for suicidality in adolescents.

NO: Regina Taurines, Manfred Gerlach, Andreas Warnke, Johannes Thome, and Christoph Wewetzer provide a general framework, therapeutic strategies, and the issues of antidepressant pharmacotherapy for the treatment of depression in childhood and adolescence.

Researchers have estimated that about 5 percent of children and adolescents suffer from depression at any given point in time (American Academy of Child and Adolescent Psychiatry (AACAP), 2013). Depressive disorders are generally chronic among adolescent, with an average episode in a clinical setting lasting 8 months. Unfortunately, children and adolescents with clinical depression and anxiety often go untreated, putting them at risk for substance abuse, school failure, impaired relationships, and personality disorders. Depression is also a strong predictor of suicidal ideation, attempts, and completions; completions are the second leading cause of death in 10- to 24-year olds (Heron, 2016). Furthermore, depression during adolescence is a major risk for suicide and long-term psychosocial impairment in adulthood.

Given the serious nature of these disorders, along with the fact that the peak onset of depression is in adolescence, early recognition and effective treatment are crucial. Effective treatments for children and adolescents with depressive disorders most often include psychotherapy and antidepressant medications. Studies have indicated that a combination of both treatments is most effective, although studies have also found antidepressants alone to convey almost as much benefit as the combined treatment.

Antidepressants introduced since 1990, especially SSRIs, have become a preferred treatment option for children and adolescents with depression. SSRIs are also used to treat anxiety disorders and obsessive-compulsive disorder (OCD). Compared to their predecessors, the tricyclic antidepressants (TCAs), SSRIs such as fluoxetine (Prozac), sertraline (Zoloft), paroxetine (Paxil), and citalopram (Celexa) are better tolerated, have a lower frequency of cardiac events and sudden death, fewer anticholinergic effects (dry mouth, somnolence, and constipation), and superior efficacy (Hamrin & Scahill, 2005). SSRIs work by blocking the reuptake of serotonin (5HT), a neurotransmitter in the central nervous system involved in a range of physiological and behavioral functions including sleep, wakefulness, appetite, emotional response, and thought process. Although the etiology of depression and some anxiety disorders is unknown, serotonin is believed to play an important role: for example, depression may be associated with reduced serotoninergic function. Therefore, antidepressants such as SSRIs appear to be effective in treating the disorder. However, the safety of prescribing antidepressants to children and adolescents has been the subject of increasing concern. Specifically, these drugs may be associated with an increased risk of suicidal ideation and behavior (suicidality) in pediatric clients.

The controversy about the safety and efficacy of antidepressants, particularly SSRIs and newer antidepressants such as selective norepinephrine reuptake inhibitors (SNRIs), began in June 2003. At that time, the U.S. Food and Drug Administration (FDA) conducted an investigation of antidepressants, including citalopram, fluoxetine, fluvoxamine (Luvox), nefazodone (Serzone), sertraline, and paroxetine. The meta-analysis of 24 SSRI trials resulted in the FDA issuing a black-box warning describing an increased risk of worsening of depression and suicidality for all current and future antidepressants used in those under the age of 18. The FDA investigation resulted in only fluoxetine receiving approval for depression in children and adolescents. Of note, however, is that of all the data reviewed by the FDA, no completed suicides were reported in any of the randomized controlled trials (RCTs) of adolescents taking any of the above medications.

The controversial black-box warning describing the possible link between use of the antidepressants and suicide in adolescents has since led to an active debate regarding the appropriate treatment of depression and anxiety in younger clients. Just how safe and effective are SSRIs in children and adolescents? Do antidepressants, such as SSRIs, increase the risk of suicidal behavior? Ecological studies provide mixed evidence on the risks and benefits of SSRIs. Arguments against their use focus on the increased risk of suicidal behaviors, while those in favor argue that untreated adolescents are at greater risk for long-term psychiatric problems and suicide.

In the YES selection, Camenisch and Hilt argue that SSRIs have been found to be more clinically beneficial for children than TCAs and SNRIs, despite an increased risk of suicidal thoughts in adolescents treated with SSRIs. They believe that it is prudent to inform families that their child may experience irritability, agitation, or suicidal thinking after starting the medication and that it is important to monitor the clients on these medications, especially in the beginning of treatment.

In the NO selection, Taurines and colleagues argue that SSRIs show an acceptable risk-benefit relationship in the treatment of depression and that the combination of psychopharmacology and psychotherapy seems to minimize the emergence of suicidal ideation. They go on to state that SSRIs are generally safe, well tolerated, and have less of a chance of overdose when compared to the TSAs and SNRIs. They also advocate that all clients should be monitored for all potential side effects and effectiveness of treatment interventions.

YES ↵

David R. Camenisch and Robert J. Hilt

SSRIs for Anxiety and Depression in Children and Adolescents

Selective serotonin reuptake inhibitors are the most commonly prescribed medications for pediatric anxiety and depression. Despite widespread use, providers who primarily work with adults can vary widely in their knowledge base about use of this class of medication for children. This article therefore reviews the child-specific indications, side effects, and recommended monitoring parameters that prescribers should know when prescribing this class of medication to young people.

Selective serotonin reuptake inhibitors (SSRIs) are once-a-day medications that selectively inhibit the reuptake of serotonin from neuronal synapses in the brain. This selectivity distinguishes them from the older tricyclic antidepressants (TCAs) and certain newer antidepressants such as the serotonin-norepinephrine reuptake inhibitors (SNRIs), both of which are less selective and impact both the serotonin and norepinephrine systems. Although less selectivity may contribute to unique benefits in certain circumstances (eg, neuropathic pain, treatment-resistant obsessive-compulsive disorder),[1-3] this characteristic is also responsible for a higher side-effect burden that has limited the use of these other agents in children.

SSRIs are also generally preferred over TCAs and the SNRIs because they have generally been found to be more clinically beneficial for children. For instance, every published randomized controlled trial using TCAs to treat childhood depression found that they had no treatment benefits.[4-6] And despite SNRIs such as venlafaxine being shown to be a valid treatment option for adolescents who fail to respond to SSRI treatment, venlafaxine poses a higher risk of treatment- emergent suicidal ideation and more discomfort on discontinuation.[7-9] As a result, SSRIs are more widely used than other agents for pediatric depression and anxiety due to better overall tolerability, less severe adverse side effects, and greater treatment effectiveness.

Despite their fairly widespread use, there are relatively few US FDA-approved indications for SSRIs in children. Fluoxetine, fluvoxamine, and sertraline are approved for the treatment of pediatric obsessive-compulsive disorder (OCD), and fluoxetine and escitalopram are approved for the treatment of adolescent depression.

This limited number of specific FDA approvals means that SSRIs are commonly being used off-label, despite a significant amount of randomized controlled trial evidence that demonstrates benefits for children.

SSRI use should ideally not occur in isolation, but rather in conjunction with evidence-based psychotherapy such as cognitive-behavior therapy (CBT).[10,11] For instance, one study of different types of childhood anxiety found 55% of sertralineonly patients improved, whereas 81% of sertraline plus CBT patients improved.[12] In a different study of adolescent major depression, 61% of the fluoxetine-only group improved and 71% of the fluoxetine-plus-CBT group improved as well as having a lower incidence of suicidal thinking.[13] Using an SSRI medication along with CBT is therefore preferred because of greater overall clinical effectiveness and because a psychotherapist can help support treatment plans and monitoring.[12,13]

Anxiety Treatment

Common anxiety disorders in childhood include OCD, generalized anxiety, social anxiety, and panic disorder. They are a potentially very disabling group of problems, and collectively occur in approximately 20% of children under the age of 18 years. In addition to discomfort and suffering, anxiety disorders can significantly impact social success, emotional development, and academic performance. Family functioning can also be greatly impacted as anxiety takes a toll on caregivers and siblings. Increasing recognition of the early onset of anxiety disorders has driven the need to identify effective treatments in younger and younger populations.

A systematic review of pharmacotherapy for pediatric anxiety disorders in 2010 identified that the pediatric anxiety treatment response to SSRIs was significantly greater (58.1%) than with placebo (31.5%).[14] Relatively greater treatment effects were seen in studies of pediatric OCD, but benefits were demonstrated across the range of anxiety disorders. It should be noted that among randomized controlled trials, there have been a total of four fluoxetine studies, four sertraline studies, two paroxetine studies, and two fluvoxamine studies that demonstrated a treatment response over

Camenisch D, Hilt R. SSRIs for Anxiety and Depression in Children and Adolescents. *Pediatr Ann.* 2013; 42: e62-e66. Reprinted with permission from SLACK Incorporated.

placebo.[15] Because of this data, FDA approvals, and certain additional side-effect issues that exist for paroxetine and fluvoxamine, we recommend that fluoxetine and sertraline be considered as the first-line agents to try for childhood anxiety disorders.

Depression Treatment

Like the anxiety disorders, major depression is both disabling and commonly occurs in children. Point prevalence of depression is about 2% in prepubertal children and 8% in adolescents. During adolescence, approximately 20% of teenagers experience clinically significant depression, with girls being diagnosed twice as often as boys.[16] As with the anxiety disorders, depression causes discomfort and suffering and can impact social success, emotional development, and academic performance. Left untreated, episodes of moderate to severe childhood depression are likely to take 6 to 12 months to resolve on their own, and future relapse is more the rule than the exception.

The seminal nonindustry-sponsored research studies in pediatric depression demonstrate that there is a role for SSRIs in the treatment of adolescent depression, and that they are safe and generally well tolerated. For instance the Treatment for Adolescents with Depression Study (TADS)[13] demonstrated that 60% to 70% of teens with moderate to severe depression will respond to fluoxetine alone or fluoxetine plus CBT. The Treatment of Resistant Depression in Adolescents (TORDIA) study[7] demonstrated that 40% of depressed adolescents who did not respond to their initial SSRI trial will respond to a second SSRI, with or without receiving adjunctive CBT. Clinically, this means it is best to try at least two different SSRIs before trialing a non-SSRI or concluding that usual medication treatment is ineffective.

First-line options for pediatric depression treatment are fluoxetine and escitalopram, which are the only two that carry FDA approvals for pediatric depression. Other second-line SSRI options that have at least one randomized control trial demonstrating efficacy over placebo are citalopram, sertraline, and paroxetine. Most child psychiatric specialists prefer not to use paroxetine to treat depression due to the fact that only one of three controlled trials with children had a positive outcome. As a class, SSRIs have been reported to be roughly twice as effective for pediatric anxiety disorders as they are for pediatric major depression,[17] so although we commonly refer to the SSRIs as "antidepressants," in the case of children they might more accurately be thought of first as "anxiolytics" that also work for depression.

Selection of Correct SSRI

Although the SSRIs have similar side effect profiles overall, individual patients can vary greatly in their response to particular agents, both in terms of clinical benefits and tolerability. Unfortunately, there are limited data to guide decisions about which particular SSRI will be best for a particular patient. There are no head-to-head studies that compare response rates to different SSRIs, nor are there head-to-head side-effect comparisons. Response can sometimes be predicted based on the experience of a first-degree relative (a familial biological response) or influenced by patient/parent preference for a particular medication (influencing observed placebo effects), so it is reasonable to take into consideration family history of response to specific SSRIs and to some extent, patient/caregiver preference. Unless there are specific family reasons against it, the aggregate of research supports that fluoxetine or escitalopram/citalopram should be the first-line options for depression, and sertraline or fluoxetine should be the first-line option for anxiety.

Side Effects

Common SSRI side effects include headaches, mild gastrointestinal discomfort (nausea, diarrhea, constipation), and a change in level of alertness. Despite being fairly innocuous and typically transient, these common side effects can contribute to discontinuation, and discussing them beforehand as part of informed consent can reduce the likelihood of premature discontinuation. Nontransient behavioral activation or mood irritability occurs at a rate of around 5%. Although these are reversible with discontinuation, this occurrence might be related to the rare but potentially serious treatment-emergent suicidal ideation (discussed further below).[4,18] The intensity of behavioral activation can range from trouble falling asleep and feeling restless, to the less common disinhibition or full hypomanic symptoms (mood elevation, talkativeness, accelerated thinking, increased energy). The development of a full manic episode—"mood flipping"—is a rare but potentially serious side effect. Although the development of manic symptoms may indicate an underlying bipolar diathesis, most children who experience manic symptoms from an SSRI do not go on to develop bipolar disorder.[18]

Insomnia is common, and it can be addressed by giving medication in the morning or by adding melatonin at night. Temporary sexual dysfunction also occurs, but the frequency in adolescent populations is not clear. The potential for sexual side effects should be discussed but not overemphasized as it can pose a barrier to treatment. Increased bleeding and bruising is a very rare side effect in children, presumably related to altered platelet serotonin function. This is typically only clinically relevant in the context of an underlying clotting disorder (eg, hemophilia) or major surgery while receiving an SSRI.

All SSRIs with the exception of paroxetine are pregnancy risk category C (some animal studies show adverse effects; no controlled studies in humans). Paroxetine is risk category D (positive evidence of risk to human fetus; potential benefits may justify use during pregnancy), so alternatives should be used instead.[19] Mothers using SSRIs at the end of pregnancy may be at increased risk of bleeding during delivery, and their infants may experience transient irritability perinatally. Neonatal exposure to SSRIs has also been associated with prolonged hospitalizations, breathing difficulties, poor feeding, and pulmonary hypertension.[19] Although there was one report that maternal antidepressant use in the year before delivery is associated with autism spectrum disorder, epidemiologic data do not suggest this is a clear causal factor.[20] Despite these concerns, maternal depression itself negatively impacts developing neonates, so the use of SSRIs during pregnancy is often recommended for mothers failing to respond to nonpharmacological strategies.

Other rare but potentially serious SSRI side effects include hyponatremia, prolonged QT interval, and serotonin syndrome. Serotonin syndrome symptoms include agitation, ataxia, diarrhea, diaphoresis, hyperreflexia, mental status changes, tremor, and hyperthermia. It is usually only seen in the context of either very high SSRI doses or the concomitant use of other proserotonergic medications such as trazodone, tricyclic antidepressants, meperidine, St. Johns Wort, melatonin, and some atypical antipsychotics.[4]

SSRIs and Suicidality

There is a small but increased risk of suicidal thoughts in adolescents treated with SSRIs, as outlined in the 2004 FDA "black-box warning," so prescribing SSRIs needs to include a discussion of this as a possible side effect. The FDA's warning on suicidal ideation was based on a review of 24 short-term randomized controlled trials with SSRIs in children for any indication, which found there was a twofold (2% in placebo versus 4%) increased risk of suicidal thoughts or behaviors while taking an SSRI versus taking a placebo.[21] Since that time, subsequent research looking specifically at this issue has found different results. At the case series level, such as youth suicide autopsies, there is little signal of SSRI use triggering suicide (ie, a large series found only 1.6% of adolescent suicides had recent exposure to SSRIs).[22] At the broader population level, repeated analyses of data from Western countries show that more use of SSRIs is associated with fewer completed youth suicides.[23,24]

Despite this discrepancy, it is prudent to inform all families prior to initiating use of an SSRI that their child may experience irritability, agitation, or suicidal thinking after starting the medication and to document that this discussion occurred. Typically when these problems appear, it is within the first month of initiation or following a dose increase. If new suicidal thoughts occur that are attributable to the SSRI, it is usually advised to stop administering the medication and reevaluate your treatment strategy.

Right after the black-box warning was issued, the FDA made a monitoring suggestion that children starting an SSRI should be seen weekly for the first 4 weeks, and then seen every other week over the next 4 weeks. This specific monitoring recommendation was later changed to the more generic recommendation that patients be "monitored appropriately and observed closely" during the initial

few months of treatment.[25] To most child psychiatric and/or pediatric specialists, "appropriate" monitoring of SSRI initiation means screening for the rapidly emergent side effects of concern like irritability, agitation, or suicidality 1 to 2 weeks after starting treatment in the office or over the phone, and then having another appointment 4 to 6 weeks after the SSRI was started.

SSRIs in Combination with Psychotherapy

As stated earlier, the added benefit of psychotherapy and medication is most clear for the treatment of anxiety disorders and for moderate to severe depression. In situations where suicidality is a concern, psychotherapy provides a very practical means of treatment monitoring and it may be the most effective intervention for reducing the risk of suicide. Despite professional consensus that combined treatment is generally preferable, it is not uncommon to encounter patient or caregiver resistance to using either medications or psychotherapy. Respecting this patient treatment preference in the initial treatment plan may increase the chance of a positive response (for instance, even placebo effects are "real" responses) and supports your therapeutic alliance.

The good news is that the literature does support medication-only and therapy-only approaches, depending on the circumstances. For adolescents and parents who want to use medication alone, the results of the Adolescent Depression Antidepressant and Psychotherapy Trial (ADAPT)[26] suggest that the addition of psychotherapy to medication sometimes does not substantially change outcomes. For those who want to use psychotherapy alone, TADS[13] demonstrated that CBT alone for mild depression produced similar outcomes as CBT plus medication. Even with the use of either medication or psychotherapy alone to treat depression or anxiety, it is generally recommended that if no improvement is seen after 8 to 12 weeks of an evidence-supported therapy, there should be a reconsideration of using combined treatment. However, for more severely depressed adolescents, the evidence does not support using CBT as monotherapy treatment.[27]

Treatment Response

Periodically monitoring response to treatment for depression or anxiety is a good idea regardless of the treatment approach. Both anxiety and depression can be chronic conditions, and as such benefit from surveillance and support. With medication starts, a check-in should ideally occur in 1 to 2 weeks to screen for side effects, and from there re-screening for side effects, assessing response, and considering dose increases should occur at roughly 4-week intervals (as it takes 4 to 6 weeks to see a treatment response from a given SSRI dosage). Given some evidence that more rapid titration leads to quicker response in some patients, patients with severe symptoms may benefit from more rapid initial titration to reduce the chance that a child will have a long duration of inadequately treated symptoms.[28]

Prior to starting an SSRI, the child's weight should be checked for the purpose of tracking any weight loss or gain associated with the medication or the depression. It is also important to establish if there is any current or past suicidal thinking or behavior. This can help reduce the chance that you, the parents, or your patient will unnecessarily implicate medication as the cause of subsequently reported suicidal thoughts. At follow-up appointments, patients should be weighed, asked about new onset of easy bruising (until bruising is demonstrated not to be a concern), asked about any emergence of suicidal thoughts, irritabliity, sleep problems, or high energy-like manic symptoms.[11,15]

In the ongoing assessment of clinical response, it is helpful to follow the same primary symptoms (ie, mood, concentration, panic episodes, obsessive worry) or markers of functioning (socializing with friends, participation in school and sports) at each visit. Because it is common that caregivers will observe positive benefits well before patients, be sure to get this information from both parents and child. It may be particularly helpful in assessing response to treatment to quantify symptom responses through repeated administration of a disorder-specific rating scale such as the Patient Health Questionnaire-9 (PHQ-9) for adolescent depression or the Self-Report for Childhood Anxiety-Related Emotional Disorders (SCARED) for anxiety.

Conclusion

It is important to identify and to treat both anxiety and depression early in children. Although initial treatment may or may not include medication, early treatment does minimize morbidity and can prevent progression to more serious and persistent dysfunction. If either anxiety or depression progresses to the point that medications are considered, co-treatment with psychotherapy is recommended both for the purposes of maximizing response to treatment and increasing monitoring. Although other SSRIs may be equally effective, the research evidence base and FDA approvals support that fluoxetine, escitalopram/citalopram, and sertraline are first-line choices that should serve most pediatric anxiety and depression patients very well, and as such should be the agents to become familiar with using in children.

References

1. Flament MF, Rapoport JL, Berg CJ, et al. Clomipramine treatment of childhood obsessive compulsive disorder: A double-blind controlled study. *Arch Gen Psychiatry.* 1985;42(10):977–983.

2. Leonard HL, Rapoport JL. Pharmacotherapy of childhood obsessive compulsive disorder. *Psychiatr Clin North Am.* 1989;12(4):963–970.

3. Leonard HL, Sevedo SE, Lenane MC, et al. A double-blind desipramine substitution during long-term clomipramine treatment in children and adolescents with obsessive compulsive disorder. *Arch Gen Psychiatry.* 1991;48(10):922–927.

4. Connor D, Meltzer BM. *Pediatric Psychopharmacology: Fast Facts.* New York, NY: WW Norton & Company, Inc.; 2006.

5. Cheung AH, Emslie GJ, Mayes TL. Review of the efficacy and safety of antidepressants in youth depression. *J Child Psychol Psychiatry.* 2005;46(97):735–754.

6. Hazell P, Connell D, Heathcote D, Henry D. Tricyclic drugs for depression in children and adolescents. Cochrane Depression, Anxiety and Neurosis Group. 2006. Available at: ccdan.cochrane.org/our-reviews. Accessed Feb. 20, 2013.

7. Brent D, Emslie G, Clarke G, et al. The treatment of adolescents with SSRI-resistant depression (TORDIA): A comparison of switch to venlafaxine or to another SSRI, with or without additional cognitive behavioral therapy. *JAMA.* 2008;299(8):901–913.

8. Hammad TA, Laughren T, Racoosin J. Suicidality in pediatric patients treated with antidepressant drugs. *Arch Gen Psychiatry.* 2006;63(3):332–339.

9. Hosenbocus S, Chahal R. SSRIs and SNRIs: A review of the discontinuation syndrome in children and adolescents. *J Can Acad Child Adolesc Psychiatry.* 2011;20(1):60–67.

10. Connolly SD, Bernstein GA. Work Group on Quality Issues. Practice parameter for the assessment and treatment of children and adolescents with Anxiety Disorders. *J Am Acad Child Adolesc Psychiatry.* 2007; 46(2):267–283.

11. Birmaher B, Brent D. AACAP Work Group on Quality Issues, et al. Practice parameter for the assessment and treatment of children and adolescents with depressive disorders. *J Am Acad Child Adolesc Psychiatry.* 2007;46(11):1503–1526.

12. Walkup JT, Albano AM, Piacentini J, et al. Cognitive behavioral therapy, sertraline, or a combination in childhood anxiety. *N Engl J Med.* 2008;359(26):2753–2766.

13. March J, Silva S, Petrycki S, et al. Fluoxetine, cognitive-behavioral therapy, and their combination for adolescents with depression: Treatment for Adolescents with Depression Study (TADS) randomized controlled trial. *JAMA.* 2004;292(7):807–820.

14. Ipser et al. Pharmacotherapy for Anxiety Disorders in Children and Adolescents. 2010. Available at: ccdan. cochrane.org/our-reviews. Accessed Feb. 20, 2013.

15. Ronsely R, Elbe D, Smith DH, Garland EJ. Do Hospital and Community SSRI Usage Patterns in Children and Adolescents Match the Evidence? *J Can Acad Child Adolesc Psychiatry*. 2010;19(3):218–226.

16. National Alliance on Mental Illness. Available at: www.nami.org. Accessed Feb. 20, 2013.

17. Bridge JA, Iyengar S, Salary CB, et al. Clinical response and risk for reported suicidal ideation and suicide attempts in pediatric antidepressant treatment: A meta-analysis of randomized controlled trials. *JAMA*. 2007;297(15):1683–1696.

18. Aronson JK, ed. *Meyler's Side Effects of Psychiatric Drugs*. Oxford: Elsevier; 2009.

19. Stahl S. *The Prescribers Guide: Stahl's Essential Psychopharmacology*. 3rd ed. Cambridge: Cambridge University Press; 2009.

20. Croen L, Grether JK, Yoshida CK, Odouli R, Hendrick V. Antidepressant use during pregnancy and childhood autism spectrum disorders. *Arch Gen Psychiatry*. 2011;68(11):1104–1112.

21. Hammad TA, Laughren T, Racoosin J. Suicidality in pediatric patients treated with antidepressant drugs. *Arch Gen Psychiatry*. 2006;63(3):332–339.

22. Isacsson G, Holmgren P, Ahlner J. Selective serotonin reuptake inhibitor antidepressants and the risk of suicide: a controlled forensic database study of 14,857 suicides. *Acta Psychiatr Scand*. 2005;111(4):286–290.

23. Gibbons RD, Brown CH, Hur K, et al. Early evidence on the effects of regulators' suicidality warnings on SSRI prescriptions and suicide in children and adolescents. *Am J Psychiatry*. 2007;164(9):1356–1363.

24. Olfson M, Shaffer D, Marcus SC, Greenberg T. Relationship between antidepressant medication treatment and suicide in adolescents. *Arch of Gen Psychiatry*. 2003;60(10):978–982.

25. Food and Drug Administration (FDA). Antidepressant Use in Children, Adolescents and Adults: Revisions to Product Labeling. 2007. Available at: www.fda.gov/Drugs/DrugSafety/InformationbyDrugClass/ucm096273.htm. Accessed Feb. 20, 2013.

26. Goodyer I, Dubicka B, Wilkinson P, et al. Selective serotonin reuptake inhibitors (SSRIs) and routine specialist care with and without cognitive behaviour therapy in adolescents with major depression: Randomised controlled trial. *BMJ*. 2007;335(7611):142.

27. Walkup JT. Treatment of depressed adolescents. *Am J Psychiatry*. 2010;167(7):734–737.

28. March JS, Silva S, Petrycki S, et al. The Treatment for Adolescents with Depression Study (TADS): Long-term effectiveness and safety outcomes. *Arch Gen Psychiatry*. 2007;64(10):1132–1143.

DAVID R. CAMENISCH, MD, MPH, is PAL Consultant and Autism Center Child Psychiatrist, at Seattle Children's Hospital. Robert J. Hilt, MD, FAAP, is Associate Professor of Psychiatry at the University of Washington and Seattle Children's Hospital.

Regina Taurines, et al.  **NO**

Pharmacotherapy in Depressed Children and Adolescents

Introduction

The chemically and pharmacologically heterogeneous class of anti-depressants are nowadays used not only in the treatment of depressive symptoms, but in diverse child psychiatric disorders, such as obsessive compulsive disorder (OCD), anxiety disorders, eating disorders, mutism, attention deficit/hyperactivity disorder (ADHD), enuresis and posttraumatic stress disorder (PTSD). In the following overview, however, our focus will be the use of antidepressants with the indication unipolar depression.

In adults, antidepressants exhibit a positive effect on the whole set of depressive symptoms, such as a low mood, irritability, reduction of energy, low self-esteem, feeling of hopelessness, psychomotor retardation, loss of interest and pleasure in normally enjoyable activities and social withdrawal. Antidepressive drugs improve somatic symptoms and loss of libido in the context of depression as well as agitation, low appetite and sleep disturbances. Major target symptoms are also suicidal ideations (Baldessarini 1989; Mulrow et al. 1998; Edwarts and Anderson 1999). In meta-analyses on the treatment of juvenile depression, however, limited efficacy of antidepressants in short-term randomised controlled trials was reported; especially in the age group of children (Schulte-Markwort et al. 2008; Tsapakis et al. 2008). Possible explanations for these observations might include developmental aspects of the brain and a higher response rates to placebo and other non-specific interventions in children compared to adolescents and adults (Tsapakis et al. 2008). Additionally, results have to be interpreted with causion as there are major study limits such as missing subgrouping into child- and adolescent- as well as gender-groups, inadaequate dosing with lack of data on corresponding plasma concentrations, inadequate treatment duration, etc.

General Framework of Therapy

Depressive symptoms always demand a multimodal treatment including psychoeducation and psychotherapeutic interventions. Psychotherapy alone may be sufficient in mild to moderate depression, in the case of severe symptoms of major depressive disorders (MDD) mostly the combination with an antidepressant

pharmacology is needed. Before starting with antidepressants, organic diseases, drug abuse, side effects, as well as intoxication have to be ruled out as underlying cause of symptomatology. Depending on severity of symptoms the clinical setting has to be chosen. In case of acute suicidality a treatment on the intensive ward may be necessary. In the onset of therapy, the child and the persons having care and custody have to be thoroughly informed about diagnosis and treatment options.

Pharmacotherapy of Depressive Symptoms in Childhood and Adolescence

Treatment Strategies

Frequently antidepressants are used "off-label" in children and adolescents, they are prescribed without official approval. When informing about an intended drug treatment, the "off-label" use has to be explicitly referred to, the explanatory discussion and informed consent by patient and/or parent has to be well documented and written informed consent gained.

In terms of selection of the substance, the specific profiles of effects, side effects and potential interactions as well as the patient or family history on antidepressant response should be considered. In case of suicidal ideations an initial sedation and anxiolysis with a comedication of benzodiazepines and a thoroughly controlled initiation of antidepressants are necessary; furthermore agreement on an emergency plan in the outpatient setting in case suicidal urges are getting too strong, perhaps even an initial treatment on the intensive ward. In order to find the optimal treatment, the dosage of all antidepressants should be very carefully and stepwise increased in order to avoid seizures and drug-induced delirium. If available, for dosage optimization, control of drug interactions as well as in the case of non-response a therapeutic drug monitoring (TDM) should be performed in the steady state (Laux et al. 2007; Gerlach et al. 2009). In general, the antidepressant effect is seen after 1–4 weeks of treatment, sedation and improvement of sleep disorders already before that. After the first or second episode of unipolar depressive symptoms, a minimum of 6 months of antidepressant therapy with the finally effective dosage is recommended. In case of subsequent symptom remission a slow drug tapering for about 25% of the dosage per week may be initiated to minimize the risk of withdrawal symptoms.

In the case of non-response after monotherapy at a sufficient dose over 4–6 weeks, after revision of diagnosis and treatment compliance, an antidepressant with a different profile should be chosen. But changing from one to another SSRI also might be beneficial. If antidepressant monotherapy stays ineffective, results from studies on adult patients might be carefully interpreted for potential augmentation strategies in children; e.g., with atypical neuroleptics (off-label use!), a mood stabilizer or a combination of two antidepressants (such as, e.g., an SSRI with a tricyclic antidepressant or mirtazapine) under thorough monitoring of potential interactions and side effects (Carvalho et al. 2007; Schmauss and Messer 2007).

For a long-term treatment or phase prophylaxis, substances such as lithium, carbamazepine, oxcarbazepine, valproic acid or lamotrigine are proven to be beneficial in adults. For this indication in children—after at least three episodes of unipolar depression, especially in presence of severe symptoms, psychotic features and suicidality—most studies exist for lithium (Campbell and Cueva 1995; Weller and Weller 2000; Gerlach et al. 2006). Due to its low therapeutic index, serum concentrations for this indication should be 0.6–0.8 mmol/l and regularly controlled by TDM.

Antidepressants of Choice for the Monotherapy of Unipolar Depression

The antidepressant of choice is fluoxetine due to its efficacy, proven repeatedly by randomized-controlled studies, already in children younger than 12 years (Emslie et al. 1997, 2002, 2008; Bridge et al. 2007) and its authorization by the Food and Drug-Administration (FDA) and the European Medicines Agency (EMEA) for the treatment of depression in subjects from the age of 8 years on. In off-label use, second choice antidepressants are SSRI such as sertraline, citalopram and es-citalopram, the eutomer of the racemic drug citalopram. As alternatives, but not antidepressants of first or second choice—due to their potentially severe side effects—tricyclic antidepressants and α_2-adrenoceptor antagonists may be used, the latter especially in the treatment of agitation and sleep disturbances connected to depression. Although study results on the safety of the selective noradrenalin-reuptake inhibitor (SNRI) venlafaxine are not yet finally resolved, a positive treatment effect is seen in adolescents, but not in children (Emslie et al. 2007). The effect of St. John's Wort has not yet been studied in controlled trials. A positive effect in the treatment of mild depression might be achieved (Simeon et al. 2005; Jorm et al. 2006); however, accompanied by a high potential of pharmacological interactions (Kölch and Fegert 2006). There are also no findings from controlled trials on monoamine oxidase inhibitors, which nowadays play a minor role in the treatment of juvenile depression due to their potential of severe interactions and side effects.

SSRIs as First and Second Choice Antidepressants in the Treatment of Unipolar Depression

The efficacy of the SSRI fluoxetine in treating juvenile depression has been proven in several controlled studies (Emslie et al. 1997, 2002, 2008; TADS team 2009). However, SSRI in general show higher effect sizes in the treatment of anxiety disorders and OCD in childhood and adolescence, compared to depression (Bridge et al. 2007). Sertraline, citalopram and es-citalopram are reported in some trials to be superior to placebo (Papanikolaou et al. 2006; Pössel and Hautzinger 2006; Wagner 2005; Wagner et al. 2003, 2004); however, their overall effectiveness according to the review of present study results is suggested to be limited (Tsapakis et al. 2008). They may be used as antidepressants of second choice, e.g., when fluoxetine does not show a treatment effect.

A controversial debate on a potentially increased risk of suicidality under SSRI treatment started with results of the FDA meta-analysis on 24 placebo-controlled studies on the use of antidepressants in children and adolescents (Hammad et al. 2006; Andrade et al. 2006). As SSRI may trigger behavioural activation—significantly more in children and adolescents compared to adults (Safer and Zito 2006)—they might facilitate the realization of suicidal impulses. In the FDA meta-analysis, a nearly two-fold increased risk of suicidal events under SSRIs was reported. After re-analysing the data and according to the newest meta-analyses, however, SSRI show an acceptable risk–benefit relationship in the treatment of depression. Furthermore, in none of the former trials were completed suicides reported (Bridge et al. 2007; Fegert and Herpertz-Dahlmann 2005; Pössel and Hautzinger 2006). The combination of psychopharmacology and psychotherapy additionally seems to minimize the emergence of suicidal ideation (March et al. 2007). Safety in the case of overdose is still a strong argument favouring SSRI over tricyclic or α_2-adrenoceptor antagonists in patients with unclear suicidality.

Although SSRI are in general safe and well tolerated in children and adolescents (Fleischhaker et al. 2003), initially in the treatment the potential increase of behavioural activation, moodiness, suicidal thoughts, anxiety and sleep problems should be thoroughly monitored. As children often resorb and metabolize faster than adults, higher dosages than recommended for adults might be necessary. For most of the SSRI one dosage in the morning is sufficient, only fluvoxamine should be administered twice a day due to its half-life of 10–22 h. Fluoxetine might be started with (5–) 10 mg/day depending on the age and weight of the patient and increased every 5–7 days for 5–10 mg. For most children/adolescents 20 mg in the morning are effective, in case of insufficient response dosage might be increased up to 40–60 mg/day. For therapy of OCD and bulimia higher dosages are needed than for treating depression.

Toxicity of SSRI is low and rarely a serotonin syndrome occurs, however with—in the course-potentially life-threatening arrhythmia, seizures and coma. In case of a central serotonin overactivity, SSRI have to be discontinued immediately and intensive care might be needed. Pharmacokinetic interactions of SSRI with legal and illegal drugs and food have to be considered and have been discussed elsewhere in extensor (Lane 1996).

SSRI should be thoroughly discussed and carefully monitored in patients with epileptic seizures, brain damages, suicidality and comedication with drugs that might increase central serotonin activity and not be utilized in case of intoxication with sedating agents. If tapering is necessary, dosage should be reduced slowly, especially of those SSRI with a short half-life. Before starting an SSRI, in the first month of treatment and in the course, each 6 months, controls of blood pressure, heart rate and routine blood tests should be performed. Additionally, if clinically indicated, an EEG and ECG should be performed; the ECG necessarily in case of pre-existing cardiac problems or a positive family history for cardiac disorders.

Alternative Antidepressants in the Treatment of Monopolar Depression

Trycyclic antidepressants did not show benefit, or only limited efficacy in comparison to placebo in the treatment of child and adolescent depression (Hazell 1995, 2002; Ambrosini 2000; Papanikolaou et al. 2006; Tsapakis et al. 2008). The lacking proof of efficacy might though be due to above-mentioned methodological study limitations. Clinical experience supports trycyclic antidepressants to be effective alternatives in the treatment of MDD. However, due to the potentially serious side effects, including cardiotoxic effects, and higher risk of intoxication they are not antidepressants of first or second choice. They might be used in patients with lethargy (e.g., clomipramine) and serious sleeping problems in the context of depression (e.g., doxepine). After starting with a low dose, dosage might be increased every 4–5 days. Due to their long half-life a single intake in the morning or at night is sufficient.

If suicidal ideation is suspected, tricyclic antidepressants should not at all be presribed or just in small amounts under narrow monitoring, as already a dose "3 times the normal" might cause life-threatening side effects. Overdosage leads to increased anticholinergic effects, finally with central temperature increase, tachycardia and arrhythmia, symptoms of delirium, seizures, somnolence and coma. Central anticholinergic syndrome demands immediate drug discontinuation and intensive care. The risk of side effects due to tricyclic antidepressants may be reduced by prescribing long-acting formulas. Trycyclic antidepressants interact with other antidepressants, anticholinergics, contraceptives, mood stabilizers, neuroleptics and methylphenidate, causing altered serum concentrations, partly increased side effects or reduced effectiveness. Smoking seems to alter serum levels of at least some antidepressants (Lind et al. 2009).

In the case of cardiac diseases the use of tricyclic antidepressants is strongly limited. The FDA describes the following

events as serious: a QRS intervall >30% of the norm or >120 ms, PR interval >200 ms, systolic blood pressure >140 mmHg or diastolic >90 mmHg, heart beat in rest >130/min. Treatment has to be carefully considered and monitored in case of comedication with sedating drugs, pre-occurring seizures and myoclonia (decreased seizure threshold), bipolar disorder (induction of mania) and suicidality (initially activating effect). A rushed tapering may lead to deteriorated mood and symptoms such as fever, sweating, headache and muscle pain, nausea and anxiety.

Before initiation of the tricyclic antidepressant, repeatedly in the first month, later every 3 and 6 months, controls of blood pressure, pulse and blood tests as well as an ECG and EEG are necessary. Furthermore, the patients' history and family history for cardiac diseases, especially sudden unexplained deaths, have to be taken.

The α_2-adrenoceptor antagonists, such as mianserine and mirtazapine are mainly indicated in anxious and agitated depression with associated sleeping problems, as from non-controlled studies a positive effect on depressive symptomatology including sleep problems has been reported (Dugas et al. 1985; Schlamp 1999; Haapasalo-Pesu et al. 2004). Mirtazapine, e.g., may be started at 15 mg and slowly increased to 45 mg, a single dosage per day is sufficient. Main side effects, especially at the beginning of treatment, are sedation and reduced reaction time, further possible side effects are discussed elsewhere (Masand and Gupta 2002). An advantage of this substance class might be the reduced potential for sexual dysfunction.

In controlled studies the SNRI venlafaxine has been shown to be clearly effective in depressed adults (Smith et al. 2002). In children, no benefit in comparison to placebo could be reported; however, a positive effect in adolescents was observed (Mandoki et al. 1997; Courtney 2004; Emslie et al. 2007; Bailly 2008). Due to a potentially increased risk of suicidal ideations and lack of approval, venlafaxine is at the moment not an antidepressant of first or second choice in juvenile depression.

For adults, initial dose is 37.5 mg with stepwise increasing dosage for 37.5 mg if needed. There is no official dose recommendation in children and adolescents. From our clinical experience in children, a standard dose of 37.5–75 mg, and in adolescents 75–150 mg might be used. Long-lasting formulas may reduce possible side effects of sedation, agitation, weight gain, sleep problems, vegetative symptoms, sexual dysfunction, etc.

References

Ambrosini PJ. 2000. A review of pharmacotherapy of major depression in children and adolescents. Psychiat Serv 51: 627–633.

Andrade C, Bhakta SG, Singh NM. 2006. Controversy revisited: Selective serotonin reuptake inhibitors in paediatric depression. World J Biol Psychiatry 7:251–260.

Bailly D. 2008. Benefits and risks of using antidepressants in children and adolescents. Expert Opin Drug Saf 7:9–27.

Baldessarini RJ. 1989. Current status of antidepressants: clinical pharmacology and therapy. J Clin Psychiatry 50:117–126.

Bridge JA, Jyengar S, Salary CB, Barbe RP, Birmaher B, Pincus HA, et al. 2007. Clinical response and risk for suicidal ideation and suicide attempts in pediatric antidepressant treatment. J Am Med Assoc 297:1683–1696.

Campbell M, Cueva JE. 1995. Psychopharmacology in child and adolescent psychiatry: a review of the past seven years. Part II. J Am Acad Child Adolesc Psychiatry 34:1262–1272.

Carvalho AF, Cavalcante JL, Castelo MS, Lima MC. 2007. Augmentation strategies for treatment-resistant depression: a literature review. J Clin Pharm Ther 32:415–428.

Courtney DB. 2004. Selective serotonin reuptake inhibitor and venlafaxine use in children and adolescents with major depressive disorder: a systematic review of published randomized controlled trials. Can J Psychiatry 49:557–563.

Dugas M, Mouren MC, Halfon O, Moron P. 1985. Treatment of childhood and adolescent depression with mianserin. Acta Psychiatr Scand Suppl 320:48–53.

Edwarts JG, Anderson I. 1999. Systematic review and guide to selection of selective serotonin reuptake inhibitors. Drugs 57:507–533.

Emslie GJ, Rush AJ, Weinberg WA, Kowatch RA, Hughes CW, Carmody T, et al. 1997. A double-blind, randomized, placebo-controlled trial of fluoxetine in children and adolescents with depression. Ach Gen Psychiatry 54:1031–1037.

Emslie GJ, Heiligenstein JH, Wagner KD, Hoog SL, Ernest DE, Brown E, et al. 2002. Fluoxetine for acute treatment of depression in children and adolescents: a placebo-controlled, randomized clinical trial. J Am Acad Child Adolesc Psychiatry 41:1205–1215.

Emslie GJ, Findling RL, Yeung PP, Kunz NR, Li Y. 2007. Venlafaxine ER for the treatment of pediatric subjects with depression: results of two placebo-controlled trials. J Am Acad Child Adolesc Psychiatry 46:479–488.

Emslie GJ, Kennard BD, Mayes TL, Nightingale-Teresi J, Carmody T, Hughes CW, et al. 2008. Fluoxetine versus placebo in preventing relapse of major depression in children and adolescents. Am J Psychiatry 165:459–467.

Fegert JM, Herpertz-Dahlmann B. 2005. Serotoninwiederaufnah-mehemmer im Kindes- und Jugendalter.

Warnhinweise der Behörden, Analyseergebnisse und Empfehlungen. Nervenarzt 76:1330–1339.

Fleischhaker Ch, Herpertz-Dahlmann B, Holtkamp K, Mehler- Wex, Warke A, Schulz E, et al. 2003. Indikationsspektrum und Nebenwirkungen von "neuen" Antidepressiva im Rahmen eines multizentrischen Arzneimittelmonitorings—eine Pilots- tudie. In Lemkuhl U, editor. Psychotherapie und Psychophar- makotherapie im Kindes- und Jugendalter. Göttingen: Vandenhoeck & Ruprecht.

Gerlach M, Baving L, Fegert J. 2006. Therapie mit Lithium-Salzen in der Kinder- und Jugendpsychiatrie—Klinische Wirksamkeit und praktische Empfehlungen. Z Kinder-Jugendpsychiatrie 34:181–189.

Gerlach M, Klampfl K, Mehler-Wex C, Warnke A. Besonderheiten der Therapie mit Psychopharmaka im Kindes- und Jugendalter. 2009. In: Gerlach M, Mehler-Wex C, Walitza S, Warnke A, Wewetzer C, editors. Psychopharmaka im Kindes- und Jugendalter. 2nd ed. Wien, New York: Springer. p. 73–88.

Haapasalo-Pesu KM, Vuola T, Lahelma L, Marttunen M. 2004. Mirtazapine in the treatment of adolescents with major depression: an open-label, multicenter pilot study. J Child Adolesc Psychopharmacol 14:175–184.

Hammad TA, Laughren T, Racoosin J. 2006. Suicidality in pediatric patients treated with antidepressant drugs. Arch Gen Psychiatry 63:332–339.

Hazell P, O'Connell D, Heathcote D, Robertson J, Henry D. 1995. Efficacy of tricyclic drugs in treating child and adolescent depression: a meta-analysis. Br Med J 310:897–901.

Hazell P, O'Connell D, Heathcote D, Henry D. 2002. Tricyclic drugs for depression in children and adolescents. Cochrane Database Syst Rev 2:CD002317.

Jorm AF, Allen NB, O'Donnell CP, Parslow RA, Purcell R, Morgan AJ. 2006. Effectiveness of complementary and self- help treatments for depression in children and adolescents. Med J Aust 185:368–372.

Kölch M, Fegert JM. 2006. [Medical treatment of depression in children and adolescents] Prax Kinderpsychol Kinderpsychiatr 56:224–233 [Review, in German].

Lane RM. 1996. Pharmacokinetic drug interaction potential of selective serotonin reuptake inhibitors. Int Clin Psychopharmacol Suppl 5:31–61, and Int Clin Psychopharmacol 1997;12:126.

Laux G, Baumann P, Hiemke C. 2007. TDM group of the Arbeitsgemeinschaft Neuropsychopharmakologie und Pharmakopsychiatrie. Therapeutic drug monitoring of antidepressants—clinical aspects. J Neural Transm Suppl 72:261–267 [Review].

Lind AB, Reis M, Bengtsson F, Jonzier-Perey M, Powell Golay K, et al. 2009. Steady-state concentrations of mirtazapine, N-desmethylmirtazapine, 8-hydroxymirtazapine and their enantiomers in relation to cytochrome P450 2D6 genotype, age and smoking behaviour. Clin Pharmacokinet 48:63–70.

Mandoki MW, Tapia MR, Tapia MA, Sumner GS, Parker JL. 1997. Venlafaxine in the treatment of children and adolescents with major depression. Psychopharmacol Bull 33:149–154.

March JS, Silva S, Petrycki S, Curry J, Wells K, Fairbank J, et al. 2007. The Treatment for Adolescents With Depression Study (TADS): long-term effectiveness and safety outcomes. Arch Gen Psychiatry 64:1132–1143. Erratum in: Arch Gen Psychiatry 2008;65(1):101.

Masand PS, Gupta S. 2002. Long-term side effects of newer-generation antidepressants: SSRIs, venlafaxine, nefazodone, bupropion, and mirtazapine. Ann Clin Psychiatry 14:175–182.

Mulrow CD, Williams JW Jr, Trivedi M, Chiquette E, Aguilar C, Cornell JE, et al. 1998. Treatment of depression—newer pharmacotherapies. Psychopharmacol Bull 34:409–795.

Papanikolaou K, Richardson C, Pehlivanidis A, Papadopoulou-Daifoti Z. 2006. Efficacy of antidepressants in child and adolescent depression: a meta-analytic study. J Neural Transm 113:399–415.

Pössel P, Hautzinger M. 2006. Effekte pharmakologischer und psychotherapeutischer Interventionen auf Depressionen bei Kindern und Jugendlichen. Z Kinder Jugendpsychiatr Psychother 34:243–255.

Safer DJ, Zito JM. 2006. Treatment-emergent adverse events from selective serotonin reuptake inhibitors by age group: children versus adolescents. J Child Adolesc Psychopharmacol 16:159–169.

Schlamp D. 1999. Remergil in der Kinder- und Jugendpsychiatrie. Psychiatr Dialog 3:8–9.

Schmauss M, Messer T. 2007. [Augmentation strategies for therapy resistant depression—a review]. Psychiatr Prax 34:165–174.

Schulte-Markwort M, Richterich A, Forouher N. 2008. Affektive Störungen. In: Herpertz-Dahlmann B, Resch F, Schulte- Markwort M, Warnke A, editors.

Entwicklungspsychiatrie. Bio- psychologische Grundlagen und die Entwicklung psychischer Störungen. 2nd ed. Stuttgart: Schattauer. p. 784–792.

Simeon J, Nixon MK, Milin R, Jovanovic R, Walker S. 2005. Open-label pilot study of St. John's wort in adolescent depression. J Child Adolesc Psychopharmacol 15:293–301.

Smith D, Dempster C, Glanville J, Freemantle N, Anderson I. 2002. Efficacy and tolerability of venlafaxine compared with selective serotonin reuptake inhibitors and other antidepressants: a meta-analysis. Br J Psychiatry 180:396–404.

Treatment for Adolescents With Depression Study (TADS) Team, March J, Silva S, Curry J, Wells K, Fairbank J, Burns B, et al. 2009. The Treatment for Adolescents With Depression Study (TADS): outcomes over 1 year of naturalistic follow-up. Am J Psychiatry 166:1141–1149.

Tsapakis EM, Soldani F, Tondo L, Baldessarini RJ. 2008. Efficacy of antidepressants in juvenile depression: meta-analysis. Br J Psychiatry 193:10–17.

Wagner KD. Pharmacotherapy for major depression in children and adolescents. 2005. Prog Neuropsychopharmacol Biol Psychiatry 29:819–826.

Wagner KD, Ambrosini P, Rynn M, Wohlberg C, Yang R, Greenbaum MS, et al. 2003. Sertraline Pediatric Depression Study Group. Efficacy of sertraline in the treatment of children and adolescents with major depressive disorder: two randomized controlled trials. J Am Med Assoc 290:1033–1041.

Wagner KD, Robb AS, Findling RL, Jin J, Gutierrez MM, Heydorn WE. 2004. A randomized, placebo-controlled trial of citalopram for the treatment of major depression in children and adolescents. Am J Psychiatry 161:1079–1083.

Weller EB, Weller RA. 2000. Treatment options in the management of adolescent depression. J Affect Disord Suppl 1:23–28.

REGINA TAURINES, MANFRED GERLACH, AND ANDREAS WARNKE are at the Hospital of Child and Adolescent Psychiatry, Psychosomatics and Psychotherapy at the University of Wurzburg in Wurzburg, Germany. Johannes Thome is at the Hospital of Psychiatry, Psychosomatics and Psychotherapy at the University of Rostock in Rostock, Germany. Christoph Wewetzer is at the Hospital of Child and Adolescent Psychiatry and Psychotherapy in Koln, Germany.

EXPLORING THE ISSUE

Do Selective Serotonin Reuptake Inhibitors (SSRIs) Increase Adolescent Suicide Risk?

Critical Thinking and Reflection

1. You are surfing the Internet for news stories and come across the headline "Kids and Antidepressants: Why They Are Harmful." Before reading the article, what about this statement pops into your mind? What evidence would you be looking for in the article to support the title?
2. Given the controversy regarding the use of SSRIs for adolescents and children coupled with the need for medications for many mood and anxiety disorders, what health care procedures could be implemented to lessen the risk while maximizing treatment?
3. If you were to design a study examining the efficacy of SSRIs on adolescent depression and/or anxiety, what variables would you measure and what variables would you control for?
4. If you were designing a suicide prevention program, who would be your targeted audience? What variables do you think need to be included within your program?

Is There Common Ground?

Major depression is a serious illness in children and adolescents and, therefore, it is important to identify safe and effective medications for the treatment of this disorder in our youth. Past warnings and continued mixed results in the literature related to the potential serious negative effects of antidepressants, especially SSRIs, raise questions about the risk-benefit ratio of these drugs. The YES and NO selections discuss the potential side effects associated with SSRIs in the use of treating these disorders and more importantly, they both discuss the need to closely monitor and follow up with clients who may be suffering from depression and anxiety for safety and effectiveness reasons.

It is clear from the research and the continued use of "off-label" antidepressants in the treatment of depression and anxiety (and other disorders) in children and adolescents that continued research into the efficacy and safety of antidepressants needs to continue. With more research, especially of sound clinical trials, the costs and benefits of SSRIs will become clearer. Future research needs to explore further the relationship between psychopharmacology and psychotherapy.

Additional Resources

Miller, M., Pate, V., Swanson, S. A., Azrael, D., White, A., & Sturmer, T. (2014). Antidepressant class, age, and the risk of deliberate self-harm: A propensity score matched cohort study of SSRI and SNRI users in the USA. *CNS Drugs, 28*, 79–88.

Wagner, K. D., Rosenbaum Asarnow, J., Vitiello, B., Clarke, G., Keller, M., Emsile, et al. (2012). Out of the black box: Treatment of resistant depression in adolescents and the antidepressant controversy. *Journal of Child and Adolescent Psychopharmacology, 22*(1), 5–10.

References

American Academy of Child and Adolescent Psychiatry. (2013, July). Depression in children and teens. Retrieved from http://www.aacap.org/AACAP/Families_and_Youth/Facts_for_Families/FFF-Guide/The-Depressed-Child-004.aspx

Hamrin, V. & Scahill, L. (2005). Selective serotonin reuptake inhibitors for children and adolescents with major depression: Current controversies and recommendations. *Issues in Mental Health Nursing, 26*, 433–450.

Heron, M. (2016). Deaths: Leading causes for 2014. *National Vital Statistics Report, 65*(5), 1–94.

Internet References . . .

American Academy of Child and Adolescent Psychiatry

www.aacap.org

Mental Disorders

http://teenmentalhealth.org/learn/mental-disorders/

Mental Health Disorders—Office of Adolescent Health

http://www.hhs.gov/ash/oah/adolescent-health-topics
/mental-health/mental-health-disorders.html

National Center for the Prevention of Youth Suicide

http://www.suicidology.org/NCPYS

Parent's Guide to Depression

http://www.helpguide.org/articles/depression
/teen-depression-signs-help.htm

Selected, Edited, and with Issue Framing Material by:
Scott R. Brandhorst, *Southeast Missouri State University*

ISSUE

Should the Human Papillomavirus (HPV) Vaccine Be Mandatory for Early Adolescents Girls?

YES: Cynthia Dailard, from "Achieving Universal Vaccination Against Cervical Cancer in the United States: The Need and the Means," *Guttmacher Policy Review* (2006)

NO: Gail Javitt, Deena Berkowitz, and Lawrence O. Gostin, from "Assessing Mandatory HPV Vaccination: Who Should Call the Shots?" *Journal of Law, Medicine and Ethics* (2008)

Learning Outcomes
After reading this issue, you will be able to:
• Explain what human papillomavirus (HPV) is and how people become infected with it.
• Understand the relationship between HPV and both cervical cancer and genital warts.
• Describe the economics related to mandating an HPV vaccine.
• Understand the gender-equality concerns related to the HPV vaccine.

ISSUE SUMMARY

YES: Cynthia Dailard, a senior public policy associate at the Guttmacher Institute, argues that making universal vaccination against HPV mandatory for school attendance is a necessary step in preventing cervical cancer and other HPV-related problems. Rebuttals to the issues of the high cost as well as the suitability for the vaccination in schools are presented, and she marks universal vaccination as a key step in future vaccination policy reform.

NO: Gail Javitt, Deena Berkowitz, and Lawrence O. Gostin argue that while the risks of contracting HPV are high, and its demonstrated link to cervical cancer has proven strong, it is both unwarranted and unwise to force mandatory vaccination on minor females. They discuss the potential adverse health effects, both long- and short-term risks, the lack of support for the HPV vaccine within the justifications for state-mandated vaccination, the consequences of a vaccination targeted solely at females, as well as the economic impact that would result from making the HPV vaccination mandatory.

Cervical cancer is largely a preventable cancer; it is the second most common cancer among women worldwide. It is generally accepted by the medical community to be caused by HPV, which is the virus that causes genital warts. HPV is considered the most common sexually transmitted infection (STI) in both Canada and the United States with an estimated 75 percent of sexually active people being infected with HPV at some point in their lives, and that percentage is higher for adolescents and young adult women. Rates for adolescent and young men are not as definite and the severe health consequences of HPV infection for males (e.g., penile, anal, and throat cancers) are less common occurrences relative to females.

Adolescent and young women—relative to older adults and males—may be more prone to contracting HPV because of biological reasons associated with the developing cervix. The good news is that, in healthy younger individuals, the immune system can "clear" the body of HPV infection in many cases (Moscicki, 2005).

In 2006, Merck & Co., a major pharmaceutical company, introduced the first vaccine for HPV. While there are almost 200 types of HPV, the vaccine has been demonstrated as effective at preventing the strains of HPV that cause 70 percent of cervical cancers. The American Academy of Pediatrics recommends that girls start the vaccine at ages 11 or 12 years (and possibly as young as 9) because to be most effective, the vaccine's three doses must be given to girls before they ever have sex. Besides 11- or 12-year-old girls, other candidates for HPV include females ages 11–26. More recently, a third group—males ages 9–26 years—was approved for the vaccination. HPV vaccine can prevent genital warts in males, and can help decrease the spread of HPV to women.

While some people question the safety of the vaccine, the existing studies warrant global introduction (Agosti & Goldie, 2007) and the Society of Obstetricians and Gynaecologists of Canada calls it ". . . one of the most extensively tested vaccine[s] to ever come [on] the . . . market" (2007). The major safety concern is that the drug has been studied in highly controlled laboratory conditions but needs to demonstrate "real-world" success (Borgmeyer, 2007). The American Association of Family Physicians has characterized mandates for vaccinations as "premature" because of the need for further data on the longer-term effects of the vaccination, yet they have included the HPV vaccination on their recommended schedule of immunizations for adolescents.

Some of the issues associated with the widespread implementation of a mandatory vaccination program include the cost of the drug. Requiring three doses, the total cost in the United States is estimated to be $360 (over €250) per person vaccinated, while the cost in Canada is approximately $450 per person. In some cases, parents would have to pay for the drugs or their daughter would be prohibited from attending school. This is not a concern in Canada where HPV vaccination is voluntary currently. A major concern of conservative groups is that, in recommending a mandatory HPV vaccination, girls will view this as adults condoning teenage sexuality (Sprigg, 2007). This "encouraging sex" worry is not likely to be realized; sexual health education and condom distribution programs, which have been implemented to help reduce the incidence of STIs (e.g., HIV, herpes) or unintended pregnancy, have not been shown to be associated with an increase in sexual activity (Charo, 2007). Also, vaccination for Hepatitis B has not resulted in rampant sexual activity or drug use (Borgmeyer, 2007). Others worry that vaccinated women will no longer value Pap smears and, as a result, will neglect their gynecological health (Zimmerman, 2006). A further concern is that the government may be mandating HPV vaccinations as a result of underlying pressure by and financial weight of the pharmaceutical companies. Thus, the mandating program is viewed as nefariously financial.

While most people do not debate the value of the HPV vaccination, per se, the controversy lies in the *mandating* of a vaccination for a number of reasons. By creating conditions where children will not be allowed to attend school unless they are vaccinated for HPV creates a lack of parental rights regarding their children's health care (Charo, 2007). The mandatory HPV vaccination program becomes a question of more complex politics and moral objections rather than simply a public health issue. The YES and NO selections provide evidence to support both sides of this debate.

Dailard presents facts that display the high infection rate of HPV—at an estimated 75 percent among Americans—as well as the strong connection to cervical cancer—HPV is responsible for 70 percent of all cervical cancer cases. These, coupled with the virtual 100-percent efficacy of current HPV vaccinations, provide, according to Dailard, a clear validation for the need for universal vaccination. She addresses the common argument against universal vaccination, that being the high cost, in a twofold manner. First, she provides evidence for the high cost and impact of medical care related to HPV infections that would be negated by the vaccine and possibly counterbalance some of the cost related to the vaccination. Next, she looks at the policies for private insurance for HPV vaccinations as well as public efforts that could reduce the cost for those who do not have coverage or the ability to afford the vaccination. The issue of school-entry requirements for the vaccination is addressed, wherein she describes the requirements as possibly the most effective way of ensuring widespread immunity. Dailard also brings up the potential future benefits the universal vaccination for HPV could bring for currently under-developed vaccinations for other STIs and diseases.

Javitt, Berkowitz, and Gostin, while not antivaccination, argue that the efforts to mandate HPV vaccination are premature and raise legal, ethical, and social concerns. As the vaccine is still new, there is little evidence to suggest that the vaccine does in fact prevent cervical cancer instead of simply the early symptoms. Additionally, possible long-term adverse reactions are not yet known, neither are the effects of the vaccine on a much wider patient pool. Javitt et al. also bring up the issue of the lack of data for long-term efficacy of the vaccination; the immunity duration has not been defined beyond a few years. Further complications arise from HPV's inability to fulfill the historic requirements for mandated vaccination. It is neither a "public health necessity," nor are children most at risk in school settings. Final issues brought to light by Javitt et al. are the issues of gender inequality from a vaccine targeted primarily at females, a potential public backlash against an aggressive push for mandatory vaccination, and the negative economic impact that could affect government vaccination programs as well as private physicians and the families of patients. As you consider these two viewpoints, is there a compromise between the two positions?

YES ↵

Cynthia Dailard

Achieving Universal Vaccination Against Cervical Cancer in the United States: The Need and the Means

The advent of a vaccine against the types of human papillomavirus (HPV) linked to most cases of cervical cancer is widely considered one of the greatest health care advances for women in recent years. Experts believe that vaccination against HPV has the potential to dramatically reduce cervical cancer incidence and mortality particularly in resource-poor developing countries where cervical cancer is most common and deadly. In the United States, the vaccine's potential is likely to be felt most acutely within low-income communities and communities of color, which disproportionately bear the burden of cervical cancer.

Because HPV is easily transmitted through sexual contact, the vaccine's full promise may only be realized through near-universal vaccination of girls and young women prior to sexual activity—a notion reflected in recently proposed federal guidelines. And history, as supported by a large body of scientific evidence, suggests that the most effective way to achieve universal vaccination is by requiring children to be inoculated prior to attending school. Yet the link between HPV and sexual activity—and the notion that HPV is different than other infectious diseases targeted by vaccine school entry requirements—tests the prevailing justification for such efforts. Meanwhile, any serious effort to achieve universal vaccination among young people with this relatively expensive vaccine will expose holes in the public health safety net that, if left unaddressed, have the potential to exacerbate longstanding disparities in cervical cancer rates among American women.

The Case for Universal Vaccination

Virtually all cases of cervical cancer are linked to HPV, an extremely common sexually transmitted infection (STI) that is typically asymptomatic and harmless; most people never know they are infected, and most cases resolve on their own. It is estimated that approximately three in four Americans contract HPV at some point in their lives, with most cases acquired relatively soon after individuals have sex for the first time. Of the approximately 30 known types of HPV that are sexually transmitted, more than 13 are associated with cervical cancer. Yet despite the prevalence of HPV, cervical cancer is relatively rare in the United States; it

generally occurs only in the small proportion of cases where a persistent HPV infection goes undetected over many years. This is largely due to the widespread availability of Pap tests, which can detect precancerous changes of the cervix that can be treated before cancer sets in, as well as cervical cancer in its earliest stage, when it is easily treatable.

Still, the American Cancer Society estimates that in 2006, almost 10,000 cases of invasive cervical cancer will occur to American women, resulting in 3,700 deaths. Significantly, more than half of all U.S. women diagnosed with cervical cancer have not had a Pap test in the last three years. These women are disproportionately low income and women of color who lack access to affordable and culturally competent health services. As a result, the incidence of cervical cancer is approximately 1.5 times higher among African American and Latina women than among white women; women of color are considerably more likely than whites to die of the disease as well. Two new HPV vaccines—Gardasil, manufactured by Merck & Company, and Cervarix, manufactured by GlaxoSmithKline—promise to transform this landscape. Both are virtually 100% effective in preventing the two types of HPV responsible for 70% of all cases of cervical cancer; Gardasil also protects against two other HPV types associated with 90% of all cases of genital warts. Gardasil was approved by the federal Food and Drug Administration (FDA) in June; GlaxoSmithKline is expected to apply for FDA approval of Cervarix by year's end.

Following FDA approval, Gardasil was endorsed by the Centers for Disease Control and Prevention's Advisory Committee on Immunization Practices (ACIP), which is responsible for maintaining the nation's schedule of recommended vaccines. ACIP recommended that the vaccine be routinely administered to all girls ages 11–12, and as early as age nine at a doctor's discretion. Also, it recommended vaccination of all adolescents and young women ages 13–26 as part of a national "catch-up" campaign for those who have not already been vaccinated.

The ACIP recommendations, which are closely followed by health care professionals, reflect the notion that to eradicate cervical cancer, it will be necessary to achieve near-universal vaccination of girls and young women prior to sexual activity, when the vaccine is most effective. Experts believe that such an approach

Dailard, Cynthia, "Achieving universal vaccination against cervical cancer in the United states: The need and the means," *Guttmacher Policy Review*, vol. 9, no. 4, Fall 2006, pp. 12–16. Copyright © 2006 by Guttmacher Institute. Reprinted by permission.

has the potential to significantly reduce cervical cancer deaths in this country and around the world. Also, high vaccination rates will significantly reduce the approximately 3.5 million abnormal Pap results experienced by American women each year, many of which are caused by transient or persistent HPV infections. These abnormal Pap results require millions of women to seek follow-up care, ranging from additional Pap tests to more invasive procedures such as colposcopies and biopsies. This additional care exacts a substantial emotional and even physical toll on women, and costs an estimated $6 billion in annual health care expenditures. Finally, widespread vaccination fosters "herd immunity," which is achieved when a sufficiently high proportion of individuals within a population are vaccinated that those who go unvaccinated—because the vaccine is contraindicated for them or because they are medically underserved, for example—are essentially protected.

The Role of School Entry Requirements

Achieving high vaccination levels among adolescents, however, can be a difficult proposition. Unlike infants and toddlers, who have frequent contact with health care providers in the context of well-child visits, adolescents often go for long stretches without contact with a health care professional. In addition, the HPV vaccine is likely to pose particular challenges, given that it must be administered three times over a six-month period to achieve maximum effectiveness.

A large body of evidence suggests that the most effective means to ensure rapid and widespread use of childhood or adolescent vaccines is through state laws or policies that require children to be vaccinated prior to enrollment in day care or school. These school-based immunization requirements, which exist in some form in all 50 states, are widely credited for the success of immunization programs in the United States. They have also played a key role in helping to close racial, ethnic and socioeconomic gaps in immunization rates, and have proven to be far more effective than guidelines recommending the vaccine for certain age-groups or high-risk populations. Although each state decides for itself whether a particular vaccine will be required for children to enroll in school, they typically rely on ACIP recommendations in making their decision.

In recent months, some commentators have noted that as a sexually transmitted infection, HPV is "different" from other infectious diseases such as measles, mumps or whooping cough, which are easily transmitted in a school setting or threaten school attendance when an outbreak occurs. Some socially conservative advocacy groups accordingly argue that the HPV vaccine does not meet the historical criteria necessary for it to be required for children attending school; many of them also contend that abstinence outside of marriage is the real answer to HPV. They welcome the advent of the vaccine, they say, but will oppose strenuously any effort to require it for school enrollment.

This position reflects only a limited understanding of school-based vaccination requirements. These requirements do not exist solely to prevent the transmission of disease in school or during childhood. Instead, they further society's strong interest in ensuring that people are protected from disease throughout their lives and are a highly efficient means of eradicating disease in the larger community. For example, states routinely require school-age children to be vaccinated against rubella (commonly known as German measles), a typically mild illness in children, to protect pregnant women in the community from the devastating effects the disease can have on a developing fetus. Similarly, states currently require vaccination against certain diseases, such as tetanus, that are not "contagious" at all, but have very serious consequences for those affected. And almost all states require vaccination against Hepatitis B, a blood borne disease which can be sexually transmitted.

Moreover, according to the National Conference of State Legislatures (NCSL), all 50 states allow parents to refuse to vaccinate their children on medical grounds, such as when a vaccine is contraindicated for a particular child due to allergy, compromised immunity or significant illness. All states except Mississippi and West Virginia allow parents to refuse to vaccinate their children on religious grounds. Additionally, 20 states go so far as to allow parents to refuse to vaccinate their children because of a personal, moral or other belief. Unlike a medical exemption, which requires a parent to provide documentation from a physician, the process for obtaining nonmedical exemptions can vary widely by state.

NCSL notes that, in recent years, almost a dozen states considered expanding their exemption policy. Even absent any significant policy change, the rate of parents seeking exemptions for nonmedical reasons is on the rise. This concerns public health experts. Research shows that in states where exemptions are easier to obtain, a higher proportion of parents refuse to vaccinate their children; research further shows that these states, in turn, are more likely to experience outbreaks of vaccine-preventable diseases, such as measles and whooping cough. Some vaccine program administrators fear that because of the social sensitivities surrounding the HPV vaccine, any effort to require the vaccine for school entry may prompt legislators to amend their laws to create nonmedical exemptions where they do not currently exist or to make existing exemptions easier to obtain. This has the potential not only to thwart the effort to stem the tide of cervical cancer, but to foster the spread of other vaccine-preventable diseases as well.

Financing Challenges Laid Bare

Another barrier to achieving universal vaccination of girls and young women will be the high price of the vaccine. Gardasil is expensive by vaccine standards, costing approximately $360 for the three-part series of injections. Despite this high cost, ACIP's endorsement

THE POTENTIAL ROLE OF FAMILY PLANNING CLINICS
IN AN HPV VACCINE 'CATCH-UP' CAMPAIGN

Family planning clinics, including those funded under Title X of the Public Health Service Act, have an important role to play in a national "catch-up" campaign to vaccinate young women against HPV. This is particularly true for women ages 19–26, who are too old to receive free vaccines through the federal Vaccines for Children program but still fall within the ACIP-recommended age range for the HPV vaccine.

Almost 4,600 Title X–funded family planning clinics provide subsidized family planning and related preventive health care to just over five million women nationwide. In theory, Title X clinics are well poised to offer the HPV vaccine, because they already are a major provider of STI services and cervical cancer screening, providing approximately six million STI (including HIV) tests and 2.7 million Pap tests in 2004 alone. Because Title X clients are disproportionately low income and women of color, they are at particular risk of developing cervical cancer later in life. Moreover, most Title X clients fall within the ACIP age recommendations of 26 and under for the HPV vaccine (59% are age 24 or younger, and 18% are ages 25–29); many of these women are uninsured and may not have an alternative source of health care.

Title X funds may be used to pay for vaccines linked to improved reproductive health outcomes, and some Title X clinics offer the Hepatitis B vaccine (which can be sexually transmitted). Although many family planning providers are expressing interest in incorporating the HPV vaccine into their package of services, its high cost—even at a discounted government purchase price—is likely to stand in the way. Clinics that receive Title X funds are required by law to charge women based on their ability to pay, with women under 100% of the federal poverty level (representing 68% of Title X clients) receiving services completely free of charge and those with incomes between 100–250% of poverty charged on a sliding scale. While Merck has expressed an interest in extending its patient assistance program to publicly funded family planning clinics, it makes no promises. In fact, a statement on the company's Web site says that "Due to the complexities associated with vaccine funding and distribution in the public sector, as well as the resource constraints that typically exist in public health settings, Merck is currently evaluating whether and how a vaccine assistance program could be implemented in the public sector."

means that Gardasil will be covered by most private insurers; in fact, a number of large insurers have already announced they will cover the vaccine for girls and young women within the ACIP-recommended age range. Still, the Institute of Medicine estimates that approximately 11% of all American children have private insurance that does not cover immunization, and even those with insurance coverage may have to pay deductibles and copayments that create a barrier to care.

Those who do not have private insurance or who cannot afford the out of pocket costs associated with Gardasil will need to rely on a patchwork system of programs that exist to support the delivery of subsidized vaccines to low-income and uninsured individuals. In June, ACIP voted to include Gardasil in the federal Vaccines for Children program (VFC), which provides free vaccines largely to children and teenagers through age 18 who are uninsured or receive Medicaid. The program's reach is significant: In 2003, 43% of all childhood vaccine doses were distributed by the VFC program.

The HPV vaccine, however, is not just recommended for children and teenagers; it is also recommended for young adult women up through age 26. Vaccines are considered an "optional"

benefit for adults under Medicaid, meaning that it is up to each individual state to decide whether or not to cover a given vaccine. Also, states can use their own funds and federal grants to support the delivery of subsidized vaccines to low-income or uninsured adults. Many states, however, have opted instead to channel these funds toward childhood-vaccination efforts, particularly as vaccine prices have grown in recent years. As a result, adult vaccination rates remain low and disparities exist across racial, ethnic and socioeconomic groups—mirroring the disparities that exist for cervical cancer.

In response to all this, Merck in May announced it would create a new "patient assistance program," designed to provide all its vaccines free to adults who are uninsured, unable to afford the vaccines and have an annual household income below 200% of the federal poverty level ($19,600 for individuals and $26,400 for couples). To receive free vaccines, patients will need to complete and fax forms from participating doctors' offices for processing by Merck during the patients' visits. Many young uninsured women, however, do not seek their care in private doctors' offices, but instead rely on publicly funded family planning clinics for their care, suggesting the impact of this program may be limited (see box).

Thinking Ahead

Solutions to the various challenges presented by the HPV vaccine are likely to have relevance far beyond cervical cancer. In the coming years, scientific breakthroughs in the areas of immunology, molecular biology and genetics will eventually permit vaccination against a broader range of acute illnesses as well as chronic diseases. Currently, vaccines for other STIs such as chlamydia, herpes and HIV are in various stages of development. Also under study are vaccines for Alzheimer's disease, diabetes and a range of cancers. Vaccines for use among adolescents will also be increasingly common. A key question is, in the future, will individuals across the economic spectrum have access to these breakthrough medical advances or will disadvantaged individuals be left behind?

When viewed in this broader context, the debate over whether the HPV vaccine should be required for school enrollment may prove to be a healthy one. If the HPV vaccine is indeed "the first of its kind," as some have characterized it, it has the potential to prompt communities across the nation to reconsider and perhaps reconceive the philosophical justification for school entry requirements. Because the U.S. health care system is fragmented, people have no guarantee of health insurance coverage or access to affordable care. School entry requirements might therefore provide an important opportunity to deliver public health interventions that, like the HPV vaccine, offer protections to individuals who have the potential to become disconnected from health care services later in life. Similar to the HPV vaccine's promise of cervical cancer

prevention, these benefits may not be felt for many years, but nonetheless may be compelling from a societal standpoint. And bearing in mind that school dropout rates begin to climb as early as age 13, middle school might be appropriately viewed as the last public health gate that an entire age-group of individuals pass through together—regardless of race, ethnicity or socioeconomic status.

Meanwhile, the cost and affordability issues raised by the HPV vaccine may help draw attention to the need to reform the vaccine-financing system in this country. In 2003, the Institute of Medicine proposed a series of reforms designed to improve the way vaccines are financed and distributed. They included a national insurance benefit mandate that would apply to all public and private health care plans and vouchers for uninsured children and adults to receive immunizations through the provider of their choice. Legislation introduced by Rep. Henry Waxman (D-CA) and Sen. Edward Kennedy (D-MA), called the Vaccine Access and Supply Act, adopts a different approach. The bill would expand the Vaccines for Children program, create a comparable Vaccines for Adults program, strengthen the vaccine grant program to the states and prohibit Medicaid cost-sharing requirements for ACIP-recommended vaccines for adults.

Whether the HPV vaccine will in fact hasten reforms of any kind remains to be seen. But one thing is clear: If the benefits of this groundbreaking vaccine cannot be enjoyed by girls and women who are disadvantaged by poverty or insurance status, then it will only serve to perpetuate the disparities in cervical cancer rates that have persisted in this country for far too long.

Gail Javitt, Deena Berkowitz,
and Lawrence O. Gostin

Assessing Mandatory HPV Vaccination: Who Should Call the Shots?

I. Introduction

The human papillomavirus (HPV) is the most common sexually transmitted infection worldwide. In the United States, more than six million people are infected each year. Although most HPV infections are benign, two strains of HPV cause 70 percent of cervical cancer cases.[1] Two other strains of HPV are associated with 90 percent of genital warts cases.[2]

In June 2006, the Food and Drug Administration (FDA) approved the first vaccine against HPV. Sold as Gardasil, the quadrivalent vaccine is intended to prevent four strains of HPV associated with cervical cancer, precancerous genital lesions, and genital warts.[3] Following FDA approval, the national Advisory Committee on Immunization Practices (ACIP) recommended routine vaccination for girls ages 11–12 with three doses of quadrivalent HPV vaccine.[4] Thereafter, state legislatures around the country engaged in an intense effort to pass laws mandating vaccination of young girls against HPV. This activity was spurred in part by an intense lobbying campaign by Merck, the manufacturer of the vaccine.[5]

The United States has a robust state-based infrastructure for mandatory vaccination that has its roots in the 19th century. Mandating vaccination as a condition for school entry began in the early 1800s and is currently required by all 50 states for several common childhood infectious diseases.[6] Some suggest that mandatory HPV vaccination for minor females fits squarely within this tradition.

Nonetheless, state efforts to mandate HPV vaccination in minors have raised a variety of concerns on legal, ethical, and social grounds. Unlike other diseases for which state legislatures have mandated vaccination for children, HPV is neither transmissible through casual contact nor potentially fatal during childhood. It also would be the first vaccine to be mandated for use exclusively in one gender. As such, HPV vaccine presents a new context for considering vaccine mandates.

In this paper, we review the scientific evidence supporting Gardasil's approval and the legislative actions in the states that followed. We then argue that mandatory HPV vaccination at this time is both unwarranted and unwise. While the emergence of an HPV vaccine reflects a potentially significant public health advance, the vaccine raises several concerns. First, the long-term safety and effectiveness of the vaccine are unclear, and serious adverse events reported shortly after the vaccine's approval raise questions about its short-term safety as well. In light of unanswered safety questions, the vaccine should be rolled out slowly, with risks carefully balanced against benefits in individual cases. Second, the legal and ethical justifications that have historically supported state-mandated vaccination do not support mandating HPV vaccine. Specifically, HPV does not threaten an imminent and significant risk to the health of others. Mandating HPV would therefore constitute an expansion of the state's authority to interfere with individual and parental autonomy. Engaging in such expansion in the absence of robust public discussion runs the risk of creating a public backlash that may undermine the goal of widespread HPV vaccine coverage and lead to public distrust of established childhood vaccine programs for other diseases. Third, the current sex-based HPV vaccination mandates present constitutional concerns because they require only girls to be vaccinated. Such concerns could lead to costly and protracted legal challenges. Finally, vaccination mandates will place economic burdens on federal and state governments and individual practitioners that may have a negative impact on the provision of other health services. In light of these potentially adverse public health, economic, and societal consequences, we believe that it is premature for states to add HPV to the list of state-mandated vaccines.

II. Background

Before discussing in detail the basis for our opposition to mandated HPV vaccination, it is necessary to review the public health impact of HPV and the data based on which the FDA approved the vaccine. Additionally, to understand the potentially widespread uptake of HPV vaccine mandates, we review the state legislative activities that have occurred since the vaccine's approval.

A. HPV Epidemiology

In the United States, an estimated 20 million people, or 15 percent of the population, are currently infected with HPV.[7] Modeling

Javitt, Gail et. al., From *Journal of Law, Medicine and Ethics*, vol. 36, issue 2, Summer 2008, pp. 384–395. Copyright © 2008 by American Society of Law, Medicine & Ethics. Reprinted by permission.

studies suggest that up to 80 percent of sexually active women will have become infected with the virus at some point in their lives by the time they reach age 50.[8] Prevalence of HPV is highest among sexually active females ages 14–19.[9]

Human papillomavirus comprises more than 100 different strains of virus, of which more than 30 infect the genital area.[10] The majority of HPV infections are transient, asymptomatic, and cause no clinical problems. However, persistent infection with high risk types of HPV is the most important risk factor for cervical cancer precursors and invasive cervical cancer. Two strains in particular, 16 and 18, have been classified as carcinogenic to humans by the World Health Organization's international agency for research on cancer.[11] These strains account for 70 percent of cervical cancer cases[12] and are responsible for a large proportion of anal, vulvar, vaginal, penile, and urethral cancers.[13]

More than 200,000 women die of cervical cancer each year.[14] The majority of these deaths take place in developing countries, which lack the screening programs and infrastructure for diagnosis, treatment, and prevention that exist in the United States. In the United States, it is estimated that there were about 9,700 cases of invasive cervical cancer and about 3,700 deaths from cervical cancer in 2006, as compared with 500,000 cases and 288,000 deaths worldwide.[15]

Two other HPV types, 6 and 11, are associated with approximately 90 percent of anogenital warts. They are also associated with low grade cervical disease and recurrent respiratory papillomatosis (RRP), a disease consisting of recurrent warty growths in the larynx and respiratory tract. Juvenile onset RRP (JORRP), a rare disorder caused by exposure to HPV during the peripartum period, can cause significant airway obstruction or lead to squamous cell carcinoma with poor prognosis.[16]

Although HPV types 6, 11, 16, and 18 are associated with significant morbidity and mortality, they have a fairly low prevalence in the U.S. population. One study of sexually active women ages 18 to 25 found HPV 16 and 18 prevalence to be 7.8 percent.[17] Another study found overall prevalence of types 6, 11, 16, and 18 to be 1.3 percent, 0.1 percent, 1.5 percent, and 0.8 percent, respectively.[18]

B. Gardasil Safety and Effectiveness

Gardasil was approved based on four randomized, double blind, placebocontrolled studies in 21,000 women ages 16 to 26. Girls as young as nine were included in the safety and immunogenicity studies but not the efficacy studies. The results demonstrated that in women without prior HPV infection, Gardasil was nearly 100 percent effective in preventing precancerous cervical lesions, precancerous vaginal and vulvar lesions, and genital warts caused by vaccine-type HPV. Although the study period was not long enough for cervical cancer to develop, the prevention of these cervical precancerous lesions was considered a valid surrogate marker for cancer prevention. The studies also show that the vaccine is only effective when given prior to infection with high-risk strains.[19]

Gardasil is the second virus-like particle (VLP) vaccine to be approved by the FDA; the first was the Hepatitis B vaccine. VLPs consist of viral protein particles derived from the structural proteins of a virus. These particles are nearly identical to the virus from which they were derived but lack the virus's genetic material required for replication, so they are noninfectious and nononcogenic. VLPs offer advantages over more traditional peptide vaccines as the human body is more highly attuned to particulate antigens, which leads to a stronger immune response since VLP vaccines cannot revert to an infectious form, such as attenuated particles or incompletely killed particles.

No serious Gardasil-related adverse events were observed during clinical trials. The most common adverse events reported were injection site reactions, including pain, redness, and swelling.[20] The most common systemic adverse reactions experienced at the same rate by both vaccine and placebo recipients were headache, fever, and nausea. Five vaccine recipients reported adverse vaccine-related experiences: bronchospasm, gastroenteritis, headache with hypertension, joint movement impairment near injection site, and vaginal hemorrhage. Women with positive pregnancy tests were excluded from the studies, as were some women who became pregnant following receipt of either vaccine or placebo. The incidence of spontaneous pregnancy loss and congenital anomalies were similar in both groups.[21] Gardasil was assigned pregnancy risk category B by the FDA on the basis that animal reproduction studies failed to demonstrate a risk to the fetus.[22]

As of June 2007, the most recent date for which CDC has made data available, there were 1,763 reports of potential side effects following HPV vaccination made to the CDC's Vaccine Adverse Event Reporting System (VAERS). Ninety-four of these were defined as serious, including 13 unconfirmed reports of Guillain-Barre syndrome (GBS), a neurological illness resulting in muscle weakness and sometimes in paralysis. The CDC is investigating these cases. Seven deaths were also reported among females who received the vaccine, but the CDC stated that none of these deaths appeared to be caused by vaccination.[23]

Although the FDA approved the vaccine for females ages 9–26, based on the data collected in those age groups, the ACIP recommendation for vaccination is limited to females ages 11–12. This recommendation was based on several considerations, including age of sexual debut in the United States and the high probability of HPV acquisition within several years of sexual debut, cost-effectiveness evaluations, and the established young adolescent health care visit at ages 11–12 when other vaccines are also recommended.

C. State Legislative Activities

Since the approval of Gardasil, legislators in 41 states and the District of Columbia have introduced legislation addressing the

HPV vaccine.[24] Legislative responses to Gardasil have focused on the following recommendations: (1) mandating HPV vaccination of minor girls as a condition for school entrance; (2) mandating insurance coverage for HPV vaccination or providing state funding to defray or eliminate cost of vaccination; (3) educating the public about the HPV vaccine; and/or (4) establishing committees to make recommendations about the vaccine.

In 2007, 24 states and the District of Columbia introduced legislation specifically to mandate the HPV vaccine as a condition for school entry.[25] Of these, only Virginia and Washington, D.C. passed laws requiring HPV vaccination. The Virginia law requires females to receive three properly spaced doses of HPV vaccine, with the first dose to be administered before the child enters sixth grade. A parent or guardian may refuse vaccination for his child after reviewing "materials describing the link between the human papillomavirus and cervical cancer approved for such use by the Board of Health."[26] The law will take effect October 1, 2008.

Additionally, the D.C. City Council passed the HPV Vaccination and Reporting Act of 2007, which directs the mayor to establish an HPV vaccination program "consistent with the standards set forth by the Centers for Disease Control for all females under the age of 13 who are residents of the District of Columbia."[27] The program includes a "requirement that the parent or legal guardian of a female child enrolling in grade 6 for the first time submit certification that the child has received the HPV vaccine" and a provision that "allows a parent or guardian to opt out of the HPV vaccination requirement." It also directs the mayor to develop reporting requirements "for the collection and analyzation [sic] of HPV vaccination data within the District of Columbia Department of Health," including "annual reporting to the Department of Health as to the immunization status of each female child entering grade 6." The law requires Congressional approval in order to take effect.

In contrast, an Executive Order issued by the Texas governor was thwarted by that state's legislature. Executive Order 4, signed by Governor Rick Perry on February 4, 2007, would have directed the state's health department to adopt rules mandating the "age appropriate vaccination of all female children for HPV prior to admission to the sixth grade."[28] It would have allowed parents to "submit a request for a conscientious objection affidavit form via the Internet." However, H.B. 1098, enacted by the Texas state legislature on April 26, 2007, states that HPV immunization is "not required for a person's admission to any elementary or secondary school," and "preempts any contrary order issued by the governor."[29] The bill was filed without the governor's signature and became effective on May 8, 2007.

Of the 22 other states in which legislation mandating HPV vaccination was introduced in 2007, all would have required girls to be vaccinated somewhere between ages 11 and 13 or before entry into sixth grade. Most would have provided for some sort of parental or guardian exemption, whether for religious, moral, medical, cost,

or other reasons. However, vaccine mandate bills in California and Maryland were withdrawn.

Bills requiring insurance companies to cover HPV vaccination or allocating state funds for this purpose were enacted in eight states.[30] Eight states also enacted laws aimed at promoting awareness of the HPV vaccine using various mechanisms, such as school-based distribution of educational materials to parents of early adolescent children.[31] Finally, three states established expert bodies to engage in further study of HPV vaccination either instead of or as an adjunct to other educational efforts.[32]

In total, 41 states and D.C. introduced legislation addressing HPV vaccination in some manner during the 2007 legislative session, and 17 of these states enacted laws relating to HPV vaccination.

III. Why Mandating HPV Is Premature

The approval of a vaccine against cancer-causing HPV strains is a significant public health advance. Particularly in developing countries, which lack the health care resources for routine cervical cancer screening, preventing HPV infection has the potential to save millions of lives. In the face of such a dramatic advance, opposing government-mandated HPV vaccination may seem foolhardy, if not heretical. Yet strong legal, ethical, and policy arguments underlie our position that state-mandated HPV vaccination of minor females is premature.

A. Long-Term Safety and Effectiveness of the Vaccine Is Unknown

Although the aim of clinical trials is to generate safety and effectiveness data that can be extrapolated to the general population, it is widely understood that such trials cannot reveal all possible adverse events related to a product. For this reason, post-market adverse event reporting is required for all manufacturers of FDA-approved products, and post-market surveillance (also called "phase IV studies") may be required in certain circumstances. There have been numerous examples in recent years in which unforeseen adverse reactions following product approval led manufacturers to withdraw their product from the market. For example, in August 1998, the FDA approved Rotashield, the first vaccine for the prevention of rotavirus gastroenteritis in infants. About 7,000 children received the vaccine before the FDA granted the manufacturer a license to market the vaccine. Though a few cases of intussusception, or bowel obstruction, were noted during clinical trials, there was no statistical difference between the overall occurrence of intussusception in vaccine compared with placebo recipients. After administration of approximately 1.5 million doses of vaccine, however, 15 cases of intussusception were reported, and were found to be causally related to the vaccine. The manufacturer subsequently withdrew the vaccine from the market in October 1999.[33]

In the case of HPV vaccine, short-term clinical trials in thousands of young women did not reveal serious adverse effects.

However, the adverse events reported since the vaccine's approval are, at the very least, a sobering reminder that rare adverse events may surface as the vaccine is administered to millions of girls and young women. Concerns have also been raised that other carcinogenic HPV types not contained in the vaccines will replace HPV types 16 and 18 in the pathological niche.

The duration of HPV vaccine-induced immunity is unclear. The average follow-up period for Gardasil during clinical trials was 15 months after the third dose of the vaccine. Determining long-term efficacy is complicated by the fact that even during naturally occurring HPV infection, HPV antibodies are not detected in many women. Thus, long-term, follow-up post-licensure studies cannot rely solely upon serologic measurement of HPV-induced antibody titers. One study indicates that protection against persistent HPV 16 infection remained at 94 percent 3.5 years after vaccination with HPV 16.[34] A second study showed similar protection for types 16 and 18 after 4.5 years.[35]

The current ACIP recommendation is based on assumptions about duration of immunity and age of sexual debut, among other factors. As the vaccine is used for a longer time period, it may turn out that a different vaccine schedule is more effective. In addition, the effect on co-administration of other vaccines with regard to safety is unknown, as is the vaccines' efficacy with varying dose intervals. Some have also raised concerns about a negative impact of vaccination on cervical cancer screening programs, which are highly effective at reducing cervical cancer mortality. These unknowns must be studied as the vaccine is introduced in the broader population.

At present, therefore, questions remain about the vaccine's safety and the duration of its immunity, which call into question the wisdom of mandated vaccination. Girls receiving the vaccine face some risk of potential adverse events as well as risk that the vaccine will not be completely protective. These risks must be weighed against the state's interest in protecting the public from the harms associated with HPV. As discussed in the next section, the state's interest in protecting the public health does not support mandating HPV vaccination.

B. Historical Justifications for Mandated Vaccination Are Not Met

HPV is different in several respects from the vaccines that first led to state mandated vaccination. Compulsory vaccination laws originated in the early 1800s and were driven by fears of the centuries-old scourge of smallpox and the advent of the vaccine developed by Edward Jenner in 1796. By the 1900s, the vast majority of states had enacted compulsory smallpox vaccination laws.[36] While such laws were not initially tied to school attendance, the coincidental rise of smallpox outbreaks, growth in the number of public schools, and compulsory school attendance laws provided a rationale for compulsory vaccination to prevent the spread of smallpox among school

children as well as a means to enforce the requirement by barring unvaccinated children from school.[37] In 1827, Boston became the first city to require all children entering public school to provide evidence of vaccination.[38] Similar laws were enacted by several states during the latter half of the 19th century.[39]

The theory of herd immunity, in which the protective effect of vaccines extends beyond the vaccinated individual to others in the population, is the driving force behind mass immunization programs. Herd immunity theory proposes that, in diseases passed from person to person, it is difficult to maintain a chain of infection when large numbers of a population are immune. With the increase in number of immune individuals present in a population, the lower the likelihood that a susceptible person will come into contact with an infected individual. There is no threshold value above which herd immunity exists, but as vaccination rates increase, indirect protection also increases until the infection is eliminated.

Courts were soon called on to adjudicate the constitutionality of mandatory vaccination programs. In 1905, the Supreme Court decided the seminal case, *Jacobson v. Massachusetts,*[40] in which it upheld a population-wide smallpox vaccination ordinance challenged by an adult male who refused the vaccine and was fined five dollars. He argued that a compulsory vaccination law was "hostile to the inherent right of every freeman to care for his own body and health in such way as to him seems best." The Court disagreed, adopting a narrower view of individual liberty and emphasizing the duties that citizens have towards each other and to society as a whole. According to the Court, the "liberty secured by the Constitution of the United States . . . does not import an absolute right in each person to be, at all times and in all circumstances, wholly freed from restraint. There are manifold restraints to which every person is necessarily subject for the common good." With respect to compulsory vaccination, the Court stated that "[u]pon the principle of self-defense, of paramount necessity, a community has the right to protect itself against an epidemic of disease which threatens the safety of its members." In the Court's opinion, compulsory vaccination was consistent with a state's traditional police powers, i.e., its power to regulate matters affecting the health, safety, and general welfare of the public.

In reaching its decision, the Court was influenced both by the significant harm posed by smallpox—using the words "epidemic" and "danger" repeatedly—as well as the available scientific evidence demonstrating the efficacy of the vaccine. However, the Court also emphasized that its ruling was applicable only to the case before it, and articulated principles that must be adhered to for such an exercise of police powers to be constitutional. First, there must be a public health necessity. Second, there must be a reasonable relationship between the intervention and public health objective. Third, the intervention may not be arbitrary or oppressive. Finally, the intervention should not pose a health risk to its subject. Thus, while *Jacobson* "stands firmly for the proposition that police powers authorize states to compel vaccination for the public good," it also indicates that "government power must be exercised reasonably to pass constitutional scrutiny."[41] In the 1922 case *Zucht v. King*,[42] the Court reaffirmed its ruling in *Jacobson* in the context of a school-based smallpox vaccination mandate.

The smallpox laws of the 19th century, which were almost without exception upheld by the courts, helped lay the foundation for modern immunization statutes. Many modern-era laws were enacted in response to the transmission of measles in schools in the 1960s and 1970s. In 1977, the federal government launched the Childhood Immunization Initiative, which stressed the importance of strict enforcement of school immunization laws.[43] Currently, all states mandate vaccination as a condition for school entry, and in deciding whether to mandate vaccines, are guided by ACIP recommendations. At present, ACIP recommends vaccination for diphtheria, tetanus, and acellular pertussis (DTaP), Hepatitis B, polio, measles, mumps, and rubella (MMR), varicella (chicken pox), influenza, rotavirus, haemophilus Influenza B (HiB), pneumococcus, Hepatitis A, meningococcus, and, most recently HPV. State mandates differ; for example, whereas all states require DTaP, polio, and measles in order to enter kindergarten, most do not require Hepatitis A.[44]

HPV is different from the vaccines that have previously been mandated by the states. With the exception of tetanus, all of these vaccines fit comfortably within the "public health necessity" principle articulated in *Jacobson* in that the diseases they prevent are highly contagious and are associated with significant morbidity and mortality occurring shortly after exposure. And, while tetanus is not contagious, exposure to *Clostridium tetani* is both virtually unavoidable (particularly by children, given their propensity to both play in the dirt and get scratches), life threatening, and fully preventable only through vaccination. Thus, the public health necessity argument plausibly extends to tetanus, albeit for different reasons.

Jacobson's "reasonable relationship" principle is also clearly met by vaccine mandates for the other ACIP recommended vaccines. School-aged children are most at risk while in school because they are more likely to be in close proximity to each other in that setting. All children who attend school are equally at risk of both transmitting and contracting the diseases. Thus, a clear relationship exists between conditioning school attendance on vaccination and the avoidance of the spread of infectious disease within the school environment. Tetanus, a non-contagious disease, is somewhat different, but school-based vaccination can nevertheless be justified in that children will foreseeably be exposed within the school environment (e.g., on the playground) and, if exposed, face a high risk of mortality.

HPV vaccination, in contrast, does not satisfy these two principles. HPV infection presents no public health necessity, as that term was used in the context of *Jacobson*. While non-sexual transmission routes are theoretically possible, they have not been

demonstrated. Like other sexually transmitted diseases which primarily affect adults, it is not immediately life threatening; as such, cervical cancer, if developed, will not manifest for years if not decades. Many women will never be exposed to the cancer-causing strains of HPV; indeed the prevalence of these strains in the United States is quite low. Furthermore, many who are exposed will not go on to develop cervical cancer. Thus, conditioning school attendance on HPV vaccination serves only to coerce compliance in the absence of a public health emergency.[45]

The relationship between the government's objective of preventing cervical cancer in women and the means used to achieve it—that is, vaccination of all girls as a condition of school attendance—lacks sufficient rationality. First, given that HPV is transmitted through sexual activity, exposure to HPV is not directly related to school attendance.[46] Second, not all children who attend school are at equal risk of exposure to or transmission of the virus. Those who abstain from sexual conduct are not at risk for transmitting or contracting HPV. Moreover, because HPV screening tests are available, the risk to those who choose to engage in sexual activity is significantly minimized. Because it is questionable how many school-aged children are actually at risk—and for those who are at risk, the risk is not linked to school attendance—there is not a sufficiently rational reason to tie mandatory vaccination to school attendance.

To be sure, the public health objective that proponents of mandatory HPV vaccination seek to achieve is compelling. Vaccinating girls before sexual debut provides an opportunity to provide protection against an adult onset disease. This opportunity is lost once sexual activity begins and exposure to HPV occurs. However, that HPV vaccination may be both medically justified and a prudent public health measure is an insufficient basis for the state to compel children to receive the vaccine as a condition of school attendance.

C. In the Absence of Historical Justification, the Government Risks Public Backlash by Mandating HPV Vaccination

Childhood vaccination rates in the United States are very high; more than half of the states report meeting the Department of Health and Human Services (HHS) Healthy People 2010 initiative's goal of 95 percent vaccination coverage for childhood vaccination.[47] However, from its inception, state mandated vaccination has been accompanied by a small but vocal antivaccination movement. Opposition has historically been "fueled by general distrust of government, a rugged sense of individualism, and concerns about the efficacy and safety of vaccines."[48] In recent years, vaccination programs also have been a "victim of their tremendous success,"[49] as dreaded diseases such as measles and polio have largely disappeared in the United States, taking with them the fear that motivated past generations. Some have noted with alarm the rise in the number of parents opting out of vaccination and of resurgence in antivac-cination rhetoric making scientifically unsupported allegations that vaccination causes adverse events such as autism.[50]

The rash of state legislation to mandate HPV has led to sig-nificant public concern that the government is overreaching its police powers authority. As one conservative columnist has written, "[F]or the government to mandate the expensive vaccine for chil-dren would be for Big Brother to reach past the parents and into the home."[51] While some dismiss sentiments such as this one as simply motivated by right wing moral politics, trivializing these concerns is both inappropriate and unwise as a policy matter. Because sexual behavior is involved in transmission, not all children are equally at risk. Thus, it is a reasonable exercise of a parent's judgment to con-sider his or her child's specific risk and weigh that against the risk of vaccination.

To remove parental autonomy in this case is not warranted and also risks parental rejection of the vaccine because it is per-ceived as coercive. In contrast, educating the public about the value of the vaccine may be highly effective without risking public back-lash. According to one poll, 61 percent of parents with daughters under 18 prefer vaccination, 72 percent would support the inclusion of information about the vaccine in school health classes, and just 45 percent agreed that the vaccine should be included as part of the vaccination routine for all children and adolescents.[52]

Additionally, Merck's aggressive role in lobbying for the pas-sage of state laws mandating HPV has led to some skepticism about whether profit rather than public health has driven the push for state mandates.[53] Even one proponent of state-mandated HPV vaccina-tion acknowledges that Merck "overplayed its hand" by pushing hard for legislation mandating the vaccine.[54] In the face of such crit-icisms, the company thus ceased its lobbying efforts but indicated it would continue to educate health officials and legislators about the vaccine.[55]

Some argue that liberal opt-out provisions will take care of the coercion and distrust issues. Whether this is true will depend in part on the reasons for which a parent may opt out and the ease of opting out. For example, a parent may not have a religious objection to vaccination in general, but nevertheless may not feel her 11-year-old daughter is at sufficient risk for HPV to warrant vaccination. This sentiment may or may not be captured in a "religious or philo-sophical" opt-out provision.

Even if opt-out provisions do reduce public distrust issues for HPV, however, liberal opt outs for one vaccine may have a negative impact on other vaccine programs. Currently, with the exception of those who opt out of all vaccines on religious or philosophi-cal grounds, parents must accept all mandated vaccines because no vaccine-by-vaccine selection process exists, which leads to a high rate of vaccine coverage. Switching to an "a la carte" approach, in which parents can consider the risks and benefits of vaccines on a vaccine-by-vaccine basis, would set a dangerous precedent and may lead them to opt out of other vaccines, causing a rise in the transmission of these diseases. In contrast, an "opt in" approach to HPV vaccine would not require a change in the existing paradigm and would still likely lead to a high coverage rate.

D. Mandating HPV for Girls and Not Boys May Violate Constitutional Principles of Equality and Due Process

1. Vaccination of Males May Protect Them from HPV-Related Morbidity

The HPV vaccine is the first to be mandated for only one gender. This is likely because the vaccine was approved for girls and not boys. Data demonstrating the safety and immunogenicity of the vac-cine are available for males aged 9–15 years. Three phase 1 stud-ies demonstrated that safety, tolerance, and immunogenicity of the HPV vaccine were similar to men and women. The first two studies focused on HPV 16 and 11, respectively, while the third study demonstrated high levels of immunogenicity to prophylactic HPV 6/11/16/18 vaccine in 10–15-year-old males.[56] Phase III clinical trials examining the vaccine's efficacy in men and adolescent boys are currently underway, with results available in the next couple of years.[57]

HPV infection is common among men.[58] One percent of the male population aged 15–49 years has genital warts, with peak incidence in the 20–24-year-old age group.[59] A recent cohort study found the 24-month cumulative incidence of HPV infection among 240 men aged 18–20 years to be 62.4 percent, nearly double the inci-dence of their female counter-parts.[60] This result may have been due to the increased sensitivity of the new HPV-PCR-based testing pro-cedure used in the study. Nonetheless, the results reaffirm that HPV is common and multifocal in males. Males with genital warts have also been shown to carry the genital type specific HPV virus on their fingertips.[61] While HPV on fingertips may be due to autoinoculation, it may also represent another means of transmission.[62] Men are also at risk for HPV-related anogenital cancers. Up to 76 percent of penile cancers are HPV DNA positive.[63] Fifty-eight percent of anal can-cers in heterosexual men and 100 percent among homosexual men are positive for HPV DNA.[64] Therefore, assuming vaccine efficacy is confirmed in males, they also could be protected through HPV vaccination.

2. Including Males in HPV Vaccination May Better Protect the Public Than Female Vaccination Alone

As no clinical trial data on vaccine efficacy in men has been published to date, mathematical models have been used to explore the poten-tial benefits and cost effectiveness of vaccinating boys in addition to girls under various clinical scenarios. Even under the most generous assumption about vaccine efficacy in males and females, cost-effective analyses have found contradictory results. Several studies suggest that if vaccine coverage of women reaches 70–90 percent of the popula-tion, then vaccinating males would be of limited value and high cost.[65]

Ruanne Barnabas and Geoffrey Garnett found that a multivalent HPV vaccine with 100 percent efficacy targeting males and females 15 years of age with vaccine coverage of at least 66 percent was needed to decrease cervical cancer by 80 percent. They concluded that vaccinating men in addition to women had little incremental benefit in reducing cervical cancer,[66] that vaccine acceptability in males is unknown, and that in a setting with limited resources, the first priority in reducing cervical cancer mortality should be to vaccinate females.

Yet several models argue in favor of vaccinating males. Vaccination not only directly protects through vaccine-derived immunity, but also indirectly through herd immunity, meaning a level of population immunity that is sufficient to protect unvaccinated individuals. If naturally acquired immunity is low and coverage of women is low, then vaccinating men will be of significant benefit. James Hughes et al. found that a female-only monovalent vaccine would be only 60–75 percent as efficient as a strategy that targets both genders.[67] Elamin Elbasha and Erik Dasbach found that while vaccinating 70 percent of females before the age of 12 would reduce genital warts by 83 percent and cervical cancer by 78 percent due to HPV 6/11/16/18, including men and boys in the program would further reduce the incidence of genital warts, CIN, and cervical cancer by 97 percent, 91 percent, and 91 percent, respectively.[68] In all mathematical models, lower female coverage made vaccination of men and adolescent boys more cost effective, as did a shortened duration of natural immunity.

All the models include parameters that are highly inferential and lacking in evidence, such as duration of vaccine protection, reactivation of infections, transmission of infection, and health utilities. The scope of the models is limited to cervical cancer, cancer-in-situ, and genital warts. None of the models accounts for HPV-related anal, head, and neck cancers, or recurrent respiratory papillomatosis. As more data become available, the scope of the models will be broadened and might strengthen the argument in favor of vaccinating males. Given that male vaccination may better protect the public than female vaccination alone, female-specific mandates may be constitutionally suspect, as discussed below.

3. The Government Must Adequately Justify Its Decision to Mandate Vaccination in Females Only

While courts have generally been deferential to state mandate laws, this deference has its limits. In 1900, a federal court struck a San Francisco Board of Health resolution requiring all Chinese residents to be vaccinated with a serum against bubonic plague about which there was little evidence of efficacy. Chinese residents were prohibited from leaving the area unless they were vaccinated. The court struck down the resolution as an unconstitutional violation of the Equal Protection and Due Process clauses. The court found that there was not a defensible scientific rationale for the board's approach and that it was discriminatory in targeting "the Asiatic or Mongolian race as a class." Thus, it was "not within the legitimate police power" of the government.[69]

A sex-based mandate for HPV vaccination could be challenged on two grounds: first, under the Equal Protection Clause because it distinguishes based on gender and second, under the Due Process Clause, because it violates a protected interest in refusing medical treatment. In regard to the Equal Protection concerns, courts review laws that make sex-based distinctions with heightened scrutiny: the government must show that the challenged classification serves an important state interest and that the classification is at least substantially related to serving that interest. To be sure, courts would likely view the goal of preventing cervical cancer as an important public health objective. However, courts would also likely demand that the state justify its decision to burden females with the risks of vaccination, and not males, even though males also contribute to HPV transmission, will benefit from an aggressive vaccination program of females, and also may reduce their own risk of disease through vaccination.

With respect to the Due Process Clause, the Supreme Court has, in the context of right-to-die cases, recognized that individuals have a constitutionally protected liberty interest in refusing unwanted medical treatment.[70] This liberty interest must, however, be balanced against several state interests, including its interest in preserving life. Mandated HPV laws interfere with the right of girls to refuse medical treatment, and therefore could be challenged under the Due Process Clause. Whether the government could demonstrate interests strong enough to outweigh a girl's liberty interest in refusing vaccination would depend on the strength of the government's argument that such vaccination is life-saving and the extent to which opt outs are available and easily exercised in practice.

Even if courts upheld government mandates as consistent with the Due Process and Equal Protection clauses, such mandates remain troubling in light of inequalities imposed by sex-based mandates and the liberty interests that would be compromised by HPV mandates, therefore placing deeply cherished national values at risk.

E. Unresolved Economic Concerns

Mandated HPV vaccination may have negative unintended economic consequences for both state health departments and private physicians, and these consequences should be thoroughly considered before HPV vaccination is mandated. In recent years, state health departments have found themselves increasingly strapped by the rising number of mandated vaccines. Some states that once provided free vaccines to all children have abandoned the practice due to rising costs. Adding HPV could drive more states to abandon funding for other vaccinations and could divert funding from other important public health measures. At the federal level, spending by the federal Vaccines for Children program, which pays for immunizations for Medicaid children and some others, has grown to $2.5 billion, up from $500 million in 2000.[71] Such rapid increases in budgetary expenses affect the program's ability to assist future patients. Thus, before HPV vaccination is mandated, a thorough consideration of its economic consequences for existing vaccine programs and other non-vaccine programs should be undertaken.

The increasing number of vaccines has also placed a burden on physicians in private practice. Currently, about 85 percent of the nation's children get all or at least some of their inoculations from private physicians' offices.[72] These offices must purchase vaccines and then wait for reimbursement from either government or private insurers. Some physicians have argued that the rising costs of vaccines and the rising number of new mandatory vaccines make it increasingly difficult for them to purchase vaccinations initially and that they net a loss due to insufficient reimbursement from insurers. Adding HPV to the list of mandated vaccines would place further stress on these practices, and could lead them to reduce the amount of vaccines they purchase or require up-front payment for these vaccines. Either of these steps could reduce access not only to HPV but to all childhood vaccines.

Access to HPV is one reason that some proponents favor state mandates. They argue that in the absence of a state mandate, parents will not know to request the vaccine, or will not be able to afford it because it will not be covered by insurance companies or by federal or state programs that pay for vaccines for the uninsured and underinsured. However, mandates are not the only way to increase parental awareness or achieve insurance coverage. In light of the potentially significant economic consequences of state mandates, policymakers should consider other methods of increasing parental awareness and insurance coverage that do not also threaten to reduce access to those who want vaccination.

IV. Conclusion

Based on the current scientific evidence, vaccinating girls against HPV before they are sexually active appears to provide significant protection against cervical cancer. The vaccine thus represents a significant public health advance. Nevertheless, mandating HPV vaccination at the present time would be premature and ill-advised. The vaccine is relatively new, and long-term safety and effectiveness in the general population is unknown. Vaccination outcomes of those voluntarily vaccinated should be followed for several years before mandates are imposed. Additionally, the HPV vaccine does not represent a public health necessity of the type that has justified previous vaccine mandates. State mandates could therefore lead to a public backlash that will undermine both HPV vaccination efforts and existing vaccination programs. Finally, the economic consequences of mandating HPV are significant and could have a negative impact on financial support for other vaccines as well as other public health programs. These consequences should be considered before HPV is mandated.

The success of childhood vaccination programs makes them a tempting target for the addition of new vaccines that, while beneficial to public health, exceed the original justifications for the development of such programs and impose new financial burdens on

both the government, private physicians, and, ultimately, the public. HPV will not be the last disease that state legislatures will attempt to prevent through mandatory vaccination. Thus, legislatures and public health advocates should consider carefully the consequences of altering the current paradigm for mandatory childhood vaccination and should not mandate HPV vaccination in the absence of a new paradigm to justify such an expansion.

Note

The views expressed in this article are those of the author and do not reflect those of the Genetics and Public Policy Center or its staff.

References

1. D. Saslow et al., "American Cancer Society Guideline for Human Papillomavirus (HPV) Vaccine Use to Prevent Cervical Cancer and Its Precursors," *CA: A Cancer Journal for Clinicians* 57, no. 1 (2007): 7–28.

2. Editorial, "Should HPV Vaccination Be Mandatory for All Adolescents?" *The Lancet* 368, no. 9543 (2006): 1212.

3. U.S. Food and Drug Administration, *FDA Licenses New Vaccine for Prevention of Cervical Cancer and Other Diseases in Females Caused by Human Papillomavirus: Rapid Approval Marks Major Advancement in Public Health*, Press Release, June 8, 2006, *available at . . .* (last visited March 5, 2008).

4. Centers for Disease Control and Prevention, *CDC's Advisory Committee Recommends Human Papillomavirus Virus Vaccination*, Press Release, June 29, 2006, *available at . . .* (last visited March 5, 2008).

5. A. Pollack and S. Saul, "Lobbying for Vaccine to Be Halted," *New York Times*, February 21, 2007, *availiable at . . .* (last visited March 14, 2008).

6. Centers for Disease Control and Prevention, *Childcare and School Immunization Requirements, 2005–2006*, August 2006, *available at . . .* (last visited March 5, 2008).

7. Centers for Disease Control and Prevention, "A Closer Look at Human Papillomavirus (HPV)," 2000, *available at . . .* (last visited March 5, 2008); Centers for Disease Control and Prevention, "Genital HPV Infection—CDC Fact Sheet," May 2004, *available at . . .* (last visited March 5, 2008).

8. See Saslow et al., *supra* note 1.

9. S. D. Datta et al., "Sentinel Surveillance for Human Papillomavirus among Women in the United States, 2003–2004," in Program and Abstracts of the 16th Biennial Meeting of the International Society for Sexually Transmitted

Diseases Research, Amsterdam, The Netherlands, July 10–13, 2005.

10. Centers for Disease Control and Prevention, "Human Papillomavirus (HPV) Infection," July 2, 2007, *available at* . . . (last visited March 5, 2008).

11. J. R. Nichols, "Human Papillomavirus Infection: The Role of Vaccination in Pediatric Patients," *Clinical Pharmacology and Therapeutics* 81, no. 4 (2007) 607–610.

12. See Saslow et al., *supra* note 1.

13. J. M. Walboomers et al., "Human Papillomavirus Is a Necessary Cause of Invasive Cervical Cancer Worldwide," *Journal of Pathology* 189, no. 1 (1999) 12–19.

14. J. K. Chan and J. S. Berek, "Impact of the Human Papilloma Vaccine on Cervical Cancer," *Journal of Clinical Oncology* 25, no. 20 (2007): 2975–2982.

15. See Saslow et al., *supra* note 1.

16. B. Simma et al., "Squamous-Cell Carcinoma Arising in a Non-Irradiated Child with Recurrent Respiratory Papillomatosis," *European Journal of Pediatrics* 152, no. 9 (1993): 776–778.

17. E. F. Dunne et al., "Prevalence of HPV Infection among Females in the United States," *JAMA 297*, no. 8 (2007): 813–819.

18. L. E. Markowitz et al., "Quadrivalent Human Papillomavirus Vaccine: Recommendations of the Advisory Committee on Immunization Practices (ACIP)," *Morbidity and Mortality Weekly Report* 55, no. RR-2 (2007): 1–24.

19. L. A. Koutsky et al., "A Controlled Trial of a Human Papillomavirus Type 16 Vaccine," *New England Journal of Medicine* 347, no. 21 (2002): 1645–1651; D. R. Brown et al., "Early Assessment of the Efficacy of a Human Papillomavirus Type 16L1 Virus-Like Particle Vaccine," *Vaccine* 22, nos. 21–22 (2004): 2936–2942; C. M. Wheeler, "Advances in Primary and Secondary Interventions for Cervical Cancer: Human Papillomavirus Prophylactic Vaccines and Testing," *Nature Clinical Practice Oncology* 4, no. 4 (2007): 224–235; L. L. Villa et al., "Prophylactic Quadrivalent Human Papillomavirus (Types 6, 11, 16, and 18) L1 Virus-Like Particle Vaccine in Young Women: A Randomized Double-Blind Placebo-Controlled Multicentre Phase II Efficacy Trial," *The Lancet Oncology* 6, no. 5 (2005): 271–278; see Saslow, *supra* note 1.

20. *Id.* (Villa).

21. See Wheeler, *supra* note 19.

22. N. B. Miller, *Clinical Review of Biologics License Application for Human Papillomavirus 6, 11, 16, 18 L1 Virus Like Particle Vaccine (S. cerevisiae) (STN 125126 GARDASIL),*

Manufactured by Merck, Inc.," Food and Drug Administration, June 8, 2006, *available at* . . . (last visited March 5, 2008).

23. Centers for Disease Control and Prevention, *HPV Vaccine—Questions and Answers for the Public*, June 28, 2007, available at . . . (last visited April 2, 2008).

24. National Conference of State Legislatures, "HPV Vaccine," July 11, 2007, *available at* . . . (last visited March 5, 2008).

25. *Id.*

26. S.B. 1230, 2006 Session, Virginia (2007); H.B. 2035, 2006 Session, Virginia (2007).

27. *HPV Vaccination and Reporting Act of 2007*, B.17–0030, 18th Council, District of Columbia (2007).

28. Governor of the State of Texas, Executive Order RP65, February 2, 2007, *available at* . . . (last visited March 5, 2008).

29. S.B. 438, 80th Legislature, Texas (2007); H.B. 1098, 80th Legislature, Texas (2007).

30. The states are Colorado, Maine, Nevada, New Mexico, New York, North Dakota, Rhode Island, and South Carolina. See National Conference of State Legislatures, *supra* note 24.

31. The states are Colorado, Indiana, Iowa, North Carolina, North Dakota, Texas, Utah, and Washington. *Id.* (National Conference of State Legislatures).

32. The states are Maryland, Minnesota, and New Mexico. *Id.* (National Conference of State Legislatures).

33. Centers for Disease Control and Prevention, *RotaShield (Rotavirus) Vaccine and Intussusception*, 2004, *available at* . . . (last visited March 14, 2008); M. B. Rennels, "The Rotavirus Vaccine Story: A Clinical Investigator's View," *Pediatrics* 106, no. 1 (2000): 123–125.

34. C. Mao et al., "Efficacy of Human Papillomavirus-16 Vaccine to Prevent Cervical Intraepithelial Neoplasia: A Randomized Controlled Trial," *Obstetrics and Gynecology* 107, no. 1 (2006): 18–27.

35. L. L. Villa et al., "Immunologic Responses Following Administration of a Vaccine Targeting Human Papillomavirus Types 6, 11, 16 and 18," *Vaccine* 24, no. 27–28 (2006): 5571–5583; D. M. Harper et al., "Sustained Efficacy Up to 4.5 Years of a Bivalent L1 Virus-Like Particle Vaccine against Human Papillomavirus Types 16 and 18: Follow Up from a Randomized Controlled Trial," *The Lancet* 367, no. 9518 (2006): 1247–1255.

36. J. G. Hodge and L. O. Gostin, "School Vaccination Requirements: Historical, Social, and Legal Perspectives," *Kentucky Law Journal* 90, no. 4 (2001–2002): 831–890.

37. J. Duffy, "School Vaccination: The Precursor to School Medical Inspection," *Journal of the History of Medicine and Allied Sciences* 33, no. 3 (1978): 344–355.

38. See Hodge and Gostin, *supra* note 36.

39. *Id.*

40. *Jacobson v. Commonwealth of Massachusetts*, 197 U.S. 11 (1905).

41. L. O. Gostin and J. G. Hodge, "The Public Health Improvement Process in Alaska: Toward a Model Public Health Law," *Alaska Law Review* 17, no. 1 (2000): 77–125.

42. *Zucht v. King*, 260 U.S. 174 (1922).

43. A. R. Hinman et al., "Childhood Immunization: Laws that Work," *Journal of Law, Medicine & Ethics* 30, no. 3 (2002): 122–127; K. M. Malone and A. R. Hinman, "Vaccination Mandates: The Public Health Imperative and Individual Rights," in R. A. Goodman et al., *Law in Public Health Practice* (New York: Oxford University Press, 2006).

44. See Centers for Disease Control and Prevention, *supra* note 6.

45. B. Lo, "HPV Vaccine and Adolescents' Sexual Activity: It Would Be a Shame If Unresolved Ethical Dilemmas Hampered This Breakthrough," *BMJ* 332, no. 7550 (2006): 1106–1107.

46. R. K. Zimmerman, "Ethical Analysis of HPV Vaccine Policy Options," *Vaccine* 24, no. 22 (2006): 4812–4820.

47. C. Stanwyck et al., "Vaccination Coverage Among Children Entering School—United States, 2005–06 School Year," *JAMA* 296, no. 21 (2006): 2544–2547.

48. See Hodge and Gostin, *supra* note 36.

49. S. P. Calandrillo, "Vanishing Vaccinations: Why Are So Many Americans Opting Out of Vaccinating Their Children?" *University of Michigan Journal of Legal Reform* 37 (2004): 353–440.

50. *Id.*

51. B. Hart, "My Daughter Won't Get HPV Vaccine," *Chicago Sun Times, February* 25, 2007, at B6.

52. J. Cummings, "Seventy Percent of U.S. Adults Support Use of the Human Papillomavirus (HPV) Vaccine: Majority of Parents of Girls under 18 Would Want Daughters to Receive It," *Wall Street Journal Online* 5, no. 13 (2006), *available at . . .* (last visited March 5, 2008).

53. J. Marbella, "Sense of Rush Infects Plan to Require HPV Shots," *Baltimore Sun*, January 30, 2007, *available at . . .* (last visited March 14, 2008).

54. S. Reimer, "Readers Worry about HPV Vaccine: Doctors Say It's Safe," *Baltimore Sun*, April 3, 2007.

55. A. Pollack and S. Saul, "Lobbying for Vaccine to Be Halted," *New York Times*, February 21, 2007, available at . . . (last visited March 14, 2008).

56. J. Partridge and L. Koutsky, "Genital Human Papillomavirus in Men," *The Lancet Infectious Diseases* 6, no. 1 (2006): 21–31.

57. See Markowitz et al., *supra* note 18.

58. *Id.*

59. See Partridge and Koutsky, *supra* note 56.

60. J. Partridge, "Genital Human Papillomavirus Infection in Men: Incidence and Risk Factors in a Cohort of University Students," *Journal of Infectious Diseases* 196, no. 15 (2007): 1128–1136. It should be noted that the higher incidence might be due to the increased sensitivity of the HPV-PCR-based testing procedure used in this recent study.

61. *Id.*

62. J. Kim, "Vaccine Policy Analysis Can Benefit from Natural History Studies of Human Papillomavirus in Men," *Journal of Infectious Diseases* 196, no. 8 (2007): 1117–1119.

63. See Partridge and Koutsky, *supra* note 56.

64. *Id.*

65. R. V. Barnabas, P. Laukkanen, and P. Koskela, "Epidemiology of HPV 16 and Cervical Cancer in Finland and the Potential Impact of Vaccination: Mathematical Modeling Analysis," *PLoS Medicine* 3, no. 5 (2006): 624–632.

66. *Id.*

67. J. P. Hughess, G. P. Garnett, and L. Koutsky, "The Theoretical Population Level Impact of a Prophylactic Human Papillomavirus Vaccine," *Epidemiology* 13, no. 6 (2002): 631–639.

68. D. Elbasha, "Model for Assessing Human Papillomavirus Vaccination Strategies," *Emerging Infectious Diseases* 13, no. 1 (January 2007): 28–41. Please note that these researchers are employed by Merck, the producer of Gardasil vaccine.

69. *Wong Wai v. Williamson*, 103 F. 1 (N.D. Cal. 1900).

70. *Vacco v. Quill*, 521 U.S. 793 (1997); *Washington v. Glucksberg*, 521 U.S. 702 (1997).

71. A. Pollack, "Rising Costs Make Doctors Balk at Giving Vaccines," *New York Times*, March 24, 2007.

72. *Id.*

EXPLORING THE ISSUE

Should the Human Papillomavirus (HPV) Vaccine Be Mandatory for Early Adolescents Girls?

Critical Thinking and Reflection

1. If early adolescent girls (with their parents/caregivers) are to make an informed decision regarding receiving the HPV vaccine, what information should they be given?
2. Are HPV vaccines safe and effective? Do we have enough data (research and clinical trials) to draw a conclusion on safety and effectiveness?
3. Why is the HPV vaccine licensed for use and recommended for preadolescent girls as young as 9 years of age?
4. Recently, the HPV vaccine has been approved for adolescent boys. If the vaccine is mandated for girls, should it also be mandated for boys?
5. If an adolescent—who refuses to get the HPV vaccine—is infected with the virus and spreads it to others, should they be held accountable in the same way that someone with HIV "knowingly" spreads HIV?

Is There Common Ground?

An ounce of prevention is worth a pound of cure. . . . Who would disagree that we should prevent cervical cancer in women as opposed to treating it after cancer has occurred? The authors of both YES and NO selections certainly agree on this and other points. They support a vaccine that would eliminate cervical cancer. They agree that the HPV is widespread and is responsible for cervical cancer. Additionally, they agree the HPV vaccine is a significant health advance for women and the medical community. Hence, the debate is not about the vaccine itself but instead about "mandating" it—especially before long-term safety and effectiveness are known. The two authors subscribe to different theoretical frameworks that include social and economic issues in order to make their cases. When reading Dailard's analysis favoring mandatory HPV vaccinations, it appears that she subscribes to a utilitarian theoretical perspective. In this theoretical paradigm, the rightness or wrongness of a particular action is based on a cost–benefit analysis. In this case, the many benefits of universal mandated HPV vaccination (e.g., prevention of cancer with consequent reduced human suffering, long-term health care cost savings, etc.) outweigh the costs in terms of minor side-effects (e.g., pain at the injection site). In contrast, Javitt, Berkowitz, and Gostin's discussion (2008) of the reasons against mandatory HPV vaccinations seems to appeal to the bioethical principles of beneficence (do good), nonmaleficence (do no harm), justice, and autonomy (Zimmerman, 2006). While the principle of beneficence is met with mandatory vaccines (i.e., preventing cervical cancer), the principle of nonmaleficence is not met when one considers possible negative side-effects result-

ing from the mandatory vaccination. In terms of justice, there may be a "lower class" (financial hardship) that does not have equal access to the vaccine. Finally, mandating HPV vaccination violates the issue of autonomy.

Additional Resources

Bryer, J. (2010). Human papillomavirus health policy. *Policy, Politics, and Nursing Practice, 11*(1), 23–28.

Jennifer Bryer addresses the HPV health policy in this article. She concludes that the HPV vaccine could significantly reduce cervical cancer but to do so would require broad mandated vaccination coverage. She further argues that health care providers are in a position to educate adolescents and their parents about the benefits of the vaccine.

Caseldine-Bracht, J. (2010). The HPV vaccine controversy. *The International Journal of Feminist Approaches to Bioethics, 3*(1), 99–112.

This article presents an argument for why feminists have reason to be concerned about mandatory HPV vaccinations. The author discusses the potential conflict of interest that could arise given the cost associated with mandating the vaccine, the fact that men can also be infected yet there is no push to mandate a vaccine for them; and finally, that empirical evidence regarding women's safety is lacking.

Gostin, L. O. (2011). Mandatory HPV vaccination and political debate. *The Journal of the American Medical Association, 306*(15), 1699–1700.

Gostin provides a commentary regarding the attention mandatory HPV vaccination received during recent debates among U.S. republican presidential candidates.

Szarewski, A. (2010). HPV vaccine: Cervarix. *Expert Opinion on Biological Therapy, 10*(3), 477–487.

Szarewski presents his expert opinion regarding the HPV vaccine. His take-home message is that the vaccine Cervarix has been proven highly effective against diseases associated with HPV. He further states that because the vaccine is not a live virus, it is reassuring in terms of safety.

Vamos, C. A., McDermott, R. J., & Daley, E. M. (2008). The HPV vaccine: Framing the arguments FOR and AGAINST mandatory vaccination of all middle school girls. *Journal of School Health, 78*(6), 302–309.

This article presents arguments used by advocates who either oppose or endorse routine, mandatory HPV vaccine to school-aged girls. The arguments can assist school health personnel in being effective participants in understanding the debate.

Zimmerman, R. (2006). Ethical analysis of HPV vaccine policy options. *Vaccine, 24*(22), 4812–4820.

References

Agosti, J. M., & Goldie, S. J. (2007). Introducing HPV vaccine in developing countries—Key challenges and issues. *New England Journal of Medicine, 356*(19), 1908–1910.

Borgmeyer, C. (2007). Many states are moving to require HPV vaccination for school entry: AAFP calls such mandates 'premature'. *American Association of Family Physicians News Now.* Retrieved December 10, 2007 from http://www.aafp.org/online/en/home.html

Charo, R. A. (2007). Politics, parents, and prophylaxis—Mandating HPV vaccination in the United States. *New England Journal of Medicine, 356*(19), 1905–1908.

Charo offers a perspective.

Javitt, G., Berkowitz, D., & Gostin, L. O. (2008). Assessing mandatory HPV vaccination: Who should call the shots? *Journal of Law, Medicine, & Ethics, 36*(2), 384–395.

The authors review the scientific evidence supporting the approval of the HPV vaccine Gardasil. They also review the legislative actions that followed the approval of Gardasil. Their take home message is that mandatory HPV vaccination is unwarranted and unwise at this time. One reason among several they list is that both short-term and long-term safety is unclear.

Moscicki, A.-B. (2005). Impact of HPV infection in adolescent populations. *Journal of Adolescent Health, 37,* S3–S9.

Society of Obstetricians and Gynaecologists of Canada (August 14, 2007). Positioning Statements & Guidelines: SOGC Statement on CMAJ Commentary, "Human papillomavirus, vaccines and women's health: questions and cautions." Retrieved December 11, 2007 from www.sogc.org/media/guidelines-hpv-commentary_e.asp

Internet References . . .

For Parents: Vaccines for Your Children

http://www.cdc.gov/vaccines/parents/diseases/teen/

HPV Vaccines: Vaccinating Your Preteen or Teen

http://www.cdc.gov/hpv/parents/vaccine.html

Preteen and Teen Vaccine Resources

http://www.cdc.gov/vaccines/parents/resources/teen.html

Vaccine Impact

http://vaccineimpact.com/2016/american-college-of-pediatricians-latest-to-warn-of-hpv-vaccine-dangers/

Vaccine Information You Need

http://www.vaccineinformation.org/teens/resources.asp

Selected, Edited, and with Issue Framing Material by:
Scott R. Brandhorst, *Southeast Missouri State University*

ISSUE

Should Terminally Ill Adolescents Have End-of-Life Decision-Making Rights?

YES: Jo Cavallo, from "The Importance of Including Adolescents and Young Adults with Cancer in Their Advance Care Planning: A Conversation with Chris Feudtner, MD, PHD, MPH," *The ASCO Post* (2015)

NO: Lainie Friedman Ross, from "Against the Tide: Arguments against Respecting a Minor's Refusal of Efficacious Life-Saving Treatment, *Cambridge Quarterly of Healthcare Ethics* (2009)

Learning Outcomes
After reading this issue, you will be able to:
• Outline and describe the benefits of including adolescents in medical decision-making.
• Outline and describe the risks of including adolescents in medical decision-making.
• Analyze and critically evaluate the different positions of the issue.

ISSUE SUMMARY

YES: Jo Cavallo in his conversation with Chris Feudtner discusses the importance of including adolescents and young adults in advance care planning and potential ethical dilemmas posed by these conversations. Dr. Feudtner argues that taking part in this helps them gain some sense of independence and control and provides them with a chance to write their legacy and feel less alone or isolated.

NO: Lainie Friedman Ross debates different scenarios that are possible in treating adolescents with life-threatening illnesses and states that courts and state legislatures are mistaken in their polices to respect family refusals of treatments aimed at treating these illnesses. Dr. Ross concludes that mature minor laws that permit refusals of effective life-saving treatments by adolescents alone or in conjunction with their parents are morally unjustified.

Should adolescents have a role in the decision-making process related to their medical care? From a legal standpoint, one could argue that since adolescents are considered minors they do not have the legal capability of making informed consent related to their care. Just like in psychotherapy, legally the adolescent's parents or legal guardian have the legal right to know all that discussed in the session. However, some state legislatures have begun to follow what is known as the "mature minor" doctrine/statue, which allows someone who has not reached adulthood to be considered an adult in special circumstances (i.e., medical decision-making).

If an adolescent is given the legal right, does the adolescent have the cognitive and/or emotional maturity to make these decisions? Developmentally are they advanced enough to fully comprehend the potential consequences to their decisions? Anderson (2015) argues adolescents do not have the same ability to reason and make decisions as adults do because the adolescent's frontal lobe is immature and not fully developed. The frontal lobe is considered the executive control center of the brain and influences many aspects of an adolescent's rational processes (i.e., judgment, abstract reasoning, and personality). Another area of the brain that is immature and impacts decision-making is the cerebellum, which impacts the adolescent's ability to understand the subtleties of social and emotional interactions. Given the overall immaturity of the brain, along with the fact that the adolescent's neurotransmitters are overly active, Dr. Anderson argues that adolescents are incapable of independent medical decision-making without parental involvement.

Given these concerns and the belief regarding the necessity for adolescents to pursue their autonomy, some argue for a shared decision-making perspective when it comes to making decision regarding medical care. This perspective states that adolescents should be involved during the decision-making process, at least when appropriate (Coyne & Harder, 2011). Walker-Wilson (2015) puts forth the belief that including parents' and adolescents' perspectives (together) improves the decision-making process and helps protect against the potential biases (i.e., confirmation bias, over-optimism bias) or immaturity (i.e., underdeveloped frontal lobe) that may interfere with rational decision-making.

In the YES selection, the authors discuss the importance of adolescents being involved in their end-of-life care. They propose that it helps the adolescents have a sense of control and independence and feel less alone and isolated. The authors discuss the importance of helping the adolescents build autonomy and include parents and other important figures and they discuss the importance of the relationship between the adolescent and his or her physicians within the process of making end-of-life decisions.

In the NO selection, the author discusses the different types of scenarios available and various different state and legislative issues (i.e., mature minor) that influence the outcome, but argues the position that allowing adolescents to have the ability to refuse or reject a treatment/care is morally unjustified. She puts forth the position that it is our obligation (parents and physicians) to promote and protect the basic medical needs of adolescents and to give them the capability to refuse treatment is not in their best interest.

YES

Jo Cavallo

The Importance of Including Adolescents and Young Adults with Cancer in Their Advance Care Planning

A Conversation with Chris Feudtner, MD, PhD, MPH

Three years ago, a study of adolescents and young adults aged 16 to 28 with metastatic or recurrent cancer or HIV/AIDS compared the usefulness of two previously developed advance care planning guides—one prepared specifically for adolescents and young adults and one specifically for adults. The study revealed that at the top of the list of concerns by adolescents and young adults were that they be allowed to choose the kind of care and medical treatment they wanted and to express their wishes to family and friends about how they wanted to be remembered.[1]

The result of the study findings is *Voicing My Choices™: A Planning Guide for Adolescents & Young Adults,* which includes areas for adolescents and young adults to provide input on their medical care decisions, such as the type of life support treatment they want, how they want to be cared for and supported during their illness, who they want making medical decisions if they no longer can make them, and how they want to be remembered after death. The booklet can be previewed and ordered at agingwithdignity.org.

According to the National Cancer Institute, over 69,000 adolescents and young adults between the ages of 15 and 39 were diagnosed with cancer in 2011, about six times the number of cases diagnosed in children under the age of 15. Only accidents, suicide, and homicide claimed more lives in this age group than cancer.[2]

Being able to participate in their own care plan and state their end-of-life wishes while they are still healthy enough to take part helps young patients get back some sense of independence and control and provides them with a chance to write their legacy and feel less alone or isolated, according to Chris Feudtner, MD, PhD, MPH, Director of the Department of Medical Ethics; Attending Physician and Director of Research for the Pediatric Advance Care Team at the Children's Hospital of Philadelphia; and Professor of Pediatrics, Medical Ethics and Health Policy at the Perelman School of Medicine at the University of Pennsylvania.

Although end-of-life directives have largely focused on the medical wishes of adult patients, over the past decade, there has been a growing movement by physicians to include discussions about advance care planning with their terminally ill young patients, said Dr. Feudtner. *The ASCO Post* talked with Dr. Feudtner about the importance of talking with adolescents and young adults about their end-of-life wishes and the potential ethical dilemmas posed by these conversations.

Emotionally Difficult Conversations

Please talk about the attention now being paid to the end-of-life concerns of adolescents and young adults with terminal cancer.

Health-care providers have been discussing the need to talk to children, adolescents, and young adults about the nature of their health in compassionate but truthful terms for 40 years. About 10 years ago, a broader movement started taking shape regarding how to take the adult concept of advance care planning and customize it for young patients.

Although it sounds like a good thing to do in theory, there are logistical challenges to overcome, such as where to record these directives and how to cope with the emotional challenges of having these conversations. Even if it is ethically the right thing to do, these conversations are emotionally difficult for physicians.

Many physicians think of these conversations as depressing and disturbing, but they can have good outcomes for both adolescents and young adults, who are given an opportunity to have this important discussion, and their family members, because their loved ones also benefit from learning about patients' wishes for end-of-life care.

A Matter of Control

Is one of the main benefits of including adolescents and young adults in discussions about their end-of-life care that it gives them back some sense of control over their life?

That is one important aspect of advance care planning discussions. Adolescents and young adults often report that they feel these conversations give them a voice and some control. They feel empowered to be who they are and also to express the reality of the situation; and given that reality, they have the opportunity to express what they care about.

This is their experience; they are the ones who are most intimately involved with the situation, and this gives them an avenue to talk about it. So, yes, it's a control issue, but it also gives young patients the ability to be who they are and provides them the chance to leave a written legacy of their life, how they want to be remembered, and their hopes for their loved ones.

When to Talk: Sooner Than Later

How can oncologists start this difficult dialogue with their patients, and when should these conversations begin?
Some physicians are reluctant to initiate advance care planning conversations because they think the timing is not right, or maybe it is going to be too upsetting for patients and their family members. We all should look at this as an area of medical care that can be improved and search for ways to get better at having these conversations.

For example, physicians can introduce the topic by saying: "I promised you I'd always be straightforward. While there is nothing new that we need to worry about, I feel that I owe it to you to have a 'just in case' discussion about how you would want me to take care of you if you were to get really sick and were unable to tell me what you wanted."

Physicians can also say, "Many patients with cancer appreciate having the chance to talk about what matters most to them in case some day they get really sick and can't tell people what they want in terms of their care." They can also use some of the tools available in Voicing My Choices to help guide these conversations.

If a physician does not personally feel comfortable facilitating this type of discussion, he should enlist the help of someone on the interdisciplinary clinical team who does, because the comfort level of the facilitator will have a big impact on how comfortable the adolescents and young adults feel about engaging in the discussion.

In terms of when to start the talk about death and dying, the answer is we don't know for sure. There is no evidence to show that there is a "best time." What I can say is that when adolescents and young adults are given an opportunity to think about advance care planning while they are still fairly healthy, they do not object to it. They seem gratified to be given the chance to talk about something they know is a scary possibility and don't slip into magical thinking that because they are talking about death when they are still healthy, it inevitably means they are not going to survive. In addition, they also may not be depressed by the conversation.

I don't know that we will ever be able to say with certainty what the best timing is for such a conversation, but the feeling among many physicians that having these discussions too early is somehow a bad thing does not seem to be true. The conversation

should be offered as an option sooner rather than later because it does not appear to be harmful. But you must keep in mind that adolescents and young adults are individuals, and they should have a say in when this conversation would make sense and be meaningful to them.

The Ethics of Patient Autonomy

If a patient is under the age of 18, do you need permission from the parents before these discussions can begin?
This question addresses the ethics of autonomy of the patient, specifically for a child or adolescent who over time has an emerging capacity for autonomy, and how to respect this emerging autonomy while at the same time also respecting the responsibility and authority of parents to safeguard the well-being of their child. At both a conceptual and a practical level, it does not make sense to disregard parents by not involving them in the timing of these conversations. So one wants to approach parents with deep respect for their commitment to their children and their authority to make treatment decisions until their children are 18 or emancipated.

At the same time, you want be aware this is a very stressful situation for parents, and the conversation is going to be difficult not just potentially for the adolescent and young adult, but also for the parents. So what we want to do is support all of them in having this conversation and help them to realize that although the conversation will be challenging, it is something they may have already been thinking and worrying about. If they can hear each other talk through the issues they are confronting, it allows them the opportunity to join together and support each other, rather than be opposed or apart from each other.

What are some other ethical issues physicians may confront as a result of initiating end-of-life discussions with their young patients?
There are basically two issues. One is how to navigate the space between a child's emerging autonomy of adolescence and not just respect that autonomy but enable it to develop. If you don't engage younger adolescents in discussions about what they are going through and the treatments they are going to receive—and elicit their input—it is going to be difficult later on as their cancer progresses to transition them suddenly to the point where they have to cope with the inevitability of what is happening and make all of their decisions on their own.

It is better for younger patients to acquire the ability to make good choices for their own health by giving them the chance to have real informed input about what types of choices will be made on their behalf and that informed input might actually shift from decisions that are made for them to decisions that are made by them.

There is more of a role over time for informed input in medical decisions. Some people call it "informed assent," but I would broaden that concept beyond informed assent. It is rather "informed input," which means that rather than giving someone an option either to assent or not, the patient can talk about what matters to him (or her) in terms of treatment or end-of-life care, is informed about the process of figuring out what is the right thing to do, and is given the opportunity to be involved in care decisions.

In other words, before children or adolescents are developmentally ready to assent or dissent to a particular treatment course, they may be developmentally ready and eager to be given the chance to provide input regarding how they want to be treated.

The second ethical consideration is to be honest with them about the degree to which they are going to be able to craft the treatment to fit their preference. We have to be sure not to overpromise or misrepresent our commitment to honor their preferences.

If we are going to seek patients' assent, we also need to honor their "dissent" about what they do not want at the end of life. And since we often are not willing to honor patients' dissent, we have to be careful not to make promises we are not willing to keep.

The bottom line is if we are going to involve adolescents in decisions about what the best thing is to do for them, we have to involve them with the utmost integrity, assuring them that we will honor our commitments to the promises we made about their preferences and their views. It is better to be straightforward about our lack of commitment to honor our young patients' preferences than to make a promise and not live up to it.

A Sense of Connectedness

Does including adolescents and young adults in the decision-making of their end-of-life care help them accept death?
I don't use the phrase "accept death." I don't believe we fully understand what goes on in the minds of people as they actively start to die. In my practice, I have observed that sometimes when patients decline, they often become isolated and lonely. Having a conversation about what might happen once this process begins and asking patients how they want to be cared for allow them to have a stronger connectedness with their loved ones, and then they don't feel as isolated. And because of that connectedness, I have observed that patients are calmer and more comforted.

I think people want to believe their loved one accepted death, because it is easier to cope with the loss of that person, but I don't

know that it is true. Our goal is to figure out whether we can help people feel connected vs separate and calm vs panicky as they are dying.

We have no scientific evidence that having these conversations results in end-of-life care that helps patients feel more connected and calmer, but we have reason to believe that it is true. What scientific data do show is that having these conversations does not appear to upset people and that there is a general sense of appreciation for having had the conversation.

Disclosure: Dr. Feudtner reported no potential conflicts of interest.

References

1. Wiener L, Zadeh S, Battles H, et al: Allowing adolescents and young adults to plan their end-of-life care. Pediatrics 130:897–905, 2012.

2. National Cancer Institute: A snapshot of adolescent and young adult cancers. Available at http://www.cancer.gov/research/progress/snapshots/adolescent-young-adult. Accessed July 14, 2014.

Adolescent and Young Adult Oncology explores the unique physical, psychosocial, social, emotional, sexual, and financial challenges adolescents and young adults with cancer face. The column is guest edited by Brandon Hayes-Lattin, MD, FACP, Associate Professor of Medicine and Medical Director of the Adolescent and Young Adult Oncology Program at the Knight Cancer Institute at Oregon Health and Science University in Portland, Oregon; Senior Medical Advisor to the LIVESTRONG Foundation; and Chief Medical Officer of Critical Mass: The Young Cancer Alliance.

Jo Cavallo is a writer for the *ASCO Post* and *Life Matters Media*. Dr. Chris Feudtner is the Director of the Department of Medical Ethics; Attending Physician and Director of Research for the Pediatric Advance Care Team at the Children's Hospital of Philadelphia; and Professor of Pediatrics, Medical Ethics and Health Policy at the Perelman School of Medicine at the University of Pennsylvania.

Lainie Friedman Ross

Against the Tide: Arguments Against Respecting a Minor's Refusal of Efficacious Life-Saving Treatment

In October 1994, Billy Best, a 16-year-old adolescent from Boston, made national television skateboarding in Texas. Billy had been diagnosed with Hodgkin's disease earlier that year. After five sessions of chemotherapy, he had lost 20 pounds and his hair.[1] Billy had observed his aunt die after chemotherapy made her sick, and he too felt the chemotherapy was killing him. He decided to run away after he was told that most of the cancer was gone, but that he would need to continue chemotherapy and receive radiation therapy over the next four months.[2]

A self-described born-again Christian, Billy packed his skateboard and $300 into a small duffle bag, left home, and "put his life in God's hands."[3] His parents, heartbroken and stricken with fear, made an appeal in the national media for him to come home and promised not to force more chemotherapy on him.[4] When Billy returned from Houston to Boston, he and his parents met with the oncologists and explained that they would seek out complementary and alternative medicines (CAM) and use prayer. The physicians reported the family to the Department of Social Services, which tried to have Billy removed from his parents' custody and to have treatment forced upon him.[5] The State of Massachusetts dismissed the case after intense media coverage of the case.[6] Although initially the claim was that Billy would probably die without treatment,[7] the physicians eventually acknowledged that he had received enough chemotherapy that he had a good chance of survival.[8] Billy and his family, on the other hand, claim that he was cured by the CAM and prayer.[9]

Fourteen years later, Billy is, according to his own web site, healthier than ever.[10] He takes two to four ounces of Essiac a day "to keep his immune system boosted" and also does at least two 21-day cycles of 714X per year for the same reason. Billy avoids processed food, red meat, dairy products, and sugar and takes lots of Shaklee supplements. He also continues to enjoy skateboarding. On his web site are links to his book, published by his parents, and to 714X and Essiac herbal formula.[11]

Billy Best is not the only adolescent to make the media for treatment refusal. In 2005, 15-year-old Starchild Abraham Cherrix was diagnosed with Hodgkin's disease.[12] He underwent chemotherapy but was told in 2006 that the cancer had returned. He refused a second round of chemotherapy and the recommendation to add radiation treatment. Instead he and his father traveled to Mexico to try the Hoxsey method,[13] a combination of an herbal tonic and organic diet. Upon their return, his parents were accused of medical neglect and he was ordered by a judge to undergo chemotherapy.[14] Eventually a compromise of radiation therapy plus CAM was approved by the courts.[15] In February 2007, the Virginia state legislature passed what has come to be known as "Abraham's Law," which allows teenagers 14 years or older and their parents to refuse medical treatments for cancer and other diseases.[16] Today, Abraham is still fighting his cancer and remains optimistic that he will win the battle.[17]

In November 2007, Dennis Lindberg, a 14-year-old Jehovah's Witness with leukemia, was granted the right by a Washington State court to refuse a blood transfusion, even though the refusal was expected to kill him.[18] Dennis was supported by his aunt and legal guardian, Dianna Mincin, who is also a Jehovah's Witness. Less than 12 hours later, Dennis was dead.[19]

The trend is clear: The courts and state legislatures are becoming more tolerant of permitting refusal of efficacious treatment for minors (any individual younger than 18 years) with life-threatening illnesses, particularly when the minor and parents (or legal guardians) are in agreement.[20] In this article, I will argue why the courts and state legislatures are mistaken in their policies to respect family refusals of well-established, highly efficacious medical treatment for adolescents with life-threatening illnesses like childhood leukemia and lymphoma. For the purposes of this article, I consider a treatment "highly efficacious" if there is a greater than 75% chance of cure (75% overall survival) with the proposed medical treatment. The issue of line drawing will be discussed in the section "Pediatric Decisionmaking for Life-Threatening Illnesses When Effective Therapy Does Not Exist," below.

Adult Versus Pediatric Decisionmaking with Respect to Effective Life-Saving Therapies

Imagine Steve has low-risk acute lymphoblastic leukemia (ALL) that has a 90% overall survival. (How decision-making is modified when treatment is less effective is addressed in the section

Table 1

Decisionmaking by Competent Adults with Respect to Effective Life-Saving Therapies		
Adult's preferences	Yes	No
Physician's actions	Treat	Do not treat; try to convince but in the end, respect patient's wishes.

"Pediatric Decisionmaking for Life- Threatening Illnesses When Effective Therapy Does Not Exist," below.) The physician recommends chemotherapy and blood transfusions as necessary. If Steve is an adult, then the wishes of the competent adult are decisive on procedural grounds: The competent adult has the right to accept or refuse all treatment, including life-saving treatment (Table 1).

However, if Steve is a minor, traditionally his parents would be expected to make decisions for him. If parental autonomy to make healthcare decisions for a child were absolute, the response to the parents' wishes would look the same as in Table 1: Physicians would treat when parents authorized treatment on behalf of their child and would not treat when parents refused. But parents, as surrogate decision-makers, are held to a "best interest" standard. Although the presumption is that parents know what is best for their child, the state has the authority to intervene when the parents' decision falls below some threshold that qualifies their decision as abusive or neglectful. This is permitted because the child is not only a member of a family but also a member of a larger community, and the state has the authority to intervene when the parents fail to protect members of their family who are also community members. Thus, if Steve has a life-threatening illness for which an effective treatment exists, his parents' failure to authorize treatment is generally regarded as neglectful, and the state would take custody and consent for treatment (Table 2). However, as the treatment becomes more drastic (e.g., involves amputation) or less successful (e.g., the likelihood of overall survival is <10%), physicians may not seek court intervention. Even if the physicians seek court intervention, whether the state would or should override the parents is more ambiguous (discussed in the section "Pediatric Decisionmaking for Life-Threatening Illnesses When Effective Therapy Does Not Exist," below).

Some may object that if Table 2 is valid, then pediatric decisionmaking is not about respecting parental autonomy. Table 2 shows that parents can authorize effective life-saving treatment and have their permission respected, but they cannot refuse or their decisions are overridden. The objection is that the parents do not really have decisional authority, because authority to make the "right" decision is not authority at all. Nevertheless, even if parents do not have substantive decisional discretion, consent is needed and the physicians will seek parental consent first. If the parents refuse, physicians will often work with the parents to convince them to do otherwise and only seek legal intervention as a last resort. The belief is that the parent's consent is not just symbolic but is consistent with the respect that we give to parents in their authority over their child's life.[21]

The difference in how a refusal is handled in Tables 1 and 2 represents the difference in who determines what is in the patient's best interest. In adult medicine, a competent patient has the right to accept or refuse any treatment, including life-saving treatment. The solution to physician–patient disagreement is procedural: Physicians must respect the competent patient's wishes because it is presumed that the competent patient knows what is best for himself. This does not mean that the physician should accept all refusals as final, but after attempts at convincing the patient to change his mind, the physician must ultimately respect his refusal. A competent adult's decision is respected because, even if the physicians are sure that a medical treatment would serve the patient's medical best interest, physicians do not know what is best for any particular patient, all things considered. Steve may be a Jehovah's Witness and refuse treatment on the grounds that accepting blood will damn him for eternity, or Steve may refuse treatment because he believes that he can be cured with less toxic medicines as prescribed by his CAM provider. Either decision reflects his own evaluation of what is best for him, all things considered.

In pediatrics, determining who is the appropriate decisionmaker is more complex. Traditionally, parents were presumed to be the decisionmakers, but this presumption is being challenged in two ways. First, it is challenged if the physicians believe that the parents are not acting in the child's "best interest," or, more accurately, if they believe that the parents' refusal is neglectful or abusive. In these cases, the state may be asked to take medical custody of the child and override the parents' refusal. More recently, parental authority is being challenged by those who seek to empower minors with healthcare decisionmaking autonomy.[22] The trend to respect

Table 2

Decisionmaking for Children by Parents with Respect to Effective Life-Saving Therapies		
Parents' preferences	Yes	No
Physician's actions	Treat	Court order to treat over parental objections

Table 3

Decisionmaking with and on Behalf of Children with Respect to Life-Saving Therapies

		Minor's preferences	
		Yes	No
Parents' preferences	Yes	Best interest	Minor refusal
	No	Parental refusal	Family refusal

adolescent autonomy means that Table 2 must be reconsidered in light of the minor's own preferences. Table 3 provides labels to represent each potential decisionmaking scenario.

Pediatric Decisionmaking with Respect to Effective Life-Saving Treatment

Now imagine our patient Steve with cancer is 6 years old. There are very few who would argue that a 6-year-old boy has the capacity to understand what it means to have a diagnosis of cancer and what the proposed treatments entail. Few would argue that Steve could make an independent assessment of the risks, benefits, and alternatives of treatment. Therefore, as depicted in Table 4, the preferences of the child has a minimal role in the decisionmaking process. The reasons for acceding to a parent's wishes to treat are respect for parental autonomy and the parents' ability to assess what is best for the child. The parents' decision is overridden when they refuse life-saving treatment because their action is determined to be neglectful, and this holds regardless of the child's stated preference for or against treatment.

Table 4, however, is no different than Table 2: Parental permission is respected and refusal is overridden by court intervention. The child's own opinion about treatment or refusal has no impact on the outcome, even if it might have some impact on the process (particularly with minor refusal).

Now consider the trend to support adolescent autonomy in healthcare decisionmaking that is justified on the grounds that some

adolescents are "mature minors" who know best what is in their best interest.[23] A "mature minor" refers to someone who has not reached adulthood (as defined by state law), but who may be treated as an adult for certain purposes (e.g., consenting to certain types of medical care). Mature minor statutes now exist in many states and courts have frequently sided with the mature minor's right to define his own best interest and to make his own healthcare decisions.[24] Thus, it may be more accurate to state that medical decisionmaking for children historically was understood by Table 4, but that Table 4 now only applies to immature and/or young children.

If adolescents are deemed "mature" and are allowed to make decisions based on their own judgment of what is in their best interest, the decision-making process would empower the adolescent to make healthcare decisions just like his adult counterpart. The algorithm for Steve at age 16 years if he were granted decisionmaking authority, then, would be depicted by Table 5. It demonstrates that the parent's preferences serve an advisory function for the child, but only to the extent that the minor is willing to involve his parents, regardless of the fact that he lives in their house, they pay the healthcare bills, and they have responsibility for providing for their child's basic needs.[25] And when the parents' duty to promote their child's basic needs conflicts with the minor's right to define his own best interest, the minor's right would trump.

It is important to realize how Tables 4 and 5 differ. The presumption of Table 4 is that parents have authority to act in the child's best interest, and when they fall short by failing to provide for their child's basic medical needs, that the state will promote the child's "best interest" (i.e., the child's basic medical needs). In Table 5

Table 4

Decisionmaking with and on Behalf of Children with Respect to Effective Life-Saving Therapies

		Minor's preferences	
		Yes	No
Parents' preferences	Yes	Treat. Respect for parental authority in defining a child's best interest. Good to have the child on board.	Treat. Respect parental wishes on the grounds of the minor's best interest and the child's immaturity. Try to convince the child to see the utility of treatment.
	No	Treat with court order. Parents are failing to provide for their child's basic interests, which is medical neglect. Good to have the child on board.	Treat with court order. Parental medical neglect. The fact that the child agrees with parents is not perceived to be an independent decision.

the presumption is that the mature minor knows what is best and is acting in his own best interest and that his judgment trumps third-party duties to protect his basic needs. That is, the mature minor is being given the same decisional authority as the adults in Table 1.

Although the scenarios in which the minor seeks treatment (best interest and parental refusal) lead to treatment in both Tables 4 and 5, the justifications that support the decision to treat differ. When the child and parent consent to treatment (best interest), the focus in Table 4 is that the parents have appropriately defined the child's best interest and the child's agreement facilitates the treatment. In Table 5, the focus is that the minor has best determined his best interest and his judgment is corroborated by his parents' support. When the minor consents to treatment and the parents refuse (parental refusal), the reason for treating in Table 4 is that the parents are neglectful and they must be overridden, whereas in Table 5, the argument is that the minor has defined his best interest and the physician and his parents' should respect his autonomy. Attempts can be made to convince the parents to support their adolescent's decision, but if they continue to refuse, the physicians can treat based on the adolescent's consent.

Tables 4 and 5 have different outcomes in the scenarios in which the minor objects to treatment (minor refusal and family refusal). In actuality, in the case of minor refusal, most physicians would side with the parents and treat the minor over his objections, regardless of the minor's age. That is, most physicians would act according to Table 4 and not Table 5. This is not to say that physicians and parents would just ignore the adolescent. They would seek to get his support and to convince him to get treatment. Although the physicians and parents would do this for all children, they would be even more willing to engage a mature child and to use arguments and reasoning that are appropriate to his maturity.[26] But if a stalemate remained, the adolescent would get treated unless he could convince his parents and the physicians that the treatment was unnecessary. The minor could also avoid treatment by running away, like Billy Best.

So what does this mean about decisional authority? On first glance it suggests that the practice of respecting the mature minor does not hold when the minor has an available parent who concurs with the physicians. However, recall that in cases of parental refusal, the physicians will support the adolescent and take the parents to court, and the parents' decision will not be respected. That is, it seems that the physicians are not really respecting a procedural method of determining who best speaks for the minor but, rather, are targeting a substantive goal: The physicians will support whoever consents to treatment (i.e., whoever agrees with them). But that is not about respecting autonomy or about shared decisionmaking, but about making the "right" decision; more specifically, about making the same decision as the physicians.[27]

The case of family refusal, then, becomes the test case about decisional authority. Although physicians may respect adolescents and override parental objections on grounds of neglect in cases of parental refusal, and physicians may respect parents and override the minor's objections on grounds of immaturity in cases of minor refusal, in cases of family refusal, there is a minor saying that treatment is not in his best interest and his parents are in agreement. The physicians cannot claim to be respecting one party over the other. Rather, the physicians must either concede that the family knows what is best and respect its refusal or take the family to court to seek permission to override its refusal. And in more and more cases of family refusal with a mature adolescent, the courts are upholding the decision of the family. The courts may argue that their decisions are based on "mature minor" statutes, and yet it is not clear that the courts would uphold the refusal if the parents did not agree with the teenager as in the case of minor refusal.[28] This suggests that the "mature minor" doctrine is only invoked when the parents concur, which makes one question whether the courts' decisions are truly being based on respect for adolescent autonomy. This is discussed further, below.

Actual Decisional Outcomes in Refusals of Effective Life-Saving Therapies

In Table 5, the cases of minor refusal and family refusal reveal how empowering minors with decisional authority would change pediatric decisionmaking, but Table 5 does not really reflect what happens in actual practice. What happens in reality is shown in Table 6: If the parents give permission for treatment, treatment

Table 5

Decisionmaking with and on Behalf of Teenagers with Respect to Life-Saving Therapies (Algorithm IF Mature Minor Were Granted Decisionmaking Authority)

		Adolescent's preferences	
		Yes	No
Parents' preferences	Yes	Treat. Minor defines his own best interest. Good to have the parent's support.	No treat. Adolescent can make his or her own decisions, and his right to do so trumps his parents' duty to promote his basic needs.
	No	Treat on the grounds that the teen is a mature minor. Can try to help parents understand the minor's judgement.	No treat. Adolescent can make his or her own decisions. Strengthened by parents' agreement (although should be unnecessary).

Table 6

Decisionmaking with and on Behalf of Children with Respect to Effective Life-Saving Therapies
(What Actually Happens)

		Adolescent's preferences	
		Yes	No
Parents' preferences	Yes	Treat. In the minor's best interest (as determined by parents and minor).	Treat. Parents define the minor's best interest. Minor can avoid treatment by convincing parents or by running away (Billy Best).
	No	Treat. Go to court on the grounds that parents are medically neglectful. Can also assert that the minor is acting as a mature minor.	Treat/no treat based on court ruling. Argue to treat based on both (1) that parents are neglectful and (2) that teen lacks decisional capacity to make an independent decision. Courts moving to respecting the teenager's decision. This is particularly true when the teen and parent agree.

is provided whether the minor agrees (best interest) or disagrees (minor refusal). There are two ways of arguing in support of treatment in the case of minor refusal. One is to argue that the parents know what is best for the minor; the other is to argue that the child is not acting maturely. The minor can try to convince his parents that nontreatment is in his best interest (as in the case of Billy Best), but if he fails, treatment will occur. And yet, even if the minor convinces his parents to refuse treatment (family refusal), it is not clear that his and his parents' wishes will be respected. When Billy returned to Boston, attempts were made to charge Billy's parents with child neglect, to take legal custody of Billy, and to force him to undergo further chemotherapy. The case was dismissed, however, due to intense public pressure.

The courts' typical response to family refusal differs from their response to parental refusal. In the case of parental refusal, parents are often overridden by courts that find the parents neglectful. That is, the focus is less on parental authority and more about what is in the minor's best interest. When both minor and parent refuse (family refusal), the courts might still force treatment on young children on the grounds of what is in the child's best interest, but do not necessarily assert their authority to promote the adolescent's best interests, even if the result is that the minor, like Dennis Lindberg, dies from a treatable condition (compare family refusal in Tables 4 and 6, respectively).

One may argue that the different responses of the courts towards family refusal with a young child (override the refusal) versus with an older adolescent (respect the refusal) make sense pragmatically because it is more difficult to impose treatment on an unwilling teenager than on an unwilling younger child and because it is more difficult to take a teenager away from parents to force treatment because the teenager may run away. Morally, however, it is not clear that it makes sense. When parents refuse life-saving therapy, they are failing to promote their child's basic medical needs.[29] The fact that the minor agrees with his parents does not change the fact that treatment promotes his basic medical needs. Refusal of life-saving therapy may promote other interests and needs of the

minor and his parents (e.g., religious beliefs), but basic needs have lexical priority over other needs and interests.[30] Therefore, effective treatment for a life-threatening illness must be provided even if it requires overriding the minor's religious beliefs.

The case of minor refusal, on the other hand, shows the legal contradiction toward respecting "mature minors" because these cases rarely go to court. They do not get to court as the minor often does not have the where-withal or means to challenge both his physicians and parents and insist upon a guardian *ad litem* to take him to court to promote his autonomy. Even if the minor gets to court, it is not clear that a judge would uphold the adolescent's decision to refuse treatment and die when he is pitted against his parents and his physicians, who seek treatment to save his life, which, they argue, is in the minor's best interest. Thus, the current pediatric decisionmaking model is inconsistent with the moral principle of adolescent autonomy with which it is justified. Although it is claimed that a mature adolescent's autonomy should be respected because a mature adolescent knows what is in his own best interest, the fact is that the mature adolescent's autonomy is overridden when his actions are against his parents' perception of what is in his best interest (minor refusal). Rather, the adolescent is only heard when he agrees with his parents. An alternative decisionmaking model and/or moral principle is needed.

Constrained Parental Autonomy

Elsewhere I have developed a model of decisionmaking for pediatrics that I called constrained parental autonomy.[31] The model presumes that parents should have the authority to make life-saving treatment decisions for their children. Parental authority, however, is not absolute but is constrained by the respect that is owed to the child. There is both a positive and negative conception of respecting the child. The negative conception has lexical priority and requires that parents not harm their child's basic needs. The positive conception requires that parents help their child develop the skills to become an independent and autonomous decision-maker when he attains adulthood. But the positive conception is not limited to the child's future needs and interests, but also requires respect for the minor's present projects, although not to the extent that we would respect these projects if they were the goals of a competent adult.[32]

What does this mean for the minor and his role in the decision-making process regarding life-saving treatment? Few would argue that at age 6, Steve could make an independent assessment of the risks, benefits, and alternatives of treatment. Therefore, the preferences of the young child play a minimal role in the decisionmaking process as depicted in Table 4. The reasons for acceding to the parent's wishes to treat are respect for parental authority and respect for the parents' ability to assess what is best for the child. The parents are overridden when they refuse treatment because their actions fail to promote the child's basic needs and are therefore neglectful. This is true regardless of the child's preferences. Although the young child's voice is overridden as immature, this does not mean we do not try to cajole him into accepting the situation. It means, however, that the child's preferences for or against treatment are nonbinding, even if they are a signal to both the parents and the physicians that the child needs further education and support.

But what about Steve at age 16? In the case of parental refusal, physicians treat Steve over his parents' objections because his parents are failing to promote his basic needs and only secondarily because Steve tells them that he wants treatment (i.e., that treatment is in his best interest). In contrast, in the case of minor refusal, physicians follow his parents' decision and treat Steve over his objections. This is not to deny that Steve may have some present projects that are thwarted, but his parents have an obligation to fulfill his basic medical needs before they can consider how and to what degree they should respect both his present and future projects. Steve can try to convince them otherwise. They should hold steadfast.

There are two arguments to justify overriding the decisions of a mature minor (minor refusal). The first argument is that the adolescent's current autonomy can be overridden to promote his long-term autonomy.[33] This is quite different from how adults are treated, but there are moral reasons for treating the decision-making capacity of adults and adolescents differently. The adolescent's relative lack of worldly experience "distorts his capacity for sound judgment."[34] In addition, adolescents need the opportunity to develop "enabling virtues" (habits, including the habit of self-control) that can advance their lifetime autonomy and opportunities.[35] Although many adults would also benefit from the development of their potential and the improvement of their skills and self-control, at some point (and it is reasonable to use the age of emancipation as the proper cutoff), the advantages of self-determination outweigh the benefits of further guidance and its potential to improve long-term autonomy.[36] Second, parental interest in raising their child according to their own vision of the good life does not abruptly terminate when the adolescent has achieved some degree of decisional capacity. If anything, his parents can now try to inculcate their beliefs through rational

discourse rather than by example, bribery, or force.[37] In other words, the mature minor doctrine fails to acknowledge the limitations of judgment seen in many adolescents and the right and responsibility of parents to promote their adolescent's long-term autonomy. Adolescent maturity is necessary but not sufficient to justify sole decision-making authority in cases where effective life-saving therapies exist.

This is not to suggest that parents should not give their adolescent's opinions serious consideration, but only that parents should retain ultimate authority to consent to effective life-saving treatment over their adolescent's refusal until the age of emancipation. One could argue that even at emancipation the adolescent may benefit from parental input, but at some point, the value of making decisions for himself trumps his parents' authority to intervene even if it would promote his best interest, all things considered. His parents should attempt to convince him to act otherwise, but the refusal by an emancipated adolescent, like the refusal of any adult, must be respected.

How does the model of constrained parental autonomy address the case of family refusal? In this case, just as in the case of parental refusal, the parents are failing to promote Steve's basic medical needs. Thus, even though Steve and his parents may believe that the refusal promotes his present and future projects (positive conception), the physicians ought to seek court permission to treat because of the lexical priority of his basic medical needs. And the courts should impose treatment. Table 4 is the algorithm that the model of constrained parental autonomy generates for pediatric decision-making for life-threatening illnesses when an effective treatment exists for all minors regardless of maturity.

Pediatric Decisionmaking for Life-Threatening Illnesses When Effective Therapy Does Not Exist

In the case of a young child or adolescent with a life-threatening illness for which effective therapy exists, the model of constrained parental autonomy does not give any decisional authority to the minors and gives only modest decisional discretion to parents. However, if we were to consider the case of a life-threatening illness for which treatment is not highly effective (e.g., prognosis is <10% overall survival) or an illness for which only experimental treatment exists, then parental discretion and the adolescent's dissent would have a more determinative role. Table 7 depicts the algorithm that the model of constrained parental autonomy generates for minors with life-threatening illnesses when therapies have low efficacy or are experimental.

As in all the previous algorithms, when the parents and child want the proposed treatment, the treatment is provided under the best interest standard (best interest). Table 7 differs from Table 4, however, with respect to greater tolerance of refusals from either the mature adolescent or his parents. For example, although parental permission alone is sufficient to consent for

Table 7

Decisionmaking with and on Behalf of Minors with Life-Threatening Illnesses When Only Low Efficacy or Experimental Life-Saving Treatment Exists

		Minor's preferences	
		Yes	No
Parents' preferences	Yes	Treat. In the child's best interest.	Treat/not treat based on benefit-to-risk ratio and the maturity of the child.
	No	Do not treat. When possible seek compromise.	Do not treat, particularly if the child is mature. When possible, seek compromise.

effective life-saving therapy for a minor of any age, when parents want their child to undergo an experimental treatment or treatment with a low probability of success, healthcare providers often seek the minor's assent, particularly of the older child. One could imagine the reluctance and even refusal of a physician to force such treatment on a mature adolescent (minor refusal). Thus, the case of minor refusal demonstrates that when the benefit-to-risk ratio decreases, the preferences of the mature adolescent have a greater role, although even the mature minor does not have sole decisional authority.

When the parents refuse low efficacious or experimental treatments, most physicians will respect the refusal given the benefit-to-risk ratio (parental refusal), even if the child would assent. Likewise, when both the parent and the minor refuse life-saving therapies of low efficacy (family refusal), the refusal is respected, particularly when the child is mature. Again, the justification is based on the lower benefit-to-risk ratio of the proposed treatment that does not justify forcing such treatment over the objections of the parents and the minor. In fact, if the physicians were to seek judicial intervention to override either a parental refusal or a family refusal on the grounds that even low efficacious treatment is in the child's best interest, it is not clear that the courts would or should find for the physicians. Although the courts are entrusted to promote the basic interests of its children citizens in its role as *parens patriae*, it may be appropriate to refuse to mandate a treatment that is unlikely to achieve its goal. The justices do not need to believe that the refusal is in the child's best interest, only that they may elect to demur when it is ambiguous whether treatment promotes the child's basic needs. This does not mean, however, that physicians must accept refusals at face value, because it is morally permissible to attempt to persuade the family to accept treatment, or at least to negotiate a time-limited trial.

The difficult practical and moral question, then, is when does the shift from highly efficacious treatment (Table 4) to inefficacious or experimental treatment (Table 7) occur. There exists great variability and disagreement within the medical profession about how ineffective a treatment must be before tolerance for pediatric refusals should occur. Other factors may also play an important role in deciding whether to respect a refusal: the likelihood of a good outcome without treatment, whether the condition is acute or chronic, whether the treatment is a one-time therapy or requires a protracted course of therapy, the invasiveness of treatment, whether the therapy can be provided as an outpatient or whether it requires one or more hospitalizations, to what extent treatment must be continued at home, and whether mandated treatment would require separating the child from his family.[38] Individual cases may require line drawing determined by the courts.

Reevaluation of the Three Cases

Let us return, then, to the three cases presented in the introduction. In the case of Billy Best, the physicians thought it was neglectful not to continue chemotherapy and asked the state to take custody of Billy so his course of therapy could be completed. The fact that the physicians were wrong in their prognosis is wonderful for Billy and humbling for the medical profession. But that should serve as a warning: Before attempting to retake custody, the physicians had the obligation to consider how much treatment Billy had received and how much greater benefit would accrue from continued treatment. Had they acknowledged that he had obtained most of the necessary treatment, they may have decided that the costs of going to court were outweighed by the marginal benefit that additional chemotherapy would provide. That is, they should have realized that the appropriate decisionmaking algorithm was Table 7 and no longer Table 4. In a sense, this is what happened when Starchild Abraham Cherrix and his parents went to court. Rather than having a court decide whether or not to force additional chemotherapy and radiation, the physicians, family, and the state came to a compromise that included both allopathic therapy (radiation) and CAM. It is not clear that Abraham's family would have agreed to any allopathic therapy without the legal ordeal and threat of losing custody, which is what disturbs Mark Mercurio. As he explains, "I am struck by the thought that if Abraham's Law had been in effect when Abraham's diagnosis was made, he might have died as a result"[39] because the law makes it more difficult for physicians to seek third-party intervention in protecting minors from themselves and their well-intentioned but misguided families.

The death of Dennis Lindberg should not surprise us given the use by the courts of the algorithm depicted in Table 6. Refusals by mature minors are respected when their parents support their refusal (family refusal). The mistake occurs in believing that we have an obligation to respect Dennis' autonomy or the autonomy of his guardians when their decision violates his basic medical needs. Rather, I have argued that Table 4 ought to be the guiding algorithm and that Dennis should have been treated over his refusal despite his guardian's support. The court's decision demonstrates a failure to provide effective treatment over family refusal that a coherent moral framework and analysis would demand. Again, this does not mean that all minors must be treated in all cases: As the likelihood of successful treatment decreases, whether the treatment promotes the child's basic needs becomes more ambiguous, and physicians and courts should respect broader discretion to a parental determination of the child's best interest (Table 7).

Conclusion

The evolving position of many courts, state legislatures, and healthcare providers to respect family refusals in cases of life-threatening illness when an effective treatment exists (Table 6) is morally inconsistent with our obligation to protect and promote the basic medical needs of minors (Table 4). Basic medical needs have lexical priority over other interests and needs, both present and future regarding. Mature minor laws that permit refusals of effective life-saving treatments by adolescents alone (minor refusal) or in conjunction with their parents (family refusal) are morally unjustified.

Notes

1. Nealon P. Runaway teen-ager calls family in Norwell; Youth left home over cancer treatments. *The Boston Globe* 1994 Nov 6: Metro p. 34.

2. Weary of chemotherapy, teenager with cancer runs away. *The New York Times* 1994 Nov 6:A15.

3. See note 1, Nealon 1994.

4. Negri G. Parents beg ill Norwell youth to call home. *The Boston Globe* 1994 Nov 4: Metro p. 34.

5. Best B, Best S. Billy's story. Last revised August 27, 2006. Available at http://www.billybest.net/BillysStory.htm (last accessed 14 March 2009).

6. See note 5, Best, Best 2006.

7. Hart J. Cancer patient beating odds. *The Boston Globe* 1999 Mar 7:B2.

8. See note 7, Hart 1999; Kong D. Specialists express concern over youth's cancer treatments. *The Boston Globe* 1995 Apr 7:Metro p. 25.

9. See note 5, Best, Best 2006.

10. See note 5, Best, Best 2006.

11. See note 5, Best, Best 2006.

12. The Abraham Cherrix story; available at http://www.angelfire.com/az/sthurston/abraham_cherrix.html (last accessed 14 March 2009).

13. Markon J. Fight over a child's care ends in compromise; Va. judge's order could have forced teen to get chemotherapy. *The Washington Post* 2006 Aug 17:A01.

14. See note 13, Markon 2006.

15. Craig T. Kaine signs tax cut for poor, medical rights for sick teens. *The Washington Post* 2007 Mar 22:B02.

16. Markon J. Update: Teen who fought cancer regimen feeling 'amazing'. *The Washington Post* 2006 Oct 15:C02.

17. Associated Press. Chemotherapy case: Teen who fought treatment is in remission. *The Washington Post* 2007 Sep 15:B05.

18. Black C. Boy dies of leukemia after refusing treatment for religious reasons. *Seattle Post-Intelligencer* 2007 Nov 29; available at http://seattlepi.nwsource.com/local/341458_leukemia 29.html (last accessed 14 March 2009).

19. See note 18, Black 2007.

20. For the purposes of this document, the term "minor" refers to any individual less than 18 years old. The term "child" also refers to any individual less than 18 years, although I prefer to use the term "minor" when referring to all individuals under the age of 18 because "child" also contrasts with "adolescent" and the dual meaning of the term "child" can be confusing. However I do use the term "child" to refer to all individuals under the age of 18 when discussing the child's role and relationship with his or her parents.

     Some of the court decisions and Abraham's law use the age cutoff of 14 years to distinguish between children and adolescents, but mature minor statutes may include minors as young as 11 or 12 as "adolescents."

21. Buchanan AE, Brock DW. *Deciding for Others: The Ethics of Surrogate Decision Making*. Cambridge MA: Cambridge University Press; 1989:233–5; Ross LF. *Children, Families and Health Care Decision Making*. Oxford, UK: Oxford University Press; 1998:50–2; Goldstein J, Freud A, Solnit A. *Beyond the Best Interests of the Child* (new edition with epilogue). New York: The Free Press; 1979:7.

22. American Academy of Pediatrics (AAP), Committee on Bioethics. Informed consent, parental permission, and assent in pediatric practice. *Pediatrics* 1995;95:314–7; Alderson P. *Children's Consent to Surgery*. Oxford, UK:

Open University Press; 1993; Weir RF, Peters C. Affirming the decisions adolescents make about life and death. *Hastings Center Report* 1997;27(6):29–40.

23. See note 22, American Academy of Pediatrics 1995; see note 22, Weir, Peters 1997.

24. Slonina MI. *State v. Physicians* et al.: Legal standards guiding the mature minor doctrine and the bioethical judgment of pediatricians in life-sustaining medical treatment. *Health Matrix* 2007;17:181–214; Derish MT, Heuvel KV. Mature minors should have the right to refuse life-sustaining medical treatment. *Journal of Law, Medicine & Ethics* 2000;28: 109–24; Sigman GS, O'Connor C. Exploration for physicians of the mature minor doctrine. *Journal of Pediatrics* 1991;119:520–5.

25. Basic needs refer to primary goods as described by John Rawls (Rawls J. *A Theory of Justice.* Cambridge, MA: Belknap Press of Harvard University Press; 1971:62). Health is a primary good and medical care is one way to fulfill the child's basic medical needs. Parents have a duty to provide a threshold of healthcare services to ensure that the child's basic medical needs are met. See note 21, Ross 1998:5–6.

26. See note 21, Ross 1998:62.

27. Engelhardt HT Jr. Freedom vs. best interest: A conflict at the roots of health care. In: Kliever LD, ed. *Dax's Case: Essays in Medical Ethics and Human Meaning.* Dallas, TX: Southern Methodist University Press; 1989:79.

28. Consider, for example, the case of *In re E.G.*, which was decided by the Illinois Supreme Court in 1989. EG was a 17-year-old Jehovah's Witness with acute lymphocytic leukemia who went to court to be allowed to refuse blood transfusions. The Court concluded that EG had the right to refuse blood transfusions but that she required her parents' concurrence (*In re E.G.*, 549 N.E.2d (Ill. 1989) at 328).

29. Again, as defined in note 25, health is a primary good, and medical care is one way to fulfill this basic need. When a child has a life-threatening illness for which effective treatment exists, parents authorize medical care to promote their child's basic medical needs. Sometimes, however, as discussed in the section "Pediatric Decision-making for Life-Threatening Illnesses When Effective Therapy Does Not Exist," below, treatment may not achieve cure and may cause more harm than good. In those cases, promoting the child's basic medical needs may mean refusing low-efficacy or experimental treatment and authorizing palliative care instead.

30. Rawls uses the term "lexical order" to refer to the requirement to satisfy the first principle before one can move to the second principle (note 25, Rawls 1971:42–3). Rawls explains that the correct term is "lexicographical order" but that this term is too cumbersome (note 25, Rawls 1971:43). Likewise, I hold that basic needs must be satisfied before one considers other needs and interests, and therefore refer to the lexical priority of basic needs over other needs and interests.

31. See note 21, Ross 1998:50–2.

32. See note 21, Ross 1998:66–9.

33. See note 21, Ross 1998:61–2.

34. Gaylin W. Competence: No longer all or none. In: Gaylin W, Macklin R, eds. *Who Speaks for the Child: The Problems of Proxy Consent.* New York: Plenum Press; 1982:35.

35. Purdy LM. *In Their Best Interest? The Case Against Equal Rights for Children.* New York: Cornell University Press; 1992:76–84.

36. See note 21, Ross 1998:61.

37. See note 21, Ross 1998:62; see note 34, Gaylin 1982:31.

38. Diekema DS. Parental refusals of medical treatment: The harm principle as threshold for state intervention. *Theoretical Medicine & Bioethics* 2004;25:243–64; Burt RA. Resolving disputes between clinicians and family about "futility" of treatment. *Seminars in Perinatology* 2003;27:495–502; Clark PA. Medical futility in pediatrics: Is it time for a public policy? *Journal of Public Health Policy* 2002; 23:66–89; Antommaria AH, Bale JF Jr. Ethical issues in clinical practice: Cases and analyses. *Seminars in Pediatric Neurology* 2002; 9:67–76.

39. Mercurio MR. An adolescent's refusal of medical treatment: Implications of the Abraham Cheerix case. *Pediatrics* 2007;120:1357–8.

Dr. Lainie Friedman Ross is the Carolyn and Matthew Bucksbaum Professor of Clinical Medical Ethics; a Professor of Pediatrics, Medicine, Surgery and the College Associate Director at the MacLean Center for Clinical Medical Ethics and Co-Director at the Institute for Translational Medicine. She also serves on the Secretary Advisory Committee on Human Research Protections (SACHRP) and as the chair of the American Academy of Pediatrics Section on Bioethics Executive Committee. She currently practices at the University of Chicago Medicine.

EXPLORING THE ISSUE

Should Terminally Ill Adolescents Have End-of-Life Decision-Making Rights?

Critical Thinking and Reflection

Imagine you are a 16-year-old adolescent who just found out you were diagnosed with cancer, which, if you receive treatment, you have a great chance to survive. However, treatment involves chemotherapy and all of the side effects associated with that treatment:

1. Should you be able to make the decision to refuse or receive treatment? What considerations should be included in your decision?
2. Does the research on cognitive development and psychosocial maturity support allowing adolescents to make these decisions or does it support that adolescents should not (or somewhere in between)?
3. If a parent refuses the treatment recommended by the adolescent's health care provider, should the courts be allowed to intervene based on legal standards or precedence? Should the courts be allowed to intervene if a parent refuses to comply with the adolescent's wishes?
4. An oncologist comes to you expressing a desire to develop a resource for parents and adolescents who are dealing with end-of-life issues, what information do you feel is important to include in the resource?

Is There Common Ground?

Both the YES and NO selections take different positions on should adolescents be included in end-of-life decision-making. The YES selection argues they should be included and it is necessary for the adolescent to feel in control. Furthermore, the authors discuss the ethical dilemmas of autonomy and informed consent and the importance these play in the adolescent's wellbeing. In the NO section, the position is that including adolescents in decision-making is morally inconsistent with our obligation to protect and promote the basic needs of minors. However, even though both sets of authors take different positions on the matter, they both discuss the importance of adolescent input on his/her care.

Regardless of which side of the issue you fall on, the researchers agree that it is important that adolescents should be able to share their wishes in terms of end-of-life care. It is important to allow adolescents to have at least a say in the process and the research has started to develop guidelines within the community on how best to handle these situations. Future research should continue to examine how the various roles and expectations influence decision-making processes and what impact this may have on the outcome of such decisions.

Additional Resources

Grineyer, A. (2012). *Palliative and end of life care for children and young people: Home, hospice, hospital.* Hoboken, NJ: Wiley-Blackwell.

Partridge, B. (2014). Adolescent pediatric decision-making: A critical reconsideration in the light of the data. *HEC Forum, 26*(4), 299–308.

References

Anderson, J. F. (2015). Brain development in adolescents: New research—implications for physicians and parents in regard to medical decision making. *Issues in Law & Medicine, 30*(2), 193–196.

Coyne, I. & Harder, M. (2011). Children's participation in decision-making: Balancing protection with shared decision-making using a situational perspective. *Journal of Child Health Care, 15*, 312–319.

Walker-Wilson, M. J. (2015). Legal and psychological considerations in adolescents' end of life choice. *Northwestern Law Review, 109*, 203–222.

Internet References . . .

Adolescents and Young Adults (AYA)

https://www.caresearch.com.au/Caresearch/tabid/1567
/Default.aspx

End of Life Issues in Clinical Research

https://www.socra.org/publications/past-socra-source
-articles/end-of-life-issues-in-clinical-research/

**Office of End-of-Life and Palliative Care
Research (OEPCR)**

http://www.ninr.nih.gov/researchandfunding/dea/desp
/oepcr#.V7EvNWU9a0M

**Palliative Care in Adolescents and Young Adults
Needs, Obstacles, and Opportunities**

https://www.nationalacademies.org/hmd/~/media/Files
/Activity%20Files/Disease/NCPF/2013-JUL-15
/5B_Baker.pdf

Voicing My Choices

https://agingwithdignity.org/shop/product-details
/voicing-my-choices

Should Schools Be Responsible for Completing Body Mass Index (BMI) Report Cards in the Fight Against Youth Obesity? by Brandhorst

63

Selected, Edited, and with Issue Framing Material by:
Scott R. Brandhorst, *Southeast Missouri State University*

ISSUE

Should Schools Be Responsible for Completing Body Mass Index (BMI) Report Cards in the Fight Against Youth Obesity?

YES: Cynthia I. Joiner, from "Writing for the PRO Position—Body Mass Index (BMI) Report Cards: Should Schools Be Responsible for Screening?" *The American Journal of Maternal Child Nursing* (2009)

NO: Betsy Di Benedetto Gulledge, from "Writing for the CON Position," *The American Journal of Maternal Child Nursing* (2009)

Learning Outcomes
After reading this issue, you will be able to:
• Gain an understanding of the school's role in children's health. • Assess the role of the school system in the fight against obesity. • Critically consider the research that supports and challenges the usefulness of BMI report cards. • Analyze the benefits and risks of conducting BMI screening in the schools.

ISSUE SUMMARY

YES: Cynthia I. Joiner, MPH, RN and nurse research manager at the University of Alabama, views having body mass index (BMI) report cards in the schools as an extension of what schools are already managing to highlight the important role they play in helping to address childhood obesity.

NO: Betsy Di Benedetto Gulledge, an instructor of nursing at Jacksonville State University, highlights what she sees as the disadvantages of having body mass index (BMI) report cards in the schools; she challenges the accuracy of BMI measures and notes the risks of labeling on children's psychological well-being.

Obesity is a growing concern in North America and around the world. According to the Centre for Disease Control and Prevention (CDC), the obesity rate among children and adolescents has almost tripled in the last 30 years. Using data from the National Health and Nutrition Examination Survey, the CDC reports that about 17 percent of 12–19-year-old Americans are obese. When expanded to include young people who are overweight and at-risk for obesity, the statistic rises to almost 32 percent of American children/youth (Ogden, Carroll, & Flegal, 2008). Overweight and obesity issues are not limited to developed countries; their prevalence is increasing in developing countries, such as the Middle East and Central and Eastern Europe as well (Dehghan et al., 2005). Children who are overweight and obese are at risk for a range health issues and illness, including diabetes, high blood pressure, sleep apnea, cardiovascular disease, joint problems, and gallstones, and a range of psychosocial difficulties such as low self-esteem, poor body image, discrimination, and depression (see CDC; Evans & Sonneville, 2009; Justus et al., 2007). Furthermore, children who are obese and overweight are more likely to become overweight or obese adults, and to suffer from a variety of adult health conditions (CDC; Evans & Sonneville, 2009).

According to the CDC, assessment of overweight and obesity draws on the measure of Body Mass Index (BMI), which is the ratio of a person's weight to height (kg/m^2). Although it is not a direct measure of body fat, the CDC considers BMI "a reasonable indicator of body fatness for most children and teens." Others argue that while BMI may be a useful measure for adults, its use with children may not be appropriate given their changing bodies as they move through the growth cycle and into puberty (Dehghan et al., 2005). Children's and adolescents' weight status is calculated by plotting their BMI scores against a growth chart by gender and age to account for such developmental changes and physical differences across boys and girls (CDC). According to these CDC growth charts, weight status for 2–19-year-olds is defined as follows:

- *Overweight* is defined as a BMI at or above the 85th percentile and lower than the 95th percentile for children of the same age and sex.
- *Obesity* is defined as a BMI at or above the 95th percentile for children of the same age and sex.

However, there are no universal standards currently in place to assess weight status. For example, whereas the United States follows the CDC definitions of weight status, the UK draws on BMI reference curves that classify children with a BMI between the 91st and 97th percentiles as overweight, and those with a BMI at or above the 98th percentile as obese (Whitney & Kendrin, 2009).

Given the prevalence rate of obesity and overweight in young people, it is no surprise that this has become a social concern. How to address this issue and who should be involved are fodder for much debate. At a global level, the World Health Organization held a meeting of experts on childhood obesity in 2005 in order to better understand its contributing factors, assessment, and interventions (Ikeda et al., 2006). In 1998, the U.S. government named childhood obesity as an epidemic, and by 2003 the state of Arkansas passed a law requiring schools to expand their heath monitoring to include BMI assessments and a resulting "Report Card" be sent to families (Evans & Sonneville, 2009; Ikeda et al., 2006). According to Nihiser et al. (2009), at least 13 U.S. states have introduced legislation to implement similar school-based screening initiatives. The use of BMI report cards is grounded in a Health Belief Model whereby behavior changes are preceded by recognitions of vulnerability to illness; for young people who are obese and overweight, the recognition process often rests on parents and caregivers who must first perceive their child as overweight and at risk before behavioral changes can be initiated (Evans & Sonneville, 2009). Herein lies a problem. Research has repeatedly demonstrated that parents are not the best judges of whether their child is overweight or obese. For example, in a study by Chomitz and colleagues, 43 percent of parents inaccurately classified their overweight children as being a healthy weight. Similarly, Newmark-Sztainer et al. (2008) found that over half of parents of overweight adolescents (52.8 percent) did not label them as such. Low parental awareness and inaccurate perceptions are problematic in the fight against obesity; if a child's weight status is not classified correctly, how can behavioral changes to improve health be implemented?

How might BMI screening and subsequent report cards introduce a more objective measure of weight status and marker by which to generate a behavioral change? Many argue that because children and youth spend so much time in school, schools can play an integral role in preventing obesity (Nihiser et al., 2009). In addition to providing healthy foods and promoting physical activity, some schools have expanded their role to include BMI screening and report cards. According to Nihiser et al. (2009), BMI screening programs in schools have the following goals:

- Preventing and reducing obesity in a population;
- Correcting misperceptions of parents and children about the children's weight;
- Motivating parents and their children to make healthy and safe life-style changes;
- Motivating parents to take children at risk to medical care providers for further evaluation and, if needed, guidance and treatment; and
- Increasing awareness of school administrators and school staff of the importance of addressing obesity.

(pp. 590–591)

Research on the efficacy of BMI screening programs in schools does not exist; however, issues related to in-school screening programs, such as student perceptions and comfort (Kalich et al., 2008), parental use of information (Chomit et al., 2003; Newmark-Sztainer et al., 2008), and possible harm have been studied (see Ikeda et al., 2006 for a review). It is not clear whether such programs do, indeed, prevent or reduce obesity. What makes this particularly difficult to evaluate is that many schools who have introduced BMI screening have not done so in isolation. They have also implemented changes in physical activity required of students, nutritional contents of foods served, and snack selections in school vending machines.

BMI screening and report cards in schools are becoming a widespread practice in the fight against obesity. Researchers, health practitioners, and the general public seem to endorse the need to reduce overweight and obesity, especially in our young; however, they do not agree on how to do this. Whereas schools can be part of the screening and reporting process, the question on the table is *should* they? Do screening and reporting fall under the responsibility of the school system? Are there measures in place to control for confidentiality of the information gathered and shared? Are parents adequately supported when they do receive BMI report cards from schools? What do they do with this information? Are schools "meddling" where they don't belong—in parents/caregivers parenting practices OR are they "stepping up to the plate" as part of a holistic approach to reducing childhood obesity?

While reading the YES and NO selections, consider the pros and cons of BMI screening in the schools and the role this process plays in helping to address childhood obesity. Weigh the advantages and disadvantages, and decide where you stand on the issue.

Should Schools Be Responsible for Completing Body Mass Index (BMI) Report Cards in the Fight Against Youth Obesity? by Brandhorst

65

YES ↵

Cynthia I. Joiner

Writing for the PRO Position—Body Mass Index (BMI) Report Cards: Should Schools Be Responsible for Screening?

In my opinion, body mass index (BMI) report cards in schools offer an opportunity to help tackle childhood obesity and should be encouraged. Among children 6 to 11 years of age, the prevalence of obesity has increased from 6.5% to 17% over the past three decades, and among adolescents aged 12 to 19 years of age, the rate of obesity has more than tripled, increasing from 5% in 1980 to 17.6% in 2006 (Ogden, 2008). Childhood obesity has reached epidemic proportions.

BMI report cards can provide a means to annually gather detailed data on childhood obesity, and to follow individual and group trends. The data collected can include information on all ages, gender, race, and ethnicity, and can thus provide valuable data necessary to monitor obesity trends at both the state and local level where data often is limited. Information obtained from the report cards can be used to help plan and target public health interventions for specific populations. Although BMI is not a perfect measurement, the BMI report card is intended to be used as a screening tool to help identify potential health risks, identifying the percent of students who are underweight, normal weight, overweight, and obese, detecting those children who are at risk for weight-related health problems (Nihiser, 2007).

Schools are well equipped to take on the responsibility of BMI screening and reporting. They manage other screening programs using standardized protocols (such as those for vision, hearing, and scoliosis), and BMI screening is no different. Managing the assessment and findings in a private, sensitive manner, and including education as a key component of the screening and assessment helps to insure that children would not be emotionally harmed or threatened by the process.

BMI screening and reporting programs need to be comprehensive in nature, and should be administered and managed with the assistance of healthcare professionals. School nurses are the appropriate professionals to perform the BMI screening, for accuracy in measurements is essential. Results of the assessment should be individualized and sent to parents in a confidential manner; the findings should include educational information about healthy diet, physical activity, and referral information for those who might wish additional assistance in managing their child's weight.

The Institute of Medicine (IOM) endorses BMI reporting and recommends that schools measure children's weight, height, and BMI annually. Underscoring the importance of BMI screening in preventing childhood obesity, the Institute of Medicine (2005) has called upon the federal government to develop guidance for measuring BMI in schools, where children spend a majority of their developmental years; 95% of American children ages 5 to 17 are enrolled in school (Institute of Medicine, 2005). Since schools strongly influence a child's health, diet, and physical activity for a greater part of their youth, they are the perfect place for promoting a healthy lifestyle. Schools also have frequent contact with and access to parents, so BMI assessments can be discussed with them along with other health issues they may not have considered to be a problem for their child.

Schools already manage other screening programs using standardized protocols such as those for vision, hearing, and scoliosis. BMI screening is no different.

If school-based BMI screening and report cards are part of a comprehensive program, including other strategies such as limiting access to low-nutrient, high-sugar foods during the school day and increasing the frequency and duration of school-based physical exercise, they can provide important information about the effectiveness of interventions to prevent childhood obesity.

References

Institute of Medicine. (2005). *Preventing childhood obesity: Health in the balance*. Washington, DC: National Academies Press.

Nihiser, A. J., Lee, S. M., Wechsler, H., McKenna, M., Odom, E., Reinhold, C., Thompson, D., & Grummer-Strawn, L. (2007). Body mass index measurement in schools. *Journal of School Health*, 77, 651–671.

Ogden, C. L., Carroll, M. D., Flegal, K. M. (2008). High body mass index for age among US children and adolescents. 2003–2006. *JAMA, 299*, 2401–2405.

Joiner, Cyntha I. From *American Journal of Maternal Child Nursing*, vol. 34, no. 4, July/August 2009, p. 208. Copyright © 2009 by Lippincott, Williams & Wilkins/Wolters Kluwer Health—Journals. Reprinted by permission.

Betsy Di Benedetto Gulledge    **NO**

Writing for the CON Position

The inclusion of body mass index (BMI) report cards as a component of a school's responsibility is disadvantageous on multiple levels. Several states have already implemented BMI report cards as a component of a state-wide initiatives to fight obesity; thus far only Arkansas has demonstrated significant change in BMI among students from 2003 to 2005 (Story, Nanney, & Schwartz, 2009). Does sending home a report of a child's weight classification really contribute to preventing overweight and obese children? Some parents of overweight children who have been a part of BMI report card program have reported that they feel the assessments are counterproductive and perhaps even harmful (Story et al., 2009). Parents of overweight and obese children do not need anyone pointing out the obvious. What they need are real solutions that can be incorporated into real life.

In a society intent on *labeling* every child, such approaches as BMI report card can have disastrous consequences including low self-esteem. In my opinion, the role of the school environment is primarily education, not health assessment. There is also a great irony in the prospect of schools assuming the responsibility of determining body mass index when many school systems have significantly limited the amount of instructional time spent engaged in physical education. Parents who are concerned about their child's weight might desire the school's input, but it would be more appropriately focused on how the school can provide additional educational opportunities about health and wellness, not measuring BMI.

An additional concern is the maintenance of confidentiality. Although schools are accountable to provide privacy for student information, there is the significant concern students may disclose such personal information to one another and then suffer the consequences in the form of bullying, thus being further ostracized from their peer group (Story et al., 2009). Children may also experience feelings of fear and anxiety related to a weight classification associated with serious health issues. These feelings may then lead to the development of psychological distress and associated eating disorders.

Opposition to BMI report cards has also come from healthcare practitioners. BMI has not been shown to be the most accurate measure of body composition in children. When considering body size, stature, and muscle composition, BMI, has questionable validity (Maynard et al., 2001). The use of BMI during childhood, particularly adolescence, can contribute to over-estimations in level of body fat (Kimm et al., 2005). Healthcare practitioners also caution against the use of BMI as a definitive measurement tool since there is a distinguishable difference in body mass and body fat. Whereas obesity refers to the amount of body fat, BMI refers to body weight, and the relationship between age and body fat versus body mass may significantly change as the child ages.

Finally, research on childhood overweight and obesity has yet to reach any causal conclusions. Disagreement exists over the classifications of at-risk for overweight, overweight, obese, and severely obese categories. There is, however, consensus that prevalence rates of unhealthy weight among children have increased and there is an immediate need for solutions. However, solutions do not lie in merely the identification and reporting of those children meeting criteria for a high BMI. If the healthcare and education communities are to unite in assisting parents and children achieve a healthy lifestyle, initiatives should be focused on interventions and education, not counterproductive labeling.

References

Kimm, S., Glynn, N., Obarzanek, E., Kriska, A., Daniels, S., Barton, B., & Liu, K. (2005). Relation between the changes in physical activity and body mass index during adolescence: a multicentre longitudinal study. *Lancet, 366*(9482), 301–307.

Maynard, L., Wisemandle, W., Roche, A., Chumlea, W., Guo, S., & Siervogel, R. (2001). Childhood body composition in relation to body mass index. *Pediatrics, 107*(2), 344–350.

Story, M., Nanney, M. S., & Schwartz, M. B. (2009). Schools and obesity prevention: Creating school environments and policies to promote healthy eating and physical activity. *The Milbank Quarterly, 87*(1), 71–100.

Should Schools Be Responsible for Completing Body Mass Index (BMI) Report Cards in the Fight Against Youth Obesity? by Brandhorst

67

EXPLORING THE ISSUE

Should Schools Be Responsible for Completing Body Mass Index (BMI) Report Cards in the Fight Against Youth Obesity?

Critical Thinking and Reflection

1. Given the controversy regarding whether schools should be responsible for BMI screening and report cards, what safeguards need to be put in place to protect young people's privacy and confidentiality surrounding their medical information?
2. If you were to empirically examine the impact of BMI report cards on youth obesity and overweight, how would you design the study? Who would comprise your sample? What variables would you include and why? How would you measure them?
3. Imagine that you are a parent of an early adolescent and that your child brings home a BMI report card, alongside the academic one. This document informs you that your child's BMI is above average for his/her age and labels your child overweight, bordering on obese. Your child reads this and becomes very upset. Take a moment to critically self-reflect on what your response might be: What are your beliefs about the roles of parents and the school system in socializing and caring for our young? Where do your beliefs align with, or diverge from, research data? What actions would you take and why?
4. Consider the role of schools beyond the initial BMI screening process. Should the school's responsibility end at screening? How can schools, parents, and health care practitioners work together beyond the screening process to incorporate prevention and intervention strategies to decrease youth obesity and overweight?

Is There Common Ground?

Childhood and youth obesity and overweight are serious health concerns. Words like "crisis" and "epidemic" have been used to describe the growing concern around the health risks (for both youth and adults) that weight issues in childhood and adolescence pose. Are BMI screening in the schools and subsequent report cards helpful in the fight against obesity? The YES and NO selections hold opposing views. Cynthia Joiner argues that the school system is a logical system to include in this effort, in part, because it is well within the school's ability to conduct BMI screening, and children/youth spend the majority of their time in school. Furthermore, she highlights that the data gathered through such efforts are integral to monitoring obesity trends, and can thus be used to support intervention strategies. Arguing for the CON position, Betsy Di Benedetto Gulledge draws attention to concerns that BMI is a less-than-ideal measuring tool, especially for young people, and that schools are not adept to handle the follow-through of such screening, particularly in terms of ensuring confidentiality of results and preventing the potential negative outcomes of labeling. An additional concern is how the information is used; specifically, how parents are supported in understanding and acting upon the results. Although intuitively reasonable, the efficacy of BMI screening programs

and report cards in the schools has not been fully established in the research. Methodological issues are partially at play here—whereas associations between screening programs and decreases in obesity and overweight have been noted, the data do not support inferences regarding causality.

So where does that leave us? Should BMI screening and report cards be standard protocol in all schools? Do the benefits outweigh the risks? Should the responsibility for monitoring and decreasing obesity and overweight concerns in young people move beyond the family to include a more "objective" or "neutral" third party—the school? If so, how should this process be managed (and by whom) in order to protect against the possible negative outcomes, including breach of confidentiality and labeling?

Additional Resources

Centre for Disease Control and Prevention. (CDC, 2012). Basics about childhood obesity. Retrieved from http://www.cdc.gov/obesity/childhood/basics.html

Grimmett, C., Croker, H., Carnell, S., & Wardle, J. (2008). Telling parents their child's weight status: Psychological impact of a weight-screening program. *Pediatrics*, *122*(3), 682–688.

References

Chomitz, V. R., Collins, J., Kim, J., Kramer, E., & McGowan, R. (2003). Promoting healthy weight among elementary school children via a health report card approach. *Archives of Pediatrics and Adolescent Medicine, 157*(8), 765–772.

Dehghan, M., Akhtar-Danesh, N., & Merchant, A. T. (2005). Childhood obesity, prevalence and prevention. *Nutrition Journal, 4*(24), 1–8. doi:10.1186/1475–2891-4-24

Evans, E. W., & Sonneville, K. R. (2009). BMI report cards: Will they pass or fail in the fight against pediatric obesity? *Current Opinion in Pediatrics, 21*(4), 431–436.

Ikeda, J. P., Crawford, P. B., & Woodward-Lopez, G. (2006). BMI screening in schools: Helpful or harmful. *Health Education Research, 21*(6), 761–769.

Justus, M. B., Ryan, K. W., Rockenback, J., Katterapalli, C., & Card-Higginson, P. (2007). Lessons learned while implementing a legislated school policy: Body mass index assessments among Arkansas's public school students. *School of Health Policy, 77*(10), 706–713.

Kalich, K. A., Chomitz, V., Peterson, K. E., McGowan, R., Houser, R. F., et al. (2008). Comfort and utility of school-based weight screening: The student perspective. *BMC Pediatrics, 8:9*, doi:10.1186/1471–2431-8-9.

Newmark-Sztainer, D., Wall, M., Story, M., & van den Berg, P. (2008). Accurate parental classification of overweight adolescents' weight status: Does it matter? *Pediatrics, 121*(6), 1495–1502.

Nihiser, A. J., Lee, S. M., Wechsler, H., McKenna, M., Odom, E., Reinold, C., et al. (2009). BMI measurement in schools. *Pediatrics, 124,* 589–597. doi: 10.1542/peds.2008–3586L.

Ogden, C. L., Carroll, M. D., & Flegal, K. M. (2008). High body mass index for age among US children and adolescents, 2003-2006. *Journal of American Medical Association, 299*(20), 2401–2405.

Internet References . . .

Body Mass Index (BMI) Measurement in Schools

http://www.cdc.gov/healthyschools/obesity/BMI/BMI
_measurement_schools.htm

Childhood Overweight

http://www.obesity.org/obesity/resources/facts-about
-obesity/childhood-overweight

Do Schools' BMI Screenings of Students Even Work?

http://www.cnn.com/2016/03/17/health/bmi-screenings
-schools-students/

Prevention Strategies and Guidelines

https://www.cdc.gov/obesity/resources/strategies
-guidelines.html

Weight Management for Youth

https://www.nutrition.gov/weight-management/weight
-management-youth

Unit 2

UNIT

Sex, Sexuality, and Gender

A very important part of an adolescent's development is sexuality. Unfortunately, many textbooks regarding adolescence will gloss over the topics of sex, sexuality, and sometimes gender issues pertaining to youth because of the controversial nature of these topics. Learning about sex and sexuality is of critical importance to youth. Developing sexual and romantic relationships with peers is considered a critical part of youth development. Adolescence is a time when sexual identity and gender roles are explored and formed. This unit examines some of the key issues surrounding sexuality and gender in adolescence.

Selected, Edited, and with Issue Framing Material by:
Scott R. Brandhorst, *Southeast Missouri State University*

ISSUE

Is There Cause for Concern About an "Oral-Sex Crisis" for Teens?

YES: Sharlene Azam, from *Oral Sex Is the New Goodnight Kiss: The Sexual Bullying of Teenage Girls* (2008)

NO: SIECCAN (The Sex Information and Education Council of Canada), from "Do You Think 'Oral Sex' Is 'Having Sex'? Does the Answer Matter?" *The Canadian Journal of Human Sexuality* (2011)

Learning Outcomes

After reading this issue, you will be able to:

- Summarize the two "case studies" provided by Sharlene Azam that illustrate the "casual attitude" that youth take toward oral sex.
- Describe and evaluate the academic research outlined by the Sex Information and Education Council of Canada with regard to how adolescents view oral sex.
- Compare and contrast the positions of the two different authors.
- Reconcile the two positions and draw conclusions about the state of oral sex and adolescents.
- Explore the role of intimacy and romance in sexual behaviors such as oral sex, intercourse, and anal sex.

ISSUE SUMMARY

YES: Journalist Sharlene Azam, in a book about teen prostitution, discusses the cavalier attitude toward oral sex that some girls report. As well, she discusses a famous Canadian case of oral sex with under-aged girls that had major press coverage.

NO: The Research Coordinator of the Sex Information and Education Council of Canada reviews the academic research regarding oral-sex practices and their associated meaning for youth. Their take-home message is that oral sex among teens is not at "epidemic" levels and that many youth feel that oral sex is an intimate sexual behavior.

For the past decade or so, there has been a surge in media attention given to the "problem" of teen oral sex. Much of this interest started with an *Oprah Winfrey* show (circa, Fall 2003) when she discussed the existence of "Rainbow" clubs—parties for teens where girls wear different colored lipstick and fellate boys. The "goal" is for boys to have many different colors of lipstick on their penis at the end of the party. Oral sex has been called the new "spin the bottle" of teenagers. A book for teens by Paul Ruditis, entitled *Rainbow Party* (2005), brought with it a flurry of discussion on the topic of teen oral sex. Discussion of these rainbow parties continues on popular television shows (e.g., *Maury Povich*, Fall 2009). Consider this quote from a "psychotherapist"

(presumably a reputable source) who appeared on a 2010 episode of *The Doctors* (May 27, 2010; www.thedoctorstv.com/main/show_synopsis/408?section=synopsis):

> Another trend gaining traction among teens is the rainbow party, an oral sex party during which each girl wears a different shade of lipstick and each boy attempts to collect every shade.
>
> "Back in the day, liwwke five years ago, you were hearing about parties where people played spin the bottle and truth or dare, and now it's escalated to a whole other level," says psychotherapist Stacy Kaiser. "There's definitely a competition in how many girls [a boy] can get, how many different colors you can get. I want you all to

know this is happening everywhere. It's happening in private schools. It's happening in the suburbs. It's happening in the cities. Kids are doing it everywhere."

Very clearly, the media is keen to keep this issue in the forefront of parents' minds. This "crisis" attracts viewer's/reader's attention and the "sex" sells the show, magazine, book, etc.

But, is there any real cause for concern? When questioned about sex, Michael Learned, a television star of the 1970s, stated in an interview in the 1980s that she thought kids today are doing the same thing that she and her peer group were doing as kids—only the kids of the 1980s talked about their sexual activities more than her cohorts did. Is that the case with oral sex of the "Internet generation" of today's teens? Are they simply talking about oral sex more as opposed to "doing it" more, compared to past generations? And, is oral sex simply an activity that is not considered terribly intimate—akin to a goodnight kiss?

A variety of studies have been conducted recently in North America that have garnered some information about oral sex and adolescents. In a large sample of 12–14-year-olds, De Rosa et al. (2010) found that few (i.e., less than 10 percent) young adolescents have had oral sex. Chandra et al. (2011), in a National Health Statistics Report, found that just under two-thirds of youth and young adults (aged 15–24 years) have had some sort of oral sex. A few points of interest from this study: There were no gender differences in oral-sex incidence: the figures for males and females were essentially the same. A comparison of the national statistics from 2002 to data from 2006–2008 indicated that youth engaged in oral sex (indeed, in all forms of sexual contact) slightly less in more recent years (e.g., oral sex in 2002: 69 percent versus 2006–2008: 63–64 percent). Exploring oral sex further, Chandra et al. found that only 5–7 percent of youth had engaged in oral sex without vaginal sex. About half of youth who have had intercourse have engaged in oral sex. Others have concluded that oral sex and vaginal intercourse tend to occur close together (i.e., within 6 months of each other; Lindberg et al., 2008). Similarly, in a sample comprising mostly older teens, Chambers (2007) found that the majority of youths (95 percent) who had had intercourse had also had oral sex at some point in their lives; however, most (around 60 percent) "virgins" (i.e., those who had not had intercourse) had not had oral sex. Most of these aforementioned studies have been cross-sectional (i.e., at one time point) in nature. Song and Halpern-Felsher (2011) present one of the only studies to date that is longitudinal. Following students from 9th grade through 11th grade, they found that oral sex either preceded or occurred at the same time for youth. Having oral sex during the study time period predicted having vaginal sex later during the study time period. While more longitudinal studies are necessary, it seems that oral sex is part of a sexual repertoire of behaviors as opposed to an alternative to vaginal sex (i.e., it appears that most adolescents are having oral and vaginal sex together rather than using oral sex as a means of maintaining virginity).

In terms of changes over time, there does seem to be somewhat of an increase in oral sex, in recent times. Gindi et al. (2008) compared adolescent and young adult women in 1994 to adolescent and young adult women in 2004 and found that women in 2004 were three times more likely to report performing oral sex than women in 1994. Men in 2004 were twice as likely to report performing oral sex compared to men in 1994. This study, along with others (e.g., Remez, 2000), presents some evidence of a trend for an increase in oral sex for adolescents—but it should be noted that there has been a modest increase in oral sex for adults, too (see McKay, 2004).

An aspect of "concern" regarding oral sex raised by some is that youth view this sexual behavior in a cavalier fashion. Studies of youth attitudes toward oral sex do indicate that adolescents believe having oral sex is more acceptable for their age group than having vaginal sex (Halpern-Felsher et al., 2005). In this study, youth also perceived fewer negative emotional and social consequences of oral sex relative to vaginal sex. Ethically, morally, and religiously, oral sex was rated as more personally acceptable than vaginal sex. In her study of older adolescents, Chambers (2007) found that over half perceived oral sex to be intimate (much lower than the 91 percent who found intercourse to be an intimate behavior). Similarly, a study of Canadian women aged 18–25 years found that about half of women think that oral sex is equally intimate or more intimate than intercourse (Malacad & Hess, 2010). When these women said that they were in love with their partners, they had more positive emotions associated with oral sex and intercourse. Chambers also addressed oral sex and relationship status; a minority of youth reported that they, personally, would be comfortable with having oral sex in a noncommitted or primarily sexually based relationship (i.e., only 12–18 percent; Chambers, 2007). Finally, De Rosa et al. (2010) found that having a boy/girlfriend increased the odds of youth reporting having had oral sex. One implication we might make from this is that oral sex, for these young adolescents (i.e., the sample consisted of middle school students), took place within the context of a relationship. However, this is purely speculative. These studies, collectively, suggest that most youth consider oral sex as an intimate behavior that takes place within the context of romantic relationships.

Given that there is some evidence of a modest increase in oral-sex performance by teens and there are a subset of youth who consider oral sex as a behavior that can take place outside of the context of a committed romantic relationship, should sex educators and those who work with adolescents be concerned about teen oral-sex activity? In the YES selection, journalist Sharlene Azam documents situations in Canada where young girls have been participants in rainbow parties or where girls were "passed around" among group of older, popular boys for fellatio—illustrating the cavalier teen attitude toward oral sex. In the NO selection, the Sex Information and Education Council of Canada reviewed the research on how youth view oral sex (i.e., "is it sex?") and generally concluded that there is no "youth epidemic" of oral sex as the media might lead us to believe.

YES ↵

Sharlene Azam

Oral Sex Is the New Goodnight Kiss:
The Sexual Bullying of Teenage Girls

"**A**t one school, students formed a barrier on either side of a narrow hallway to prevent teachers from walking through. In the middle, 12-year-old girls were giving blowjobs to boys," explains Joy Becker, Director of Education for Options for Healthy Sexuality (formerly Planned Parenthood).

12-and 14-year-old campers in Ottawa made headlines when they were found having group oral sex.[1] Counselors assumed the kids were playing cards in a nearby cabin. "Camps reflect what is happening in society," says Dan Offord, executive director of Christie Lake Camp, adding that, "Childcare workers are being caught off guard by the fact that children are engaging in sexual activity. I think parents are also in denial about their children having sex."

It would be easy to believe that these girls and boys are an anomaly, but for this generation, oral sex is like kissing was to their parents.

At Lord Byng in Vancouver, the principal asked Joy Becker and Hannah Varto, a sexual assault nurse, to counsel 4 grade 8 girls who were discovered performing oral sex at school, along with the boys, and the parents.

"The girls were in the boys' bathroom on their knees in a cubicle with urine on the floor," Varto explained. "Or, the boy would stand over them as they sat on the toilet. They described the feeling of being gagged and choked because the boy was on top."

I met Rita and Crystal (names changed), 2 of the Lord Byng students . . .

Why did you do it?

"Everybody does it," Rita says

At school?

"Oral is not even like a question any more: guys want it all the time," says Crystal, . . .

"The girls told us that they loved the attention the boys would give them, which at first was very positive," Varto explained, adding, "The boys would make them feel beautiful, loved, sexy and cared for and that's what they were really needing."

"Was it worth it?"

"After each experience, I think, 'Was that really what I wanted, or was it because I was feeling lonely?' I'll look back on some experiences and think, 'It wasn't worth it. I didn't get anything out of it.' There are a lot of different moments you get caught up in, and a lot happens at parties.[2] I think if you have a spot or hole that needs to be filled, sex can replace it. I'm not saying it's one of the righter choices," Rita says.

Did the boys reciprocate?

"No," Rita says flatly.

Do they ever reciprocate?

"9 times out of 10, if you walk into a room [at a party] you'll see a girl on her knees. But you never see a guy on top of a girl eating her out. It just doesn't usually happen," Crystal explains.

"If it does happen, it's after you leave the party, and only if you're in a relationship. And then, he might do it sometimes really quickly so he can say, 'I ate you out.' But it's not like they're really into it for pleasure. It's just for 2 seconds so they can make you feel like you should give something back," Rita adds.

Why hook up when it is so dissatisfying?

"Oral is a chore. It's not the greatest thing, but you don't have to think about it the way you do with sex," Rita says. . . .

Did you have a boyfriend at the time of the incident in the boys' bathroom?

"No," Rita says softly. . . .

How many boys have you had sex with?

"I've given head to more guys than I've slept with. . . . ," Crystal says.

. . . Through role-playing, Varto and Becker learned that the 8th and 9th grade boys pursued the girls relentlessly. "After 3 hours of being followed around the school being told, 'You're so beautiful why won't you give me a blowjob,' the girls gave in," Becker explained.

Boys have long been taught how to get what they want and to "go for it" when it comes to girls, while girls are expected to be the "gatekeepers." This objectifying mentality speaks to a failure by parents to instill in boys the kind of empathy that would translate into a greater degree of caring in their sexual relationships.

After counseling, Becker and Varto say the boys understood that a girl waving or smiling at them does not mean she wants them, "For them, everything leads to sex," Varto says.

And, the girls realized that they are deserving of respect. "They told us, 'We are better than having our heads pushed down into crotches when we don't want them to be there,'" Becker says.

Although the parents of the boys were surprised their sons were having oral sex at school, they were unwillingly to fault them. "I think a lot of parents think the onus is on the girls because 'boys will be boys,'" Becker says. The girls' parents were upset and embarrassed by their daughters' involvement, but they did not think their behavior was cause for alarm.

"We've counseled girls who give oral sex to a boy leaving a lipstick rainbow on his penis. If it starts out being one blowjob here or there and then it becomes 5 or 10 in a day, it would be natural to eventually think, 'Well, why don't I just get paid for this? Why shouldn't I just take some money for it or something else that I want?' And it can be that innocent and that's where it starts. Yet, parents and schools have a hard time seeing the link between rainbow parties and being recruited into the sex trade," Becker explains.

. . . I am struck by the girls' collusion in what seems like a sexual dystopia; this collusion turns on the idea that oral sex is what girls will do, getting passed around is what girls will endure, and so getting paid is a bonus, rather than an element that further degrades the behavior.

. . . [On Prince Edward Island], a story broke that shone a spotlight on the practice of girls providing sexual favors to older guys. . . . "The girls who testified in the case said that they didn't feel coerced, in fact, there was a willingness on their part."

The case involved Los Angeles Dodgers' draft pick, Cass Rhynes, who testified in 2003 that 12-and 13-year-old girls regularly performed oral sex on him. Rhynes was in the 12th grade, at the time. In his testimony, he described in detail his sexual escapades with the adolescents Sara and Brittney (names changed).

Rhynes was caught when Annie, Sara's mother, overheard a late-night conversation between Rhynes and her daughter. . . .

"I confronted her, and she explained how she had become involved with Cass and his friend, Tyler, over the school year. When I learned their ages, that she had oral sex with 17-and 18-year-old boys, I was outraged," Annie says.

Annie contacted the boys' parents and was told that her daughter must be lying, because their sons would never become sexually involved with such young girls. She called the parents of 15 of the girls Sara claimed were also sexually involved with the boys, but they refused to discuss the issue. She then contacted the school principal. "He told me to keep it 'hush-hush,'" she says That's when I decided to call the police and press charges."

As testimony about the girls' willing participation emerged, the community became increasingly angry that 2 girls would attempt to destroy the reputation of a local hero on his way to the big leagues.

Jamie Ballem, Attorney General . . . spoke . . . about the division in the community. "Some groups are saying, 'Yes, he's guilty, but he's been punished enough by being publicly exposed. He may lose his athletic scholarship.'"

The case garnered a lot of national media attention, but there was never any mention of the negative impact of the extensive coverage on the girls. Although the girls' names were not made public, their identities are known in their city, where the feeling is that girls who "act like boys"—in other words, behave promiscuously—get what they deserve.

Some believe that the girls became sexually involved with Rhynes in a "quest for fame," and so they should not claim to be innocents. Neither of the girls presented themselves as victims. Nor did they want to go to court. Sara's mom pressed charges because the girls are minors.

"There is a lot of discussion about the responsibility of the girls' parents. Where were those girls' parents?" Ballem asks. "A lot of people don't think the courts should be used to decide these issues." Sara, like many of the girls I interviewed, comes from a broken home where her father is absent from her life.

Rhynes was convicted on 2 counts of inciting girls under 14 to touch him for sexual purposes, but the conviction was overturned on appeal. . . .

As a result of our rapidly changing sexual mores, the line between adolescents and adults is blurred. A decade ago, the notion of a 12-year-old giving an 18-year-old, 200-pound, 6-foot athlete oral sex would have enraged most of society and the courts. Today, the girl is vilified and he is back on the field with a lucrative contract. . . .

Reporters described Sara and Brittney as little Lolitas. Rhynes even spoke to reporters about the girls' morality and how much things had changed since he was a kid. "I wasn't even thinking about sex when I was 12," he explained. And yet no one challenged his sexual mores as an 18-year-old. "All the blame is on the girls, as if it's normal for an adult man to want to have sex with 12-year-old girls," Annie says.

Complicating the Cass Rhynes case is the fact that Rhynes falls under the extraordinary protection that is handed out to professional athletes who get caught deviating from the straight and narrow. In *Out of Bounds: Inside the NBA's Culture of Rape, Violence and Crime*, Jeff Benedict explains that when an athlete is accused of sexual assault there are enormous nets that go up around him. "He is a commodity. He's a product. And he's got to be protected.". . .

Increasingly, girls who are victims of sexual exploitation will find there is little incentive to come forward and tell their stories. Girls know that their worth is determined by how they appear to others; they know that fame is more valuable than romance. These are absolutes in our celebrity-obsessed culture. And yet a girl who acts on these messages will be put on the stand and made to feel as though she is in the wrong. The justice system and society, which should protect her, will, in effect, vilify her and the result is that her life will be ruined at the age of 12. . . .

Sara, 12

. . . I met Cass Rhynes through his friend Tyler who I met in September on the school bus. It was the beginning of grade 7. At first I didn't really know who Tyler was. . . . Then a couple times he sat with me and Brittney on the school bus. . . . We'd talk and he was nice to us. I thought we were just friends. I guess he took it a different way.

Tyler added us on his MSN buddy list (Hotmail's chat service) and we would talk online a lot. The fact that I was getting attention from a 17-year-old was big. . . .

Then he got into sex talk. At first I thought it was disgusting, but then he kept on asking. He just kept saying, "Do you think you could give me head?" He was pretty blunt about it. After [a while] it started to click-in that he wasn't joking.

Then I found out that Brittney, my best friend, had done it with him and 2 of his friends. We met him on the school bus at the same time and she was 12 too. She didn't get called names and stuff and she got so much attention from everybody. . . .

When I did it, I didn't necessarily want to do it. It wasn't my main priority to have oral sex with some random guy, but it was like, "Well, my best friend did it, and if she can do it then I can do it." My first time, it was really weird because I hadn't done anything sexual before. I was terrified. I didn't know what to do. I had to ask him

what I was supposed to do. I did it, and after that, he just expected it from both of us. I didn't care about doing it. It wasn't like such a big deal, but after we would make fun of him like, "Oh my God, did you see how curly his hair is down there?" and stuff.

I didn't do it for the acceptance. I was already accepted. I wanted to do something that I wasn't supposed to do. I wanted to be a rebel. I thought this would make me greater and better. I got a rush from being with somebody older who has a car. I thought, "They really must have an interest in me, if they're hanging out with a 12-year-old. They can have any girl they want." But I guess we were just easy to get. It didn't really bother me to do It. It was like nothing.

Tyler started to pass us around to his friends after he had been with us, and that's how me and Cass Rhynes got together. Tyler would ask his friends if they wanted us to give them head and stuff. . . .

On October 22, 2003, Cass Rhynes, 18, was convicted of sex crimes involving the underage girls and sentenced to 45 days in jail. Convicted on 2 counts of inciting girls under the age of 14 to touch him for sexual purposes, he was placed on 1 year probation and required to complete 100 hours of community service. . . .

John Mitchell, Cass Rhynes's lawyer, appealed the guilty ruling to the Supreme Court, arguing that Rhynes was a passive participant. The guilty verdict was overturned. Annie, Sara's mother, says, "Most appeals can take up to 2 years to be heard. How did Rhynes get his appeal before the bench in just a few months?" . . .

Notes

1. "Kids have oral sex at summer camp." *Montreal Gazette,* 4 July 2003, P A12.

2. "Grade 9 girls were the group most likely to say, 'They first had sex because they got carried away,'" Council of Ministers of Education. 2003. *Canadian Youth, Sexual Health and HIV/AIDS Study.*

SIECCAN (The Sex Information and
Education Council of Canada)

 **NO**

Do You Think "Oral Sex" Is "Having Sex"?
Does the Answer Matter?

In recent years, the topic of oral sex among young people has been frequently discussed in the media. Some media reports have gone as far as to suggest that there is an "epidemic" of oral sex breaking out among teens. In fact, research from both Canada and the United States suggests that less than a third of younger teens (i.e., 17 and under) and about half to two-thirds of older teens (18/19) have participated in oral-genital contact one or more times (Boyce, et al., 2006: Lindberg, Jones, & Santelli, 2008). In other words, among young people, oral-genital contact is about as common as sexual intercourse and the two behaviours typically happen at about the same age (Maticka-Tyndale, 2008).

At the same time, there has also been a lot of discussion as to whether teens and young adults today classify oral-genital contact as "having sex" to the same extent that they would classify intercourse as "having sex." Is oral-genital contact now viewed as an activity that does not carry the same emotional, psychological, social, and health implications as penile-vaginal or penile-anal intercourse and, thus, not considered to be "having sex"?

We examine contemporary research on how people classify oral-genital contact as a behaviour. We will also ask whether classifying oral-genital contact as not "having sex" has implications for our health and well-being that we should be aware of.

Is It Having Sex?

Several studies have examined whether university students classify oral-genital contact as "having sex." Randal and Byers (2003) asked 197 Canadian university students to indicate from a list of 18 behaviours which ones they considered to be "having sex." Here, we will look at how the students classified three different behaviours. As you can see in Table 1, both male and female students were much more likely to classify penile-vaginal and penile-anal intercourse as "having sex" than they were to classify it has "having sex" when a partner performed oral-genital contact.

In a similar study, Hans, Gillen, and Akande (2010) asked 477 students at a university in the United States the

Table 1

Percentage of University Students Classifying Behaviours As "Having Sex"*

	Male	Female	Total
Oral contact with genitals	24%	24%	23.2%
Penile-vaginal intercourse	98%	97%	97.6%
Penile-anal intercourse	84%	83%	83.3%

*These results are for the behaviours "with orgasm"; "no orgasm" had similar percentages.
Source: Randall & Byers (2003)

question "Would you say you 'had sex' with someone if the most intimate behavior you engaged in was," followed by a list of 11 different behaviours. The vast majority of the students said that having penile-vaginal (98%) and penile-anal (78%) intercourse was "having sex" but only about 20% said that oral-genital contact was "having sex." Interestingly, when the researchers compared their results to a very similar study conducted in 1991, they discovered that current university students are about twice as likely than students in the early 1990's to not consider oral-genital contact as "having sex."

Does It Matter That Many Young People Do Not Consider Oral Sex To Be Having Sex?

At first glance we might say that it really doesn't matter whether we label a particular behaviour as "having sex" or not. On the other hand, if saying that oral-genital contact is not "having sex" means that the activity has fewer, if any, implications for our lives, then we may want to examine the issue a little more closely.

First, it is interesting to note that although most of the students in the Randall and Byers (2003) study did not classify oral-genital contact as "having sex," 99% said that if their relationship partner had oral-genital contact with someone else, they would view their partner as having been "unfaithful." For most people, being monogamous means, among other things, that the partners do not have sex with other people. But with so many people not classifying oral-genital contact as "having sex," it might be a good idea for partners at the beginning of a relationship to clarify with each other that they are on the same page on what it means to be monogamous.

Second, some people might assume that if oral-genital contact is not "having sex" then the behaviour has less emotional significance and is less intimate than "having sex" (e.g. intercourse). Malacad and Hess (2010) examined these issues in a study of 181 18 to 25-year-old Canadian women. The authors found that about half (49.7%) indicated that "I think oral sex is a less intimate activity than intercourse," 40.7% said that oral sex and intercourse were equally intimate and about 8% believed that oral sex is more intimate than intercourse. In sum, the women in this study were split about evenly as to whether oral-genital contact is a less intimate behaviour than intercourse.

Malacad and Hess (2010) also found that, overall, the women expressed positive emotions (e.g., excited) about their most recent experiences of both intercourse and oral-genital contact (especially if they were on the receiving end). As might be expected, the women reported more positive emotions about having intercourse if they were "in love" with their partner. However this was also the case for oral-genital contact: those who said they were "in love" with their partner were more likely to express positive emotions about the activity. Similarly, women who were not "in love" with their partner were more likely to express negative emotions (e.g., disappointment, guilt) for both oral-genital contact and intercourse. These findings indicate that, for these women, some considered oral-genital contact less intimate than intercourse, and some didn't, but, overall, the emotional implications of the two activities were similar.

Third, we might assume that if oral-genital contact is not "having sex" then there is no risk of transmitting a sexually transmitted infection (STI) through oral-genital contact. There is, in fact, some risk. According to the U.S. Centers for Disease Control and Prevention (2009), the risk of transmitting HIV through oral-genital contact is "much less" than for penis-vagina or penis-anus intercourse but there have been cases where it has occurred through oral-genital contact and there is some risk of transmission for other STI (herpes, syphilis,

gonorrhea, HPV, hepatitis A, intestinal parasites) through oral-genital contact.

What's The Take Home Message?

Oral-genital contact is about as common as penile-vaginal intercourse among young people. Increasingly, young people do not consider oral-genital contact as "having sex." However, we need to be aware that even if we do not classify oral-genital contact as "having sex" this does not mean that we should ignore the potential emotional, relationship, and health implications of the behaviour.

References

Boyce, W. et al. (2006). Sexual health of Canadian youth: Findings from the *Canadian Youth, Sexual Health and HIV/AIDS Study. The Canadian Journal of Human Sexuality*. 15, (2), 59–68. http://www.sieccan.org/pdf/boyce_cjhs2006_sexualhealth.pdf

Centers for Disease Control and Prevention. (2009). *Oral Sex and HIV Risk*. http://www.cdc.gov/hiv/resources/factsheets/PDF/oralsex.pdf

Hans, J. D., Gillen, M., & Akande, K. (2010). Sex redefined: The reclassification of oral-genital contact. *Perspectives on Sexual and Reproductive Health*, 42, (2), 74–78.

Lindberg, L. D., Jones, R., & Santelli, J. S. (2008). Noncoital sexual activities among adolescents. *Journal of Adolescent Health*, 43, 231–238.

Malacad, B. L. & Hess, G. C. (2010). Oral sex: Behaviours and feelings of Canadian young women and implications for sex education. *The European Journal of Contraception and Reproductive Health Care*, 15, 177–185.

Maticka-Tyndale, E. (2008). Sexuality and sexual health of Canadian adolescents. *The Canadian Journal of Human Sexuality*, 17, (3), 85–95. http://www.sieccan.org/pdf/maticka-tyndale_cjhs2008_commentary.pdf

Randall, H. & Byers, E. S. (2003). What is sex? Students' definitions of having sex, sexual partner, and unfaithful sexual behaviour. *The Canadian Journal of Human Sexuality*, 12, (2), 87–96.

EXPLORING THE ISSUE

Is There Cause for Concern About an "Oral-Sex Crisis" for Teens?

Critical Thinking and Reflection

1. Do youth today have a "casual" attitude about oral sex? Is oral sex the new "goodnight kiss" as Sharlene Azam's book title suggests? How does intimacy factor into adolescent sexual behavior?

2. What is the role of morals and ethics in the interpretation of the meaning of sexual behavior? In particular, why is oral sex and youth such an ethically charged, emotionally hot issue? Consider how your own morals, values, ethics, and principles influence your reading and assessment of these two selections. Consider how the morals, values, ethics, and principles of the authors affected their writing. How would different morally inclined audiences interpret these two selections?

3. Sharlene Azam's piece may be taken as evidence of a sexual double standard (i.e., ". . . girls who act like boys, promiscuously, get what they deserve . . ."). Is there a double standard with regard to oral sex? How does the media influence this double standard? Is the double standard different for adolescents versus adults?

4. What is "sex"? If oral sex is not classified as "having sex" by some, then why would many view oral–genital contact outside the primary relationship as "cheating"? Why don't people tend to think of oral sex as "sex"?

5. There is no academic literature that supports the existence of "rainbow parties." Does this mean such parties do not exist? Are "rainbow parties" an urban myth (give a rationale for your answer)?

6. If middle and high school sex educators and teachers were to ask you what should be done (i.e., what they should do) about "the problem of adolescent oral sex," what would your advice be, based on your reading of these two selections? Why is oral sex a topic that is rarely addressed in sex education curricula?

Is There Common Ground?

Is there a teen oral sex crisis? Extreme situations such as the group oral sex that occurred at the Ottawa summer camp and the oral sex that occurred in the bathroom at Lord Byng High School certainly point to some sort of "moral emergency." The Cass Rhynes case, which made national headlines, illustrates that young girls are in danger of being enticed into sexual acts by young men—despite the illegality of these actions under the federal Criminal Code of Canada. Both Azam and SIECCAN would agree that these situations are extreme, exploitive, and unacceptable. The two diverge on other conclusions: Azam's book goes further into depth by discussing even greater sexual exploitation of girls—that this oral sex phenomenon can lead to, ultimately, prostitution of these girls. Azam would likely view casual attitudes toward oral sex by adolescents as a slippery slope into moral sexual depravity. In contrast, SIECCAN's review of the empirical research suggests that most youth consider oral sex as at least somewhat of an intimate sexual behavior that usually occurs within a romantic relationship. The research does suggest that there is a small subset of youth who view oral sex as a casual behavior (see Chambers, 2007). Perhaps it is this group that needs further study to understand how their perceptions of oral sex differ from their peers who consider oral sex an intimate

sexual behavior. Perhaps it is these youth who are the subject of Azam's book; perhaps it is these youth who need to be targeted for differential sex education.

Additional Resources

Barrett, A. (2004). Teens and oral sex: A sexual health educator's perspective. *Canadian Journal of Human Sexuality*, *13*, 197–200.

Brady, S. S., & Halpern-Felsher, B. L. (2007). Adolescents' reported consequences of having oral sex versus vaginal sex. *Pediatrics*, *119*(2), 229–236.

Brewster, K. L., & Tillman, K. H. (2008). Who's doing it? Patterns and predictors of youths' oral sexual experiences. *Journal of Adolescent Health*, *42*, 73–80.

Burns, A., Futch, V. A., & Tolman, D. L. (2011). "It's like doing homework": Academic achievement discourse in adolescent girls' fellatio narratives. *Sexual Research and Social Policy*, *8*, 239–251.

In contrast to many of the articles cited in this section, this piece involved a qualitative, phenomenological investigation of oral sex. That is, the researchers spoke to a large number of girls about their experience of performing oral sex. Many likened performing oral sex to academic tasks such as taking tests and used learning as a framework for explaining their experiences.

Halpern-Felsher, B. L. (2008). Oral sexual behavior: Harm reduction or gateway behavior? *Journal of Adolescent Health, 43,* 207–208.

Halpern, C. T., & Haydon, A. A. (2012). Sexual time-tables for oral-genital, vaginal, and anal intercourse: Sociodemographic comparisons in a nationally representative sample of adolescents. *American Journal of Public Health*, e1-e8. doi:10.2105/AJPH.2011.300394

An analysis of the prevalence and timing of, among other sexual behaviors, oral sex for a nationally representative sample of 18-year-olds. They found that oral sex rarely was a "sole" sexual behavior—it tended to co-occur with vaginal sex (for 50–55 percent of these youth).

References

Chambers, W. C. (2007). Oral sex: Varied behaviors and perceptions in a college population. *Journal of Sex Research, 44*(1), 28–42.

This was a survey of youth (late teens, emerging adults) regarding oral sex—assessed was the level of perceived intimacy of oral sex (20 percent viewed oral sex as not intimate), the type of relationship in which oral sex occurred (oral sex tended to occur in committed relationships), and reasons for having oral sex (pleasure rationales were the most frequently endorsed reasons for oral sex).

Chandra, A., Mosher, W. D., Copen, C., & Sionean, C. (2011). Sexual behavior, sexual attraction, and sexual identity in the United States: Data from the 2006–2008 National Survey of Family Growth. *National Health Statistics Reports, 36.* Hyattsville, MD: National Center for Health Statistics.

Using national data, these researchers describe the sexual behavior of a national representative sample. Embedded in the report is a section on youth (i.e., 15–24 years of age) sexual behavior. The authors were able to compare data of 2006–2008 with that of 2002.

De Rosa, C. J., Ethier, K. A., Kim, D. H., Cumberland, W. G., Abdelmonem, A. A., Kotlerman, J., et al. (2010). Sexual intercourse and oral sex among public middle school students: Prevalence and correlates. *Perspectives on Sexual and Reproductive Health, 42*(3), 197–205.

This study investigated the oral and vaginal sexual activity of students in grades 6 to 8. They found that the overall prevalence of oral and vaginal sex was low (i.e., less than 10 percent) and that there were differences based on demographic characteristics (e.g., there were large differences between grades 6 and 8, which might indicated that this is a key developmental stage; racial differences were evident, too).

Gindi, R. M., Ghanem, K. G., & Erbelding, E. J. (2008). Increases in oral and anal sexual exposure among youth attending sexually transmitted diseases clinics in Baltimore, Maryland. *Journal of Adolescent Health, 42,* 307–308.

A brief report where the investigators analyzed medical records from youth (12–25 years of age) who had been seen at a reproductive health clinic. Significant increases in receptive oral and anal sex were documented in youth across the decade under study.

Halpern-Felsher, B. L., Cornell, J. L., Kropp, R. Y., & Tschann, J. M. (2005). Oral versus vaginal sex among adolescents: Perceptions, attitudes, and behavior. *Pediatrics, 115*(4), 845–851.

Investigators were interested in adolescent perceptions of oral-sex acceptability. Oral sex was more prevalent than vaginal sex with these grade 9 youth. Oral sex attitudes were more liberal relative to perceptions of vaginal sex.

Lindberg, L. D., Jones, R., & Santelli, J. S. (2008). Noncoital sexual activities among adolescents. *Journal of Adolescent Health, 43,* 231–238.

Using nationally representative youth data, these researchers investigated the prevalence of oral sex (among other behaviors). They found that slightly over half had had oral sex. When comparing those who had had vaginal sex, 87 percent had had oral sex, too. Only 23 percent of virgins, on the other hand, had experienced oral sex. Other demographic variables and their relation to oral sex were discussed.

McKay, A. (2004). Oral sex among teens: Research, discourse and education. SIECCAN Newsletter, 39(12) in The Canadian Journal of Human Sexuality, 13, 201–203.

Malacad, B. L., & Hess, G. C. (2010). Oral sex: Behaviours and feelings of Canadian young women and implications for sex education. *European Journal of Contraception and Reproductive Health Care, 15,* 177–185.

This was a study of female youth (late teens, emerging adults) assessing prevalence of oral sex (75 percent of young women reported having engaged in oral sex), casual attitudes toward/casual performance of oral sex (25 percent had not engaged in either oral or vaginal sex, while those who had engaged in oral sex within serious relationships), and the emotions associated with oral sex (vaginal intercourse and cunnilingus were associated with positive emotions, while fellatio tended to be associate with more negative emotions and fewer positive emotions, relatively speaking).

Remez, L. (2000) Oral Sex Among Adolescents: Is It Sex or Is It Abstinence? Family Planning Perspectives, 43(6).

Ruditis, P. (2005). *Rainbow party*. New York: Simon & Schuster.

A fictional account of a "rainbow party" marketed toward adolescents. This book has created a great deal of controversy.

Song, A. V., & Halpern-Felsher, B. L. (2011). Predictive relationship between adolescent oral and vaginal sex: Results from a prospective, longitudinal study. *Archives of Pediatric Adolescent Medicine, 165*(3), 243–249.

The first study to follow the sexual behavior of the same adolescents across three grades (i.e., for about 2.5 years). The researchers were able to document when many of the adolescents first had oral sex and vaginal sex. Three key findings from the study were: (1) having oral sex in grades 9 and 10 increased the likelihood that youth would have vaginal sex; (2) adolescents usually had vaginal and oral sex for the first time within the same 6-month period; and (3) oral sex usually occurred first.

Internet References . . .

Adolescent Sexual Behavior

http://www.hhs.gov/ash/oah/resources-and-publications
/info/parents/just-facts/adolescent-sex.html

Reproductive Health

http://yth.org/resources/youth-reproductive-health/

Science Daily

https://www.sciencedaily.com
/releases/2010/08/100811162350.htm

Sex Education: Talking to Your Teen About Sex

http://www.mayoclinic.org/healthy-lifestyle
/sexual-health/in-depth/sex-education/art-20044034

Teens and Oral Sex: It Is Not Safe

http://kingwoodmedical.com/hl/?/2010815904
/Teens-and-Oral-Sex—It-s-Not-Safe

Selected, Edited, and with Issue Framing Material by:
Scott R. Brandhorst, *Southeast Missouri State University*

ISSUE

Is "Coming Out" As a Sexual Minority Earlier in Adolescence Detrimental to Psychological Well-Being?

YES: Justin Jager and Pamela E. Davis-Kean, from "Same-Sex Sexuality and Adolescent Psychological Well-Being: The Influence of Sexual Orientation, Early Reports of Same-Sex Attraction, and Gender," *Self and Identity* (2011)

NO: Margaret Rosario, Eric W. Schrimshaw, and Joyce Hunter, from "Different Patterns of Sexual Identity Development over Time: Implications for the Psychological Adjustment of Lesbian, Gay, and Bisexual Youths," *Journal of Sex Research* (2010)

Learning Outcomes

After reading this issue, you will be able to:

- Describe and deconstruct different ways of defining the "coming out" process in research.
- Compare the similarities and differences between the two studies and their findings.
- Critique the studies such that you are able to form an opinion on which piece most adequately addresses the question posed in this issue.

ISSUE SUMMARY

YES: Using the ADD Health longitudinal dataset, researchers Justin Jager and Pamela E. Davis-Kean investigated the association of early same-sex attraction on mental health outcomes of depressive affect and self-esteem. Those who had early (12–15 years) same-sex attractions and whose attraction remained stable throughout adolescence had the most negative psychological well-being. However, this group of adolescents gained or "recovered" the most, in terms of psychological well-being, over time.

NO: In a longitudinal study, Professor Margaret Rosario and colleagues found that early versus later acknowledgment of one's minority sexual orientation was not related to psychological distress; thus, sexual-minority identity formation was unrelated to psychological distress. Rather, identity integration—how well one accepts and integrates that sexual-minority status into one's life—was predictive of psychological well-being. Those who had a well-integrated sexual-minority identity had the most favorable measure of psychological well-being, while those with lower sexual-minority identity integration had the poorest measures of psychological well-being.

Coming out is the term used to describe a process of self-identification as a lesbian, gay, bisexual, or transgender person. Coming out typically involves forming an LGBT identity and integrating this into one's sense of self. Stage theorists describe the coming out process as a set of stages through which a person progresses. While coming out is not necessarily linear or a stage process, psychosexual stage-theorist psychologists generally agree that there are a series of steps that a person typically goes through when self-identifying as LGBT (Clarke et al., 2010). People who come out with a queer identity experience self-discovery whereby they come to realize that they may be or are LGBT (i.e., awareness). Upon this realization, people can go on to develop a sense of self as LGBT, investigating what this identity means for them (i.e., exploration). Adopting the identity is another step in the process (i.e., acceptance). Finally, this identity becomes a solid, permanent part of the definition of self (i.e., integration). This process can be "shut down" by the person; when this happens, the identity is said to be foreclosed (i.e., rejected and developed no further; Clarke et al., 2010). This identity formation process is probably less stage-like and more dynamic (Shapiro et al., 2010). Regardless of theoretical stance, successful sexual-minority identity development is thought to be marked by such milestones as having successful romantic relationships with people of the same sex, developing a positive sense of self (i.e., deal at least somewhat successfully with internalized homophobia), and integrating one's homosexual self-identity into the overall or more general identity (e.g., Floyd & Stein, 2002). The process may have different content for transgender people but is somewhat parallel to the coming out of GLB people (Bockting & Coleman, 2007). Coming out is an internal process involving the synthesis of being gay, lesbian, bisexual, or transgender into one's sense of self. The person who has come out tends to feel authenticated; typically, most adolescents who come out feel good about their sexual orientation (Savin-Williams, 2005).

Coming out also has a public aspect. However, people have different levels of being "out." That is, some people have only told a few close friends (maybe queer friends) and no one else knows. These people are often referred to as being "in the closet" or "closeted." There are a whole host of stressors associated with being in the closet (Cox et al., 2011; LaSala, 2010). Typically, public disclosure of sexual orientation to others proceeds in a particular order with close friends and family being told first, and then more peripheral friends, workmates/classmates, and/or acquaintances being told next. Telling parents of one's sexual-minority status is often a seminal event in an LGBT person's life (Floyd & Stein, 2002; LaSala, 2010). Finally, complete outness would entail being out to strangers or upon meeting people. An out person might also be involved in LGBT community events or organizations (e.g., online groups, pride celebrations; Clarke et al., 2010). Generally, this kind of disclosure to social sources is viewed as a positive aspect of sexual-minority identity development (LaSala, 2010; Savin-Williams, 2005).

Many LGBT individuals begin this identity process as youth or young adults (Calzo et al., 2011). Retrospective research suggests that LGBT people typically come out at a variety of ages; Calzo et al. conducted a study that investigated "groupings" of when people came out in a large sample of Californians aged 18–84 years. They found that three developmental "groups" of people were evident: those who came out early in life (i.e., first same-sex attraction at 12.5 years and identifying as queer at 16.5 years, on average), those who came out in later adolescence or early adulthood (i.e., first same-sex attraction at 18 years and identifying as queer at 25.5 years, on average), and the "older" group, who came out, on average, at 40 years of age. The early group constituted over 75 percent of the sample. The group who came out in late adolescence/early adulthood made up 19 percent of the sample. Many queer individuals report feeling "different" as young as 5 or 6 years of age (D'Augelli & Hershberger, 1993). In short, coming out is a process that primarily affects youth with 9 out of 10 people beginning the coming-out process in the teen years.

Coming out or disclosing one's sexual orientation to significant others is thought to have beneficial effects, while concealing one's sexual orientation is thought to have many negative effects

(see Legate et al., 2012). Harvey Milk, a 1970s' gay icon/political leader who was assassinated, encouraged people to "come out . . . and once you do, you will feel so much better." Being public about one's sexual-minority status or even being perceived as a sexual minority often has a dark side: being on the recipient of prejudice toward and discrimination based on sexual-minority status. This seems particularly true when adolescents come out in school settings; this sets the stage for potential bullying based on sexual orientation (Clarke et al., 2010). The supportive context of the situation in which a person comes out interacts with levels of sexual orientation disclosure to have a differential impact on emotional and health-related outcomes. Legate et al. (2012) found that being out was only really beneficial to a person when a social environment was supportive of the individual. The school climate is not known for being a positive atmosphere for LGBT students (Clarke et al., 2010; Taylor et al., 2011).

The YES and NO selections address timing of coming out as beneficial or detrimental to the mental health outcomes of youth. Using a longitudinal design, Rosario et al. (2011) investigated the impact of coming out earlier—defined by both identity formation and identity integration—on depression, anxiety, and self-esteem relative to coming out later. Rosario et al. found that identity formation was not an issue, per se, in terms of psychological distress. Rather, they found that how well-integrated one's sexual orientation was into one's sense of self was the key predictor of psychological well-being. In fact, having a well-integrated sexual-minority sense of self as early as possible is probably a protective factor for youth's psychological adjustment, based on Rosario et al.'s findings. In contrast, Jager and Davis-Kean (2011) compared sexual-minority youth to sexual-majority youth in terms of the psychological outcomes of depression and self-esteem at different points during adolescence. They found that sexual-minority youth had significantly higher levels of depression and lower self-esteem than sexual-majority youth at the earliest time point in the study. Also, the younger the person was when coming out, the greater the level of depression the person exhibited. The sexual-minority youth "gained" or "recovered" a lot over time in terms of having reduced depression and increased self-esteem relative to the sexual-majority control group. As you are reading the two selections, consider the role of how "coming out" is defined by the two sets of authors and how differences in the research design might contribute to what seem like contradictory results.

Terminology

LGBT is an umbrella term representing lesbian, gay, bisexual, transsexual, and transgender. Sometimes, this is written as LGBTQ and also can include two-spirited, queer, and/or questioning. While being transgender or transsexual involves gender identity and biological disparity—more so than sexual orientation—trans people have communalities with LGB people in that all are sexual minorities. All LGBT people experience a coming-out process—a process of self-discovery of their sexual-minority status. In some instances, this is written as GLBT.

Queer has often been used as a pejorative insult to refer to LGBTQ people. Many LGBT people have "taken back the word"—adopted its use in a positive fashion so that it may lose its pejorative meaning.

Questioning describes those who are in the exploration stage of coming out, those who are unsure, those who have not adopted a sexual-minority status label, or those who eschew such labels.

Homophobia is a bit of a misnomer as it implies an irrational fear of homosexuality. However, this is the term that is common vernacular. **Homonegativity** would be a better term to describe negative attitudes and feelings toward homosexuals. **Internalized homophobia** refers to internalizing negative feels and attitudes toward oneself as a result of one's sexual-minority status. This is often a reflection of negative attitudes toward homosexuality of significant others and of wider societal attitudes.

YES

Justin Jager and Pamela E. Davis-Kean

Same-Sex Sexuality and Adolescent Psychological Well-Being: The Influence of Sexual Orientation, Early Reports of Same-Sex Attraction, and Gender

Developmental research suggests that the period between late childhood and early adolescence is a time when disparities across race, gender, socioeconomic status (SES), and overweight status have a profound influence on psychological well-being. . . . [M]iddle childhood and early adolescence are vulnerable times for youth, when being different from those around them can cause anxiety and stress.

An emerging area of particular concern for psychological well-being is the issue of same-sex sexuality or what is termed sexual minority status (SM). The majority status is exclusive heterosexual attraction or attraction to the opposite sex, and the minority status refers to those who are attracted to the same sex either in combination with an attraction to the opposite sex or solely to the same sex. Emerging research suggests that, on average, SM report somewhat lower levels of psychological well-being than do sexual majorities (Cochran, [et al.], 2003; Fergusson, [et al.], 2005; Galliher, [et al.], 2004; Russell, 2006; Sandford et al., 2003). However, researchers have yet to examine how the relation between SM status and psychological well-being varies across middle childhood and adolescence. Since this particular period proves formative for these other social statuses, perhaps this pattern generalizes to all social statuses, including SM status. Thus, the goal of this study was to examine how, if at all, the relation between SM status and psychological well-being varies across middle childhood and adolescence, with a particular focus on the adolescent years. . . .

Why Are Middle Childhood and Early Adolescence So Important?

While there may be many reasons why middle childhood is an important developmental period with respect to the relation between social status and psychological well-being, two likely reasons for its importance are: (1) advances in cognitive development during this period that render one's social status(es) more

personally relevant to one's sense of self; and (2) increases in the size and instability of the peer network. . . .

Sexual-Minority Status

In terms of the emergence of disparities in psychological well-being, it is not clear whether middle childhood is an important time period for SM as it is for race, gender, overweight status, and SES. An important question regarding SM status is as follows: When does one's awareness of one's SM status emerge? Is it early on in development like one's awareness of race and gender, or is it later on in development like one's awareness of being a college student or a parent? Retrospective reports indicate that SM individuals recall being treated differently by others, often as early as age 8, before they develop or are even aware of their attractions to the same sex (Bell, [et al.], 1981; Zucker, [et al.], 1993). They recall feeling different from their peers, and often this sense of feeling different has a negative valence and is centered around atypical, gender-related traits (Savin-Williams, 2005; Troiden, 1989). Retrospective reports also indicate that around the age of 10 or 11, many SM individuals recall their first awareness of attraction to the same sex (D'Augelli & Hershberger, 1993; Floyd & Stein, 2002; Friedman, [et al.], 2008; Rosario, [et al.], 1996; Savin-Williams & Diamond, 2000). Thus, there is some evidence to suggest that awareness of one's SM status may emerge during the middle-childhood years. . . .

Though one may acquire a vague sense of SM status during middle childhood (i.e., a sense of difference or initial awareness of feelings of same-sex attraction), coming to grips with one's own sexuality does not end there. A subset of youth go on to realize during early adolescence that this attraction to the same sex is what society deems as homosexual, and then an even smaller subset go on to actually identify themselves (as opposed to just their sexual attractions) as homosexual or bisexual (D'Augelli & Hershberger; 1993; Rosario et al., 1996; Savin-Williams & Diamond, 2000). Awareness of SM status is a prerequisite for others' messages regarding sexual minorities to be internalized as personally meaningful, and the period when one's awareness of one's SM status appears to form extends into late adolescence or even early adulthood. Thus, the relation between SM status and psychological well-being may itself be in flux through late adolescence/early adulthood.

Complicating things further is the possibility that growing awareness of one's SM status during adolescence will be accompanied by social isolation as well as victimization and stigmatization. . . . [At] a time when SM adolescents are coming to grips with their status, they are typically doing so alone, perhaps in the face of heightened harassment and aggression. As a consequence, the influence of SM status on psychological well-being may prove stronger between mid- to late-adolescence than between middle childhood and early adolescence.

Moderators of Sexual-Minority Status and Psychological Well-Being

Available cross-sectional research has identified three factors that moderate the relation between SM status and psychological well-being: (1) sexual identification or orientation; (2) age of first awareness/disclosure; and (3) gender status. Importantly, to date the extent to which, if at all, these factors moderate the relation between SM status and growth in psychological well-being is unknown.

Sexual Identification

While all those that exhibit same-sex sexuality share the *status* of SM, they vary dramatically as to whether or not they hold an SM *identity* as well as the nature of that identity, if any. Among those exhibiting same-sex sexuality, some identify as heterosexual, some as homosexual, and others as bisexual (Diamond, 2006). This heterogeneity in identification among those who exhibit same-sex sexuality could have implications for the relation between SM status and psychological well-being. . . .

Age of First Awareness/Disclosure

[R]esearch . . . indicates that coming to terms with one's sexual orientation and integrating it within one's sense of self is associated with higher psychological well-being. However, the extent to which this is the case may vary with age. There are risks associated with disclosing your sexual orientation to others. . . .

Hypotheses and Key Questions

. . . [T]he following hypotheses guided our examination, (1a) By early adolescence, we expected SM youth to report lower levels of psychological well-being than those of sexual-majority status; (1b) Disparities in psychological well-being among SM and sexual-majority individuals were predicted to increase during adolescence. By comparing the size of disparities at early

adolescence (i.e., Hypothesis 1a) to the extent, if any, that those disparities increase over adolescence (i.e., Hypothesis 1b), we evaluated the relative influence of middle childhood and adolescence on the relation between SM status and psychological well-being. (2) Among those of SM status, we expected those of bisexual status to report lower psychological well-being at the onset of adolescence as well as lower growth in well-being across adolescence. (3a) In terms of initial status differences and growth differences, we expected earlier awareness of same-sex attractions to be associated with lower psychological well-being; and (3b) we expected that the disparities in psychological well-being between SM and non-SM would be larger among those SM reporting earlier awareness of same-sex attractions. (4) In terms of both intercept differences and growth differences, we expected psychological well-being disparities between SM and non-SM to be more pronounced among males.

Methods

Sample

The data for this study came from the National Longitudinal study of Adolescent Health (Add Health), a multi-wave, nationally representative sample of American adolescents. . . . [After] initial assessment (Wave 1), . . . [t]wo additional waves of data are available, each taking place approximately one (Wave 2) and six years later (Wave 3). . . . For the present study, only those respondents who completed a sexual-orientation measure at Wave 3, completed same-sex attraction measures at Waves 1, 2, and 3, [and] had data for age . . . were included in the study ($N = 7733$). . . .

Measures

Psychological Well-Being
We focused on two indices of psychological well-being: depressive affect and self-esteem. . . .

Sexual Orientation and Sexual-Minority Status
Based on the distinction between SM status (those exhibiting versus those not exhibiting same-sex sexuality) and sexual orientation (those identifying versus those not identifying as an SM), we classified individuals into one of four groups. Classification was based on a single question that was asked at Wave 3 only. . . . All who identified themselves as 100% heterosexual . . . were classified as *Heterosexual identified/non-SM* ($n = 6889$). All who indicated some level of same-sex sexuality . . . qualified as an SM ($n = 844$). Of these individuals, those who identified as gay . . . were classified as *Homosexual-identified/SM* ($n = 129$), those who identified as bisexual . . . were classified as *Bisexual-identified/ SM* ($n = 140$), and those who identified as straight but indicated an attraction to the same sex . . . were classified as *Heterosexual-identified/SM* ($n = 575$).

Instability of Reported Same-Sex Attractions

At Wave 1 respondents were asked two yes/no questions: (1) "Have you ever had a romantic attraction to a female?" and (2) "Have you ever had a romantic attraction to a male?" For Waves 2 and 3 respondents were asked the same questions but were asked to indicate if they experienced these attractions since the last time they were interviewed. Using the reported same-sex attraction (or lack thereof) associated with one's Wave 3 sexual orientation as the reference point, we created three variables to assess instability in same-sex attraction—one for each wave. . . .

In concrete terms, relative to the reported same-sex attraction (or lack thereof) associated with one's Wave 3 sexual orientation, these . . . variables were an indication of inconsistency in reported same-sex attraction . . . [T]he Wave 1 and 2 instability [variables] may have reflected developmental changes or instability in awareness of and/or willingness to report same-sex attractions. For example, among those reporting a sexual orientation at Wave 3 that includes same-sex attractions, those who also reported same-sex attractions at Waves 1 and/or 2 may have become aware of their same-sex attractions at an earlier age than those who did not report same-sex attractions at Waves 1 and 2 . . . .

Cohort

Although age at Wave 1 ranged between 12 and 20 years of age, over 95% of the sample ranged between 13 and 18 ($M = 15.60$, $SD = 1.73$). We dichotomized the sample so that we could more closely examine how the relation between SM status and psychological well-being varied across adolescence. A dichotomous cohort variable was created: Those between the ages of 12 and 15 (51% of the sample) were classified as young, whereas those between the ages of 16 and 20 (49% of the sample) were classified as old. . . .

Results

. . .

Sexual Orientation at Wave 3 and Adolescent Trajectories of Psychological Well-Being

. . .

Depressive Affect

. . . Among the entire sample, intercept levels of depressive affect were low . . . and growth in depressive affect was negative. . . . Intercept levels of depressive affect were equivalent across the three SM groups. . . . However, collectively the three SM groups reported higher intercept levels of depressive affect . . . than Heterosexual-identified/non-SM. . . . Among the three SM groups, growth of depressive affect was more negative among the Bisexual-identified/SM . . . and Homosexual-identified/SM . . . groups than it was among the Heterosexual-identified/SM

group. . . . Also, only the Heterosexual-identified/SM group differed from the Heterosexual-identified/non-SM group. . . . In sum, at intercept the three SM groups did not differ from one another, but they collectively reported higher levels than Heterosexual-identified/non-SM. For Heterosexual-identified/SM these initial differences increased over time, but for Homosexual-identified/SM and Bisexual-identified/SM these differences remained stable over time. [Intercept level merely means depressive affect at the beginning of the study i.e., at wave 1 Negative growth in depressive affect means youth become less depressed over time]

Self-Esteem

In the sample as a whole, intercept levels of self-esteem were high . . . , and growth in self-esteem was positive but moderate. Intercept levels of self-esteem were equivalent across the three SM groups. . . . However, collectively the three SM groups reported lower intercept levels of self-esteem . . . than did Heterosexual-identified/non-SM. . . . With respect to growth in self-esteem, none of the four sexuality groups differed from one another.

The Influence of Instability in Reported Same-Sex Attractions

The above analyses suggested that reported sexual orientation during early adulthood (i.e., Wave 3) was associated with psychological well-being during adolescence. Next we examined (1) whether instability in reported same-sex attractions was related to adolescent patterns of psychological well-being, and (2) whether that instability influenced the relation between declared sexual orientation at Wave 3 and psychological well-being during adolescence, We did so by repeating the analyses above but including . . . instability . . . variables . . .: (1) unstable at Waves 1 and 2; (2) unstable at Wave 1 or 2, but not both; and (3) unstable at Wave 3. . . .

[T]he relation between the instability . . . variables and depressive affect did not differ across the three SM groups. However, the relation did differ between the SM groups and Heterosexual-identified, non-SM. The same was true for self-esteem. . . . Focusing first on SM, in reference to those who persistently reported same-sex attractions at all three waves, those who reported no same-sex attractions at Waves 1 and 2 reported higher psychological well-being at intercept (i.e., lower depressive affect and higher self-esteem). However, they reported smaller increases in psychological well-being over time. Among Heterosexual-identified/non-SM the relation between instability in reported same-sex attractions was much more muted, with those reporting same-sex attractions at both Waves 1 and 2 reporting lower depressive affect at intercept.

Controlling for instability in reported same-sex attractions did alter the relation between reported sexual orientation at Wave 3 and adolescent psychological well-being. . . . Concerning depressive affect, intercept levels among the Heterosexual-identified/ SM group and the Bisexual-identified/SM group were equivalent. . . . Collectively, however, they were higher than levels of depressive affect among both the Homosexual-identified/SM group . . . and the Heterosexual-identified/non-SM group. . . . In addition, the Homosexual-identified/SM group reported higher intercept levels than the Heterosexual-identified/non-SM group. . . . Taken together, at intercept the Heterosexual-identified/non-SM group reported the lowest depressive affect, followed by the Homosexual-identified/SM group, followed by the Heterosexual-identified/SM and Bisexual-identified/SM groups, who reported equivalent levels to one another as well as the highest levels overall. Growth in depressive affect was equivalent across the three SM groups. . . . However, declines in depressive affect over time were more evident among the SM groups . . . than among the Heterosexual-identified/non-SM group. . . . There were fewer group differences in self-esteem. At intercept the three SM groups reported equivalent levels of self-esteem, . . . but collectively they reported lower levels of self-esteem than the Heterosexual-identified/non-SM group. . . . There were no group differences in the growth of self-esteem.

Summary

Wave 3 sexual orientation was associated with psychological well-being. It appeared to have a stronger relation with intercept levels than with growth, with SM reporting lower psychological well-being at intercept. Among the SM groups, early and stable reporting of same-sex attractions was associated with lower initial levels of psychological well-being but greater increases in psychological well-being over time. Within the Heterosexual-identified/non-SM group, early and stable reporting of no same-sex attractions was associated with lower initial levels of depressive affect. Relative to cases of unstable same-sex attractions, the relation between Wave 3 sexual orientation and adolescent depressive affect was different among those who reported stable same-sex attractions. Specifically, after controlling for instability in reported same-sex attractions, the discrepancy between SM and Heterosexual-identified/non-SM was larger at the intercept; however, SM also reported greater increases in psychological well-being over time relative to Heterosexual-identified/non-SM. Thus, relative to those reporting unstable sexual attractions over time, among those reporting stable sexual attractions over time, the initial gap in psychological well-being between SM and Heterosexual-identified/non-SM was larger; however, that gap also closed at a faster rate over time.

Sexual-Minority Status and Psychological Well-Being: Cohort and Gender Differences

. . . The relation between SM status and psychological well-being varied across both cohort and gender. In the case of depressive affect, patterns evident among the entire sample when instability controls were not included (i.e., greater increases in depressive

affect over time among SM—Heterosexual-identified/SM in particular) were more evident among those in the young cohort and females. However, in the case of self-esteem, patterns found among the entire sample (i.e., intercept differences across SM and Heterosexual-identified/non-SM) were more evident among the young cohort. A pattern that was not evident among the entire sample emerged as well: Among the entire sample there was no instance when growth in self-esteem varied across any of the sexual orientation groups. However, among the young cohort, growth in self-esteem was more positive among SM. Growth in self-esteem was equivalent across SM status among the old cohort. This differential growth pattern across cohort only emerged when controls for instability in reported same-sex attractions were included. Finally, the relation between early and stable reports of same-sex attractions and psychological well-being (i.e., lower initial levels but greater increases over time) was more pronounced among males.

Discussion

Overall, four main conclusions can be drawn from this study: (1) Psychological well-being disparities between SM and non-SM are in place by early adolescence, and then for many the remainder of adolescence is a recovery period when the disparities narrow over time. (2) Early and stable reporting of same-sex attractions is associated with a greater initial deficit in psychological well-being, but because it is also associated with a quicker recovery over time, the effects are often not long lasting. (3) Though the relation between sexual orientation during early adulthood (i.e., Wave 3) and adolescent psychological well-being was quite similar across gender, the negative relation between psychological well-being and early, stable awareness of same-sex attractions was more pronounced among males. (4) Relative to Bisexual- and Homosexual-identified/SM, the understudied yet relatively sizable group of Heterosexual-identified/SM appeared to be at equal risk for deficits in psychological well-being. . . .

The Emergence of the Negative Relation Between SM Status and Psychological Well-Being

The driving motivation for this study was to examine whether the negative relation between SM status and psychological well-being (1) is similar to that of other social statuses where differences are primarily in place by early adolescence; or (2) continues to emerge through the adolescent years when SM are thought to encounter unique developmental challenges. The findings suggest that the negative relation between SM status (based on the declaration of a sexual orientation that includes same-sex attractions during early adulthood) and psychological well-being is largely in place by early adolescence. This is evidenced by the fact that among both the young and old cohorts, and regardless of adolescent patterns of reported same-sex attractions, the discrepancies in psychological well-being were largest at the study's onset (when those among the young and old cohorts ranged between 12 and 15, and 16 and 19 respectively). Moreover, middle childhood and early adolescence appear to be more of a struggle for those who report early and stable same-sex attractions, since by early adolescence these individuals report the greatest deficits in psychological well-being relative to Heterosexual-identified/non-SM.

Across adolescence the negative relation between SM status (again based on declared sexual orientation during early adulthood) and psychological well-being either remained stable or decreased. Among those who reported early and stable same-sex attractions, the negative relation between SM status and psychological well-being decreased across time. Importantly, among the young cohort (12–15 years of age at Wave 1), this pattern held true for both depressive affect and self-esteem. This finding suggests that for those who reported early, stable same-sex attractions, the negative relation between SM status and psychological well-being decreased across time, even among those who were early adolescents at the onset of the study. . . .

Why Is the Negative Relation in Place by Early Adolescence?

Most of the challenges associated with being a sexual minority (e.g., dealing with homophobia and bullying, trying to find other SM peers, navigating romantic relationships, coming out) are confronted over the course of adolescence, not prior to it. The relation between declared sexual orientation during early adulthood and psychological well-being seems to manifest by early adolescence and does not increase thereafter, which speaks to the deleterious effects of feeling different from others during middle childhood and early adolescence. Though individuals must deal throughout the lifespan with being members of devalued groups and the sense of difference that accompanies those memberships, middle childhood is the first time individuals are confronted with this sense of difference. After all, it is not until middle childhood that youth are cognitively capable of internalizing this sense of difference as meaningful to their own personal sense of value (Harter, 2006). Consequently, they likely have not yet acquired the tools for dealing with this sense of difference. As a result those in middle childhood may be more likely to have their sense of well-being negatively influenced by that sense of difference.

Potentially compounding the deleterious effects of this sense of difference during middle childhood is the fact that unlike individuals of other stigmatized groups, SM often deal with this sense of difference in isolation, since those around them are predominantly, if not completely, of the sexual majority (D'Augelli & Hershberger, 1993). Contrast this to other youth of at-risk social status, such as females or members of racial minorities, who (1) are likely to have role models in the home or at school as well as peers and friends who share their status; and (2) are likely to have parents or extended family members actively socializing them to deal

with the challenges associated with their social status (Bowman & Howard, 1985; Cross, 1991; Thornton, 1997). Finally, the initial deficits may be larger among those SM reporting early and stable same-sex attractions because they are more likely to be dealing with this novel sense of difference at an even earlier age, an age at which they are even more likely to be isolated from others in the SM community (D'Augelli, 1996; Friedman et al., 2008).

Who "Recovers" and Why?

The negative relation between a declared sexual orientation during early adulthood that includes same-sex attractions and adolescent psychological well-being did decrease across adolescence, but only for a select group. The "recovery" or narrowing of psychological well-being deficits between SM and Heterosexual-identified/non-SM was limited to those who reported early and stable same-sex attractions. In the case of self-esteem, the recovery was limited to the young cohort, those who ranged between 12 and 15 at the onset and between 18 and 23 at the conclusion of the study. Why the recovery was limited to those who reported early, stable same-sex attractions requires further examination, but we offer two possible explanations. First, SM who reported early, stable same-sex attractions had farther to recover. That is, relative to Heterosexual-identified/non-SM, SM who reported early and stable same-sex attractions reported far lower initial levels of psychological well-being than did SM who did not report early and stable same-sex attractions. Second, SM who reported early and stable same-sex attractions may have benefited from having longer to adjust to their status and incorporate it into their sense of self (Floyd & Bakeman, 2006; Savin-Williams, 1995). Regardless of the reason, it seems that the earlier the awareness of same-sex attractions, the greater the initial deficit in psychological well-being, but also the steeper the recovery. This pattern of recovery among those reporting early, stable same-sex attraction is inconsistent with Friedman et al.'s (2008) findings that those progressing through gay-related developmental milestones at earlier ages tended to report lower functioning during adulthood. Respondents included in the Friedman et al. (2008) study were teenagers in the early to mid 1980s, whereas respondents in Add Health were teenagers in the mid to late 1990s. Perhaps historical increases in the acceptance of homosexuality (Savin-Williams, 2005) have contributed to reductions in the long-term consequences of an early awareness of same-sex sexuality.

In cases where there was a recovery, such recovery was generally not complete. SM still reported deficits in psychological well-being during early adulthood; those deficits were simply smaller than they were during early adolescence. . . .

Overall Lack of Gender Differences

The relation between sexual orientation during early adulthood (i.e., Wave 3) and adolescent psychological well-being was largely equivalent across gender. . . .

Conclusions and Next Steps

Sexual minorities or those exhibiting same-sex sexuality are a heterogeneous group who vary not only in sexual orientation but also in the developmental course they follow in terms of their awareness and acceptance of their sexual orientation. Among those exhibiting same-sex sexuality, there also is heterogeneity in terms of developmental patterns of psychological well-being. Across adolescence, trajectories of psychological well-being converge, such that by early adulthood those exhibiting same-sex sexuality look more similar to both one another and those not exhibiting same-sex sexuality. In developmental science this phenomenon is termed *equifinality* (Bertalanffy, 1968)—multiple pathways to the same (or similar) end point. This pattern of findings highlights the important contributions that developmental theory and longitudinal data can make to our understanding of same-sex sexuality, sexual orientation, and psychological well-being.

More specifically, the pattern of results suggests that: (1) the negative relation between SM status and psychological well-being is in place by early adolescence; and (2) the exact pathway or trajectory that one follows across adolescence is more a function of the timing of awareness of same-sex attractions than it is of actual sexual orientation (as declared during early adulthood). These results raise the possibility that community resources and social support groups geared towards SM youth, now available in many high-schools, may benefit students in grade school and middle school as well. . . .

References

Bell, A., Weimberg, M., & Hammersmith, K. (1981). *Sexual preference: Its development in men and women.* Bloomington, IN: Indiana University Press.

Bertalanffy, L. V. (1968). *General systems theory: Foundations, development, applications.* New York: George Braziller.

Bowman, P., & Howard, C. (1985). Race-related socialization, motivation, and academic achievement: A study of Black youths in three-generation families. *Journal of the American Academy of Child Psychiatry, 24*(2), 134–141.

Cross, W. (1991). *Shades of Black diversity in ethnic-minority identity.* Philadelphia: Temple University Press.

D'Augelli, A. (1996). Enhancing the development of lesbian, gay, and bisexual youths. In E. Rothblum & L. A. Bond (Eds.), *Preventing heterosexism and homophobia.* Thousand Oaks, CA: Sage.

D'Augelli, A., & Hershberger, S. (1993). Lesbian, gay, and bisexual youth in community settings: Personal challenges and mental health problems. *American Journal of Community Psychology, 21*(4), 421–448.

Diamond, L. (2006). What we got wrong about sexual identity development: Unexpected findings from a longitudinal study of women. In A. Omoto & H. Kurtzman (Eds.), *Recent research on sexual orientation, mental health, and substance use.* Washington, DC: American Psychological Association.

Fergusson, D., Horwood, L., Ridder, E., & Beautrais, A. (2005). Sexual orientation and mental health in a birth cohort of young adults. *Psychological Medicine, 35,* 971–981.

Floyd, F., & Bakeman, R. (2006). Coming-out across the life course: Implications of age and historical context. *Archives of Sexual Behavior, 35*(3), 287–296.

Floyd, F., & Stein, T. (2002). Sexual orientation identity formation among gay, lesbian, and bisexual youths: Multiple patterns of milestone experiences: *Journal of Research on Adolescence, 12*(2), 167–191.

Friedman, M., Marshal, M., Stall, R., Cheong, J., & Wright, E. (2008). Gay-related development, early abuse and adult health outcomes among gay males. *AIDS and Behavior, 12*(6), 891–902.

Galliher, R., Rostosky, S., & Hughes, H. (2004). School belonging, self-esteem, and depressive symptoms in adolescents: An examination of sex, sexual attraction status, and urbanicity. *Journal of Youth and Adolescence, 33*(3), 235–245.

Harter, S. (2006). The self. In N. Eisenberg, W. Damon, & R. Lerner (Eds.), *Handbook of child psychology.* (Vol. III). Hoboken, NJ: Wiley.

Rosario, M., Meyey-Bahlburg, H., Hunter, J., & Exner, T. (1996). The psychosocial development of urban lesbian, gay, and bisexual youths. *Journal of Sex Research, 33*(2), 113–126.

Russell, S. (2006). Substance use and abuse and mental health among sexual minority youth: Evidence from Add Health. In A. Omoto & H. Kurtzman (Eds.), *Recent research on sexual orientation, mental health, and substance use.* Washington, DC: American Psychological Association.

Sandfort, T., de Graaf, R., & Bijl, R. (2003). Same-sex sexuality and quality of life: Findings from the Netherlands mental health survey and incidence study. *Archives of Sexual Behavior, 32*(1), 15–22.

Savin-Williams, R. (1995). Lesbian, gay male, and bisexual adolescents. In A. D'Augelli & C. Patterson (Eds.), *Lesbian, gay, and bisexual identities over the lifespan: Psychological perspectives* (pp. 165–189). New York: Oxford University Press.

Savin-Williams, R. (2005). *The new gay teenager.* Cambridge, MA: Harvard University Press.

Savin-Williams, R., & Diamond, L. (2000). Sexual identity trajectories among SM youths: Gender comparisons. *Archives of Sexual Behavior, 29*(6), 607–627.

Thornton, M. (1997). Strategies of racial socialization among Black parents: Mainstream, minority, and cultural messages. In R. Taylor (Ed.), *Family life in Black America* (pp. 201–215). Thousand Oaks, CA: Sage.

Troiden, R. (1989). The formation of homosexual identities. In G. Herdt (Ed.), *Gay and lesbian youth.* New York: Hayworth Press.

Zucker, K., Wild, J., Bradley, S., & Lowry, C. (1993). Physical attractiveness of boys with gender identity disorder. *Archives of Sexual Behavior, 22*(1), 23–26.

Margaret Rosario, Eric Schrimshaw, and Joyce R. Hunter

 **NO**

Different Patterns of Sexual Identity Development over Time: Implications for the Psychological Adjustment of Lesbian, Gay, and Bisexual Youths

... This report examines whether differences in the formation and integration of an LGB identity are associated with the subsequent psychological adjustment of LGB youths.

We base our conceptualization of sexual identity development on the work of Erik Erikson. The process of identity development consists of identity formation in which the internal reality of the individual begins to assert and demand its expression as earlier identifications are discarded or reconfigured (Erikson, 1968, 1956/1980). Identity development also consists of identity integration, in which a commitment to and integration of the evolving identity with the totality of the self are expected, although not guaranteed (e.g., Kroger, 2007; Marcia, 1966). Identity integration involves an acceptance of the unfolding identity, its continuity over time and settings, and a desire to be known by others as such, none of which is surprising given identity integration concerns an inner commitment and solidarity with who one is (Erikson, 1968, 1946/1980). The antithesis of identity integration is diffusion or confusion; a sense of self as other or inauthentic either because an invalid identity has been assumed or foisted upon one, or because one is searching for a meaningful identity (Erikson, 1968, 1946/1980, 1956/1980). Although most theories of LGB identity development do not explicitly reference Erikson's more general theory of identity development, the general notions of identity formation and integration are implicit in the models (Cass, 1979; Chapman & Brannock, 1987; Fassinger & Miller, 1996; Troiden, 1989).

In keeping with Erikson, sexual identity development is conceived as having two related developmental processes (Morris, 1997; Rosario, [et al.], 2006). The first, identity formation, is the initiation of a process of self-discovery and exploration of one's LGB identity, including becoming aware of one's sexual orientation, questioning whether one may be LGB, and having sex with members of the same sex (e.g., Chapman & Brannock, 1987; Fassinger & Miller, 1996; Troiden, 1989). The second, identity integration, is a continuation of sexual identity development as individuals integrate and incorporate the identity into their sense of self and thereby increase their commitment to the new LGB identity (Morris, 1997; Rosario, [et al.], 2001,

Rosario et al., 2006). Specifically, identity integration is composed of engaging in LGB-related social activities, working through negative attitudes toward homosexuality, feeling more comfortable with other individuals knowing about their LGB identity, and disclosing that identity to others (Morris, 1997; Rosario et al., 2001, 2006). . . .

Several studies of LGB youths and adults have examined the relations between sexual identity development and psychological adjustment. . . . Despite the lack of research identifying an association between identity formation and adjustment, the broader literature on identity development of other groups (e.g., adolescent identity, ethnic identity, and general sexual identity) has demonstrated that a stagnated identity development is associated with poorer adjustment (Adams et al., 2001; Archer & Grey, 2009; Kiang, Yip, & Fuligni, 2008; Marcia, 1966; Muise, [et al.] in press). . . .

In contrast to identity formation, aspects of identity integration have been linked to psychological adjustment among both LGB youths and adults. More positive attitudes toward homosexuality (e.g., Balsam & Mohr, 2007; Morris, Waldo, & Rothblum, 2001; Rosario et al., 2001; Wright & Perry, 2006), greater openness and disclosure of one's sexuality (D'Augelli, 2002; Jordan & Deluty, 1998; Morris et al., 2001), and greater involvement in the LGB community (Morris et al., 2001) have each been found to be associated with greater psychological adjustment. Relatedly, LGB individuals who are further along in integrating their sexual identity have been found to have higher self-esteem (Halpin & Allen, 2004; Swann & Spivey, 2004). . . .

[T]his report investigates the heretofore unexamined roles of identity formation and changes in identity integration on the subsequent psychological adaptation of LGB youths. Specifically, we hypothesized that LGB youths who begin identify formation more recently than other youths may be at risk for poorer psychological adjustment. Further, we hypothesized that greater identity integration and increases in identity integration over time will be associated with higher subsequent psychological adjustment. We also examine whether and how different patterns of sexual identity development are associated with psychological adjustment after accounting for other important social-context factors known to be critical for the

Rosario, Margaret; Schrimshaw, Eric; Hunter, Joyce R, "Different patterns of sexual identity development over time: Implications for the psychological adjustment of lesbian, gay, and bisexual youths," *Journal of Sex Research*, Vol. 48, No. 1, December 21, 2010. Copyright © 2010 Society for the Scientific Study of Sexuality. pp 3–15. Reproduced by permission of Taylor & Francis LLC, http://www.tandfonline.com

psychological adjustment of LGB youths (i.e., family and friend support, negative social relationships, and experiences of gay-related stress). Similarly, we control for sociodemographic characteristics (e.g., sex) that covary with sexual identity development or adjustment.

Method

Participants [were] 156 youths (49% female), with a mean age of 18. 30 years (SD =1.65 years). . . .

A two- to three-hour structured interview was conducted at recruitment, with follow-up interviews occurring . . . 12 months later. . . .

Measures of Sexual Identity Formation

Milestones of sexual identity formation were assessed by . . . ask[ing] the ages when they were first erotically attracted to, fantasized about, and were aroused by erotica focusing on the same sex. The mean age of these three milestones was computed to obtain the age of first awareness of same-sex sexual orientation. . . . In addition, youths were asked about the age when they first thought they "might be" lesbian, gay, or bisexual and when they first thought they "really were" lesbian, gay, or bisexual. Finally, they were asked about the age when they first experienced any of several sexual activities with the same sex, with the earliest age in which they engaged in any of these sexual activities used as the age of their first same-sex sexual encounter. . . . [F]or all four developmental milestones, we computed the number of years since the youth first experienced the various milestones by subtracting the age at each milestone from the youth's age at Time 1.

Measures of Sexual Identity Integration

Involvement in LGB-Related Activities
A 28-item checklist assessed lifetime involvement in gay-related social and recreational activities at all assessments (Rosario et al., 2001). At follow-up assessments, youths were asked about their activity involvement . . . since their last assessment. . . .

Positive Attitudes Toward Homosexuality or Bisexuality
. . . 11 items assessed attitudes toward homosexuality (e.g., "My [homosexuality/bisexuality] does not make me unhappy"). . . .

Comfort with Others Knowing About Your Homosexuality or Bisexuality
. . . 12 items assessed comfort with other individuals knowing about the youth's sexuality (e.g., "If my straight friends knew of my [homosexuality/bisexuality], I would feel uncomfortable"). . . .

Disclosure of Homosexuality or Bisexuality to Others
Youths were asked at Time 1 to enumerate "all the people in your life who are important or were important to you and whom you told that you are (lesbian/gay/bisexual)." . . . Subsequently, youths were asked about the number of new individuals to whom the youth had disclosed . . . since their last assessment. . . .

Measures of Psychological Adjustment

Psychological Distress
Depressive and anxious symptoms during the past week were assessed by means of the Brief Symptom Inventory (BSI; Derogatis, 1993). . . .

As the BSI assesses only internalized distress, conduct problems were included as indicators of externalized psychological distress. A 13-item index . . . was created to assess the number of conduct problems experienced by the youths such as skipping school, vandalism, stealing, fighting, and running away. . . .

Self-Esteem
Rosenberg's (1965) 10-item scale was administered at all assessments. . . .

Measures of Social Context and Other Potential Covariates

Social Support from Family and Friends
Procidano and Heller's (1983) measures of perceived social support from family and from friends were adapted, deleting items that might be confounded with psychological health. . . .

Negative Social Relationships
The 12-item Social Obstruction Scale (Gurley, 1990) was administered at Time 1 to assess the presence of negative social relationships with others, including being treated poorly, being ignored, and being manipulated by others (e.g., "Somebody treats me as if I were nobody"). . . .

Gay-Related Stressful Life Events
A 12-item checklist of stressful events related to homosexuality was administered at Time 1 (e.g., "Losing a close friend because of your [homosexuality/bisexuality];" Rosario, [et al.], 2002). . . .

Social Desirability
The tendency to provide" socially desirable responses was assessed at Time 1 by means of the Marlowe–Crowne Social Desirability Scale (Crowne & Marlowe, 1964). . . .

Data Analysis

Cluster analysis was used to identify naturally occurring subgroups of LGB youths on sexual identity formation and integration. Cluster analysis is a . . . procedure to determine whether groups exist. . . . Rather than imposing a priori categories on the data, cluster analysis allows for the identification of potentially heretofore unidentified groups based on the data themselves. . . .

Results

To examine potential patterns of LGB identity formation and identity integration, indicators of sexual identity development were cluster analyzed. . . . In summary, three sets of cluster analysis were conducted. First, an analysis of length of time since achieving each of four identity formation milestones (i.e., years since first being attracted to the same sex, years since first thinking one might be LGB, years since first thinking one really was LGB, and years since first same-sex sexual encounter) generated two clusters: one composed of youths whose identity developed earlier (33%) and a second of youths whose identity formation was more recent (67%). . . .

Second, four aspects of identity integration at Time 1 (i.e., involvement in gay-related social activities, positive attitudes toward homosexuality or bisexuality, comfort with other individuals learning about one's homosexuality or bisexuality, and disclosing that sexuality to others) were cluster analyzed. Three clusters emerged: high, middling, and low integration. . . .

Third, the cluster analysis of identity integration at Time 2 (one year later) was conducted relative to . . . Time 1 clusters. Thus, this analysis took into account potential change in clusters from Time 1 to Time 2. Three clusters were found at Time 2, consisting of youths low, middling, or high on identity integration. . . .

Identity Groups and Psychological Adjustment

. . . A comparison of youths whose LGB identity formation had occurred earlier vs. more recently found that the two groups did not differ significantly on any indicator of psychological adjustment at Time 1 or Time 2.

Significant differences were found in psychological adjustment by identity integration groups. The three integration groups at Time 1 differed on their concurrent (Time 1) and subsequent (Time 2) distress and self-esteem. [C]omparison found that highly integrated youths reported significantly less anxious and depressive symptoms, fewer conduct problems, and higher self-esteem, especially at Time 2, than did youths with low integration. Youths with middling integration sometimes differed significantly from youths with high integration, reporting more distress or lower self-esteem than highly integrated peers.

Identity integration groups at Time 2 also differed on psychological distress and self-esteem at Time 2. By Time 2, psychological distress, with the exception of anxiety, did not differ significantly between the high and middling integrated youths, but both groups of youths differed from youths low in integration. All groups differed on self-esteem, with the highly integrated group reporting the highest self-esteem and the low-integrated group reporting the lowest self-esteem.

Individual Change in Identity Integration and Psychological Adjustment

Close examination of the integration data at the individual level indicated that youths followed a number of different patterns of change over time in identity integration, including a large number who remained consistent over time (see Rosario et al., 2008, for details). . . .

A comparison of . . . five integration-change groups on subsequent psychological distress and self-esteem at Time 2 was conducted . . . indica[ting] that youths who were consistently high in integration generally reported lower psychological distress than other youths, with the exception of youths who decreased from high to middling, who often did not differ from consistently high youths. Youths who were consistently high, those who increased from low or middling to high, or those who decreased from high to middling reported higher self-esteem at Time 2 than youths who were consistently middling or low in integration over time.

Social-Context Factors

Social relationships and gay-related stress at Time 1 were related significantly to psychological adjustment at Time 2. Youths with more family and friend support experienced less depressive symptoms. . . . Friend support was related to fewer conduct problems . . . and family support was related to higher self-esteem. . . . Conversely, youths with more negative social relationships reported more anxious and depressive symptoms, more conduct problems, and lower self-esteem. . . . Youths who experienced gay-related stress reported more anxious symptoms ($r = .17$). . . .

Multivariate Analyses Predicting Psychological Adjustment

To examine whether individual-level changes in identity integration over time were associated with youths' psychological adjustment at Time 2, over and above that already accounted for by social-context factors and other potential covariates, multiple linear regression analyses were conducted. First, we controlled for sex, sexual identity, social desirability, and the social-context factors. We then entered the identity–integration–change groups. . . .

[I]mportantly changes in identity integration over time were consistently associated with psychological adjustment, even after controlling for the social-context factors. . . . Specifically, LGB youths who were consistently high in identity integration over time reported less anxious symptoms and higher self-esteem than youths who were consistently low in integration. There was also a . . . trend for consistently high-integration youths to report less depressive symptoms and fewer conduct problems than consistently low-integration youths. This pattern was not restricted to just the consistently high youths. Youths who increased from low or middling to high integration, youths who decreased from high to middling integration, and youths who were consistently middling in their integration were also found to report significantly less anxious symptoms and higher self-esteem than consistently low youths. In addition, consistently middling youths reported fewer conduct problems than consistently low youths.

Discussion

There has been increasing recognition that the sexual identity development of LGB youths may follow multiple paths. . . . [T]his report examined the associations of LGB identity development with psychological distress (i.e., symptoms of anxiety, depression, and conduct problems) and self-esteem. Given that LGB youths followed different developmental patterns, we hypothesized that psychological adjustment would differ by the developmental patterns.

Identity Development and Psychological Adjustment

Consistent with some past research (e.g., D'Augelli, 2002; Floyd & Stein, 2002), we found that patterns of identity formation (early vs. recent development) were not significantly related to psychological distress and self-esteem. This may be because too much time had elapsed since experiencing even "recent" identity formation and subsequent psychological adjustment, resulting in a dilution of the relations between formation and adaptation. . . .

In contrast to the formation findings, different identity integration groups were found to significantly differ on all four indicators of psychological adjustment, both cross-sectionally and over time. Thus, identity integration has short-term and long-term implications for the psychological adjustment of LGB youths.

The relation of identity integration to adjustment also was evident when individual changes in identity integration over time were examined. These findings indicated that youths who were consistently high in integration or had previously been high in integration experienced greater psychological adjustment than other youths. The finding suggests that the latter youths were protected by the immunity afforded by being highly integrated at one point. By comparison, youths who were consistently low in integration reported the highest levels of distress and the lowest self-esteem. The totality of these findings underscores both the benefits of achieving and maintaining identity integration and the costs associated with low identity integration. Such findings are supported by similar findings on heterosexual youths with respect to other identities including ethnic, family, and religious identities (e.g., Adams et al., 2001; Kiang et al., 2008). . . .

Covariates of Adjustment and Changes in Individual-Level Identity Integration

Despite the strong associations found between identity integration and psychological adjustment, we also recognize that the social contexts in which LGB youths live can have important implications for their psychological adjustment. Indeed, we found that supportive relationships were related to better psychological adjustment and that negative social relationships were related to poorer adjustment. In addition, supportive and negative social relationships were related to change in individual-level identity integration. Therefore, it was possible that the association between sexual identity integration and adjustment might be due to social relationships.

. . . As valuable as supportive relationships are for the individual's mental and physical well-being our findings suggest that identity integration captures much more than can be explained solely by social relationships. LGB identity integration, as stated at the beginning of this report, involves both acceptance and commitment to one's sexuality. Social relationships may affect the individual's identity integration (e.g., retarding it for some time), . . . but they do not exclusively determine it.

. . . [I]t was hardly surprising that youths who were consistently high on integration reported higher psychological adjustment than youths who were consistently low in integration, after controlling for social relationships, gay-related stress, and other covariates. . . . [T]here are psychological taxes to be paid for stagnation at low levels of identity integration. As such, the findings suggest that LGB youths who are consistently low in integration should be identified and targeted for interventions. . . .

Conclusion

Our findings underscore the importance of sexual identity development for understanding the adjustment of LGB youths. They suggest that the poor psychological adjustment that has been found among LGB youths relative to heterosexual peers may be attributed to a subset of youths whose identity integration has stagnated, especially at low levels. Indeed, a comparison of our youths' anxious and depressive symptoms with adolescent norms for these symptoms indicates that consistently low and middling youths were more symptomatic than normative peers. By comparison, consistently high youths reported lower levels of anxious and depressive symptoms than normative peers. Moreover, the findings held even when the means were adjusted for social context and other [variables]. . . .

References

Adams, G. R., Munro, B., Doherty-Poirer, M., Munro, G., Petersen, A.-M. R., & Edwards, J. (2001). Diffuse-avoidance, normative, and informational identity styles: Use of identity theory to predict maladjustment. *Identity, 1,* 307–320.

Archer, S. L., & Grey, J. A. (2009). The sexual domain of identity: Sexual statuses of identity in relation to psychosocial sexual health. *Identity, 9,* 33–62.

Balsam, K. F., & Mohr, J. J. (2007). Adaptation to sexual orientation stigma: A comparison of bisexual and lesbian/gay adults. *Journal of Counseling Psychology, 54,* 306–319.

Cass, V. C. (1979). Homosexual identity formation: A theoretical model. *Journal of Homosexuality, 4,* 219–235.

Chapman, B. E., & Brannock, J. C. (1987). Proposed model of lesbian identity development: An empirical examination. *Journal of Homosexuality, 14,* 69–80.

Crowne, D. P., & Marlowe, D. (1964). *The approval motive: Studies in evaluative dependence.* Westport, CT: Greenwood.

D'Augelli, A. R. (2002). Mental health problems among lesbian, gay, and bisexual youths ages 14 to 21. *Clinical Child Psychology and Psychiatry, 7,* 433–456.

Derogatis, L. R. (1993). *BSI, Brief Symptom Inventory: Administration, scoring, and procedures manual.* Minneapolis, MN: National Computer Systems.

Erikson, E. H. (1968). *Identity: Youth and crisis.* New York: Norton.

Erikson, E. H. (1980). Ego development and historical change. In *Identity and the life cycle* (pp. 17–50). New York: Norton. (Original work published 1946).

Erikson, E. H. (1980). The problem of ego identity. In *Identity and the life cycle* (pp. 107–175). New York: Norton. (Original work published 1956).

Fassinger, R. E., & Miller, B. A. (1996). Validation of an inclusive model of sexual minority identity formation on a sample of gay men. *Journal of Homosexuality, 32,* 53–78.

Floyd, F. J., & Stein, T. S. (2002). Sexual orientation identity formation among gay, lesbian, and bisexual youths: Multiple patterns of milestone experiences. *Journal of Research on Adolescence, 12,* 167–191.

Gurley, D. N. (1990). *The context of well-being after significant life stress: Measuring social support and obstruction.* Unpublished doctoral dissertation, University of Kentucky, Lexington.

Halpin, S. A., & Allen, M. W. (2004). Changes in psychosocial well-being during stages of gay identity development. *Journal of Homosexuality, 47,* 109–126.

Jordan, K. M., & Deluty, R. H. (1998). Coming out for lesbian women: Its relation to anxiety, positive affectivity, self-esteem, and social support. *Journal of Homosexuality, 35,* 41–63.

Kiang, L., Yip, T., & Fuligni, A. J. (2008). Multiple social identities and adjustment in young adults from ethnically diverse backgrounds. *Journal of Research on Adolescence, 18,* 643–670.

Kroger, J. (2007). *Identity development: Adolescence through adulthood* (2nd ed.). Thousand Oaks, CA: Sage.

Marcia, J. E. (1966). Development and validation of ego-identity status. *Journal of Personality and Social Psychology, 3,* 551–558.

Morris, J. F. (1997). Lesbian coming out as a multidimensional process. *Journal of Homosexuality, 33,* 1–22.

Morris, J. F., Waldo, C. R., & Rothblum, E. D. (2001). A model of predictors and outcomes of outness among lesbian and bisexual women. *American Journal of Orthopsychiatry, 71,* 61–71.

Muise, A., Preyde, M., Maitland, S. B., & Milhausen, R. R. (in press). Sexual identity and sexual well-being in female heterosexual university students. *Archives of Sexual Behavior.*

Procidano, M. E., & Heller, K. (1983). Measures of perceived social support from friends and from family: Three validation studies. *American Journal of Community Psychology, 11,* 1–24.

Rosario, M., Hunter, J., Maguen, S., Gwadz, M., & Smith, R. (2001). The coming-out process and its adaptational and health-related associations among gay, lesbian, and bisexual youths: Stipulation and exploration of a model. *American Journal of Community Psychology, 29,* 133–160.

Rosario, M., Schrimshaw, E. W., & Hunter, J. (2008). Predicting different patterns of sexual identity development over time among lesbian, gay, and bisexual youths: A cluster analytic approach. *American Journal of Community Psychology, 42,* 266–282.

Rosario, M., Schrimshaw, E. W., Hunter, J., & Braun, L. (2006). Sexual identity development among lesbian, gay, and bisexual youths: Consistency and change over time. *Journal of Sex Research, 43,* 46–58.

Rosario, M., Schrimshaw, E. W., Hunter, J., & Gwadz, M. (2002). Gay-related stress and emotional distress among gay, lesbian, and bisexual youths: A longitudinal examination. *Journal of Consulting and Clinical Psychology, 70,* 967–975.

Rosenberg, M. (1965). *Society and adolescent self-image.* Princeton, NJ: Princeton University Press.

Swann, S. K., & Spivey, C. A. (2004). The relationship between self-esteem and lesbian identity during adolescence. *Child and Adolescent Social Work Journal, 21,* 629–646.

Troiden, R. R. (1989). The formation of homosexual identities. In G. Herdt (Ed.), *Gay and lesbian youth* (pp. 43–73). New York: Haworth.

Wright, E. R., & Perry, B. L. (2006). Sexual identity distress, social support, and health of gay, lesbian, and bisexual youth. *Journal of Homosexuality, 51,* 81–110.

EXPLORING THE ISSUE

Is "Coming Out" As a Sexual Minority Earlier in Adolescence Detrimental to Psychological Well-Being?

Critical Thinking and Reflection

1. Consider how Jager and Davis-Kean would define "coming out" at least from their research perspective. What is the role of sexual-minority status in this definition? What is the role of "questioning" individuals in this research? Are Jager and Davis-Kean participants who are labeled as heterosexual-identified/SM really just "questioning" sexual minorities? How might excluding this group (heterosexual-identified/SM) from the study impact Jager and Davis-Kean's findings?

2. Consider how Rosario et al. would define "coming out"—at least from their research perspective. Compare and contrast sexual-identity formation to sexual-identity integration. Why would identity formation (early versus later) show no differences in psychological adjustment but identity integration would? Are less integrated individuals "questioning" sexual minorities? What about low-integration individuals? Are they "questioning" or "closeted"?

3. Are the YES and NO selections really addressing the same issue? Are these two studies comparable with each other? Why or why not? Compare and contrast the two studies in terms of their similarities and their differences.

4. Based on Jager and Davis-Kean's study, what queer teen would have the greatest need for intervention? Based on their findings, what form should that intervention take? What might the unique barriers be for alleviating depression in the different sexual orientation groupings? At what point should intervention occur? Should interventions at different time points take different forms?

5. Based on Rosario et al.'s study, what queer teen would have the greatest need for intervention? Based on their findings, what form should that intervention take? What might the barriers be to further identity integration? How might these be addressed?

Is There Common Ground?

Both sets of authors would likely agree that it is in a person's best interest to come out, and that foreclosing on a sexual-minority self-identity is detrimental to the psychological well-being of the individual. They would agree that coming out is a very important process in the identity development of sexual-minority youth. They would want their research used to better the adolescent experience for sexual-minority youth.

Both studies used longitudinal designs: Both sets of authors would agree that this is an advantageous way of assessing the impact of maturation on psychological adjustment outcomes. It is critically important to view coming out as a developmental process rather than a discrete moment in time.

Jager and Davis-Kean found that there was a subset of their sample who had unstable sexual attractions to the same sex across the three time points. Rosario et al. found that there was variability in integration of sexual identity. These two findings seem very congruent with each other: Both studies found that the instable or the less integrated individuals had poorer mental health outcomes.

Finally, both sets of authors would agree that it is insufficient to simply look at "the age of coming out" (as implied by the question addressing the issue herein). Rather, both sets of authors would agree that there are different developmental trajectories to coming out and multiple factors must be taken into consideration to address the impact of coming out on mental health outcomes of youths. Social context, such as having friend and familial support, is one such factor that may impact mental health outcomes during the coming-out process (see Legate et al., 2012).

Additional Resources

D'Augelli, A. R., & Patterson, C. J. (Eds.). (2001). *Lesbian, gay, and bisexual identities and youth: Psychological perspectives*. New York: Oxford University Press.

Drasin, H., Beals, K. P., Elliot, M. N., Lever, J., Klein, D. J., & Schuster, M. A. (2008). Age cohort differences in the developmental milestones of gay men. *Journal of Homosexuality*, *54*(4), 381–399.

This study concluded that younger gay men are reaching coming-out developmental milestones at earlier ages relative to older cohorts, particularly in the area of social milestones (e.g., went to a gay bar, came out to a family member).

Graham, G., et al. (2011). *The health of lesbian, gay, bisexual, and transgender people: Building a foundation for better understanding.* Washington, DC: National Academies Press.

A very thorough book addressing issues of health, which has chapters relevant to sexual-minority development during different stages in life—including childhood and adolescence.

Halverson, E. R. (2005). InsideOut: Facilitating gay youth identity development through a performance-based youth organization. *Identity: An International Journal of Theory and Research, 5*(1), 67–90.

A very interesting study about a performance art program and how it facilitated identity development in sexual-minority youth. This is an example of a unique form of identity-integration intervention.

References

Bockting, W. O., & Coleman, E. (2007). Developmental stages of the transgender coming-out process: Toward an integrated identity. In R. Ettner, S. Monstrey, & E. Evan (Eds.), *Principles of transgender medicine and surgery* (pp. 185–208). New York: Haworth Press.

Calzo, J. P., Antonucci, T. C., Mays, V. M., & Cochran, S. D. (2011). Retrospective recall of sexual orientation identity development among gay, lesbian, and bisexual adults. *Developmental Psychology, 47*(6), 1658–1673.

A study of age of coming-out milestones in a large sample of lesbian, gay, and bisexual Californians. Results indicated the majority began the coming-out process in their childhood or adolescent years. Authors also investigated generational effects (Great Generation, Boomers, Gen X, and Y) and concluded early development is common regardless of age cohort.

Clarke, V., Ellis, S. J., Peel, E., & Riggs, D. W. (2010). *Lesbian, gay, bisexual, trans, and queer psychology: An introduction.* New York: Cambridge University Press.

Cox, N., Dewaele, A., Van Houtte, M., & Vincke, J. (2011). Stress-related growth, coming out, and internalized homonegativity in lesbian, gay, and bisexual youth. An examination of stress-related growth within the minority stress model. *Journal of Homosexuality, 58*, 117–137.

D'Augelli, A. R., & Hershberger, S. L. (1993). Lesbian, gay, and bisexual youth in community settings: Personal challenges and mental health problems. *American Journal of Community Psychology, 21*, 421–448.

Floyd, F. J., & Stein, T. S. (2002). Sexual orientation identity formation among gay, lesbian and bisexual youths: Multiple patterns of milestone experiences. *Journal of Research on Adolescence, 12*, 167–191.

These researchers investigate 10 different coming-out events. Analyses identified five unique "clusters" of individuals, which suggest that there are different experiences of the milestones of coming out.

Jager, J. & Davis-Kean, P. E. (2011). Same-sex sexuality and adolescent psychological well-being: The influence of sexual orientation, early reports of same-sex attraction, and gender. *Self identity, 10*(4), 417–444.

LaSala, M. C. (2010). *Coming out, coming home: Helping families adjust to a gay or lesbian child.* New York: Columbia University Press.

Legate, N., Ryan, R. M, & Weinstein, N. (2012). Is coming out always a "good thing"? Exploring the relations of autonomy support, outness, and wellness for lesbian, gay, and bisexual individuals. *Social Psychological and Personality Science, 3*(2), 145–152.

This research investigated the impact of coming out in different (e.g., more versus less supportive) social contexts. They found social context of coming out was very important.

Rosario, M., Schrimshaw, E. W., & Hunter, J. (2011). Different patterns of sexual identity development over time: Implications for the psychological adjustment of lesbian, gay, and bisexual youths. *Journal of Sexual Research, 48*(1), 3–15.

Savin-Williams, R. (2005). *The new gay teenager.* Cambridge, MA: Harvard University Press.

Shapiro, D. N., Rios, D., & Stewart, A. J. (2010). Conceptualizing lesbian sexual identity development: Narrative accounts of socializing structures and individual decisions and actions. *Feminism & Psychology, 20*(4), 491–510.

Using qualitative research methodology, these researchers argue in favor of more dynamic models of coming out.

Taylor, C., Peter, T., McMinn, T. L., Elliott, T., Beldom, S., Ferry, A., et al. (2011). *Every class in every school: The first national climate survey on homophobia, biphobia, and transphobia in Canadian schools.* Final report. Toronto, ON: Egale Canada Human Rights Trust.

Internet References . . .

Adolescent Sexual Orientation

http://www.ncbi.nlm.nih.gov/pmc/articles
/PMC2603519/

Coming Out

http://kidshealth.org/en/teens/coming-out.html

Coming Out as a LGBT Teen

http://teens.webmd.com/features/coming-out-as
-lgbt-teen

**Resources for Gay, Lesbian, Bisexual and
Transgender Youth: Select Organizations, Web
Sites, and Videos**

http://www.advocatesforyouth.org/publications
/publications-a-z/727-resources-for-gay-lesbian
-bisexual-and-transgender-youth-select-organizations
-web-sites-videos

The Trevor Project

http://www.thetrevorproject.org/section/YOU

Selected, Edited, and with Issue Framing Material by:
Scott R. Brandhorst, *Southeast Missouri State University*

ISSUE

Does a Strong and Costly Sexual Double Standard Still Exist Among Adolescents?

YES: Derek A. Kreager and Jeremy Staff, from "The Sexual Double Standard and Adolescent Peer Acceptance," *Social Psychology Quarterly* (2009)

NO: Heidi Lyons et al., from "Identity, Peer Relationships, and Adolescent Girls' Sexual Behavior: An Exploration of the Contemporary Double Standard," *Journal of Sex Research* (2011)

Learning Outcomes
After reading this issue, you will be able to:
• Identify the key components involved in the sexual double standard.
• Critically analyze the gendered nature of this double standard.
• Interpret and assess the research on the contemporary double standard and its origins.
• Explain the impact of the sexual double standard on contemporary youth.

ISSUE SUMMARY

YES: Derek A. Kreager and Jeremy Staff, both associate professors of sociology and crime, law, and justice at Pennsylvania State University, used data from the National Longitudinal Study of Adolescent Health to examine the existence of a contemporary double standard among adolescents. They found significant differences in peer acceptance among sexually experienced males and females, with higher numbers of sexual partners associated with significantly greater peer acceptance for boys than for girls.

NO: Heidi Lyons, assistant professor of sociology and anthropology at Oakland University, and her colleagues, Peggy C. Giordano, Wendy D. Manning, and Monica A. Longmore, all of Bowling Green State University's Department of Sociology, examined the sexual double standard in a longitudinal, mixed-method study of adolescent girls' popularity and lifetime number of sexual partners. The results paint a nuanced picture of the contemporary sexual double standard. Number of sexual partners was not associated with negative peer regard, and whereas young women acknowledged the existence of a sexual double standard, violating it did not seem to be associated with significant social costs. In fact, these authors highlight the buffering role of friendships against possible negative outcomes.

"What do you call a girl with many sexual partners? A slut. What do you call a guy with many sexual partners? A stud." This quote, taken directly from students in a psychology of gender class, illustrates how easily young people can identify the key constructs involved in the sexual double standard. The sexual double standard, put simply, is that the same heterosexual behavior is judged differently depending on whether a male or a female is engaging in the behavior. That is, boys who are sexual are celebrated or rewarded for their behavior, whereas girls who are similarly sexual are censured or punished for their behavior. While the "line" is arguable for what sexual behaviors by girls is acceptable across history and social groups, girls and boys can readily identify what is and is not permissible regarding girls' sexual activity. For example, in the 1950s, a Catholic school girl whose skirt was too short and showed "too much leg" would have been branded "loose." In contrast, sexual intercourse may be permissible for a girl of the 2000s, *if* she is in a romantic relationship with a boy; otherwise, she might also be labeled as "loose" (i.e., in today's language, a slut, whore, etc.). Today's language may be different (e.g., a sexually experienced boy who has had many partners, most of them in noncommitted relationships, may be called a "player"), but the concepts remain the same. That said, it is important to highlight that the English words used to describe similarly promiscuous girls and boys are qualitatively different. Words like "player" and "stud" are far less negative and pejorative than their female-oriented counterparts, such as "whore" and "slut."

Sociologist Ira Reiss was one of the first people to write about the sexual double standard from an academic viewpoint. In his classic 1967 work, *The Social Context of Premarital Sexual Permissiveness*, Reiss discussed the double standard in relation to premarital intercourse and divided the double standard into "orthodox" and "transitional" categories. The orthodox standard viewed premarital intercourse as permissible for males but not for females under *any* circumstance, while the transitional double standard viewed premarital intercourse as permissible for males under any circumstance, and permissible for females *only* if they were engaged or deeply in love. In the 1960s, Reiss optimistically predicted that North American society would move toward increasing sex-role equality and decreasing sexual double standards.

Research on the double standard continued into the 1970s and beyond. A meta-analysis by Oliver and Hyde (1993) found a gender difference in the endorsement of the sexual double standard. Reiss's 1960 studies found that men were more likely than women to endorse the double standard (while women were more likely to endorse total abstinence for all). In contrast, Oliver and Hyde found that women were more likely to endorse the double standard than men. This gender effect became stronger across the years. Thus, both men and women were becoming more permissive in their sexual attitudes, *but* men were dropping their endorsement of the double standard, while women were moving from an abstinence-only

attitude to a more double-standard–based attitude. It is noteworthy that this gender difference in double-standard endorsement was only moderate to small, which is not surprising as there is strong and consistent research that men are more sexually liberal than women (i.e., if we consider the double standard as a form of sexist sexual conservatism). Many different types of studies today seem to suggest that the sexual double standard was and is alive and well in the 1980s, 1990s, and 2000s.

In contrast, other researchers maintain that, while lay people believe that the sexual double standard exists and are able to articulate the double standard easily, a sexual double standard does not exist in terms of its application to the evaluation of others. For example, Marks and Fraley (2005) interpret the existing research as failing to support the sexual double standard. Even in considering Reiss's 1967 data, students did not endorse the double standard to any great extent. In fact, only 25 percent endorsed a double standard (either orthodox or transitional; almost half [42 percent] endorsed abstinence from sexual intercourse for all). While reading the YES and NO selections, consider whether the evidence presented can be interpreted as supporting or refuting the existence of the sexual double standard.

In the YES selection Derek Kreager and Jeremy Staff examined the existence of a contemporary double standard among adolescents and the relationship between a double standard and peer acceptance. They found significant differences in peer acceptance among sexually experienced males and females, with higher numbers of sexual partners associated with significantly greater peer acceptance for boys than for girls. Heidi Lyons and colleagues examined the sexual double standard in relation to adolescent girls' popularity and number of sexual partners. In this study, girls with a greater number of sexual partners were not regarded negatively by peers. Whereas girls in this study acknowledged the existence of a sexual double standard, they did not punish one another for violating it.

YES ↵

Derek A. Kreager and Jeremy Staff

The Sexual Double Standard and Adolescent Peer Acceptance

In contemporary American society, it is a commonly held belief that sexual behaviors are judged differently depending on the gender of a sexual actor (Milhausen and Herold 2001). Boys and men are thought to receive praise and positive attributions from others for nonmarital sexual contacts, while girls and women are believed to be derogated and stigmatized for similar behaviors. The relevance of this double standard for sexual development and gender inequality has prompted substantial research on the topic (see Crawford and Popp 2003 for a review) along with the publication of several popular trade books with titles such as *Slut!*, *Fast Girls*, and *Promiscuities* (Tanenbaum 1999; White 2002; Wolf 1997). Although public perceptions generally support the sexual double standard, scientific evidence remains equivocal and contested. Ethnographies of secondary schools and early attitudinal studies found evidence of the double standard (Eder, Evans, and Parker 1995; Oliver and Sedikides 1992; Sprecher, McKinney, and Orbuch 1987), whereas more recent experimental vignette studies generally fail to find similar results (Gentry 1998; Milhausen and Herold 1999; Marks and Fraley 2005, 2006). The existence of a modern sexual double standard thus remains in doubt, opening the door for further research and innovative study designs.

Quantitative tests of the sexual double standard typically rely on survey instruments to directly measure respondents' judgments of male and female sexual conduct (Crawford and Popp 2003). These studies correctly locate the roots of the double standard in individuals beliefs and attitudes about "gender appropriate" sexual behaviors. However, . . . the attitudes captured in survey designs may not translate to the enactment of gendered behaviors in social situations, leading to a disjuncture between motives and outcomes (Reskin 2003). School-based ethnographies and individual case studies address this issue by focusing on the expression and consequences of gendered sexual attitudes in specific social contexts. Through participant observation, communication analyses, and retrospective interviews (Eder et al. 1995; Tanenbaum 1999), qualitative studies document the application of deleterious labels for sexual norm violations and individuals' responses to discredited sexual identities (Goffman 1963). These studies therefore link psychological concepts with their socially constructed meanings and outcomes, bringing us closer to understanding how sexuality is regulated in a given social context and who potentially benefits or is stigmatized by these processes. . . .

In this study, we build on the strengths of both survey and ethnographic research by quantitatively measuring the expected social consequences of sexual behavior in a national sample of adolescent youth. Specifically, we rely on network data collected from the National Longitudinal Study of Adolescent Health (Add Health) to test whether the association between adolescent peer acceptance and the number of self-reported sexual partners varies significantly by gender. Our use of peer-network data allows us to statistically compare the peer-status levels of sexually permissive boys and girls and their nonpermissive peers. . . .

Sex and Adolescent Peer Acceptance

The importance of peer status for adolescent development and informal school organization has prompted generations of researchers to identify the criteria underlying teenage popularity. Coleman (1961), in his seminal work *Adolescent Society*, found that social class background, athletics, physical attractiveness, and material possessions (e.g., cars, expensive clothes) were important symbols for teenage peer acceptance, providing their possessors with valued access to the leading crowds. Developmental research also suggests that prosocial behaviors and individual characteristics—such as cooperativeness, kindness, honesty, leadership, intelligence, and self-confidence—are positively associated with children's popularity across a wide variety of social settings (Coie, Dodge, and Kupersmidt 1990; Newcomb, Bukowski, and Pattee 1993). For the most part, the criteria for adolescent popularity operate in the same directions for both girls and boys, even if some characteristics or activities—such as attractiveness, athletics, or physical aggression—may have stronger associations with peer status for one gender than the other (Coleman 1961; LaFontana and Cillessen 2002; Steffensmeier and Allan 1996). Sexual behaviors may provide an exception to this pattern. According to the sexual double standard, the social consequences of early romantic and sexual experiences differ substantially by gender. Gender-specific norms govern the appropriate number of sex partners, the conditions under which it is acceptable to engage in sexual activity (e.g., on

Kreager, Derek A.; Staff, Jeremy. From *Social Psychology Quarterly*, Vol. 72, No. 2, June 1, 2009, pp. 143–164. Copyright © 2009 by American Sociological Association. Reprinted by permission of Sage Publications, Inc.

a "first-date," prior to marriage, in a non-committal relationship, etc.), and the appropriate motives for sexual behavior (e.g., a man may have sex without affection, whereas a women can only have sex when she is in love). If women and men are evaluated differently for engaging in the same sexual behaviors, then male sexual permissiveness would be tolerated, or even praised, while female permissiveness would lead to damaged reputations and "spoiled" identities (Goffman 1963).

Although gendered norms of appropriate sexual conduct have existed for centuries (e.g., the harsh penalties historically associated with female infidelity [see Wolf 1997]), it is a debatable claim that strong sexual double standards persist in contemporary, post-sexual revolution, U.S. society (Risman and Schwartz 2002). Shifts in sexual norms may result in a single standard of sexual conduct that is applied to both men and women (Marks and Fraley 2005). Accordingly, negative perceptions of sexual permissiveness may lower the social desirability of a sexual actor regardless of his or her gender.

Tests of a modern sexual double standard remain inconclusive and contested. We first review this research, paying particular attention to modern adolescent peer contexts and potential gender differences in sexual norm enforcement. We also consider sociodemographic variations in the double standard, such that gender and socioeconomic background may combine nonadditively with sexual experiences to affect adolescent peer acceptance. Finally, we discuss those individual and social characteristics that may moderate or make spurious any link between sexual behavior and peer status.

Documenting the Sexual Double Standard

Attitudinal surveys and ethnographic studies have generally found evidence of contemporary sexual double standards. In perhaps the earliest study of sexual attitudes, Reiss (1964) asked student respondents to directly comment on normative sexual behavior, finding that a majority of the respondents who did not endorse sexual abstinence agreed that it was acceptable for a male, but not a female, to have premarital intercourse. Similarly, more recent survey research suggests that respondents perceive women to be judged significantly more harshly than men for having higher numbers of sex partners (Milhausen and Herold 1999; Sheeran Spears, Abraham, and Abrams 1996). These findings are commonly confirmed in school-based ethnographies. [For example,] Eder et al. (1995) found that "what was considered acceptable behavior in boys—making sexual passes at other boy's girlfriends as well as at their own girlfriends—was definitely not considered acceptable in girls. Those girls who did initiate sexual actions were labeled 'bitches' and 'sluts'" (130). By contrast, "boys tend to perceive girls as objects for sexual conquest as they compete with other boys for sexual achievements" (128). Additional qualitative studies by Orenstein (1994), Moffat

(1989), and Tolman (2002) also suggest that young women's fears of the "slut" label curbs their sexual expressions, while young men are encouraged to demonstrate their masculinity through sexually permissive behavior.

Results from experimental vignette designs have been much less consistent. In these studies, subjects are provided with sexual information (e.g., number of intercourse partners, age at first coitus, etc.) for a hypothetical actor and asked to evaluate his or her desirability or popularity. The sexual information and gender of the target are then randomly varied to test for the existence of a double standard. . . .

Although early studies with this method tended to find evidence of the double standard, recent studies fail to find similar results. As an example of the latter, Marks and Fraley (2005) asked a sample of undergraduates and internet-based respondents to evaluate whether a target was popular and likeable based upon the target's gender and number of sexual partners. They found that respondents generally evaluated male and female targets with higher numbers of sexual partners as unpopular and unlikable, suggesting that sexual permissiveness holds a negative connotation regardless of a sexual actor's gender. . . .

A Network Approach

In this study, we extend prior research by testing the sexual double standard using a measure of peer status derived from social network data (see also Newcomer, Udry, and Cameron 1983). A *social network* consists of a set of interdependent nodes (e.g., individuals, firms, countries, etc.) and ties (e.g., friendships, communications, treaties, etc.) that combine to form a social structure. When applied to the study of school-based peer relations, a social network is created by asking each adolescent to nominate a specified number of friends from a school's attendance roster. These ties are then mapped or tallied . . . to provide an overhead view of the school's friendship system. At the level of the individual (i.e., ego), the total number of ties *received* from other students captures the extent to which that individual is socially accepted, or well-liked, within the informal organization of the school. Incoming friendship nominations thus provide a measure of peer status for each individual in the network. To test the sexual double standard, we may relate this egocentric measure of peer status with students' self-reported sexual partnerships. If a "strong" double standard exists, then increased numbers of sexual partners should be positively associated with male peer status and negatively associated with female peer status. . . .

Variations by Gender of the Evaluator

. . . If sexual standards do differ by gender, then sexually permissive women may not be accepted by female peers, but be well liked by male peers. Similarly, permissive men may be accepted by other men, but be disfavored by women. Assessing whether the gender of the evaluator conditions the association between sexual partnerships and adolescent peer status is an advantage of a network approach over prior research in the area.

Variations by Socioeconomic Background

The large-scaled Add Health survey also allows us to examine whether variables beyond gender, such as socioeconomic background, potentially moderate the link between peer status and sexual behavior. . . .

Alternative Explanations

A final benefit of our study is that it allows us to control for variables that may attenuate any association between sexual permissiveness and peer acceptance. Thus far, we have presented hypotheses stating that sexual behaviors affect peer status and that this association may be conditioned by gender and socioeconomic origins. However, other scholars have argued that these correlations are explained by stable individual traits or characteristics of the sexual contacts. For example, Risman and Schwartz (2002) assert that the sexual revolution of the 1960s and 1970s altered young women's attitudes toward premarital sex, such that premarital coitus is now normative behavior for young women as long as it takes place in socially defined *steady relationships*." Girls and women who have sex in exclusive relationships may then avoid the "slut" label and maintain high-status positions in the peer structure regardless of their number of sexual partnerships. Likewise, girls and women who have sex in an uncommitted relationship may lose peer status. If this argument is accurate, then relationship exclusivity should attenuate any association between number of sexual partnerships and adolescent peer acceptance. . . .

Data

We test our hypotheses using data from the National Longitudinal Study of Adolescent Health (Add Health). Add Health is a nationally representative longitudinal study of adolescents in grades 7 to 12. From 1994 to 2001, the study collected four waves of student data, with additional surveys administered to parents, siblings, and school administrators. In the current analyses, we rely on data from the first two student surveys (e.g. the in-school and first in-home interviews), collected in 1994 and 1995.

In one class period during the fall of 1994, Add Health administered in-school surveys to all available students in each of 145 sampled schools. Approximately 80 percent of enrolled students (N = 90,118) were surveyed. The questionnaire asked respondents about basic demographic and behavioral characteristics. Students also nominated their five best male and five best female friends. . . . [O]ur analysis sample included 6,613 girls and 6,160 boys. . . .

Measures

Outcome Variable: Peer Acceptance

During the in-school survey conducted in 1994, students in the sampled schools nominated their five best male and five best female friends from a roster of all students enrolled in the respondent's school and in a sister middle or high school. Peer acceptance is measured as the total number of friendship nominations that each Add Health respondent *received* from other students in their high school or associated middle school (Wasserman and Faust 1994). . . . We also create gender-specific measures of our dependent variable. Peer status from female peers is captured by multiplying the number of received friendship nominations by the percentage of the nominations that were female. This value was then subtracted from the total number of received friendship nominations to assess peer status from males.

Predictor Variables

Our key predictor variable is student-reported numbers of lifetime sexual partners. Students were first asked to nominate up to three "special romantic partners" from the 18-month period prior to the . . . survey. If they answered affirmatively to this question, they were asked a series of relationship questions about each romantic relationship, including whether they had sexual intercourse. Following those questions, all respondents were asked if they had sexual relationships with anyone other than the three "special romantic relationships." . . . Those who answered "yes" were asked to provide the total number of lifetime sexual partnerships, including the three "special romantic relationships" and any non-romantic sexual partners. . . . [W]e recoded the number of lifetime partners into four dummy variables (i.e., none, 1 to 2, 3 to 8, and more than 8. Additionally, due to likely mis-reporting, we deleted from our analyses those outlying respondents who reported 100 or more lifetime sexual partners. Less than one percent of the sample (all males) fell into this category, dropping the final sample of boys to 5,522. [A]pproximately two-thirds of youth reported no sexual partnerships, while two percent of girls and five percent of boys fell into the highly permissive category of 8 or more partnerships. . . .

Nonromantic sexual involvement was defined as having had sexual intercourse with someone outside of a "special romantic relationship" during the past year. Respondents who reported having had a nonromantic sexual relationship were asked if they (1) held hands with the nonromantic sexual partner, (2) kissed the partner on the mouth, and (3) said "I love you" to the partner. If the respondent answered no to at least one of these items, we coded him or her as having had a nonromantic relationship (which could be ongoing). If a respondent answered yes to the three items, the relationship was coded as a "special romantic relationship" and the corresponding sexual questions were asked. Approximately 12 percent of boys and

7 percent of girls reported at least one prior or current nonromantic sexual encounter. . . .

Research finds that athletic participation is positively associated with peer status (Holland and Andre 1994) and these activities may also increase sexual opportunities, particularly for males (Miller Farrell, Barnes, Melnick, and Don Sabo 2005). We include a self-reported indicator for whether or not respondents participated in any of 12 sports during the prior year (e.g., baseball/softball, basketball, field hockey, football, ice hockey, soccer, swimming, tennis, track, volleyball, wrestling, and other sports). We also measure participation in other nonathletic extracurricular clubs or activities, as these may provide avenues for peer acceptance (Kreager 2007). Peer acceptance is also positively associated with academic achievement and adjustment (Parker and Asher 1987). Academic aptitude was captured by a vocabulary test. . . . Grades indicate the average of student-reported GPAs in four subjects—math, English, social studies, and science. . . .

Attractiveness and early physical maturity may also confound the association between number of sex partners and peer status. Physical attractiveness is based upon an interviewer-rated measure of "how physically attractive is the respondent?" . . . Our measure of female physical development is an additive scale based on three items: (1) "How advanced is your physical development compared to other girls your age?" (five-point scale from 1 = I look younger than most to 5 = I look older than most); (2) "As a girl grows up, her breasts develop and get bigger. Which sentence best describes you?" (five-point scale from 1 = my breasts are about the same size as when I was in grade school to 5 = my breasts are a whole lot bigger than when I was in grade school, they are as developed as a grown woman's breasts); and (3) "As a girl grows up, her body becomes more curved. Which sentence best describes you?" (five-point scale ranging from 1 = my body is about as curvy as when I was in grade school to 5 = my body is a whole lot more curvy than when I was in grade school). . . . For males, physical development is an additive scale based upon four items: (1) "How much hair is under your arms now" (coded on a five-point scale from 1 = I have no hair at all to 5 = I have a whole lot of hair that is very thick, as much hair as a grown man; (2) "How thick is the hair on your face?" (four-point scale ranging from 1 = I have a few scattered hairs, but the growth is not thick to 4 = the hair is very thick, like a grown man's facial hair); (3) "Is your voice lower now than it was when you were in grade school?" (five-point scale ranging from 1 = no to 5 = yes, it is as low as an adult man's voice); and (4) "how advanced is your physical development compared to other boys your age?" (five-point scale from 1 = I look younger than most to 5 = I look older than most). . . . Finally, we include a measure of body mass index (BMI), which we calculated based upon the respondent's self-reported height and weight. . . .

Results

. . . Our first goal is to document gender differences in the association between number of sex partners and peer acceptance. . . . [S]tatistics for the gender differences between lifetime sexual partners were statistically significant for all partner categories . . ., suggesting that sexual behaviors are one of the few areas where peers evaluate girls and boys differently.

[W]e find evidence that sexually permissive girls (i.e., greater than eight lifetime partners) have fewer friendship nominations than girls who report no sexual partners. This provides some evidence that permissive girls are marginalized within peer groups. In addition, we find no evidence that girls with 1 to 8 sexual partners have fewer friendship nominations than their sexually inexperienced peers.

Girls with greater than eight sexual partners are predicted to have .8 fewer peer nominations than sexually inexperienced girls, holding all other variables constant. . . . Indeed, sexual involvement outside of a romantic relationship during the past year has no direct effect on peer acceptance, failing to support the idea that intercourse outside of a committed relationship results in lowered female peer status. Looking at the remaining effects, we see . . . [f]emale adolescents receive higher numbers of peer nominations if they participate in athletics or club activities, if they are doing well in school, or if they reside with both biological parents. Body mass is inversely related to female peer acceptance, so that girls with higher weight/height ratios have fewer peer nominations. Peer status is also higher among females who perceive that they are more physically mature than other females their age and who are rated as physically attractive by interviewers. Whereas violence has a negative effect on acceptance, alcohol use in the past year is positively associated with popularity. Hispanic and Asian females have significantly fewer friendship nominations than white females.

Supporting the hypothesis that boys are rewarded for sexually permissive behavior, we find that the number of lifetime sexual partners has a positive . . . effect on male peer acceptance. Unlike the results for girls, we find that sexually inexperienced boys have significantly less peer nominations than boys with one or more sexual partners, and more partners are associated with greater numbers of peer nominations. . . . [A]mong youth who report more than 8 lifetime sexual partners, boys have approximately 1.3 additional friendship nominations than girls. By contrast, among the majority of youth who report no current or prior sexual partners, boys report 0.7 fewer friendship nominations than girls.

We next turn our attention to the question, "Which peers provide (or fail to provide) status to sexually permissive youth?" . . . [P]ermissive boys are more likely to gain status from female peers than from male peers, while permissive girls only have lower peer acceptance among other girls. These results suggest that female reactions to sexual behavior simultaneously escalate the status of permissive boys and decrease the status of permissive girls.

[S]ome research suggests that boys from disadvantaged backgrounds are the most likely to derive peer status from numerous lifetime sexual partners, in part because of the heterogeneity of gender frames and relational scripts in poor neighborhoods and urban schools (Anderson 1999; Harding 2007). Moreover, we expect that girls from advantaged backgrounds should receive more consistent messages than disadvantaged girls regarding the negative consequences of sexual permissiveness for life chances and "good" reputations. . . .

[A]mong girls from low educated families, the effect of sexual partners on peer acceptance is statistically nonsignificant. By contrast, girls from high socioeconomic backgrounds who report eight or more lifetime sexual partners have significantly lower peer status than high SES girls who report no sexual partners even after we control for relationship status, school success, physical characteristics, and adjustment.

The positive effect of more than eight lifetime sexual partners on male peer acceptance significantly varies by socioeconomic background. Boys from disadvantaged backgrounds who report eight or more sexual partners have higher peer status than disadvantaged boys who report no partners, and this effect is significantly larger for low versus high SES boys. Thus, even though the association between lifetime sexual partners and peer status differs significantly by gender, the positive effects of sexual contacts are strongest among low SES boys.

Discussion

In this study, we used social network data to explore the association between adolescent sexuality and peer acceptance at school. Our primary interest was to provide an innovative test of the sexual double standard in a nationally representative adolescent sample. Though most covariates of peer acceptance were similar for boys and girls (e.g., sports and club memberships, fighting, attractiveness, physical development, school performance, body mass index, and social background), we found strong gender differences with regard to sexual behavior, such that increased numbers of sexual partnerships were positively associated with boys' peer acceptance but negatively associated with girls' peer acceptance. Boys with many sexual "conquests" are thus expected to be well-liked at schools, while permissive girls are predicted to have low status in school-based networks, regardless of whether or not their sexual behaviors occur within "romantic" relationships. Moreover, the positive association between male sexual permissiveness and peer acceptance was strongest among disadvantaged boys. Together, these findings suggest that gendered and social class-specific perceptions of normative sexual behaviors remain alive in contemporary adolescent peer contexts. . . .

We should also make clear that we do not provide a direct test of whether permissive girls are stigmatized (i.e., rejected) for their sexual behavior. To do so, we would need nominations of peer dislike rather than peer friendships. Female stigmatization would then be apparent when disliked nominations increase with greater numbers of sexual partners. Such nominations . . . were not part of the Add Health study. . . .

Another interesting, and perhaps counterintuitive, finding is that non-romantic sexual partnerships have no net correlation with

school-based peer nominations. Several scholars point to nonromantic sexual liaisons as the clearest means for adolescent girls to be rejected by peers and earn "slut" labels (Risman and Schwartz 2002; Tolman 2002). To further explore this expectation . . . [f]or boys, we found a significant positive association between nonromantic sex and peer acceptance, but for girls this estimate was nonsignificant. . . . One possible explanation for this pattern is that boys understand that positive peer attributions follow sexual activity of any sort, and volunteer information about recent nonromantic sexual contacts, whereas girls fear public knowledge of such liaisons and therefore do not disclose the existence of nonromantic sex. Potential gender differences in sexual disclosure also emphasize the importance of social contexts for sexual double-standard research. If female actors are successful at keeping their sexual contacts secret, then they may avoid any stigma associated with permissive behaviors. Clearly, increased frequencies of sexual partners and behaviors raise the risks of public disclosure and social reaction, perhaps explaining why only the most permissive girls have significantly fewer friendship nominations than other girls. . . .

References

Anderson, Elijah. 1999. *Code of the Street; Decency, Violence, and the Moral Life of the Inner City.* New York: Norton.

Networks." *American Journal of Sociology* 11(1):44–91.

Coie, John D., Kenneth A. Dodge and J. B. Kupersmidt. 1990. "Peer Group Behavior and Social Status." pp. 17–59 in *Peer Rejection in Childhood,* edited by Steven R. Asher and John D. Coie. New York: Cambridge University Press.

Cohen, Albert K. 1955. *Delinquent Boys: The Culture of the Gang.* Glencoe, IL: Free Press.

Crawford, Mary and Danielle Popp. 2003. "Sexual Double Standards: A Review and Methodological Critique of Two Decades of Research," *Journal of Sex Research* 40(1):13–26.

Eder, Donna, Catherine C. Evans, and Stephen Parker. 1995. *School Talk: Gender and Adolescent Culture.* New Brunswick, NJ: Rutgers University Press.

Edin, Kathryn and Maria Kefalas. 2005. *Promises I Can Keep: Why Poor Women Put Motherhood Before Marriage.* Berkeley, CA: University of California Press.

Gentry, Margaret. 1998. "The Sexual Double Standard: The Influence of Number of Relationships and Level of Sexual Activity on Judgments of Women and Men." *Psychology of Women Quarterly* 22(3):505–11.

Goffman, Erving. 1963. *Stigma: Notes on the Management of Spoiled Identity.* Englewood Cliffs, NJ: Prentice-Hall.

Harding, David J. 2007. "Cultural Context, Sexual Behavior, and Romantic Relationships in Disadvantaged Neighborhoods." *American Sociological Review* 72(3):341–64.

Holland, Alyce and Thomas Andre. 1994. "Athletic Participation and the Social Status of Adolescent Males and Females." *Youth and Society* 25:388–407.

Kreager, Derek A. 2007. "When It's Good to be "Bad": Violence and Adolescent Peer Acceptance." *Criminology* 45(4):893–923.

LaFontana, Kathryn M. and Antonius Cillessen. 2002. "Children's Perceptions of Popular and Unpopular Peers: A Multimethod Assessment." *Developmental Psychology* 38(5):635–47.

Marks, Michael J. and R. Chris Fraley. 2005. "The Sexual Double Standard: Fact or Fiction?" *Sex Roles* 52:175–86.

——. 2006. "Confirmation Bias and the Sexual Double Standard." *Sex Roles* 54:19–26.

Milhausen, Robin R. and Edward S. Herold. 2001. "Reconceptualizing the Sexual Double Standard." *Journal of Psychology and Human Sexuality* 13(2):63–83.

——. 1999. "Does the Sexual Double Standard Still Exist? Perceptions of University Women." *Journal of Sex Research* 36:361–8.

Miller, Kathleen E., Michael P. Farrell, Grace M. Barnes, Merrill J. Melnick, and Don Sabo. 2005. "Gender/Racial Differences in Jock Identity, Dating, and Adolescent Sexual Risk." *Journal of Youth and Adolescence* 34(2):123–36.

Moffat, Michael. 1989. *Coming of Age in New Jersey*. New Brunswick, NJ: Rutgers University Press.

National Longitudinal Study of Adolescent Health. 2001. *Network Variables Codebook*. Chapel Hill, NC: University of North Carolina.

Newcomb, Andrew F., William M. Bukowski, and Linda Pattee. 1993. "Children's Peer Relations: A Meta-Analytic Review of Popular, Rejected, Neglected, Controversial, and Average Sociometric Status." *Psychological Bulletin* 113:99–128.

Newcomer, Susan, J. Richard Udry, and Freda Cameron. 1983. "Adolescent Sexual Behavior and Popularity." *Adolescence* 18(71):515–22.

Oliver, Mary B. and Constantine Sedikides. 1992. "Effects of Sexual Permissiveness on Desirability of Partner as a Function of Low and High Commitment to Relationship." *Social Psychology Quarterly* 55:321–33.

Orenstein, Peggy. 1994. *Schoolgirls: Young Women, Self-Esteem, and the Confidence Gap*. New York: Doubleday.

Parker, Jeffrey G. and Steven R. Asher. 1987. "Peer Relations and Later Personal Adjustment: Are Low-Accepted Children at Risk?" *Psychological Bulletin* 102(3):357–89.

Reiss, Ira L. 1964. "The Scaling of Premarital Sexual Permissiveness." *Journal of Marriage and the Family* 26(2):188–98.

Reskin Barbara F. 2003. "Including Mechanisms in our Models of Ascriptive Inequality: 2002 Presidential Address." *American Sociological Review* 68(1):1–21.

Risman, Barbara and Pepper Schwartz. 2002. "After the Sexual Revolution: Gender Politics in Teen Dating." *Contexts* 1(1):16–24.

Sheeran, Paschal, Russell Spears, Charles S. Abraham, and Dominic Abrams. 1996. "Religiosity, Gender, and the Double Standard." *Journal of Psychology* 130:23–33.

Steffensmeier, Darrell and Emilie Allan. 1996. "Gender and Crime: Toward a Gendered Theory of Female Offending." *Annual Review of Sociology* 22(1):459–88.

White, Emily. 2002. *Fast Girls: Teenage Tribes and the Myth of the Slut*. New York: Scribner.

Willis, Paul. 1977. *Learning to Labor: How Working Class Kids Get Working Class Jobs*, Farnborough, UK: Saxon House.

Wolf, Naomi. 1997. *Promiscuities: The Secret Struggle for Womanhood*. New York: Faucet Books.

Heidi Lyons et al.

 **NO**

Identity, Peer Relationships, and Adolescent Girls' Sexual Behavior: An Exploration of the Contemporary Double Standard

The double standard is a well-recognized cultural phenomenon. However, some researchers have suggested that gendered sexual standards of behavior may be undergoing change and increasing in complexity (Marks & Fraley, 2006; Milhausen & Herold, 2001; Moore & Rosenthal, 1994; Risman & Schwartz, 2002; Tolman, 1996). The classic definition of the sexual double standard focuses on the ways in which young men are socialized to value sexual experience and young women learn to emphasize committed relationships (Reiss, 1960). It is believed that, in general, this inhibits young women's sexual behavior, particularly "promiscuous" behavior, by making it socially costly. Accordingly, women who do not fit the conservative ideal are subjected to negative social sanctions or censures. Some research has suggested that this classic pattern may be eroding (Crawford, 2003; Gentry, 1998; Marks & Fraley, 2005, 2006), but more research is needed that investigates not simply whether the sexual double standard exists, but also the social and identity implications of departing from its basic tenets.

In this study, we focused on young women who report a higher number of sexual partners relative to their similarly aged counterparts. . . . [and] investigated two related research questions regarding the social and identity statuses of young women who represented a range of sexual experiences. First, . . . do young women who report a high number of sexual partners report lower popularity or other peer deficits as a result of the double standard? Further, and consistent with this idea of negative "reflected appraisals" from others, do these young women report lower self-esteem than their more sexually conservative counterparts? We tested these associations both cross-sectionally and longitudinally. The cross-sectional assessment documents whether there is a significant association between number of sex partners and perceived popularity with peers, dissatisfaction with number of friends, and level of self-esteem. A longitudinal analysis adds to the portrait by investigating whether the number of sex partners is associated with lower peer popularity as reported one year later.

We also focused the analysis on the attitudes and behaviors of the adolescent's more immediate circle of friends. This *social*

network emphasis suggests that young women who report a higher number of sexual partners may not experience the kinds of social costs or deficits described earlier (perceptions of being unpopular or low self-esteem) in large part because they receive support and reinforcement from their friends, whose attitudes about sexuality are similar to their own. This notion is more consistent with the tenets of symbolic interaction, which emphasizes the localized or "situated" nature of action (Mead, 1934), and more general social learning theories (Sutherland, 1934), which stress the role of intimate others in fostering particular patterns of behavior—even those that may be considered "deviant" by the wider society. . . . Thus, it is possible that . . . friends provide a buffer against negative attributions from the wider peer group, as well as actively fostering and reinforcing these behaviors.

Prior Research on the Double Standard

The sexual double standard has evolved over time. Early on, it was considered inappropriate for women to engage in sexual activity outside of marriage (Crawford, 2003; Reiss, 1960). Some researchers have argued that the sexual double standard has changed somewhat, but it is still in place (Milhausen & Herold, 1999; Risman & Schwartz, 2002). Maccoby (1998), for example, suggested that teenage boys who gain considerable sexual experience do not run the same risk of being labeled deviant as do their female counterparts. More specifically, young women who had a high number of sex partners were socially reprimanded for their behaviors, and young men were rewarded (Milhausen & Herold, 1999).

Some research has examined the prevalence of the sexual double standard among samples of American youth. Moore and Rosenthal (1994) focused on the attitudes of 16-year-olds and found that over one half of their sample judged girls and boys similarly regarding the issue of having many sex partners (respondents were asked the general question, "What do you think about girls/boys who sleep around?") Although this suggests some movement away from a clear double standard, nevertheless, a relatively large percentage of teenagers do evaluate males and females differently, with girls most often viewed or judged in a negative manner. One limitation of their study is that it asked respondents to reflect on a hypothetical individual, rather than on one's own behavior or that of friends and classmates.

Another study by Jackson and Cram (2003) relied on focus groups of late adolescent girls. The young women in their sample noted that women are typically labeled "sluts" for the same sexual behavior that would earn boys the label "stud." Although this reflects a continued double standard, as in the Moore and Rosenthal (1994) study, these respondents rarely used experiences from their own lives to explain how the double standard affects them personally; and, although the aforementioned studies find support for the survival of the double standard, other research suggests that this gendered normative system may be eroding. Oliver and Hyde (1993) compiled research conducted between 1966 and 1990 relating to this issue and determined that attitudes toward premarital sexual behaviors are becoming more similar across gender in more recent studies. Further, using a sample of college students and patrons at a bar, Milhausen and Herold (2001) reported that, although men were significantly more likely to endorse the sexual double standard, this nevertheless reflected only a minority of men. The authors stated that most men and women endorsed a single standard that judged men and women's sexual behavior equally.

Some of the variability in results of prior research may be related to variations in methodological approaches across the various studies. Crawford (2003) conducted a meta-analysis of research on the double standard and reported that experimentally designed studies were more likely to indicate less support for the existence of the double standard. In contrast, qualitative approaches, such as interviews and focus groups, tended to reveal that it survives. Marks and Fraley (2006) examined the possible role of confirmation bias in studying the sexual double standard. The researchers concluded that their participants recalled information from a given vignette that confirmed the sexual double standard more often than any other details. This suggests that studies which only focus on the abstract concept of the double standard do not tap into the actual ways individuals understand the sexual behavior of male and female teens and what sexual activities mean within the context of their own lives.

Recently, Kreager and Staff (2009), drawing on data from the National Longitudinal Study of Adolescent Health (Add Health), focused on adolescents' own sexual behaviors and found that those women with many sex partners do report fewer friends, whereas this association was not found for male respondents. This tends to support the idea of the survival of the double standard, particularly the notion of social costs levied against girls whose sexual behavior exceeds normative levels. However, this association with number of friends was found only for those female respondents who reported more than eight partners, a subgroup that comprises about 2% of the sample. In addition, the friends' nominations were limited to

those in schools participating in the survey, which may not provide a comprehensive portrait of the adolescent's complete social network. This study contributes beyond this prior work by considering the broader implications of girls' sexual behaviors for peer status and regard as measured by perceived *popularity*, as well as girls' own reports of the adequacy of their friendship networks (*desire for more friends*). The analysis also examines the role of friends' attitudes and behaviors (*friends' liberal sexual attitudes* and *friends' number of sexual partners*), as well as the identity implications (*levels of self-esteem*) of reporting a larger number of sexual partners. . . .

This Study

In this analysis, we explored the variability in number of sex partners girls report to determine whether those who report a greater number of partners also report lower popularity with friends and experience perceived deficits in the number of friends or lower self-esteem. These relationships would be consistent with the basic notion of a double standard and the perspective that there are social costs levied against young women who violate these conservative standards. We concentrated on the perspectives and behaviors of young women in this analysis because (a) the double standard notion emphasizes costs to young women rather than men and (b) we have focused specifically on young men's sexual attitudes and behaviors in prior analyses (Giordano, Longmore, & Manning, 2006; Giordano, Longmore, Manning, & Northcutt, 2009).

Because cross-sectional analyses undoubtedly capture reciprocal processes (less popular girls may have more partners and then experience even more decline in popularity), we also examined these associations longitudinally. Our models show how sexual behavior and popularity at Wave 1 influence popularity one year later (Wave 2). This analysis provides an indication of a decline in popularity that is more readily theorized as a consequence, rather than a cause, of the behavior of interest.

Our analysis also evaluated variability across the sample in peer normative climates, consistent with the idea of variability in friends' support for and encouragement of these sexual behaviors. A symbolic interactionist approach leads us to expect that those who report a higher number of sex partners will have friends with more liberal sexual attitudes and a higher level of sexual experience themselves. The symbolic interactionist approach also highlights the importance of identity formation processes, as self-views reflect an internalization of prior social experiences. Thus, rather than conceptualizing the self only in positive or negative terms (the self-esteem notion), theories of symbolic interaction stress that the self is comprised of multiple content areas (Matsueda, 1992), including one's sexual self (Giordano et al., 2009). These sexual self-views need not be viewed from a negative lens, but simply as self-definitions that reference the heterosexual realm. For example, young women who believe that they are "sexy" or "hot" may carry a level of confidence about their interactions with young men and engage in more activities (flirting or attending parties) that provide greater opportunities for sexual involvement. Thus, we expect that endorsement of such identities will be associated with a higher number of sex partners, controlling for traditional correlates. Thus, the analysis focuses on different aspects of the adolescent's social world and distinct features of identity. Although we have suggested that the social deficit approach focuses on different dynamics than the social learning perspective (e.g., perceived popularity with peers vs. the attitudes and behaviors of close friends), support for one set of relationships does not automatically rule-out support for the other. For example, it is possible that young women who report a larger number of sexual partners score lower on perceived popularity, but also are more likely to have close friends with more liberal attitudes and behavioral repertoires. Such a finding would be consistent with some research on early peer deficits and attachment processes, where it is argued that those who rank low in prestige or popularity with peers may gravitate toward others who tend to reinforce antisocial norms and behaviors (Asher & Coie, 1990).

The in-depth qualitative data we also elicited from a subset of the respondents provided a more multilayered view of young women's perspectives on the double standard. The qualitative data allowed us to further explore the implications of the quantitative findings as a whole, including dynamics linked to the idea of social deficits and costs, as well as those typically associated with a social learning framework. Specifically, we contrast general understandings about the double standard as a social phenomenon that exists at the societal or school level, with girls' perspectives on the acceptability of their own behaviors and that of their immediate circle of friends.

Data and Method

This article draws on the TARS. The original sample collected quantitative information on a stratified, random sample of seventh-, ninth-, and eleventh-grade adolescent boys and girls in Lucas County, Ohio, with an over sampling of the African American and Hispanic populations and with a final sample size of 1,316 total youths from the Toledo area, which included 678 girls. . . . The data collection of Wave 1 was June 2001 through February 2002. Wave 2 was collected about one year later . . . [(]August 2002 through June 2003[)]. At Wave 2, 603 girls (89% of the Wave-1 respondents) were interviewed, and our analysis is based on 600 girls with valid data on the dependent and independent indicators.

Forty-six female respondents were interviewed to provide an in-depth portrait of each respondent's romantic relationships and sexual behavior history. These young women were randomly selected from those within the larger quantitative survey sample, who reported at least some dating experience. . . .

TARS is an appropriate dataset for these analyses because the interview protocol includes respondents' subjective views of broader social concerns such as popularity, measures of friends' attitudes and behaviors, as well as several indexes tapping identity domains (self-esteem, as well as sexual identities). Further, unlike the Add Health, the TARS is not a school-based sample. This is of value because young people who do not attend school may report a larger number of sexual partners, and all respondents are able to nominate friends, regardless of whether they attend the same school.

The quantitative analysis focused on two dependent variables. The first is a continuous variable of *number of lifetime sex partners* at Wave 1. The second is a binary variable measuring perceived *unpopularity with females* as reported at Wave 2. This was constructed from responses to the following item: "Others would describe you as popular with females." . . .

There were three measures of social deficits and costs associated with having a larger number of sexual partners: perceived lack of popularity, desire for more friends, and self-esteem. For the longitudinal analysis, self-perceived *unpopularity with females* at Wave 1 was based on the following item: "Others would describe you as popular with females." . . . *Perceived lack of friends* was based on the item, "I wish I had more friends." . . . A six-item scale was used to measure *self-esteem* with items like, "I can do things as well as other people." . . .

We use four items to measure the norms and behaviors of friends and identity content that we argue may be associated with a greater number of sexual partners. *Friends' liberal attitudes* . . . is a three-item scale that taps friends' liberal attitudes toward sex with items like, "My friends think it's okay to have sex with someone you are not actually dating." *Friends' sexual behavior* was measured by the question, "How many of your friends do you think have had sex?," . . . and *sexualized identity* was measured with two items ("I am flirty" and "I am sexy or hot"). . . .

Results

The mean number of *lifetime sex partners* was less than one . . . for the full sample. . . . The majority of girls perceived themselves as popular both at Time I (85%) and Time 2 (82%). At Time 1, the mean of the self-esteem measure was 23.51 (range = 9–30), and the mean for the item indexing a desire for more friends was 2.59 (range = 1–5). The sample had a mean of 7.33 for friends' liberal attitudes, suggesting a trend toward more liberal peers. The mean for number of friends having sex was 2.85 (range = 1–6). Respondents reported a mean of 3.14 for the self-identity of flirty and 3.29 for sexy (range = 1–5). The mean number of partners was 0.90 (SD = 2.40). We first focused on the social deficit indicators, perceived popularity, desire for more friends, and self-esteem. . . . [P]erceived popularity and desire for number of friends were not significantly related to girls' reports about their number of lifetime sex partners. Further, results showed that self-esteem was not associated with the number of lifetime sex partners. This is not consistent with the notion of high social costs or a devalued or stigmatized identity, at least as measured by the idea of lower self-esteem.

The indicators associated with the social networks hypothesis are friends' liberal sexual attitudes, sexual behavior of friends, and the sexualized identity indicator. Friends' liberal sexual attitudes and sexual behavior of friends were significantly and positively related to the number of lifetime sex partners. . . . In addition, "sexy" was no longer significant . . . with the addition of friends' liberal sexual attitudes. We found that respondents' endorsement of the flirty identity was not significantly tied to the number of sex partners. . . .

Longitudinal Assessments

To determine whether the number of lifetime sex partners reported at Wave 1 is associated with a reduction in popularity at Wave 2, we relied on the former as a predictor of the latter. Net of perceived popularity with females as reported at Wave 1, the number of lifetime sex partners also reported at Wave 1 was not significantly related to subsequent popularity, as measured at Wave 2. This finding suggests that within this sample of adolescents, whether we examine the issue cross-sectionally or longitudinally, the number of lifetime sex partners does not seem to be associated with self-perceived lower peer regard, as would be predicted by the basic logic of the sexual double standard and the idea of social costs levied against young women who violate such norms. . . .

Although not a primary focus of this investigation, we also attempted to replicate Kreager and Staff's (2009) finding regarding the relationship between sexual behavior and number of friends reported. Supplemental analyses of the TARS data indicated that girls with a high number of sex partners at Wave 1 are less likely to report five or more friends at Wave 2. However, there was not a significant relationship between number of sex partners and the likelihood of reporting having a few friends compared to reporting five or more friends. It is also interesting to note that across several dimensions of relationship quality (e.g., time spent with friends or levels of intimate self-disclosure to friends), girls who reported a larger number of sexual partners did not score significantly lower on frequency of interaction with friends or intimacy of communication relative to their more sexually conservative counterparts (analyses available upon request).

The Meanings of the Double Standard

Our analyses of the qualitative data provide a more nuanced picture of the double standard—one that generally accords with the quantitative results, but shows distinctions between girls' knowledge and even acceptance of these broader normative prescriptions, on the one hand, and the behaviors of friends and their own sexual experiences, on the other. Sections of the narratives focusing on the double standard suggest that these gendered normative standards survive on many levels, and even those young women who reported a

relatively large number of sexual partners do not fully reject its basic tenets. Yet, differences across various reference points are important to consider. Thus, although young women spoke eloquently about the general existence of two standards of sexual comportment, they reserved more harsh attributions for unknown or little-known others who casually violate these standards. As discussions turned to the behavior of intimate friends, and particularly respondents' own behavior, a more measured and complex set of meanings and explanations or "disclaimers" (Scott & Lyman, 1968) often emerged. The qualitative findings complement the quantitative findings in that young women who reported a high number of sex partners did not typically develop a narrative about being unpopular or stigmatized, a desire for more friends, feelings of loneliness, or low self-worth. However, they often referenced the behavior of friends within their own networks. Thus, it is likely that adolescents focus most heavily on this immediate network as a source of reference and influence, which then serves as a form of social support and as a buffer against negative attributions associated with their own behavior.

The Double Standard as a Cultural Reality

During the in-depth interviews, respondents were asked a straightforward question regarding the double standard and whether they thought it still exists. Results of the qualitative data showed that many adolescents in the sample did recognize the survival of the sexual double standard. However, when the girls discussed the meaning of the sexual double standard, it was often viewed as a known, taken-for-granted societal reality or social dynamic that occurs in the larger school environment. . . .

Across a range of different levels of sexual experience, . . . most young women reflected a keen awareness of the core elements of the double standard in pointing out that women are held to different normative standards compared to men. They also reflect on social labeling processes, in that men are subject to social rewards for engaging in behavior that is likely to garner a bad reputation or even labels such as "whore" when enacted by women.

When girls were asked to provide specific examples that related to their school environment, however, these statements are often vague or abstract, not referencing particular girls—especially the respondent's friends or their own behaviors. Kimberly. . . . [a] senior female[,] did harshly judge the younger girls who "put themselves out there" in ways that are too overtly sexual. The narrative also suggests that she has a different orientation. Thus, it is interesting to note that Kimberly is currently dating a boy who started out as a "friends with benefits" relationship, suggesting the idea that multiple—and sometimes contradictory—meanings can be associated with the double standard concept.

This notion is also illustrated by Marie, a 17-year-old who castigated other girls who gain a negative reputation linked to their sexual behaviors[,] . . . [but has herself] had four sex partners. Thus, although castigating other girls, Marie herself scored . . . above the mean in sexual experience relative to other young women who participated in the . . . study. [T]he sexual double standard may exist on a societal or school level but often erodes, or gains a layer of complication, when the referent is one's own behavior or that of intimate friends.

The Meaning of the Sexual Double Standard on the Peer Level

Numerous scholars have pointed out that a key benefit of friendships during the adolescent period is the level of support they provide (Mortimer & Call, 2001); and, as Youniss and Smollar (1985), as well as others, have pointed out, peers, relative to one's parents or other adults, are less likely to be judgmental—a social dynamic that creates many opportunities for frank dialogue and exploration of issues, including issues of sexuality. When asked how she felt about girlfriends who want to participate in sexual behavior as much as boys do, Stephanie, a 17-year-old with six lifetime sex partners . . . did not view her friend negatively because she had engaged in such behaviors; and, . . . Stephanie's own sexual experience level coordinates well with that of her friend, providing an additional motivation to avoid levying any sort of negative social sanction or disapproval of her friend's behavior. This fits well with the quantitative results [of this study]. Along similar lines, Alexis, a 17-year-old with one lifetime sex partner, described how her peer group does not talk about or judge their female friends for the sexual activities in which they participate.

Alexis . . . did not judge her friend for the sexual behavior in which she may be involved. Even more important, she felt the need to uphold certain rules of friendship, which do not include giving the friend a derogatory name or spreading rumors about her. Another participant, Amber, a 17-year-old with two lifetime sex partners, reported that her peer group . . . offers a safe place to discuss romantic and sexual activity[;] . . . She can look to her peer group as an opportunity to discuss issues around sexuality without running the risk of getting a negative reputation. Since the peer group is often a safe haven relative to the "wider circle" of peer associations, this is a place for girls to explore their own and others' sexual feelings and experiences in ways that, to an extent, "suspend or 'bracket-off'" double standard concerns. This idea is consistent with the quantitative findings demonstrating concordance between adolescent respondents' own behaviors and those of their friends, and results that do not dovetail with the "social costs and deficits" hypothesis. . . .

Discussion

Excerpts from the qualitative narratives revealed that across a range of levels of sexual experience, young women did recognize the survival of a double standard of sexual behavior. Further, whereas some noted that it was "unfair" for others to judge

young women according to a different standard, others seemed to accept the inevitability of this gendered pattern, and often provided negative descriptions of young women whose behavior veered from what was considered acceptable within their school or neighborhood (e.g., using terms such as "slut" or describing such behavior as "nasty"). Yet, both the quantitative and qualitative data we analyzed suggest a more complex portrait: Girls who reported a relatively large number of sexual partners did not, in turn, perceive lower levels of popularity with other girls, deficits in the number of friends they had, or lower self-esteem relative to their less experienced counterparts. These findings are consistent whether we examine such relationships cross-sectionally or longitudinally. . . .

Yet, the quantitative results also show that it is important to take into account the diversity of peer climates, as friends' liberal attitudes and sexual behavior emerged as significant predictors of variations in the number of sexual partners adolescent respondents reported. . . . [T]he qualitative results highlighted that, although these young women may show disdain or otherwise negatively label others in the wider circle of peers (e.g., "those sophomore girls"), they are reluctant to do this where the referent is their friend or their own behavior. This suggests that similarly situated friends may serve as a source of support or buffer against negative attributions that may take the form of gossip or other labeling that occurs within the context of the broader school normative climate. . . .

These findings are largely based on the adolescent's own perceptions or understandings, as contrasted with objective information, such as the number of friend nominations used by Kreager and Staff (2009). They found that female respondents who reported having a large number of sexual partners received fewer school-based friend nominations relative to respondents with fewer partners. . . . Yet, the perceptual data we described earlier add to this emphasis on objective information, as the youths themselves did not perceive that they would like more friends or that they were unpopular with other girls. Similarly, such girls did not score lower than their more sexually conservative counterparts on various indexes of relationship quality. Future research should explore both objective characteristics and subjectively experienced aspects of girls' friendships and other peer relationships. . . .

References

Asher, S. R., & Coie, J. D. (1990). *Peer rejection in childhood*. New York, NY: Cambridge University Press.

Crawford, M. (2003). Sexual double standards: A review and methodological critique of two decades of research. *Journal of Sex Research*, *40*, 13–26.

Giordano, P. C., Longmore, M. A., & Manning, W. D. (2006). Gender and the meaning of adolescent romantic relationship: A focus on boys. *American Sociological Review*, *71*, 260–287.

Giordano, P. C., Longmore, M. A., Manning, W. D., & Northcutt, M. J. (2009). Adolescent identities and sexual behavior: An examination of Anderson's "player" hypothesis. *Social Forces*, *87*(4), 1813–1844.

Kreager, D., & Staff, J. (2009). The sexual double standard and adolescent peer acceptance. *Social Psychology Quarterly*, *72,* 143–164.

Maccoby, E. E. (1998). *The two sexes: Growing up apart, coming together.* Cambridge, MA: Belknap.

Marks, M., & Fraley, R. C. (2005). The sexual double standard: Fact or fiction? *Sex Roles, 52,* 175–186.

Marks, M., & Fraley, R. C. (2006). Confirmation bias and the sexual double standard. *Sex Roles, 54*, 19–26.

Milhausen, R., & Herold, E. (1999). Does the sexual double standard still exist? Perceptions of university women. *Journal of Sex Research*, *36*, 361–368.

Milhausen, R., & Herold, E. (2001). Reconceptualizing the sexual double standard. *Journal of Psychology and Human Sexuality, 13*, 63–83.

Mortimer, J., & Call, D. (2001). *Arenas of comfort in adolescence: A study of adjustment in context.* Mahwah, NJ: Lawrence Erlbaum Associates, Inc.

Oliver, M., & Hyde, J. (1993). Gender differences in sexuality: A meta-analysis. *Psychological Bulletin, 114,* 29–51.

Reiss, I. (1960). *Premarital sexual standards in America.* Glencoe, IL: Free Press.

Risman, B., & Schwartz, P. (2002). After the sexual revolution: Gender politics in teen dating. *Context, 1,* 16–24.

Scott, M., & Lyman, S. M. (1968). Accounts. *American Sociological Review*, *33*, 46–62.

Younis, J., & Smollar, J. (1985). *Adolescents' relationships with mothers, fathers, and friends.* Chicago, IL: University of Chicago Press.

EXPLORING THE ISSUE

Does a Strong and Costly Sexual Double Standard Still Exist Among Adolescents?

Critical Thinking and Reflection

1. Take a moment to think about the words you would use to describe sexually promiscuous boys and girls. Now critically examine your lists—are they equal in number, tone, and judgment? Now reflect back on the nature of this exercise. What does it illuminate for you about your own perceptions, beliefs, and biases when it comes to the sexual double standard?

2. Consider your experiences (personal or witnessing others) of how boys and girls in your peer group are/have been evaluted differently for the same behaviors. What examples come to mind of instances where a sexual double standard was operating? What were the outcomes for boys versus girls who violated sexual standards?

3. How are boys and girls socialized differently with respect to their development as sexual beings? What are the messages that girls receive about how to be sexual? Are desire and pleasure part of the sexual scripts for both boys and girls? If so, how are they communicated? If not, why not?

Is There Common Ground?

In the YES selection, Kreager and Staff presented evidence for a contemporary double standard among adolescents. They found significant gender differences in the relationship between the number of sexual partners and acceptance by peers whereby boys and girls were evaluated differently (girls more negatively) for the same behaviors. Girls who were considered sexually permissive (with more than eight sexual partners) received fewer friendship endorsements from peers than did girls with no sexual partners. The authors explained this finding to mean that girls who are sexually permissive are marginalized within their peer groups. In contrast, sexually experienced boys were rewarded with peer acceptance, and less experienced boys suffered in terms of friendship ratings from peers. Interestingly, they also found that female peers viewed sexually permissive girls more negatively than they did sexually permissive boys.

In the NO selection, Lyons and colleagues examined the association between adolescent girls' popularity and lifetime number of sexual partners. Contrary to the results of Kreager and Staff's study, in this issue, number of sexual partners was not associated with popularity among peers. They also found no differences in the quality of friendships (i.e., intimacy, time spent together) for girls with higher number of sexual partners compared to those with fewer or no sexual partners, and no differences in self-esteem. Because this was a longitudinal study, the researchers were able to examine the variables cross-sectionally and over time. They found no changes in friendship status over time for sexually permissive girls. They also included a qualitative component to their study and found that these young women

acknowledged the existence of a sexual double standard (in interviews), but they did not view themselves as less popular than other girls, or marginalized for their sexual experiences. The authors suggest that one's close network of friends provides a buffer against any possible negative outcomes.

One of the main differences between these two studies is that the second measured friends' liberal attitudes toward sexuality. Perhaps the social costs of the double standard are less and they are less severe when friendship circles consist of people with more liberal attitudes toward sex. Girls in the NO selection acknowledged the existence of a normative sexual double standard, but seemed to evaluate themselves and their sexually experienced peers less negatively than the sexual double standard would suggest. That said, the results suggested that they did not apply the same sensitivity or acceptance to "unknown" girls (girls outside their peer group) who violated sexual prescriptions and standards.

Additional Resources

Aubrey, J. S. (2004). Sex and punishment: An examination of sexual consequences and the sexual double standard in teen programming. *Sex Roles, 50,* 505–514.

Double Standard (DVD). (2002). CTV. Product information. Retrieved from www.mcintyre.ca/cgi-bin/search /mmiview.asp?ID=4736

Greene, K., & Faulkner, S. L. (2005). Gender, belief in the sexual double standard, and sexual talk in heterosexual dating relationships. *Sex Roles, 53*(3/4), 239–251.

Marks, M., & Fraley, R. C. (2006). Confirmation bias and the sexual double standard. *Sex Roles, 54*(1/2), 19–26.

Milhausen, R. R., & Herold, E. S. (1999). Does the sexual double standard still exist? Perceptions of university women. *Journal of Sex Research, 36*, 361–368.

Muehlenhard, C. L., & Quackenbush, D. M. (1998). Sexual Double Standard Scale. In C. M. Davis, W. L. Yarber, R. Bauserman, G. Scherer, & S. L. Davis (Eds.), *Handbook of sexuality-related measures* (pp. 186–188). Thousand Oaks, CA: Sage.

Schleicher, S. S., & Gilbert, L. A. (2005). Heterosexual dating discourses among college students: Is there still a double standard? *Journal of College Student Psychotherapy, 19*(3), 7–23.

Sexualityandu.ca. (February 2011). The sexual double standard: Has it disappeared? Retrieved from http://sexualityandu.ca/uploads/files/DoubleStandardfebruary2011.pdf

Welles, C. E. (2005). Breaking the silence surrounding female adolescent sexual desire. *Women & Therapy, 28*(2), 31–45.

White, E. (2001). *Fast girls: Teenage tribes and the myth of the slut.* New York: Scribner.

References

Marks, M., & Fraley, R. C. (2005). The sexual double standard: Fact or fiction? *Sex Roles, 52*(3/4), 175–186. doi: 10.1007/s11199-005-1293-5

Oliver, M. B., & Hyde, J. S. (1993). Gender differences in sexuality: A meta-analysis. *Psychological Bulletin, 114*, 29–51.

Reiss, I. (1967). *The social context of premartial sexual permissiveness.* New York: Holt, Rinehart, and Winston.

Internet References . . .

Safe Teens

http://www.safeteens.org

Sex and Sensibility: A Parent's Take on Advice from an Expert

http://www.advocatesforyouth.org/parents/141?task=view

Talking with Teens

http://www.hhs.gov/ash/oah/resources-and-publications/info/parents/

Teen Sexual Double Standard Impacts Circle of Friends

http://psychcentral.com/news/2015/08/25/teen-sexual-double-standard-impacts-circle-of-friends/91327.html

The Double Standard

http://youthvoices.net/discussion/double-standard

Selected, Edited, and with Issue Framing Material by:
Scott R. Brandhorst, *Southeast Missouri State University*

ISSUE

Do Reality TV Shows Portray Responsible Messages about Teen Pregnancy?

YES: Amy Kramer, from "The REAL Real World: How MTV's *16 and Pregnant* and *Teen Mom* Motivate Young People to Prevent Teen Pregnancy," an original essay for this edition (2011)

NO: Mary Jo Podgurski, from "Till Human Voices Wake Us: The High Personal Cost of Reality Teen Pregnancy Shows," an original essay for this edition (2011)

Learning Outcomes
After reading this issue, you will be able to:
• Explain the role of reality TV shows in educating young people about the "reality" of teenage parenthood.
• Critically analyze the possible negative outcomes associated with a "televised" picture of adolescent pregnancy and parenthood.
• Critique the ethical issues associated with "real teens" participating in reality television shows.

ISSUE SUMMARY

YES: Amy Kramer argues that reality television shows engage teens in considering the consequences of pregnancy before they are ready for it and motivate them to want to prevent it. She discusses some of the other possible influences on the decline of the teen pregnancy rate (e.g., affordable contraception), but also supports her ideas with research that shows a decline in teen pregnancy rates as a result of these shows (e.g., Kearney & Levine, 2014).

NO: Mary Jo Podgurski, founder of the Academy for Adolescent Health, Inc., argues that although such television shows have potential benefits, they inadequately address the issue and may even have a negative impact on those who participate in them.

Television has evolved during the past six decades. Just 60 years ago, families could gather around one immovable set with a limited number of channels and observe Desi Arnaz and Lucille Ball occupy different beds in the wildly popular sitcom *I Love Lucy*. Considered prudent for TV standards at the time, it would strike many today as an odd family life arrangement for the famous couple—who were married both off the air and in character! Fast forward two decades, and we see Mike and Carol Brady sharing the same bed on the *The Brady Bunch*, but neither one apparently very interested in sex (and Mike peculiarly and persistently absorbed in reading *Jonathan Livingston Seagull* in bed).

Today's TV has a much more substantial representation of sexual relationships and themes. Leaps and bounds from then landmark events such as William Shatner and Nichelle Nicholl's "first interracial kiss" on TV's *Star Trek*, Ellen DeGeneres coming out on the air in the mid-1990s, Kerr Smith and Adam Kaufman's "first gay male kiss" on prime-time TV in 2000, and Scott Evans and Brett Claywell's "first gay male sex scene" on daytime TV in 2010, many of today's TV programs include overtly sexual messages and a greater range of sexual innuendo, humor, and steamy scenes. Although the representation is greater, the *accuracy* of the portrayals is questionable. Is the infrequent gay character actually a *caricature* manifesting common stereotypes? Is sex so closely and frequently tied to crime as portrayed in various crime dramas? Does the constant use of sexual humor mirror and reinforce society's discomfort with sex? Do sexual scenes in prime-time dramas make sex appear seamless—and only for the young and beautiful?

Another way in which TV has changed is with the emergence of the so-called "reality TV show" genre. Popularized with the success of MTV's *The Real World* and CBS's *Survivor*, many reality TV shows have followed, so much so that there was even a reality TV show network channel for a while! Perhaps it was inevitable that the world of reality TV and sexuality would collide; new shows addressing specific sexual themes have emerged. Some shows address issues of pregnancy and family life. In 2007, we were introduced to the family life of parents of octuplets on Discover Health's *Jon and Kate Plus 8*. And then in 2008, we were introduced to the family life of the parents of 17 kids, then 18 kids, and finally 19 kids and counting on TLC's *19 Kids and Counting* (as it was called when cancelled in 2015). Later, MTV introduced the real-life teen focused pregnancy dramas *16 and Pregnant* and *Teen Mom,* which follow the lives of real young people dealing with teen pregnancy.

Some sexuality educators, looking for ways to connect with students in authentic, meaningful ways, have embraced the popularity of these shows for their potential as teachable moments.

Educators can show a clip to build discussion questions themed around the premise, "What would you do if . . ."

Other sexuality educators express concern over the reality and impact of the shows. Do the networks provide an adequate job of portraying all the hardships of teen pregnancy, or will students perceive the characters as TV stars to be admired and emulated?

In the YES and NO selections, Amy Kramer, the senior director of entertainment median at The National Campaign to Prevent Teen and Unplanned Pregnancy, describes the positive potential these shows can have as allies in sexuality education. She explains how the shows help motivate young people to want to prevent pregnancy before they are ready to be parents. She also provides some research to support the impact these shows have had on the decline of the teen pregnancy rate. Mary Jo Podgurski, founder of the Academy for Adolescent Health, Inc., who routinely works with pregnant and parenting teens, explains her reasons for declining the opportunity to work with *16 and Pregnant* when producers approached her. Although noting the potential benefits of the shows, she expresses reservations about the impact the shows might have on the teen that appears on a national stage.

YES

Amy Kramer

The REAL Real World: How MTV's *"16 and Pregnant"* and *"Teen Mom"* Motivate Young People to Prevent Teen Pregnancy

Like it or not, media is a huge influence in the lives of young people. Teens spend more hours each week in front of a screen than they do in a classroom.[1] Many teens know a lot more about their favorite shows than they do about any academic subject, and characters on television are often more familiar than neighbors. What young people learn in sex ed, if they have sex ed at all, is a fraction of what pop culture serves up on a daily basis. Which is why parents and educators alike should be thankful that MTV has emerged as a sort of accidental hero in the campaign against teen pregnancy.

Thanks to the reality shows *16 and Pregnant* and *Teen Mom*, millions of young people are now thinking and talking about teen pregnancy. These shows were developed as nothing more than good entertainment but they have succeeded in ways public health initiatives have not—that is getting young people to stop, pay attention, consider, and discuss what happens when someone becomes a parent before they're ready.

Although we know how to avoid teen pregnancy—get teens to avoid having sex at all or to use contraception carefully and consistently when they do have sex—prevention isn't always as easy as it looks. Getting young people to commit to waiting or protecting themselves is tough. After all, they're kids. The consequences of their actions might not seem as likely as the benefit of the risks. Nearly half of teens admit they've never thought about how a pregnancy would change their lives,[2] and most girls who get pregnant say they never thought it would happen to them. It's no wonder young people don't always take precautions to prevent pregnancy—if you never consider that something might happen to you, or what life would be like if it did, why would you consider taking steps to prevent it?

But *16 and Pregnant* and *Teen Mom* seem to be changing that. These shows are bringing the reality of too-early pregnancy and parenthood smack into the middle of the lives and minds of young people in powerful and important ways. Teens come to these shows on their own and they say they come away with a new appreciation for some of the consequences of unprotected sex. In fact, in a nationally representative poll conducted by The National

Campaign to Prevent Teen and Unplanned Pregnancy in 2010, 82% of teens who had seen *16 and Pregnant* said that watching the show "helps teens better understand the challenges of pregnancy and parenthood." Only 17% said the show makes teen pregnancy look glamorous.[3] Already, the fact that young people are tuning in week after week makes what MTV is doing more successful than many PSA campaigns could ever hope to be.

* * *

Rates of teen pregnancy and birth are higher in the United States than in any other industrialized nation. The teen birth rate in the United States is more than three times higher than the rate in Canada, and nearly twice that of the United Kingdom (which has the highest rate in Europe). One out of every ten babies born in the United States is born to a teen mother. Three out of every ten girls in the United States get pregnant before their 20th birthday—750,000 girls each year. That's 2,000 girls getting pregnant *every day*. These numbers—as shocking as they are—actually represent dramatic improvements. In the past two decades, rates of teen pregnancy and childbearing in the United States have dropped by more than one-third.[4]

According to the National Center for Health Statistics, in early-1990s America, 117 out of every 1,000 girls ages 15–19 got pregnant, and 62 out of every 1,000 girls ages 15–19 gave birth. Not even twenty years later those rates are down to 72 per 1,000 teens getting pregnant and 39 per 1,000 teens giving birth. Put another way, teen pregnancy has declined by 38% and teen births are down by one-third. Still too high, but a remarkable improvement on an issue once thought to be intractable.

To what do we owe this astonishing decline in teen pregnancy and teen births? Quite simply and perhaps not surprisingly, it's a combination of less sex and more contraception. According to the National Survey of Family Growth (NSFG), a household-based nationally representative survey conducted periodically by the Centers for Disease Control and Prevention to study families, fertility, and health in the United States, in 1988, 51% of girls and 60% of boys ages 15–19 had ever had sex. In

2006–2008 those numbers had declined to 42% of girls and 43% of boys. Condom use increased during that time as well: In 1988, 31% of girls and 55% of boys who had sex in the past 90 days said they used a condom the last time they had sex. In 2006–2008, those numbers had grown to 53% for girls and 79% for boys. So, for a complicated array of reasons, teens have been doing the only two things you can do to prevent pregnancy: delaying sex and being better about contraception when they do have sex.

It's also important to note that abortions to teens declined as well over that same time period. In 1988, 39% of pregnancies to teens ended in abortion, in 2006, it was 27%, meaning that the decline in teen births was not due to an increase in terminations.[5]

* * *

Consider the following: While rates of sexual activity, pregnancy, birth, and abortion among teens were declining enormously, the media were growing exponentially and becoming coarser and more sexualized. There are hundreds of channels now and an infinite number of websites. Finding sexually suggestive content on television and explicit content online—or it finding you—is a fact of life for many young people. If media influence on teens' decisions about sex is so direct and so negative, why might it be that teen sexual behavior has gotten more responsible at exactly the same time the media and popular culture have become more sexualized? Simply put, the media can't be solely to blame for teens having sex, or having babies. However, the media can help write the social script and contribute to viewers' sense of what's normal and acceptable—and can make sex seem casual, inconsequential, or serious. In fact, polling for The National Campaign to Prevent Teen and Unplanned Pregnancy shows that year after year, 8 in 10 teens say they wish the media showed more consequences of sex (not less sex).[6]

So television alone doesn't cause teen pregnancy, but could it actually help prevent it? Teens themselves suggest that it can. Most teens (79% of girls, 67% of boys,) say that "when a TV show or character I like deals with teen pregnancy, it makes me think more about my own risk of becoming pregnant/ causing a pregnancy, and how to avoid it," according to the National Campaign to Prevent Teen and Unplanned Pregnancy.[7] "Thinking about my own risk" is an important piece of the prevention puzzle.

In that same study from The National Campaign, three-quarters of teens (76%) and adults (75%) say that what they see in the media about sex, love, and relationships can be a good way to start conversations about these topics. Communication between parents and teens about their own views and values regarding these issues is critical. Children whose parents are clear about the value of delaying sex are less likely to have intercourse at an early age. Parents who discuss contraception are also more likely to have children who use contraception when they become sexually active.[8] These conversations can be awkward and intimidating (on both sides), but they are important. So anything that encourages such talk, or makes it easier to start the conversation, is valuable.

MTV's *16 and Pregnant* is a conversation starter, certainly among teens, but also within families. In a 2010 study of more than 150 teenagers involved with Boys & Girls Clubs' after-school programs in a southern state, 40% of teens who watched *16 and Pregnant* with their group at the Club and then talked about it in a facilitator-led discussion also talked about it again afterward with a parent. One-third discussed it with a boyfriend/girlfriend. More than half discussed it with a friend.[9] That 40% went home and talked about with mom or dad is particularly exciting—because the more opportunities parents have to discuss their own ideas and expectations about pregnancy and parenting, the better. Teens talking about these shows—articulating their own thoughts about a teen parent on MTV or a situation depicted in an episode—brings them one step closer to personalizing it, which is an important step along the behavior change continuum and the path to prevention.

Educators and leaders in youth-serving organizations are using the MTV shows as teaching tools. A social worker in the Midwest, who frequently speaks at schools in both urban and rural areas, has used episodes of *16 and Pregnant* in her work: "With the boys, we had great discussion about what makes a man a 'father'." Boys were a little defensive about the portrayal of the teen dads, but after talking it through, began to empathize more with the young women." A teacher in the South incorporated the series into high school lesson plans: "I use it as part of a unit on teen parenting and parenting readiness to discourage teen pregnancies and to encourage students to wait until they are older and 'ready' before having children. . . . Students enjoy watching the 'real-life' stories of teens and are able to really identify with them." A private special education teacher who works with a teen population especially vulnerable to abusive relationships and pregnancy has also watched the series with students: "The kids were very much engaged because it was something they would watch at home. Some of them had seen the episodes already but looked at them differently once viewed in a group, clinical setting. The conversations were often very serious and enlightening for the students. They were able to put themselves into the girls' shoes and talk about how they would feel, react, respond in each of the situations that came up." Staff at a county juvenile detention center in the Southwest includes the show in teen pregnancy prevention programs and calls it "heavy-hitting and impactful": "They cater to the very media-driven nature of teens today—they aren't dry book material, but rather a great combination of reality and entertainment in a condensed format. . . . A whole year in the life of these teen parents in just an hour of viewing."[10]

* * *

Television shows like MTV's *16 and Pregnant* and *Teen Mom* are created for entertainment purposes with the hope of attracting viewers and keeping them engaged. By that measure, these shows are indisputably successful. Millions of people tune in to each new episode—and the ratings are among the highest on the cable network. Recent episodes have drawn more viewers than even the major broadcast network competition. Public attention to the storylines extends beyond the episodes themselves and into Internet discussion forums, where theories and speculation about the lives depicted on the shows are rampant.

Thanks to these very real reality programs, teen pregnancy is no longer a mysterious topic to millions of young people. Viewers have seen in the most vivid way possible what happens when contraception fails, when babies arrive, when boyfriends leave, when money is tight, when parents are disappointed, and when graduating from high school is impossible. Conversations are happening around dinner tables and in carpools, allowing parents and teens to explore their own opinions and behavior. Parents now have an opportunity to discuss their own values and expectations as they pertain to family formation and romantic responsibility. Friends, siblings, and partners are talking to each other about what happens when young people become parents before they're ready. Maybe they're even talking about how to prevent it from happening in the first place.

Every episode of *16 and Pregnant* includes a scene in which the expectant teenager talks about how she got pregnant. Many weren't using any protection at all, others had problems remembering to take their pills every day, some found out that prescribed antibiotics can interfere with the effectiveness of birth control pills, a few missed their Depo shot appointments, others stopped using a method after a break-up and then never returned to its use after reconciliation, etc. This information is presented honestly and in peer-to-peer terms, inviting viewers to listen and learn, and perhaps explore a type of contraception they hadn't previously known about. On *Teen Mom* viewers see the young parents taking steps to prevent subsequent pregnancies: Cameras have captured the girls' discussions with their doctors about the vaginal ring, IUDs, and other long-acting methods of contraception. Even the "reunion" episodes devote time to discussion about birth control between updates on the babies and the relationship drama.

Watching what happens to girls who "never thought it would happen to them" encourages viewers to assess their own risk. When teenage fans of the shows see time and again that having a baby as an adolescent often means educational goals are abandoned, family relationships erode, financial challenges become insurmountable, and romantic fantasies are dashed, the prospect of early parenthood in their own lives becomes far less attractive. Rosier depictions of teen pregnancy and its consequences from movies, scripted television shows, and daydreams start to look silly in comparison. Seeing that teen pregnancy happens in the lives of girls from every sort of background (even a familiar one) reminds viewers that it could happen to them and it pushes them to figure out how to avoid a similar fate.

Separate from the shows themselves is the tabloid coverage they receive, though it is so pervasive right now it deserves mention here. That the tabloid media have decided to treat these struggling young mothers like celebrities is certainly unfortunate. That the real-life people around the teen mothers have obviously decided to cooperate with the tabloids (in the form of photos, tips, and other information) is sadder still. However, the bulk of even that coverage focuses on the turmoil in their lives. These are young mothers agonizing over money, men, family drama, health issues, the law, and the unending responsibility of parenthood. Followers of this often repugnant news stream may know even more about the chaos that swirls around young parents than do mere viewers of the show. Coverage does not necessarily equal glamorization. Bottom line: If you sit through a full episode, any episode, of *16 and Pregnant* or *Teen Mom*, glamour is totally absent.

* * *

MTV's *16 and Pregnant* and *Teen Mom* are not evidence-based teen pregnancy prevention programs. They aren't a substitute for talented teachers or comprehensive sex ed curricula. These shows aren't more meaningful than traditions of faith. They aren't more important than access to quality healthcare or relevant health information. They aren't more powerful than engaged parents willing to talk openly about tough topics. But teen pregnancy prevention needs to happen everywhere, including in the popular media teenagers love to consume. Everyone who cares about teens, babies, and the next generation of Americans needs to do their part to keep rates of teen pregnancy on a downward trajectory. Families, schools, health care professionals, businesses big and small, religious communities, and yes, the media, all have a role to play. Teen pregnancy prevention requires sustained effort over time by all sectors. This isn't an issue where a vaccine or a cure will lead to a drop in incidence. Even new and better methods of contraception won't do the trick if young people aren't motivated to use them. Making headway on this complex topic requires young people to make better choices over and over again. Any way they can get the message that the teen years are not the appropriate time for parenthood matters.

MTV is doing more than most—even if inadvertently—with *16 and Pregnant* and *Teen Mom*. Millions of young people tune in each week and four out of five viewers say that doing so "helps teens better understand the challenges of pregnancy and parenthood." Anyone who cares about reducing rates of teen pregnancy and teen birth should listen to what teens themselves are saying and tune out the rest.

Footnotes/Sources

1. Kaiser Family Foundation, (2010). *Generation M2: Media in the Lives of 8- to 18-Year-Olds.* http://www .kff.org/entmedia/upload/8010.pdf

2. National Campaign to Prevent Teen and Unplanned Pregnancy, (2007). *With One Voice 2007: America's Adults and Teens Sound Off About Teen Pregnancy.*

http://www.thenationalcampaign.org/resources/pdf/pubs/WOV2007_fulltext.pdf

3. National Campaign to Prevent Teen and Unplanned Pregnancy, (2010). *With One Voice 2010: America's Adults and Teens Sound Off About Teen Pregnancy.* http://www.thenationalcampaign.org/resources/pdf/pubs/WOV_2010.pdf

4. National Campaign to Prevent Teen and Unplanned Pregnancy, various fact sheets. http://www.thenationalcampaign.org/resources/fact-sheets.aspx

5. Guttmacher Institute, (2010) *U.S. Teenage Pregnancies, Births and Abortions: National and State Trends and Trends by Race and Ethnicity.* http://www.guttmacher.org/pubs/USTPtrends.pdf

6. National Campaign to Prevent Teen and Unplanned Pregnancy, (2007, 2004, 2002). *With One Voice 2007/2004/2002: America's Adults and Teens Sound Off About Teen Pregnancy.* http://www.thenationalcampaign.org/resources/pdf/pubs/WOV2007_fulltext.pdf http://www.thenationalcampaign.org/resources/pdf/pubs/WOV_2004.pdf http://www.thenationalcampaign.org/resources/pdf/pubs/WOV_2002.pdf

7. National Campaign to Prevent Teen and Unplanned Pregnancy, (2010). *With One Voice 2010: America's Adults and Teens Sound Off About Teen Pregnancy.* http://www.thenationalcampaign.org/resources/pdf/pubs/WOV_2010.pdf

8. Blum, R. W., & Rinehard, P. M. (1998). *Reducing the Risk: Connections that make a difference in the lives of youth.* Center for Adolescent Health and Development, University of Minnesota. Minneapolis, MN.

9. Suellentrop, K., Brown, J., Ortiz, R. (2010) *Evaluating the Impact of MTV's '16 and Pregnant' on Teen Viewers' Attitudes about Teen Pregnancy,* The National campaign to Prevent Teen and Unplanned Pregnancy, Washington DC. http://www.thenationalcampaign.org/resources/pdf/SS/SS45_16andPregnant.pdf

10. Telephone interviews and email inquiries by the author.

Addendum

It's now more than half a dozen years since MTV's "16 and Pregnant" and "Teen Mom" began, and evidence continues to mount showing that these programs have contributed to the decline in teen childbearing and to a change in attitudes about sex and pregnancy prevention among young people.

Since the shows premiered in 2009, teen births in the U.S. have dropped 38%—as much as they did in the two decades prior. Between 1991 and 2008, teen births declined steadily, at an annual rate of about 2.5%. But since 2009, declines have happened much more rapidly—more than twice as rapidly in fact. Teen pregnancies are also down, as are abortions to teens.

A groundbreaking study published in the National Bureau of Economic Research in 2014 found a direct link between the MTV shows and the accelerated decline in teen births. By looking at federal birth data, Nielsen ratings, social media, and online search analytics, researchers concluded that rates of teen childbearing declined faster in geographic areas where the shows were more popular, and that the shows influenced attitudes about teen pregnancy and birth control. Data from Google and Twitter allowed them to determine that relevant tweets (such as "16 and Pregnant is a great form of birth control!") and searches for information about contraception (such as "how to get birth control pills") spiked in the hours when the show was on the air and in the locations where the show was more popular. The researchers concluded that "16 and Pregnant" and "Teen Mom" led to a nearly 6 % reduction in teen births during the 18 months of their study—accounting for about one-third of the overall decline in teen childbearing during that time. In other words, the shows may have prevented as many as 20,000 births to teens during 2010 alone.[1]

To be clear, there have been other efforts made to combat high rates of teen pregnancy and childbearing during this time: the Obama Administration has devoted hundreds of millions of dollars to evidence-based teen pregnancy prevention programs in recent years, not to mention the Affordable Care Act making contraception less costly. There has also been a new emphasis on low-maintenance contraceptive methods like the IUD and implant for teens coming from experts such as the American Academy of Pediatrics. But government programs reach only about 2 % of youth, and the availability of affordable, more effective birth control methods isn't much help to people who aren't motivated to use them the first place.

The MTV shows have helped change the conversation among young people by introducing them to the realities of young parenthood and to methods of contraception they probably hadn't ever heard of before. These shows have given literally millions of viewers something real, relatable, meaningful, and motivating to consider when making decisions about their own sex lives. And that makes a big difference.

Amy Kramer
Senior Director of Entertainment Media
The National Campaign to Prevent teen and Unplanned Pregnancy

[1]Kearney, M. S., & Levine, P. B. (2014). Media influences on social outcomes: The impact of MTV's *16 and Pregnant* on teen childbearing, The National Bureau of Economic Research. http://www.nber.org/papers/w19795

Mary Jo Podgurski

 **NO**

Till Human Voices Wake Us: The High Personal Cost of Reality Teen Pregnancy Shows

Having a baby young took away my childhood and there's no way I'll ever get it back.

—16-year-old mother

I wouldn't be alive today if I hadn't had her. She's the reason I'm still alive.

—15-year-old mother

The "voices" above are direct quotes from the video I produced in 1998 entitled *Voices: The Reality of Early Childbearing—Transcending the Myths*. The video was marketed nationally by Injoy Productions until 2009 and is still used in the Lamaze teen program Creativity, Connection and Commitment: Supporting Teens During the Childbearing Year (Lamaze International, 2010). Over the course of a year my team interviewed and videotaped young parents with the intent of using their voices and wisdom as a catalyst for teen pregnancy prevention. I share these voices to underscore a acute need to protect teens. When editing the film, I discovered that the teen mothers consistently wanted to reveal very intimate aspects of their lives. Data including early drinking, number of sexual partners, an incestuous relationship, nonconsensual sex, and sexual experimentation were all freely revealed. I cautioned them to think of the future. Would their children relish such revelations a decade later? Were these details pertinent to their messages? I persisted, and only information that was truly educational and not sensationalized remained in the film. I believed then that 16-year-old parents could provide a priceless service to other teens as peer educators; I continue to believe such teaching is effective and significant. I simply refused to expose the truly personal details of their lives to scrutiny. I was interested in education, not drama.

My staff and I remain in contact with many of the teen parents in *Voices*. More than ten years after its production, they are in 100% agreement: Our careful screening spared their children (now young teens) embarrassment. The young parents I've served have taught me to put a face on the statistics surrounding teen pregnancy; while I will always strive to educate all young people about the risks associated with bearing children young, I am deeply cognizant

of the price a teen parent pays when offering his or her life as a lesson plan.

The last 30 years of my life have been dedicated to providing comprehensive sexuality education to young people; our programs reach over 18,000 youth a year in all 14 Washington County school districts. Concurrently I've mentored young parents. I served as a doula (providing labor support) for my first adolescent in the '70s; that young mother became one of many. My staff and I provide educational services and support for nearly 100 pregnant and parenting teens annually. When the MTV program *16 and Pregnant* was in its planning stages, I was approached by the producers and asked to provide teens for the show. I declined after much soul searching. This article explores my rationale for that decision.

Why Rethink Reality TV Using Teen Parents?

As an educator I seek teachable moments in everyday life. I am thrilled to have the opportunity to teach; I consider the field of sexuality education a vocation and am blessed to be in a role where life-affirming information is at my disposal and I am free to convey it to teens. I don't deny the impact reality shows like *16 and Pregnant* and *Teen Mom* (now *Teen Mom 2*) can have on teens. The April 10, 2011, edition of *The New York Times* reports anecdotes of teachers using the shows as a part of curriculum in life skills and parenting classes (Hoffman, 2011, April 10). The National Campaign to Prevent Teen and Unplanned Pregnancy has distributed DVDs and teacher guides on *16 and Pregnant* and these materials seem to be well received by educators. I also am not deterred by fears that these reality shows glamorize teen pregnancy. The Campaign conducted a national telephone poll of young people ages 12 to 19; 82% said that the shows aided their understanding of the reality of teen pregnancy. Only 17% stated that the shows gave pregnancy a glamorous spin (Albert, 2010). In the hands of a skilled educator, the shows' influence can be directed away from glamour to empathic awareness. There is no doubt that there are lessons to be learned from these shows, but at what price?

My primary concern with reality TV shows like *16 and Pregnant* and *Teen Mom* deals with the human cost of these lessons. Young parents, like most young people, are not immune to the appeal of fame. I question a teen's ability to give full permission to a life-changing activity that will reframe his or her identity on a national stage. I am concerned that these young people cannot developmentally grasp the far-reaching implications of their decision to participate. Exploitation is a strong word and I use it with a caveat: I do not believe the shows aim to exploit. I believe that their intentions are good; it is society that removes all boundaries and exposes tender lives to the scrutiny of tabloids and the manipulation of the media. When I filmed *Voices,* I stressed the need for discretion; in 10 or 20 years, I said, would your baby want to be known for the things you now reveal? In a decade and more, how will the babies in *16 and Pregnant* view their lives? How will they react to their parents, their families, and their infancy and toddler years exposed for posterity?

I am also troubled by a nagging sense that these shows hope to provide a simple solution to the problems associated with adolescent sexuality in America. There are no Band-aids that can be applied to the multi-faceted, complicated situations that arise when teens are sexually involved, yet our culture consistently seeks an easy fix. I was afforded the privilege of attending an Advocates for Youth European Study Tour in 2001. As part of that experience, I was exposed to European approaches to sexuality education. In contrast to American culture, European culture does not deny the fact that teens need education that helps them achieve sexual health; comprehensive sexuality education is the norm. Are reality TV shows that focus on the lives of young parents yet another simplistic answer that distracts from the need to mandate comprehensive sexuality education to all of our children?

No Band-Aids

Research points to antecedents to early pregnancy and risky behavior; I question whether the teen parents in reality TV shows reflect those antecedents or are selected for their "camera" quality and the appeal of their families' dramas. I also ponder the use of dollars to develop these TV shows instead of creating programs that would target youth that evidence-based data show are at risk.

Dr. Doug Kirby's work (2002, 2007) alone and with colleagues (Kirby, Lepore, & Ryan, 2006) is considered seminal in the areas of comprehensive sexuality education and teen pregnancy antecedents. Research into the role of siblings in early childbearing from East and associates (1996 through 2007) is pivotal to understanding generational teen pregnancy (East, Reyes, & Horn, 2007; Raneri & Constance, 2007). Kristen Luker (2006) is considered a founding theorist of the sociological and political theories surrounding early childbearing and linked poverty to teen pregnancy as an antecedent, not a consequence of the pregnancy. Young people who are survivors of sexual and physical abuse (Boyer & Fine, 1992) are at risk for early childbearing, as are children in placement or foster care (Kirby, et al. 2006) and children living with domestic violence, drug/alcohol abuse or incarcerated parents (Coyle, 2005; Goode & Smith, 2005; East & Khoo, 2005; Jekielek, Moore, Hair, & Scarupa, 2002). Do the teens in reality TV reflect these antecedents?

Research at the University of Arkansas showed that girls are more likely to experience teen pregnancy if they live with internal poverty (measured as a low locus of control and future expectations) as well as external poverty (Young, Turner, Denny, Young, 2004). Internal poverty "describes a person's lack of internal resources, such as attitudes and beliefs that attribute outcomes to individual effort, high future expectations, and few perceived limitations for life options" (Coles, 2005). Certainly internal and external poverty are antecedents in the pregnancies of some reality TV participants; at any time are those teens given guidance that will help them develop the skills and self-efficacy they need to succeed?

Antecedents to teen pregnancy in the United States lead dedicated sexuality educators to explore the need for education that affects behavioral change. Dr. Michael A. Carrera's Children's Aid Society is a well-respected and researched youth development approach that targets the whole child through early intervention (Children's Aid Society, 2010). On a much smaller scale, my team and I have tried to emulate his efforts. Although we remain committed to comprehensive sexuality education, we first approached teen pregnancy prevention through pro-active education in 1999 with the initiation of an early intervention educational mentoring program entitled Educate Children for Healthy Outcomes (ECHO). ECHO provides one-on-one mentoring to young people who have been identified as at risk for engaging in high-risk behavior. Specifically, we target girls in grades 2–12 who have experienced sexual abuse, abandonment issues, placement problems, truancy, early sexual acting out, and/or familial teen pregnancy and provide them with a supportive, consistent, empowering educator and role model. Our advisors educate participants on youth development topics that guide them in making healthy life choices. Our program topics include: decision making, refusal, communication, and problem-solving skills, assertiveness training, anger management, conflict resolution, puberty education, socialization skills, life skills, and prevention education. We strive to empower families to communicate well with each other, help children avoid risky behavior during their adolescent years, and strengthen the family unit as a whole. Only three of the 511 high-risk girls we've mentored since 1999 experienced a pregnancy, and all three of those young women were older than 18 when they gave birth.

Reality shows target all teens without the capacity to address the real and complicated issues that may lead to actual teen pregnancy. Focusing on sexual health for all young people is vital; providing personalized instruction to teens at highest risk, while costly, could maximize positive outcomes.

Voices to Break the Cycle: A Phenomenological Inquiry into Generational Teen Pregnancy

I completed my doctoral work late in life; my dissertation was not only informative but also humbling. I looked at the lived experiences of women who gave birth as adolescents to investigate how these adults might help their pubertal-aged children avoid teenage pregnancy. Research participants gave birth as teens (defined as under 19 years of age) and were parenting their biologic children ages 10–15. A key criteria for selection in the study was generational teen pregnancy; participants in the study came from families with a history of teen pregnancy through at least one generation prior to the former teen mother's birth. The study reinforced the antecedents of poverty, foster placement, sexual abuse, and familial patterns of early childbearing (Podgurski, 2009).

Stigmatizing women who conceive and bear children during adolescence is common in American culture and can lead to social inequalities (McDermott & Graham, 2005). Data reinforces young mothers' continuing need for support while teens (Pai-Espinosa, 2010) and as their lives move forward beyond adolescence (Jutte et al., 2010). The voices of former teen mothers in my study also revealed lives deeply affected by their adolescent pregnancies. Many women expressed a desire to move away from the community in which they gave birth; 30% of the former teen mothers in the study did relocate. One participant in the study stated: "When I got married I left the area. I found it easier to reinvent myself than deal with people who had labeled me as that pregnant girl. My life here is better than it would have been if I'd stayed where I was." Where can a teen parent whose life has been exposed on a national reality TV show relocate?

Adult empathic understanding and compassion for the lives of teen parents was not common among the participants in my study; over 80% described self-reported disrespectful treatment during their births, upon their return to school, or while seeking employment. If, as the National Campaign for Teen and Unplanned Pregnancy reports, 41% of adults report the show *16 and Pregnant* glorifies teen pregnancy (Albert, 2010), will that compassion diminish?

Till Human Voices Wake Us

What is the effect of fame on the young parents made into instant celebrities by reality TV? What do they and their children sacrifice to the altar of TV ratings?

To examine the possible long-term effects of fame and celebrity status on young parents, it is illustrative to look at fame as it is perceived in youth culture. Halpern (2007) surveyed 5th to 8th grade students in Rochester, New York, and found 29% of males and 37% of females selected fame over intelligence as a desired trait. The study participants viewed at least five hours of TV daily; that

figure is consistent with other studies of youth screen time (defined as TV and computer time). For example, Barnett and her research team (2008) found that 60% of teens spent an average of 20 hours in screen time, a full third spent closer to 40 hours per week and 7% were exposed to greater than 50 hours of viewing time weekly. Perhaps most significantly, Halbern's work showed that 17% of the students felt that celebrities owed their fame to luck, and believed that TV shows had the power to make people famous. If fame is valued over intelligence and luck is perceived as a better indicator of future well-being than industry among average children, would pregnant and parenting teens buy into that delusion as well?

An intense desire for fame can lead reality TV participants to believe that "every reality show is an audition tape for future work" (Wolk, 2010, p. 32). If adults are affected by fame hunger that directs their actions and choices, how can adolescents avoid influence from reality TV fame? The sad drama of Amber, violence, and child custody revealed on the show *Teen Mom* was popular among tabloids, magazines, and advertisers. As an educator I am troubled. Did Amber receive guidance or were her actions considered fodder for higher ratings? One need go no further than the cover story of a current *OK! Magazine* to read that "More Teen Mom Babies!" are planned, including one baby that is being conceived to save a relationship (2011, April 18). The same issue proclaims that Amber and Gary will reunite. What type, if any, relationship skill education do these young "reality celebrities" receive as their lives are broadcast nationally?

Putting a Face on the Numbers

The names of the young parents in the following anecdotes are fiction but their stories are not. Any of these young people would produce high ratings on a reality TV show. Protecting their anonymity is a fundamental educational task. Ethical treatment of pregnant and parenting youth demands that respect is rendered at all times.

Picture Tracy: This lively young woman was a National Honor Society student when she found she was pregnant at the age of 16. Articulate, empathetic, and soft-spoken, she is now a caring social worker completing her master's degree in counseling. Tracy did not disclose her history of sexual assault until the baby she birthed as a teen was four years old; she now uses her life experiences to help her connect with young women at risk for early childbearing.

Nina is a bright, intelligent 27-year-old. Her hair color and body piercings change often but her striking hazel eyes and determined expressions remain constant. She is perceptive, a hard worker, and one of the most resilient young people I've ever known. Nina is also the parent of a 12-year-old. She lived in a series of foster homes while pregnant and parenting; her mother gave birth to her as a 15-year-old and her grandmother had her first pregnancy as a 16-year-old. Nina was born into poverty and continues to struggle to make ends meet. She left school at 17 and hasn't completed the GED (General Equivalency Diploma) she frequently talks about.

She often bemoans the fact that her daughter "does without" things she too was denied as a teen. She is proud that she has been her child's only parent and that her daughter has never been in foster care. Like her own parents, Nina fights addiction to alcohol and drugs and has been in and out of rehab several times.

Meet Samantha: Sammy planned her baby to prove that she was heterosexual. Her first kiss at 11 was with a girl; she reacted violently to the fear that she was lesbian in a homophobic family and made a conscious decision to conceive a baby to a man ten years her senior. She was only 12 when her pregnancy was discovered; she didn't tell anyone until she was in her third trimester. She came out when her son was two years old and is currently in a five-year relationship with her female partner.

Jodi gave birth as a tenth grader but only disclosed her step father as her baby's daddy when he starting hitting on her younger sister. Her baby was two years old at the time. Disclosure led to her stepfather's arrest and incarceration for over four years of sexual abuse. Her five siblings were divided and sent to three different foster homes. While Jodi is intermittently proud of her disclosure, she blames herself for the dissolution of her family. She is in a new school district where few know her family's history and is starting to shine academically.

Trevor's father reacted to his girlfriend **Amy's** pregnancy by denying his parentage; within an hour he was homeless at 18. Too old for children and youth services, he wandered from one friend's sofa to another until the single mother of his girlfriend allowed him to move in with her family. The baby is due this spring. Trevor is determined to remain with his partner and states firmly that he will not "be a statistic." His girlfriend's mother, while kind and supportive, is skeptical. She sees Amy's father in Trevor. Although she hopes for the best, she expects him to leave before the baby is two.

It's Not about United States

Those of United States who have committed our lives to supporting, empowering, and educating young people approach this charge in unique ways. I humbly acknowledge that there are many paths to reaching youth. I have learned more from listening to the young people I serve than from any other resource. When I train new staff, I reinforce a common theme: Our work is not about us, it's about the young people. I am reminded of the old admonition: First, Do No Harm. As adults, we are responsible for the needs of all youth, regardless of sexual orientation, gender and gender identity, race, ethnicity, socio-economic status, religion, or level of sexual involvement. I challenge all who serve pregnant and parenting teens to examine the effects adult interventions have upon the lives of these young people and their children, bearing in mind that we do not yet have full knowledge of the long-term implications of national exposure at a time of great vulnerability. When in doubt, protect.

References

Albert, B. (2010). *With one voice 2010: Teens and adults sound off about teen pregnancy.* National Campaign to Prevent Teen and Unplanned Pregnancy. Retrieved from http://www.thenationalcampaign.org/resources/pdf/pubs/WOV_2010.pdf

Barnett, T., O'Loughlin, J., Sabiston, C., Karp, I., Belanger, M., Van Hulst, A., & Lambert., M. (2008). Teens and screens: The influence of screen time on adiposity in adolescents. *American Journal of Epidemiology, 172*(3), 255–262.

Boyer, D. & Fine, D. (1992). Sexual abuse as a factor in adolescent pregnancy and child maltreatment. *Family Planning Perspectives, 24*(1), 4–11.

Children's Aid Society. (2010). Dr. Michael A. Carrera, Retrieved from http://www.childrensaidsociety.org/carrera-pregnancy-prevention/dr-michael-carrera

Coles, C. (2005). Teen pregnancy and "internal poverty." *Futurist, 38*(7), 10.

Coyle, J. (2005, September). Preventing and reducing violence by at-risk adolescents common elements of empirically researche d programs. *Journal of Evidence-Based Social Work, 2*(3/4), 125.

Goode, W. W. & Smith, T. J. (2005). *Building from the ground up: Creating effective programs to mentor children of prisoners.* Philadelphia, PA: Public/Private Ventures.

East, P. L., & Khoo, S. (2005, December). Longitudinal pathways linkin g family factors and sibling relationship qualities to ad olescent substance use and sexual risk behaviors. *Journal of Family Psychology, 19*(4), 571–580.

East, P. L., Reyes, B. T., & Horn, E. J. (2007, June). Association between ad olescent pregnancy and a family history of teenage births. *Perspectives on sexual and reproductive health, 39*(2), 108–115.

Halpern, J. (2007). *Fame junkies: The hidden truth behind America's favor ite addiction.* New York: Houghton Mifflin Company.

Hoffman, J. (2011, April 10). Fighting teen pregnancy with MTV stars as Exhibit A. *The New York Times,* p. ST 1, 11.

Jekielek, S. M., Moore, K. A., Hair, E. C., & Scarupa, H. J. (2002, February). Mentoring: A promising strategy for youth development. *Child Trends Research Brief.* Retrieved from www.mentoring.ca.gov/pdf/MentoringBrief2002.pdf

Jutte, D., Roos, N., Brownell, M., Briggs, G., MacWilliam, L., & Roos, L. (2010). The ripples of adolescent motherhood: social, educational, and medical outcomes for children of teen and prior teen mothers. *Academic Pediatrics, 10*(5), 293–301.

Kirby, D. (2002). Antecedents of adolescent initiation of sex, contraceptive use, and pregnancy. *American Journal of Health Behavior, 26*(6), 473.

Kirby, D. (2007). *Emerging answers: Research findings on programs to reduce teen pregnancy and sexually transmitted diseases*. Washington, DC: National Campaign to Prevent Teen Pregnancy.

Kirby, D., Lepore, G., & Ryan, J. (2006). *Sexual risk and protective factors—Factors affecting teen sexual behavior, pregnancy, childbearing and sexually transmitted disease: Which are important? Which can you change?* Scotts Valley, CA: ETR Associates.

Lamaze International. (2010). *Creativity, connection and commitment: Supporting teens during the childbearing year*. Retrieved from http://www.lamaze.org/Childbirth Educators/Works hopsConference/SpecialtyWorkshops /SupportingTeen sDuringtheChildbearingYear/tabid/494 /Default.aspx

Luker, K. (2006). When sex goes to school: Warring views on sex—and sex education since the Sixties. New York: W. W. Norton & Company.

McDermott, E. & Graham, H. (2005). Resilient young mothering: Social inequalities, late modernity and the 'problem' of 'teenage' motherhood. *Journal of Youth Studies, 8*, 59–79.

(2011, April 18) More teen mom babies. *OK! Magazine, 16*, 32–35.

Pai-Espinosa, J. (2010). Young mothers at the margin: Why pregnant teens need support. *Children's Voice, 19*(3), 14–16.

Podgurski, MJ. (2009). *Voices to break the Cycle: A phenomenological inquiry into generational teen pregnancy*. (Doctoral dissertation). University of Phoenix, Phoenix, AZ. Raneri, L., & Constance, M. (2007, March). Social ecological predictors of repeat adolescent pregnancy. *Perspectives on Sexual & Reproductive Health, 39*(1), 39–47.

Young, T., Turner, J., Denny, G., Young, M. (2004, July). Examining external and internal poverty as antecedents of teen pregnancy. *American Journal of Health Behavior, 28*(4), 361–373.

EXPLORING THE ISSUE

Do Reality TV Shows Portray Responsible Messages about Teen Pregnancy?

Critical Thinking and Reflection

1. Reality television shows are growing in popularity among teenage and adult audience. How do issues around informed consent differ for adolescent versus adult participants in these shows?
2. Reality TV shows, such as *Teen Mom* and *16 and Pregnant*, feature the real-life struggles associated with becoming a parent in adolescence. The perspective featured is mainly that of the adolescent parent. What are the possible long-term implications for the children of these parents when they grow up with the legacy of having been a child reality-TV star? How might constructions of private and public life be different for these children?
3. Have you viewed a teen pregnancy reality TV show (or has someone you know viewed one)? What kind of discussion did you have about how realistic or unrealistic the show was? How might such a show impact a young person's sexual decision making?
4. Consider the "copy-cat" effect that may occur when adolescents witness other "real-life teens" becoming "famous" for their participation in reality TV shows. How might young people, with various levels of cognitive reasoning abilities, see these teenage parents as playing glamorous roles and desire to emulate them?

Is There Common Ground?

In the YES selection, Amy Kramer highlights the importance of teen-pregnancy reality TV shows in teen-pregnancy prevention efforts. She comments on the popularity of these shows, and the way they engage teenage viewers. As the MTV programs both entertain and educate, Kramer describes how they spark conversation among young people, how parents can utilize the shows as a starting point for discussion about their values, expectations, and how to prevent an unplanned pregnancy. She notes that the shows depict realistic consequences of sexual activity and teen pregnancy without glamorizing these outcomes.

Mary Jo Podgurski does not dispute the potential benefit that reality TV shows about teen pregnancy can have. She notes their merits and their good intentions. However, she is concerned about the potential for teens who appear on the show to be exploited. She says that, developmentally, teens can't fully "grasp the far-reaching implications of their decision to participate." Noting that young people may be blinded by fame, Podgurski also commented on how participants on the show may be selected for their "camera quality." She also expressed concern about society applying a "band-aid" solution to a complex, multifaceted issue, and that perhaps money would be better invested in programs that actually address the variety of antecedents to early pregnancy and risky behavior.

Is there room for *both* evidence-based, teen-pregnancy prevention programs *and* media-driven shows that open the door for discussion between parents and children? Are teen viewers able to differentiate between the "entertainment" and "education" components of these shows? What are the cautions or concerns associated with the media attention devoted to reality-TV "stars"—especially when they are adolescents?

Additional Resources

Chang, J., & Hopper, J. (2011, February 11). Pregnancy pressure: Is MTV's *Teen Mom* encouraging pregnancy for fame? Retrieved from http://abcnews.go.com/US /teen-pregnancy-fame-friends-teen-mom-star-jenelle /story?id=12891932

Dockterman, E. (2014, January 13). Does *16 and Pregnant* prevent or promote teen pregnancy? Retrieved from http://time .com/825/does-16-and-pregnant-prevent-or-promote -teen-pregnancy/

Dolgen, L. (2011, May 5). Why I created MTV's *16 and Pregnant*. Retrieved from http://www.cnn.com/2011 /SHOWBIZ/TV/05/04/teen.mom.dolgen/

Schneider, P. (2014, September/October). The "teen mom" effect. Retrieved from http://aspen.us/journal/editions /septemberoctober-2014/"teen-mom"-effect

Stanley, A. (2011, January 21). Motherhood's rough edges fray in reality TV . . . and baby makes reality TV. Retrieved from http://www.nytimes.com/2011/01/23/arts /television/23moms.html?_r=0

Internet References . . .

About Teen Pregnancy

http://www.cdc.gov/teenpregnancy/about/

MedlinePlus—Teenage Pregnancy

https://medlineplus.gov/teenagepregnancy.html

The Edna McConnell Clark Foundation

http://www.emcf.org

The National Campaign to Prevent Teen and Unplanned Pregnancy

http://www.thenationalcampaign.org/

Trends in Teen Pregnancy and Childbearing

http://www.hhs.gov/ash/oah/adolescent-health-topics
/reproductive-health/teen-pregnancy/trends.html

Selected, Edited, and with Issue Framing Material by:
Scott R. Brandhorst, *Southeast Missouri State University*

ISSUE

Is the Pressure to Have a Muscular Physique Recognized Equally Between Male and Female Adolescents?

YES: Marla E. Eisenberg, Melanie Wall, and Dianne Neumark-Sztainer, from "Muscle-enhancing Behaviors Among Adolescent Girls and Boys," *Pediatrics* (2012)

NO: Larry D. Burlew and W. Matthew Shurts, from "Men and Body Image: Current Issues and Counseling Implications," *Journal of Counseling & Development* (2013)

Learning Outcomes

After reading this issue, you will be able to:

- Demonstrate an understanding of body image as it pertains to adolescent males and females.
- Demonstrate an understanding of muscle-enhancing behaviors among adolescents.
- Critically analyze the suggestion that a drive for muscularity has infiltrated the female-ideal domain.
- Recognize similarities and differences between the genders in relation to body image.

ISSUE SUMMARY

YES: Marla E. Eisenberg, Melanie Wall, and Dianne Neumark-Sztainer looked at how the emphasis of muscularity has increased in recent decades and found muscle-enhancing behaviors were common for both boys and girls. In addition, the rates of engaging in muscle-enhancing behavior were higher than reported previously. The study also suggested that muscularity is an important component of body satisfaction for both genders.

NO: Larry D. Burlew and W. Matthew Shurts examined male adolescents and their body image dissatisfaction. More importantly, they looked at how this dissatisfaction is portrayed, and oftentimes missed by the experts in the field. The study examined reasons this occurs and discusses some interventions strategies.

The research consistently documents the fact that body image (or one's perception of his or her body image) is one of the many issues experienced by both adolescent males and females. There is some debate on the focus (i.e., thinness vs. muscularity) between the genders; however, there is an overwhelming recognition that adolescents are dissatisfied with their body image. The research examines many possible influences on the development of this dissatisfaction (i.e., social media; celebrities; parental influences; mental health issues) and the impact this dissatisfaction has on the adolescent's well-being. For example, Bearman & Stice (2008) note how body image and eating-related variables predict depression rates in adolescent females. Additionally, Rodgers, Faure, & Chabrol (2009)

discuss many sociocultural pressures and how these play in the development of body dissatisfaction, specially looking at parental attitudes and behaviors that influence this behavior.

Historically, the research has emphasized that sociocultural pressures lead more adolescent females to have a desire to be thin, while the reality is that very few have the genetic makeup to achieve this result. Furthermore, the male emphasis has been on muscularity, with more specifically achieving a V-shaped, lean, and muscular build as the body ideal. The research shows that woman have historically engaged in healthy and risky behaviors to achieve weight-loss and thinness and boys have engaged in strategies to increase muscle mass and the appearance of muscularity (Cafri et al., 2005; Riccardelli & McCabe, 2003). However, more recent research has shown that there has been a shift in terms of the focus of the ideal body image. While thinness and muscularity have major influence, we have seen these ideals replaced with a more "toned" and "fit" ideal. This can be seen by just walking down a magazine isle at a local store. There are many headlines, on both male- and female-oriented magazines, talking about how to achieve that "perfect" body—that "toned", "fit" body that everyone desires. Furthermore, many exercise, running, swimming, biking apps have been produced in the recent years to help us achieve this ideal body image. Given what we know about the profound impact sociocultural influences have on adolescents' perceptions of the ideal body image, is it safe to say that "muscularity" (or a tone, fit physique) is equally experienced across both genders? Do adolescent males and females in fact have more in common regarding shared drives for thinness and for muscularity than was once believed?

Given this information, it is important that an understanding of the influences, consequences, and outcomes related to body image in adolescents is understood. Markey (2010) provides us with knowledge in regards to the developmental precursors and consequences of body image. She provides us with a concept of what is body image, but also information related to how individuals feel about themselves as they are constantly changing throughout their lives. This is necessary to fully understand the impact of this behavior among adolescents.

In the YES and NO selections for this issue, body image and gender differences are examined. Eisenberg and colleagues examine the emphasis on muscularity within both genders and some of the correlational factors associated with this development. Furthermore, they explore specific behaviors adolescents engage in to increase their muscularity. Although Burlew and colleagues contend that the pressure for a muscular physique is primarily a male phenomenon, they do confirm the research that body image is an important issue for both genders, especially in adolescence. They also address the scarcity of understanding of how this body image phenomenon impacts males and provide further understanding and clarity on the development of this issue with this gender. Given the research on this topic and the understanding of sociocultural influences/pressures impacting adolescent development, it is safe to say that body image is one of the major influences on an adolescent's development and well-being, regardless of the type of physique they feel pressured to achieve.

YES

Marla E. Eisenberg, Melanie Wall, and Dianne Neumark-Sztainer

Muscle-enhancing Behaviors Among Adolescent Girls and Boys

In recent decades, images of men in the popular media of Western culture have grown increasingly large, lean, and muscular.[1,2] The male body has become more visible in advertising, with a stark increase in the proportion of undressed men beginning in the 1980s,[3] and representations of "ideal" physiques in children's action figures have evolved to be more muscular than even the largest human bodybuilders.[2] Boys' body dissatisfaction has simultaneously increased,[4] and research has demonstrated that exposure to images of extremely muscular models contributes to body dissatisfaction and muscle dysmorphia in young men.[5–7] Research regarding media images of women has focused almost exclusively on thinness as the cultural ideal for femininity,[8,9] but there is some indication that modern media figures combine slenderness with a toned and firm look that was not emphasized in previous generations.[10–12]

Muscle-enhancing behaviors have received considerable attention in the media and popular culture in recent years, as a steady stream of famous male and female athletes have been implicated in legal cases regarding their alleged use of performance-enhancing substances.[13–16] These cases often play out in the public arena, bringing awareness of muscle-building possibilities to young people around the United States and setting new standards for physical ability and appearance.

Given the emphasis on a muscular body in the media, questions exist about the use of muscle-enhancing behaviors among both athletes and the general population of youth. Existing research has focused largely on male athletes and bodybuilders in whom the prevalence of these behaviors is highest,[17,18] but recent studies with population-based samples of US youth indicate that 8.0% of females and 10.2% of males report using protein supplements,[19] 1.0% of females and 11.0% of males report using creatine,[20] and 2.2% of females and 4.3% of males report using steroids.[21] In a population-based study on adolescents, conducted by our research team over a decade ago (1998–1999), steroid use differed across racial/ethnic groups, with Asian American youth being more likely than other groups to report this behavior.[22,23] Adolescents participating in weight-related sports (defined as a sport in which it is

important to stay a certain weight, such as wrestling, gymnastics, or ballet) also had greater odds of steroid use than nonparticipants.[24] Existing research regarding the prevalence of more general muscle-enhancing behaviors such as changing one's diet or increasing exercise to generate muscle mass has been conducted with non-US samples[25–27] or boys only,[28,29] and research into the prevalence of unhealthy muscle-enhancing strategies, including protein powders, steroids, and other substances, requires replication and further exploration. Given the adverse health effects of steroids and other muscle-enhancing substances,[30,31] identifying populations at particular risk and understanding patterns of use hold considerable public health importance.

The current study therefore uses a recent large and diverse population-based sample of adolescents to examine the prevalence of 5 muscle-enhancing behaviors and differences across demographic characteristics, weight status, and sports team involvement.

Methods

Study Design and Population

Data come from EAT 2010 (Eating and Activity in Teens), a study of weight status, dietary intake, physical activity, weight control behaviors, and related factors among adolescents. The sample includes adolescents from 20 public middle schools and high schools in the Minneapolis/St. Paul metropolitan area of Minnesota that serve socioeconomically and racially/ethnically diverse communities. Surveys and anthropometric measures were completed by 2793 adolescents during the 2009–2010 academic year. Trained research staff administered surveys and measured adolescents' height and weight during selected health, physical education, and science classes. All study procedures were approved by the University of Minnesota's Institutional Review Board Human Subjects Committee and by the research boards of the participating school districts. Among adolescents who were at school on the days of survey administration, 96.9% had parental consent and chose to participate.

Survey and Measures

The EAT 2010 survey is a 235-item, self-report instrument assessing a range of factors of potential relevance to weight status and weight-related behaviors among adolescents.[4] Use of 5 muscle-enhancing behaviors was assessed with a question adapted from previous studies[19,25,28]: "How often have you done each of the following things in order to increase your muscle size or tone during the past year?" (never, rarely, sometimes, often for each method) and included (a) "Changed my eating," (b) "Exercised more," (c) "Used protein powder or shakes," (d) "used steroids," and (e) "used another muscle-building substance (such as creatine, amino acids, hydroxyl methylbutyrate [HMB], DHEA, or growth hormone)." For each of the 2 potentially healthy muscle-enhancing behaviors (changing eating and exercise habits), use was dichotomized as those who report the behavior "often" versus all other categories. For each of the 3 unhealthy behaviors (use of protein, steroids, or other substances), use was dichotomized as any use versus "never." A summary score indicating the use of any 3 or more behaviors was created from these items as an indicator of severity. The summary score was dichotomized as use of 3 or more behaviors versus fewer to capture a relatively high level of use.

Several demographic and personal characteristics were used as independent variables. Participants reported their gender and school level (grades 6–8 were grouped as middle school; grades 9–12 were grouped as high school). Race/ethnicity was assessed with 1 survey item "Do you think of yourself as (1) white, (2) black or African American, (3) Hispanic or Latino, (4) Asian American, (5) Hawaiian or Pacific Islander, or (6) American Indian or Native American" and respondents were asked to check all that apply. A "mixed/other" race category was created to include those who marked multiple race groups or indicated they were Hawaiian or Pacific Islander, because these groups were too small to permit meaningful analysis as separate categories. The majority (83%) of Asian participants were Hmong. Socioeconomic status was based primarily on parental education level, defined as the higher level of educational attainment of either parent. An algorithm was developed that also took into account family eligibility for public assistance, eligibility for free or reduced-cost school meals, and employment status of the mother or father.[32,33] BMI was calculated by using anthropometric data assessed by EAT 2010 staff. Height was measured without shoes (to the nearest 0.1 cm), and weight was measured without heavy outerwear or shoes (to the nearest 0.5 pound). Gender- and age-specific cut points for underweight, normal weight, overweight, and obesity were based on data from the Centers for Disease Control and Prevention.[34] Because muscle-enhancing behaviors are often associated with involvement in athletics, sports team participation was assessed by using the question, "During the past 12 months, on how many sports teams did you play?" Participants indicating they played on 1 or more teams were compared with those reporting no sports team involvement.

Data Analysis

All analyses were stratified by gender a priori because of previously observed differences in the use of each behavior. x^2 tests of association were used to compare the prevalence of each muscle-enhancing behavior (separately) across demographic and personal characteristics.

Logistic regression models in SAS version 9.1 were used to compare the odds of using each muscle-enhancing behavior across demographic characteristics, BMI categories, and sports participation. All covariates were entered simultaneously. To determine if each muscle-enhancing behavior differed by school, we examined for a significant school effect for each outcome and by each gender. These tests were nonsignificant in all but 1 case, protein powder in boys ($P < .01$); therefore, we did not control for school in the final models in the interest of simplicity.

Results

The mean age of the study population was 14.4 years (SD = 2.0); 46.1% were in middle school (6th to 8th grades) and 53.9% were in high school (9th to 12th grades). Participants were equally divided by gender (46.8% male, 53.2% female). The racial/ethnic backgrounds of the participants were as follows: 18.9% white, 29.0% African American or black, 19.9% Asian American, 16.9% Hispanic, 3.7% Native American, and 11.6% mixed or other. Sixty-two percent were in the lowest 2 categories of economic status, and 57.8% participated on at least 1 sports team.

Muscle-enhancing behaviors were common among both boys and girls (Table 1). Among boys, more than two-thirds reported changing their eating to increase their muscle size or tone, including 11.6% who did this often, and >90% exercised more to increase their muscle mass or tone, including 40.9% who reported doing so often. Unhealthy behaviors were also prevalent: 34.7% used protein powders or shakes, 5.9% reported using steroids, and 10.5% reported using some other muscle-enhancing substance. Girls were similarly involved, with a large majority changing eating and exercise habits, 21.2% reporting using protein powders, 4.6% using steroids, and 5.5% using other muscle-enhancing substances. Almost 12% of boys and 6.2% of girls reported using 3 or more of the behaviors examined here, indicating a relatively high level of use.

Associations Between Muscle-enhancing and Demographics, BMI, and Sports

Unadjusted Associations

x^2 tests indicated that rates of use (often for changing eating and exercise; "any" for protein, steroids, and other substances) were significantly higher for boys in comparison with girls ($P < .001$) for all behaviors, with the exception of changing eating ($x^2 = 0.2$, $P = .662$) and steroid use ($x^2 = 3.2$, $P = .076$). Table 2 shows the percentage of respondents reporting each type of muscle-enhancing

Table 1

Muscle-enhancing Behaviors Among Boys and Girls During the Past Year								
	Never		Rarely		Sometimes		Often	
	n	%	*n*	%	*n*	%	*n*	%
Boys (*n* = 1307)								
Change eating	410	31.5	312	24.0	426	32.8	151	11.6
Exercise more	114	8.8	146	11.3	507	39.1	530	40.9
Protein powder/shake	845	65.3	208	16.1	160	12.4	81	6.3
Steroids	1213	94.1	36	2.8	30	2.3	10	0.8
Other muscle-enhancing substances	1152	89.5	52	4.0	52	4.0	31	2.4
Girls (*n* = 1486)								
Change eating	559	37.8	279	18.9	462	31.2	180	12.2
Exercise more	286	19.4	249	16.9	539	36.5	403	27.3
Protein powder/shake	1165	78.8	193	13.1	91	6.2	29	2.0
Steroids	1410	95.6	48	3.3	13	0.9	4	0.3
Other muscle-enhancing substances	1397	94.5	47	3.2	24	1.6	10	0.7

behavior in each of the demographic and personal categories, and several significant differences are noted. In particular, those participating on sports teams were significantly more likely to report more muscle-enhancing behaviors than those not involved in sports. For example, the use of 3 or more behaviors was more than twice as high among boys who participated in sports versus nonparticipants (14.1 vs 6.7, $x^2 = 15.4$, $P < .001$).

Adjusted Associations
In models mutually adjusted for all covariates, several characteristics were significantly associated with the use of muscle-enhancing behaviors. As shown in Table 3, high school boys had significantly greater odds of using protein powders/shakes (odds ratio [OR] = 1.70, confidence interval [CI] = 1.30–2.21) and other muscle-enhancing substances (OR = 1.73, CI = 1.12–2.66) than those in middle school. Asian boys (primarily Hmong) had elevated odds of steroid use (OR = 3.51, CI = 1.13–10.92) compared with whites. BMI was significantly associated with changing eating, protein powders, and steroid use. Overweight and obese boys were more likely to report these behaviors than boys of average BMI. Sports team participation was significantly associated with all muscle-enhancing behaviors assessed here, with the exception of steroid use. For example, the odds of using protein powders or shakes were 2.05 (CI = 2.11–3.61) for boys on at least 1 sports team in comparison with those not on any sports teams.

Similar associations were found among girls (Table 3). Those in high school had lower odds of protein powders/shakes than those

in middle school. BMI category was significantly associated with changing eating, exercising, and protein powders. Asian girls stood out as having the highest odds of using steroids (OR = 3.37, CI = 1.29–8.80) and other muscle-enhancing substances (OR = 2.76, CI = 1.12–6.82). As with boys, girls who are obese (or overweight, in the case of protein use) had significantly elevated odds of reporting these behaviors than those of average weight. Sports team participation was positively associated with changing eating, exercising, and using protein powders/shakes.

Discussion

Results from the current study reveal that behaviors aimed at increasing muscle size or tone are extremely common: almost all students report doing at least 1 behavior with this as the goal, and up to one-third reported the use of unhealthy methods, such as taking steroids or other muscle-enhancing substances. Muscle enhancement is common and was particularly high among boys and those involved in sports teams, as seen previously.[19–21,23,24,29] However, use was not limited to these groups. This finding suggests that, in addition to a "thin ideal" and focus on leanness,[35,36] muscularity is an important component of body satisfaction for both genders.

The current study found reports of muscle-enhancing behaviors (ie, steroids and other substances) to be higher than other recent research with US youth.[20,21,37] These differences could be due to the demographic makeup of the different samples. The current study was almost 20% Asian youth (primarily Hmong), who reported higher rates of use

Table 2

Prevalence of Each Behavior Used to Increase Muscle Size or Tone During the Past Year

	n	Change Eating (Often) % (n)	Exercise (Often) % (n)	Protein (Ever) % (n)	Steroids (Ever) % (n)	Other Muscle Substances (Ever) % (n)	3 or More Behaviors % (n)
Boys							
School level		$x^2 = 1.37$, $P = .241$	$x^2 = 0.50$, $P = .482$	$x^2 = 12.2$, $P < .001^a$	$x^2 = 0.390$, $P = .532$	$x^2 = 2.63$, $P = .105$	$x^2 = 10.1$, $P = .002^a$
Middle school	598	10.5 (62)	39.8 (235)	29.7 (174)	5.5 (32)	9.0 (52)	8.9 (53)
High school	706	12.6 (89)	41.8 (294)	38.8 (275)	6.3 (44)	11.8 (83)	14.6 (103)
Race		$x^2 = 3.97$, $P = .554$	$x^2 = 8.03$, $P = .155$	$x^2 = 4.05$, $P = .542$	$x^2 = 19.7$, $P = .001^a$	$x^2 = 8.57$, $P = .127$	$x^2 = 4.86$, $P = .434$
White	277	12.3 (34)	46.0 (127)	32.1 (89)	1.4 (4)	6.9 (19)	12.3 (34)
African American	379	11.5 (43)	42.7 (160)	36.3 (135)	7.9 (29)	12.5 (46)	12.9 (49)
Hispanic	216	8.4 (18)	39.7 (85)	36.9 (79)	3.7 (8)	7.9 (17)	7.9 (17)
Asian	260	11.9 (31)	34.6 (90)	33.5 (87)	9.3 (24)	11.9 (31)	12.3 (32)
Native American	48	17.0 (8)	40.4 (19)	42.6 (20)	6.4 (3)	11.4 (5)	16.7 (8)
Mixed/other	124	13.1 (16)	39.0 (48)	30.6 (37)	6.7 (8)	13.3 (16)	12.1 (15)
SES	1247	$x^2 = 2.48$, $P = .647$	$x^2 = 4.26$, $P = .372$	$x^2 = 5.03$, $P = .284$	$x^2 = 12.3$, $P = .015^a$	$x^2 = 7.11$, $P = .130$	$x^2 = 4.19$, $P = .381$
Low	436	12.0 (52)	38.6 (167)	37.4 (161)	8.6 (37)	13.1 (56)	14.0 (61)
Medium-low	285	10.3 (29)	40.4 (113)	32.1 (90)	5.0 (14)	10.4 (29)	11.2 (32)
Medium	231	11.7 (27)	42.8 (98)	31.7 (73)	4.8 (11)	9.3 (21)	10.0 (23)
Medium-high	180	14.5 (26)	47.2 (85)	32.0 (57)	2.8 (5)	7.9 (14)	13.3 (24)
High	115	9.6 (11)	41.7 (48)	40.0 (46)	2.6 (3)	6.1 (7)	8.7 (10)
BMI category		$x^2 = 13.9$, $P = .003^a$	$x^2 = 4.52$, $P = .211$	$x^2 = 3.09$, $P = .379$	$x^2 = 10.5$, $P = .015^a$	$x^2 = 2.96$, $P = .398$	$x^2 = 7.0$, $P = .072$
Underweight	100	12.1 (12)	31.3 (31)	34.3 (34)	6.1 (6)	8.1 (8)	9.0 (9)
Average	647	8.9 (57)	41.2 (265)	32.3 (207)	3.8 (24)	9.3 (59)	9.9 (64)
Overweight	202	12.4 (25)	41.6 (84)	38.6 (78)	8.9 (18)	12.5 (25)	14.4 (29)
Obese	333	17.0 (56)	43.2 (142)	35.7 (117)	7.6 (25)	11.6 (38)	14.7 (49)
Sports teams		$x^2 = 8.12$, $P = .005^a$	$x^2 = 60.1$, $P < .001^a$	$x^2 = 25.2$, $P < .001^a$	$x^2 = 1.30$, $P = .254$	$x^2 = 4.80$, $P = .028^a$	$x^2 = 15.4$, $P < .001^a$
No	450	8.2 (37)	26.9 (120)	25.5 (114)	4.3 (19)	7.2 (32)	6.7 (30)
Yes	776	13.6 (105)	49.5 (381)	39.6 (304)	5.8 (44)	11.0 (84)	14.1 (109)
Girls							
School level		$x^2 = 0.01$, $P = .935$	$x^2 = 4.08$, $P = .043^a$	$x^2 = 9.26$, $P = .002^a$	$x^2 = 2.17$, $P = .141$	$x^2 = 0.62$, $P = .431$	$x^2 = 1.32$, $P = .251$
Middle school	689	12.2 (84)	29.8 (204)	24.7 (169)	5.3 (36)	6.0 (41)	7.0 (48)
High school	796	12.1 (96)	25.1 (199)	18.2 (144)	3.7 (29)	5.1 (40)	5.5 (44)
Race		$x^2 = 9.14$, $P = .103$	$x^2 = 5.60$, $P = .347$	$x^2 = 14.7$, $P = .012^a$	$x^2 = 27.5$, $P < .001^a$	$x^2 = 14.3$, $P = .014^a$	$x^2 = 10.5$, $P = .062$
White	248	12.1 (30)	30.2 (75)	17.7 (44)	2.4 (6)	2.8 (7)	4.0 (10)

Table 2

Prevalence of Each Behavior Used to Increase Muscle Size or Tone During the Past Year

	n	Change Eating (Often) % (n)	Exercise (Often) % (n)	Protein (Ever) % (n)	Steroids (Ever) % (n)	Other Muscle Substances (Ever) % (n)	3 or More Behaviors % (n)
African American	429	12.2 (52)	26.7 (113)	17.7 (75)	1.9 (8)	4.0 (17)	4.7 (20)
Hispanic	256	10.3 (26)	24.1 (61)	28.7 (73)	5.1 (13)	4.3 (11)	6.6 (17)
Asian	295	10.9 (32)	25.8 (76)	23.4 (69)	9.5 (28)	8.8 (26)	9.5 (28)
Native American	54	7.4 (4)	24.1 (13)	22.2 (12)	5.6 (3)	7.4 (4)	3.7 (2)
Mixed/other	198	18.2 (36)	32.3 (64)	19.8 (39)	3.6 (7)	7.6 (15)	7.6 (15)
SES		$x^2 = 3.22$, $P = .522$	$x^2 = 14.4$, $P = .006^a$	$x^2 = 1.43$, $P = .839$	$x^2 = 5.56$, $P = .235$	$x^2 = 5.84$, $P = .211$	$x^2 = 2.89$, $P = .576$
Low	636	12.1 (77)	24.1 (153)	21.8 (138)	4.8 (30)	6.3 (40)	6.5 (41)
Medium-low	310	11.0 (34)	24.0 (74)	20.8 (64)	5.2 (16)	4.9 (15)	4.8 (15)
Medium	240	13.9 (33)	33.1 (78)	22.3 (53)	4.7 (11)	6.3 (15)	7.9 (19)
Medium-high	167	9.6 (16)	34.7 (58)	19.8 (33)	3.0 (5)	3.6 (6)	5.4 (9)
High	88	15.9 (14)	31.8 (28)	17.1 (15)	0.0 (0)	1.1 (1)	4.6 (4)
BMI category		$x^2 = 36.1$, $P < .001^a$	$x^2 = 12.2$, $P = .007^a$	$x^2 = 15.8$, $P = .001^a$	$x^2 = 1.32$, $P = .725$	$x^2 = 0.26$, $P = .967$	$x^2 = 7.48$, $P = .058$
Underweight	61	6.6 (4)	21.3 (13)	24.6 (15)	1.6 (1)	4.9 (3)	1.6 (1)
Average	838	9.0 (75)	24.4 (203)	17.8 (148)	4.5 (37)	5.3 (44)	5.5 (46)
Overweight	286	13.3 (38)	30.6 (87)	23.9 (68)	5.0 (14)	6.0 (17)	6.3 (18)
Obese	280	22.2 (62)	33.8 (94)	28.3 (79)	4.3 (12)	5.7 (16)	9.3 (26)
Sports teams		$x^2 = 5.33$, $P = .021^a$	$x^2 = 50.5$, $P < .001^a$	$x^2 = 7.66$, $P = .006^a$	$x^2 = 1.05$, $P = .306$	$x^2 = 0.33$, $P = .567$	$x^2 = 0.02$, $P = .888$
No	666	10.0 (66)	18.3 (121)	18.2 (120)	5.1 (34)	5.9 (39)	6.3 (42)
Yes	755	14.0 (105)	35.2 (264)	24.2 (182)	4.0 (30)	5.2 (39)	6.5 (49)

SES, socioeconomic status.
[a] $P < .05$.

Table 3

Odds Ratio (and 95% CI) of Using Each Behavior to Increase Muscle Size or Tone During the Past Year, Mutually Adjusted for All Variables Shown

	Change Eating (Often)	Exercise (Often)	Protein (Ever)	Steroids (Ever)	Other Muscle Substances (Ever)	3 or More Behaviors
Boys						
School level						
Middle school	—	—	—	—	—	—
High school	1.27 (0.87–1.85)	1.05 (0.81–1.34)	1.70 (1.30–2.21)[a]	1.47 (0.83–2.62)	1.73 (1.12–2.66)[a]	2.08 (1.39–3.12)[a]
Race						
White	—	—	—	—	—	—

(continued)

Table 3

Odds Ratio (and 95% CI) of Using Each Behavior to Increase Muscle Size or Tone During the Past Year, Mutually Adjusted for All Variables Shown

	Change Eating (Often)	Exercise (Often)	Protein (Ever)	Steroids (Ever)	Other Muscle Substances (Ever)	3 or More Behaviors
African American	0.88 (0.52–1.51)	0.78 (0.54–1.12)	1.00 (0.69–1.46)	2.63 (0.85–8.07)	1.13 (0.59–2.13)	0.74 (0.43–1.28)
Hispanic	0.50 (0.25–0.99)[a]	0.75 (0.49–1.13)	1.18 (0.77–1.81)	1.23 (0.34–4.46)	0.70 (0.33–1.52)	0.42 (0.21–0.83)[a]
Asian	1.05 (0.59–1.88)	0.72 (0.48–1.08)	1.14 (0.75–1.72)	3.51 (1.13–10.92)[a]	1.53 (0.78–2.97)	0.94 (0.52–1.71)
Native American	1.18 (0.43–3.19)	0.97 (0.47–2.00)	1.75 (0.84–3.61)	1.98 (0.33–11.91)	1.06 (0.28–3.98)	1.03 (0.35–3.01)
Mixed/other	1.07 (0.53–2.16)	0.75 (0.46–1.22)	0.89 (0.53–1.49)	2.64 (0.71–9.90)	1.58 (0.72–3.48)	0.91 (0.44–1.89)
SES	1.01 (0.87–1.17)	1.05 (0.95–1.16)	1.04 (0.94–1.16)	0.74 (0.57–0.95)[a]	0.86 (0.72–1.01)	0.92 (0.79–1.07)
BMI category						
Underweight	1.64 (0.83–3.23)	0.71 (0.43–1.16)	1.18 (0.73–1.92)	2.13 (0.74–6.11)	1.12 (0.50–2.48)	1.17 (0.55–2.49)
Average	—	—	—	—	—	—
Overweight	1.27 (0.73–2.23)	1.02 (0.71–1.46)	1.61 (1.13–2.31)[a]	3.23 (1.53–6.83)[a]	1.67 (0.96–2.89)	1.70 (1.00–2.88)[a]
Obese	2.26 (1.47–3.47)[a]	1.31 (0.98–1.77)	1.21 (0.89–1.65)	2.83 (1.43–5.60)[a]	1.45 (0.89–2.36)	1.95 (1.25–3.04)[a]
Sports teams						
No	—	—	—	—	—	—
Yes	1.84 (1.21–2.79)[a]	2.76 (2.11–3.61)[a]	2.05 (1.55–2.71)[a]	1.44 (0.79–2.60)	1.66 (1.06–2.62)[a]	2.47 (1.57–3.87)[a]
Girls						
School level						
Middle school	—	—	—	—	—	—
High school	1.00 (0.72–1.41)	0.85 (0.66–1.09)	0.76 (0.58–0.99)[a]	0.75 (0.44–1.25)	0.83 (0.52–1.35)	0.76 (0.49–1.19)
Race						
White	—	—	—	—	—	—
African American	0.91 (0.54–1.55)	1.00 (0.68–1.47)	1.04 (0.66–1.62)	0.74 (0.24–2.22)	1.19 (0.47–3.06)	1.21 (0.54–2.74)
Hispanic	0.83 (0.46–1.52)	0.97 (0.63–1.51)	1.79 (1.12–2.85)[a]	1.84 (0.65–5.17)	1.34 (0.49–3.67)	1.75 (0.75–4.08)
Asian	0.97 (0.54–1.74)	1.20 (0.78–1.82)	1.49 (0.93–2.38)	3.37 (1.29–8.80)[a]	2.76 (1.12–6.82)[a]	2.54 (1.14–5.64)[a]
Native American	0.39 (0.11–1.36)	0.82 (0.39–1.72)	1.33 (0.62–2.83)	1.99 (0.46–8.58)	2.49 (0.68–9.17)	0.85 (0.18–4.13)
Mixed/other	1.45 (0.82–2.57)	1.14 (0.73–1.77)	1.09 (0.66–1.81)	0.96 (0.28–3.27)	2.10 (0.79–5.57)	1.72 (0.72–4.11)
SES	1.02 (0.88–1.17)	1.13 (1.02–1.09)[a]	0.99 (0.89–1.11)	0.90 (0.70–1.15)	0.90 (0.72–1.11)	1.06 (0.87–1.28)
BMI category						
Underweight	0.63 (0.22–1.79)	0.70 (0.37–1.35)	1.47 (0.79–2.75)	0.38 (0.05–2.85)	0.98 (0.29–3.30)	0.26 (0.04–1.95)
Average	—	—	—	—	—	—
Overweight	1.26 (0.80–1.97)	1.34 (0.97–1.84)	1.45 (1.03–2.05)[a]	1.25 (0.64–2.43)	1.12 (0.60–2.08)	1.10 (0.61–2.00)
Obese	2.76 (1.86–4.08)[a]	1.53 (1.11–2.10)[a]	1.90 (1.36–2.66)[a]	1.03 (0.51–2.10)	1.04 (0.55–1.97)	1.78 (1.05–3.03)[a]
Sports teams						
No	—	—	—	—	—	—
Yes	1.44 (1.02–2.04)[a]	2.30 (1.77–2.98)[a]	1.46 (1.11–1.92)[a]	0.89 (0.52–1.53)	0.93 (0.57–1.51)	1.06 (0.67–1.66)

SES, socioeconomic status; —, reference category
[a] $P < .05$.

of the muscle-enhancing behaviors examined here (compared with other racial groups in this study), but had lower representation in other recent studies.[20,21,37] Similarly, our sample was largely of lower economic status, a group that has not been separately reported on in earlier work. Future research including a wider variety of muscle-enhancing behaviors and using a more diverse and nationally representative sample of young people is needed to replicate the current study's findings.

This study's findings regarding associations between higher BMI and the use of muscle-enhancing behaviors are subject to possible alternate interpretations. Specifically, high BMI may reflect muscle mass rather than adiposity (particularly in males), which may result from use of the behaviors of interest. However, existing research has shown that overweight and obese young people engage in a variety of weight control and body change strategies at greater rates than their average-weight peers,[37–39] which suggests that weight status may indeed contribute to the adoption of the muscle-enhancing behaviors examined here. Further research with more comprehensive measures of body weight and composition is needed to disentangle this association.

Interestingly, this study did not find significant clustering of muscle-enhancing behaviors within schools. Rather than being driven by a particular school sports team coach or other features of a school's social landscape, this diffusion suggests that muscle-enhancing behaviors are widespread and influenced by factors beyond school, likely encompassing social and cultural variables such as media messages and social norms of behavior more broadly. As with the large body of literature investigating an array of influences on body dissatisfaction relating to thinness, continued research into media portrayals of muscularity,[5–7] as well as interpersonal interactions such as weight- and shape-teasing, or sharing muscle-enhancing substances among peers may be promising avenues for understanding the parallel phenomenon of dissatisfaction with regard to muscularity and unhealthy behaviors aimed at muscle enhancement.

Data for the current study come from a single state and, as such, may not be representative of muscle-enhancing behaviors elsewhere in the United States or in other countries. In addition, all measures were self-reported and included the use of illegal substances, which may have led to underreporting. Finally, more detailed measures of muscle-enhancing behaviors and body weight were not assessed. Specifically, we do not have data regarding whether respondents who changed their eating adopted healthy or unhealthy dietary changes, and use of several other muscle-enhancing substances were assessed in a single item. Similarly, the measure of BMI does not distinguish adiposity from weight because of muscle mass; it is therefore possible that associations seen here were due to increased muscle resulting from the behaviors under study. Future research should include other assessments of body weight and composition to further address this question.

However, the large and diverse sample from multiple schools permitted statistically valid analyses of relatively uncommon behaviors and smaller groups not typically considered in epidemiological research (eg, certain racial groups) and allowed for an examination of clustering by school. Finally, this study used 5 measures

of muscle-enhancing behavior spanning the range from general health behaviors (eg, exercising) to extremely unhealthy behaviors (eg, steroid use),which provides a more comprehensive picture of muscle-enhancing efforts among a US sample of male and female youth than has been available previously.

Conclusions

Pediatricians and other health care providers should ask their adolescent patients about muscle-enhancing behaviors. Conceptualization of these behaviors should include frequent use of seemingly healthy behaviors (eg, changing eating and exercising) done with the goal of increasing muscle mass or tone. Although these may be beneficial, compulsive or excessive use is cause for concern,[37] because they may be a precursor to the development of more severe and unhealthy behaviors over time. Health care providers should counsel adolescent patients about appropriate exercise, general nutrition, and the lack of efficacy and potential dangers of muscle-enhancement products. Given the observed associations with sports participation, sports physicals may present a particularly salient opportunity to initiate these conversations.

Prevention and intervention programs targeting muscle-enhancing behaviors among youth are needed for both boys and girls and should include parents, teachers, and coaches as well as youth themselves. Broadening existing body image programs to address muscularity as well as thinness would be an appropriate and cost-effective approach. Although it is appropriate to promote physical activity in youth, which may have desirable benefits in terms of health and body composition, care should be taken to emphasize moderation in behaviors and to focus on skill development, fitness, and general health rather than development of a muscular appearance. Significant differences found in select race categories suggest that prevention programs might be strengthened by incorporating culturally relevant messages and targeting communities where rates are highest. Similarly, although muscle enhancing behaviors were reported by young people in organized sports as well as those not on teams, prevention activities targeting coaches, sports teams, and their parents are likely to be beneficial, given the significantly higher prevalence of these behaviors among sports participants.

References

1. Leit RA, Pope HG Jr, Gray JJ. Cultural expectations of muscularity in men: the evolution of playgirl centerfolds. *Int J Eat Disord.* 2001;29(1):90–93

2. Pope HG Jr, Olivardia R, Gruber A, Borowiecki J. Evolving ideals of male body image as seen through action toys. *Int J Eat Disord.* 1999;26(1):65–72

3. Pope HG Jr, Olivardia R, Borowiecki JJ III, Cohane GH. The growing commercial value of the male body: a longitudinal survey of advertising

in women's magazines. *Psychother Psychosom.* 2001;70(4):189–192

4. Neumark-Sztainer D, Wall M, Larson N, Story M, Fulkerson JA, Eisenberg ME. Secular trends in weight status and weight-related attitudes and behaviors in adolescents from 1999-2010. *Prev Med.* 2012;54(1):77–81

5. Leit RA, Gray JJ, Pope HG Jr. The media's representation of the ideal male body: a cause for muscle dysmorphia? *Int J Eat Disord.* 2002;31(3):334–338

6. Daniel S, Bridges SK. The drive for muscularity in men: media influences and objectification theory. *Body Image.* 2010;7(1):32–38

7. Lorenzen LA, Grieve FG, Thomas A. Exposure to muscular male models decreases men's body satisfaction. *Sex Roles.* 2004;51(11–12):743–748

8. Andrist LC. Media images, body dissatisfaction, and disordered eating in adolescent women. *MCN Am J Matern Child Nurs.* 2003;28(2):119–123

9. Hogan MJ, Strasburger VC. Body image, eating disorders, and the media. *Adolesc Med State Art Rev.* 2008;19(3):521–546, x–xi

10. Grogan S. *Body Image: Understanding Body Dissatisfaction in Men, Women, and Children.* 2nd ed. London, England: Routledge; 2008

11. Gruber AJ. A more muscular female body ideal. In: Thompson JK, Cafri G, eds. *The Muscular Ideal Psychological, Social, and Medical Perspectives.* Washington, DC: American Psychological Association; 2007: 217–234

12. Homan K. Athletic-ideal and thin-ideal internalization as prospective predictors of body dissatisfaction, dieting, and compulsive exercise. *Body Image.* 2010;7(3):240–245

13. Associated Press. Barry Bonds indicted. November 15, 2007. Available at: www.sfgate.com/flat/archive/2007/11/15/news/archive/2007/11/15/state/n141013S18.html. Accessed October 5, 2011

14. Wikipedia. List of doping cases in sport. Available at: en.wikipedia.org/wiki/List_of_doping_cases_in_sport#cite_note-61 Accessed October 5, 2011

15. Baum B. Report positive doping test for Marion Jones. *USA Today.* August 19, 2006. Available at: http://usatoday30.usatoday.com/sports/Olympics/summer/track/2006-08-18-marion-jones-doping-report_x.htm. Accessed October 5, 2011

16. Puma M. Not the size of the dog in the fight. Available at: espn.go.com/classic/biography/s/Alzado_Lyle.html. Accessed October 5, 2011

17. Metzl JD, Small E, Levine SR, Gershel JC. Creatine use among young athletes. *Pediatrics.* 2001;108(2):421–425

18. Smith J, Dahm DL. Creatine use among a select population of high school athletes. *Mayo Clin Proc.* 2000;75(12):1257–1263

19. Field AE, Austin SB, Camargo CA Jr, et al. Exposure to the mass media, body shape concerns, and use of supplements to improve weight and shape among male and female adolescents. *Pediatrics.* 2005;116(2). Available at: www.pediatrics.org/cgi/content/full/116/2/e214

20. Johnston LD, O'Malley PM, Bachman JG, Schulenberg JE, eds. *Secondary School Students.* Ann Arbor, MI: Institute for Social Research, The University of Michigan; 2010. *Monitoring the Future. National Survey Results on Drug Use, 1975–2010;* vol 1

21. Centers for Disease Control and Prevention. Youth Risk Behavior Surveillance–United States, 2009. *MMWR Morb Mortal Wkly Rep.* 2010;59(SS-5):1–142

22. vandenBerg P, Neumark-Sztainer D, Cafri G, Wall M. Steroid use among adolescents: longitudinal findings from Project EAT. *Pediatrics.* 2007;119(3):476–486

23. Irving LM, Wall M, Neumark-Sztainer D, Story M. Steroid use among adolescents: findings from Project EAT. *J Adolesc Health.* 2002;30(4):243–252

24. Vertalino M, Eisenberg ME, Story M, Neumark-Sztainer D. Participation in weight-related sports is associated with higher use of unhealthful weight-control behaviors and steroid use. *J Am Diet Assoc.* 2007;107(3):434–440

25. McCabe MP, Ricciardelli LA. Body image and body change techniques among young adolescent boys. *Eur Eat Disord Rev.* 2001;9(5):335–347

26. McCabe MP, Ricciardelli LA. Parent, peer, and media influences on body image and strategies to both increase and decrease body size among adolescent boys and girls. *Adolescence.* 2001;36(142):225–240

27. McCreary DR, Sasse DK. An exploration of the drive for muscularity in adolescent boys and girls. *J Am Coll Health.* 2000;48(6):297–304

28. Smolak L, Murnen SK, Thompson JK. Sociocultural influences and muscle building in adolescent boys. *Psychol Men Masc.* 2005;6(4):227–239

29. Cafri G, van den Berg P, Thompson JK. Pursuit of muscularity in adolescent boys: relations among biopsychosocial variables and clinical outcomes. *J Clin Child Adolesc Psychol.* 2006;35(2):283–291

30. Fernandez MMF, Hosey RG. Performance-enhancing drugs snare nonathletes, too. *J Fam Pract.* 2009;58(1):16–23

31. *National Institute on Drug Abuse Research Report Series.* Anabolic Steroid Abuse. NIH Publication 00-3721. Available at: www.drugabuse.gov/sites/default/files/rrsteroids_0.pdf. Accessed September 1, 2011

32. Breiman L, Friedman J, Olshen R, Stone C. *Classification and Regression Trees.* Belmont, CA: Wadsworth International Group; 1984

33. Neumark-Sztainer D, Story M, Hannan PJ, Croll J. Overweight status and eating patterns among adolescents: where do youths stand in comparison with the healthy people 2010 objectives? *Am J Public Health.* 2002;92(5):844–851

34. Kuczmarski RJ, Ogden CL, Grummer-Strawn LM, et al. CDC growth charts: United States. *Adv Data.* 2000;(314):1–27

35. Stice E. Risk and maintenance factors for eating pathology: a meta-analytic review. *Psychol Bull.* 2002;128(5):825–848

36. Stice E, Whitenton K. Risk factors for body dissatisfaction in adolescent girls: a longitudinal investigation. *Dev Psychol.* 2002;38(5):669–678

37. Cafri G, Thompson JK, Ricciardelli L, McCabe M, Smolak L, Yesalis C. Pursuit of the muscular ideal: Physical and psychological consequences and putative risk factors. *Clin Psychol Rev.* 2005;25(2):215–239

38. Boutelle K, Neumark-Sztainer D, Story M, Resnick M. Weight control behaviors among obese, overweight, and nonover-weight adolescents. *J Pediatr Psychol.* 2002;27(6):531–540

39. Neumark-Sztainer D, Story M, Hannan PJ, Perry CL, Irving LM. Weight-related concernsand behaviors among overweight and nonoverweight adolescents: implications for preventing weight-related disorders. *Arch Pediatr Adolesc Med.* 2002;156(2):171–178

MARLA E. EISENBERG works in the Division of Adolescent Health and Medicine, Department of Pediatrics and Division of Epidemiology & Community Health, School of Public Health at the University of Minnesota, Minneapolis and has expertise in the area of adolescent development. MELANIE WALL works in the Departments of Biostatistics and Psychiatry at Columbia University, New York and has expertise in biostatistics. DIANNE NEUMARK-SZTAINER works in the Division of Epidemiology & Community Health, School of Public Health at the University of Minnesota, Minneapolis and has expertise in the area of adolescent health.

Larry D. Burlew and W. Matthew Shurts

Men and Body Image: Current Issues and Counseling Implications

*B*ody image is defined as "perceptions of and attitudes toward one's own physical appearance" (Phillips & deMan, 2010, p. 171). Historically, issues with body image were usually associated with women. However, it is apparent that men also experience body image issues related to their weight, body shape, and appearance, which can lead to detrimental physical and emotional consequences (Harvey & Robinson, 2003; Maida & Armstrong, 2005; Schneider, Cockcroft, & Hook, 2008). Grieve, Truba, and Bowersox (2009) estimated that there are millions of men who experience some level of body dissatisfaction. Approximately 10%–15% of eating disorder diagnoses are assigned to men (Carlat, Camargo, & Herzog, 1997), and 2.2% of males meet the criteria for body dysmorphic disorder (Koran, Abujaoude, Large, & Serpe, 2008). However, men may experience and manifest body image issues differently than women because of a variety of factors. This can make assessment, diagnosis, and intervention with men challenging for counselors who do not have specific knowledge of men's tendencies regarding body image issues.

Sociocultural and media representations of the ideal male body have changed and become more visible, causing men to think more critically about their bodies. The modern ideal male body image focuses on being muscular, toned, lean, physically fit, masculine, young, powerful, self-confident, and sexually desirable (Filiault, 2007; Kimmel & Mahalik, 2004; Schneider et al., 2008; Silva, 2006; Slevin, 2008). This ideal body image receives global attention, and men who internalize this ideal body image may experience body image dissatisfaction/distress (BID) at various levels (Grieve et al., 2009). Additionally, men and male adolescents feel "more pressure now to conform to a particular body type" (McCabe & McGreevy, 2010, p. 1008). Therefore, issues related to body image now occur more often among males, with a variety of labels and diagnoses assigned to the symptoms presented. This includes formal *Diagnostic and Statistical Manual of Mental Disorders–Text Revision* (*DSM-IV-TR* American Psychiatric Association [APA], 2000) diagnoses such as body dysmorphic disorder and eating disorders, non-*DSM-IV-TR* diagnoses like muscle dysmorphia, and

problematic symptoms (e.g., body shame). However, Brennen, Lalonde, and Bain (2010) noted the utility of these types of distinctions, viewing "body image as a continuum ranging from no body image disturbance to extreme body image disturbance" (p. 130).

Researchers also have shown differences in meaning and reactions to body image among various populations. For example, McCabe and McGreevy (2010) claimed that men of all ages relate body image less with appearance and more with "function, fitness and health" (p. 1003). On the other hand, Silva (2006) found that younger men were actually trying to enhance their physical image and were more concerned with their shapes (i.e., the way they physically look to others) than with their specific weights. Galli, Reel, Petrie, Greenleaf, and Carter (2011) and Lobera, Cid, Fernandez, and Rios (2011) reported that adolescents and men involved in sports felt pressure to conform to body weight expectations based on the sport being played, rather than concerns about a specific body type or physical appearance.

Culture can also play a role in differentiating issues with body image, but as Ricciardelli, McCabe, Williams, and Thompson (2007) noted, "there is no consistent pattern which summarizes the nature of body image concerns across the different cultures" (p. 582). Although a review of all applicable results is beyond the scope of our article, we present several notable findings here. The results of the most recent National Comorbidity Study (Adolescent Supplement) noted that, whereas White adolescents had the highest rates of anorexia, Hispanics had the highest rates of bulimia (Swanson, Crow, LeGrange, Swendsen, & Merikangas, 2011). Lobera et al. (2011) claimed that Latin American adolescents were more prone to greater body dissatisfaction than Spanish adolescents. Pacific Islanders seemed to prefer larger body sizes and ranked themselves as "underweight" or at the right weight when having a higher body mass index than White individuals (Ricciardelli et al., 2007).

Although BID is an issue for men, it may go unrecognized because men are less likely to present with overt symptoms, and practitioners and other professionals (e.g., college counselors or coaches) may not recognize subclinical behaviors related to BID (Davey & Bishop, 2006; Filiault, 2007; Grieve et al., 2009).

Additionally, there is no single description of body image problems that men may experience, and research on the extent of the problem and best treatment practices is lacking (Davey & Bishop, 2006; Green & Pritchard, 2003). Therefore, the purpose of this article is to provide counselors with an overview of the symptoms and risk factors associated with body image problems and recommend preliminary interventions for addressing BID in men.

Diagnoses, Symptoms, and Risk Factors Relating to Body Image Issues

Because there has been a cultural shift that emphasizes an ideal male body image, men are increasingly experiencing a variety of body image issues. Numerous factors contribute to the onset of BID, and symptoms vary across the BID continuum (Brennen et al., 2010). To increase understanding and recognition, we review some of the diagnoses and the most common BID symptoms and risk factors associated with BID.

BID-Related Diagnoses

Although BID is a general term used to describe a wide range of issues related to body image, it is not a formal *DSM-IV-TR* diagnosis. Several diagnoses are related to or comorbid with BID. According to the *DSM-IV-TR* (APA, 2000), body dysmorphic disorder (BDD) can be diagnosed when an individual is preoccupied with an imagined or slight physical defect in his appearance and the preoccupation causes clinically significant distress or impairment. BDD is classified as a somatoform disorder, a category of disorders in which physical symptoms are present without an identifiable physical cause.

Muscle dysmorphia (MD) is not included as a formal diagnosis in the *DSM-IV-TR,* although there is a substantial body of research outlining diagnostic criteria for this disorder (Grieve et al., 2009). Olivardia (2002) provided three primary components for the diagnosis: (a) a preoccupation with the idea that the body is not muscular or lean enough; (b) a clinically significant impairment in life activities due to the preoccupation; and (c) the preoccupation focuses on having insufficient musculature or being too small, rather than other aspects of appearance. Some researchers and practitioners classify MD as a subcategory of BDD (Pope & Katz, 1994), whereas others argue that MD is within the obsessive-compulsive disorder (OCD; e.g., Maida & Armstrong, 2005) or eating disorder (ED) spectra (e.g., Grieve, 2007).

The criteria presented in the DSM for each of the three types of EDs (anorexia nervosa, bulimia nervosa, and eating disorder not otherwise specified [EDNOS]) include at least one component related to body image (e.g., "intense fear of gaining weight or becoming fat, even though underweight"; "self evaluation is unduly influenced by body shape and weight"; APA, 2000). In brief, someone diagnosed with anorexia is unwilling to maintain a body weight

at or above a minimally normal weight for his age and height (e.g., refusing to eat, purging), whereas a diagnosis of bulimia involves recurrent binge eating followed by compensatory behaviors (e.g., purging, excessive exercise), but the individual is at or above a normal weight.

Although the aforementioned formal diagnoses all have body image criteria, many men with BID do not reach a formal diagnosis threshold. However, body image can still be a central and/or significant component of their presenting issue(s). Such conditions are typically termed *subclinical* to convey the lack of a formal diagnosis. For example, the core symptoms of BDD could be present but may not induce a significant impairment in functioning. Zimmerman and Mattia (1998) suggested that the rate of such subclinical conditions is quite high among psychiatric populations, noting that BDD symptoms have a comorbidity rate with other psychiatric disorders. Grieve et al. (2009) noted that there might be millions of men in this subclinical category.

Common Symptoms and Risk Factors

Although some symptoms and risk factors experienced by men mirror those presented by women, many are specific to the male population. For example, men are at greater risk for atypical eating disorders (EDNOS) as well as substance abuse issues (Carlat et al., 1997). Men with bulimia also tend to wait longer before seeking treatment because of the shame of having a "female" disorder, although men with anorexia are more likely to be referred sooner due to a primary care physician noticing the weight loss (Carlat et al., 1997). Likewise, men's and women's personal experiences of body image issues vary (Brennan, Lalonde, & Bain, 2010). Body image-related disorders and BDD specifically have a high rate of comorbidity with OCD, depression, and anxiety disorders (Veale et al., 1996). Thus, evidence of these disorders may also suggest a related body image issue. Sometimes the connection may be straightforward, like having the compulsive need to monitor weight or check appearances in a mirror, which is symptomatic of MD as well as OCD. However, symptomatology may not lead directly to a body image-related diagnosis. For example, a diagnosis of BDD has been linked to higher incidences of suicide attempts in men (Phillips et al., 2005). Although an attempt on one's life is the extreme manifestation of depression, any depressive symptomatology could be a red flag for a body image-related issue if additional factors or symptoms support such a diagnosis.

Body dissatisfaction in a man, which may present as viewing himself as obese and needing to lose weight and add muscle, underweight and desiring to gain weight and/or muscle, or striving for a more perfect body, is often a symptom of clinical significance and a primary criterion for MD. Just as Rogers (1961) noted that a discrepancy between one's real self and ideal self led to internal distress and lack of self-acceptance, the same is true with body image. The farther away a man is from his ideal, the greater his dissatisfaction, raising the likelihood of drastic and potentially dangerous actions taken to close the gap (Grieve, 2007). Dissatisfaction can yield symptoms of BID including reverse anorexia (i.e., unhealthy desire and attempts to gain muscle mass), use of steroids or other performance- or body-enhancing drugs, avoidance of body exposure, exercise dependence, appearance-related low self-esteem, mirror-checking behaviors, social alienation, greater gender role conflict, ritualistic behaviors, impaired insight, perfectionism, feelings of shame and anxiety, mood swings, sexual performance issues and dysfunctions, and excessive body comparison (Chaney, 2008; Crocker, 2002; Davey & Bishop, 2006; Harvey & Robinson, 2003; Maida & Armstrong, 2005; O'Dea & Abraham, 2002; Oney, Cole, & Sellers, 2011; Raevuori et al., 2008; Tiggemann & Kuring, 2004).

Research has shown that sexual orientation may have an effect on the prevalence of body image-related issues among men. Results suggest that gay men are at greater risk for EDs than heterosexual men are (Boisvert & Harrell, 2009), with homosexuality/bisexuality shown as a specific risk factor in men who develop bulimia (Carlat et al., 1997). In addition, Siconolfi, Halkitis, Allomong, and Burton (2009) found that White and Latino gay men reported higher ED scores than did African American gay men.

Involvement in certain sports, particularly those requiring the individual to maintain a prescribed weight (e.g., wrestling, gymnastics) or increase body mass (e.g., football, weightlifting), put men at a higher risk for developing an ED or MD (Baum, 2006; Galli et al., 2011; Grieve, 2007). For example, the estimated rate of MD in bodybuilders is as high as 10% (Pope & Katz, 1994). Additionally, athletes are more likely to use creatine in an effort to achieve their desired body type (Naylor, Gardner, & Zaichkowsky, 2001); this type of drug use could be viewed as a symptom of MD. However, the issue is by no means unique to athletes, because diagnoses of MD are increasing among the male college population (Davey & Bishop, 2006) and can have the added complication of steroid use (McCreary, Hildebrandt, Heinberg, Boroughs, & Thompson, 2007). In general, BIDs tend to be more severe among younger men (i.e., teenagers, college age, young adults) both within gay and heterosexual populations (Davey & Bishop, 2006). This leads to higher rates of formal (e.g., BDD, EDs) and informal (e.g., MD) diagnoses among these populations. However, the full range of BID can and does occur across the life span. Older gay men actually have reported more body dissatisfaction (but not necessarily a diagnosable BID) than younger cohorts (Siconolfi et al., 2009), although they tended to focus on health and well-being rather than appearance (McCabe & McGreevy, 2010).

Counseling Implications

Men with BID experience a range of unhealthy behaviors and cognitive distortions that often lead to symptoms of depression, low self-esteem, and even suicidal ideation (Kimmel & Mahalik, 2004; Raevuori et al., 2008; Wade, George, & Atkinson, 2009). Treatment

must address specific behaviors (e.g., binge eating, dieting, excessive exercising) and cognitive distortions (e.g., fixation on the ideal body image) while helping men acknowledge and normalize the concept of BID in men. When reporting to counseling or seeing a doctor, many men deny having BID or do not understand the seriousness of their symptoms (Grieve et al., 2009; O'Dea & Abraham, 2002). Additionally, professionals may not recognize or diagnose BID, associating such symptoms and/or disorders with women more than with men (Greenhill, 2003; Harvey & Robinson, 2003). From a holistic perspective, both prevention and intervention strategies are needed to help men realize that they may have body image problems and to help professionals appropriately recognize the subclinical symptoms that may be overlooked.

Prevention

Awareness of the body image issues men experience is an overriding goal for prevention strategies, especially because many people still incorrectly believe that only women experience BID. Prevention strategies can help reduce the stigma attached to BID so that men are less likely to feel shame and guilt and are more likely to seek counseling when they are symptomatic. Also, with effective prevention strategies, professionals can be more prepared to recognize clinical and subclinical BID behaviors (Davey & Bishop, 2006; Grieve et al., 2009).

Prevention Strategies

Prevention strategies are largely psychoeducational, although advocacy is also important. For psychoeducational strategies, information about BID must be shared with the general public, as well as professionals working with male adolescents and men. The strategic topics are multifaceted and include the following: distinguishing between healthy and unhealthy nutrition and eating behaviors as well as between helpful fitness routines and excessive or unproductive fitness behaviors; identifiable risk factors indicating BID or a diagnosis such as BDD; protective factors that can be nurtured to avoid BID (e.g., a stronger internal locus of control); effect of media on body image (Wade et al., 2009); racial/ethnic differences in related symptoms or disorders (Siconolfi et al., 2009); cultural differences in body image ideal (Oney et al., 2011); age differences with respect to body image issues (Siconolfi et al., 2009) and coping strategies (McCabe & McGreevy, 2010); and information about comorbid issues such as MD and mood disorders (Maida & Armstrong, 2005).

Psychoeducational programs can be presented in many formats (e.g., daylong workshop, program series of six 2-hour seminars) and may occur at schools, universities, community centers, senior centers, or young men's Christian associations (YMCAs). Large companies that sponsor wellness programs may be able to effectively reach working men. Educational strategies can be virtual, developed for popular informational websites as YouTube. Education can also occur in the form of print articles that target men, for example, the *AARP Bulletin* (for older men), student newspapers, *OUT* (for gay men), or culturally targeted magazines such as *Essence* for African Americans.

Because BID has not always been recognized as occurring among men (Davey & Bishop, 2006; Filiault, 2007), prevention strategies are not presented in the counseling literature. However, strategies suggested for related disorders or for use with women often can be modified to fit the needs of men. For example, Choate's (2007) Body Resilience Model is a prevention program designed for young women, but aspects of the model might also be helpful in treating men with BID. Choate included five protective factors as part of the program: Family and Peer Support, Gender Role Satisfaction, Global and Physical Self- Esteem, Coping Strategies and Critical Thinking Skills, and Holistic Wellness and Balance. Choate uses cognitive reinforcing exercises to "reinforce [people's] acceptance of each individual's unique body type" and trains participants to assess healthy body shape and to develop life skills, such as problem solving. Although these techniques and skills were not originally designed for the male client, they align well with the counseling needs of men who are experiencing BID (see Davey & Bishop, 2006).

In addition to Choate's model, specific prevention workshops and programs can benefit men about important issues surrounding BID. Sample workshop topics include media literacy and advocacy (Agliata & Tantleff-Dunn, 2004; Becker, Smith, & Ciao, 2006; Wade et al., 2009), building positive self-esteem not solely based on appearance (Grieve et al., 2009), healthy nutrition and fitness, and skills for making healthy lifestyle choices (Davey & Bishop, 2006; Grieve et al., 2009). Ultimately, any targeted workshop provides men with "criteria and reference values closer to psychological and human qualities, and further removed from a physical image which.., only reflects the more external and superficial part of a person" (Esnaola, Rodriguez, & Goni, 2010, p. 28).

Family members and peers also may reinforce the male sociocultural ideals for thinness or muscularity (Choate, 2007; Green & Pritchard, 2003; McCabe & McGreevy, 2010); therefore, it is important to educate them about BID. In addition, mental health professionals and others working with men (e.g., coaches, teachers, doctors, religious leaders) need to be trained to understand the seriousness of BID and recognize risk factors and symptoms of BID.

Direct Intervention

More research on effective treatment strategies for men who have BID is needed, and as Grieve et al. (2009) suggested for MD, treatment strategies will "have to [be] borrowed from established treatments that have been used with other disorders, such as eating disorders" (p. 310). Furthermore, because of this lack of evidence-based strategies with men, counselors may need to implement

interventions that were originally designed for use with women and closely monitor results. Although there are no definitive best practices for treating male clients with BID, the following treatment recommendations are suggestions for addressing BID.

Assessment

Because BID issues often are not the stated presenting problem for men, counselors can ask questions about eating patterns, exercise routines, body image, weight or shape concerns, feelings about appearance, use of enhancing supplements, importance of social interaction versus body development, sense of distress related to body image, and ideas about the ideal male body. Ideas for sample questions have been suggested by researchers (e.g., Davy & Bishop, 2006; Grieve et al., 2009; O'Dea & Abraham, 2002), including "Do you compare yourself to other men and how do you feel about the comparison?" "How often do you find yourself checking your body in the mirror or asking others about your overall appearance?" "What happens if you find that you cannot exercise for a week?" "Do you think women (or men) are as attracted to you as they are to other men?" "Do you often feel good about your body shape and weight?" We suggest that the client is asked simply, Do you like the way you look? and How much time do you spend trying to change something about yourself?. Any of these questions may begin a discussion about a client's body image and any related distress, patterns of behavior, or thinking that might indicate an assessment of BID.

Various psychological instruments have been developed to measure symptoms of BID or related disorders. For example, the Body Image Ideals Questionnaire (BIQ) was developed to "measure self-perceived discrepancies from and importance of internalized ideals for multiple physical characteristics [such as height, muscle tone, body proportions, weight]" (Cash & Szymanski, 1995, p. 468). This instrument is a subjective self-report tool that assesses a person's degree of body dissatisfaction; although BIQ was originally normed on an entirely female sample, it has been used in studies with men to measure BID (e.g., Kimmel & Mahalik, 2004). In addition, instruments that measure men's perceptions of their own masculinity have utility in assessing potential BID. For example, the Meanings of Masculinity measures "men's conceptions of masculinity" (Siconolfi et al., 2009, p. 258). Developed by Halkitis, Green, and Wilton (2004), the instrument comprises three subscales and was developed for use with gay men. The alphas for the subscales in the Siconolfi et al. (2009) study and the Halkitis et al. (2004) study were as follows, respectively: masculinity as physical appearance (.82, .81), as social behavior (.67.74), and as sexual behavior (.84, .83); scores on the Physical Appearance subscale would be especially relevant when assessing for possible BID. Other instruments measuring elements of perceived masculinity such as the Conformity to Male Norms Inventory (Mahalik, Talmadge, Locke, & Scott, 2005) and the Masculine Body Ideal Distress Scale (Kimmel & Mahalik, 2004) were designed specifically for male populations and have shown evidence of appropriate validity and reliability in assessing BID-related constructs.

Individual and Group Counseling

For men who exhibit risk factors and/or symptoms of BID, individual or group counseling is recommended. Although the focus of counseling depends on the client's symptoms, the overall goal is "to increase weight and appearance satisfaction, and decrease distress about body feelings" (Wade et al., 2009, p. 851). Counseling approaches to achieve this goal have been suggested and, in some cases, empirically validated.

The most commonly reported counseling approach for both men and women with BID is cognitive behavior therapy because counseling can focus intensely on the client's cognitive distortions and unhealthy behaviors (Grieve et al., 2009; Stewart, 2004; Wade et al., 2009). However, other approaches have also been recommended or empirically validated. For example, Wade et al. (2009) specifically found that a cognitive dissonance approach, which is having a client involved with "counter attitudinal activities such as listing physically positive characteristics" (p. 846), significantly improved weight satisfaction for female college students and that the acceptance approach (i.e., rather than trying to force away or deny negative thoughts about the body, simply acknowledge that the thoughts are there for the moment and that's the way it is) significantly improved appearance satisfaction. Although this study focused on female students, other research has shown cognitive dissonance approaches to be successful with men experiencing mental health issues (e.g., Draycott & Dabbs, 1998). Stewart (2004) recommended a mindfulness approach to BID, claiming that "the end product of mindfulness is observation of body image without judgment and emotional reaction, resulting in decreased likelihood of impulsive, destructive behaviors and increased insight about the complexity of the body image experience" (p. 788). Grieve et al. (2009) recommended the trans-theoretical model, motivational interviewing, and gender-sensitive therapies.

On the basis of the first author's clinical work with men experiencing BID, we also recommend using an existential counseling approach. This approach can be effective with a wide variety of clients and issues; however, three concepts from this approach are particularly helpful for male clients with BID. The first is "the will to meaning," because "this meaning is unique and specific in that it must and can be filled by him alone" (Frankl, 1984, p. 121). Determining the meaning of being more muscular, thinner, heavier, or leaner helps a client target the real goal (e.g., being worth something) and helps him confront distorted thinking and behavior preventing fulfillment of his meaning and explore all ways to reach his meaning. The second is Buber's (1970) concept of human encounter, because men suffering from BID either maintain It/Thou encounters with self and the world (i.e., I am an object because I cannot live up to your human concept of the ideal man) or I/It encounters through their restricted social interactions (e.g., I am human and must become fit or muscular and you are an object that I can discard in favor of my excessive exercising). Finally, Yalom's (2003) concept of death helps male clients put their actions in perspective to life's

meaning as the client considers that the current disordered behavior can lead to death, or feels a sense of urgency to complete the project related to his meaning of "being worth something." Choosing only one way to do this, for example, through being overly thin, actually slows down his achievement of meaning.

Intervention Strategies

Developing a close, trusting relationship with a male client who has BID is an important first step in the counseling process because of the stigma associated with a man having BID or a related disorder (Grieve et al., 2009; Stewart, 2004). When this has been achieved and an accurate assessment made, then a treatment plan can be developed using appropriate intervention strategies for BID.

Psychoeducational strategies are recommended as a first step in this process because many men do not understand the dynamics of BID (Greenhill, 2003; Grieve et al., 2009; Harvey & Robinson, 2003). Psychoeducation can be in the form of bibliotherapy, education from other professionals (e.g., nutritionist, doctor, exercise physiologist), meeting with a client who formerly had BID and who has successfully changed his behavior, and discussions about the effects of BID. Any topic previously identified with BID can be reviewed (e.g., how denial plays a role in BID). Depending on a client's symptoms and behaviors, psychoeducation can focus on population issues or behaviors specific to the client, for example, how sports involvement may play a role in BID (Harvey & Robinson, 2003), how racial centrality in African American men may relate to BID (Oney et al., 2011), or how gay culture may reinforce the ideal male body image, thus influencing BID behaviors or beliefs (Duggan & McCreary, 2004).

Cognitive restructuring and disputing irrational beliefs are important and commonly reported by professionals working with men experiencing BID and related symptoms (Maida & Armstrong, 2005; O'Dea & Abraham, 2002). Behavioral strategies help modify excessive/compulsive risky or unhealthy behavior. Some helpful techniques are relaxation training, exposure techniques, assertion training, behavior modification techniques to reinforce a healthier lifestyle, and self-monitoring techniques (Choate, 2007; Grieve et al., 2009; Wade et al., 2009).

As an umbrella strategy, we suggest using Lazarus's (2008) BASIC ID multimodal model because it can help the counselor assess many factors and symptoms of BID. Examples of areas the BASIC ID model might lead a counselor to address include the following: Behavior (e.g., excessive exercising), which can be treated via a self-management program; Affect (e.g., anxiety when unable to exercise), which can be treated through biofeedback or a mindfulness approach (i.e., developing awareness of gaining multiple perspectives about not exercising rather than "the simplistic . . . negative view of self" [Stewart, 2004, p. 794]); Sensation (e.g., tension in body when not exercising enough), which can be treated through massage therapy or relaxation training; Imagery (e.g., views of body as too puny or underdeveloped), which can be treated through guided imagery exercises to develop a realistic and healthier image of the body; Cognitive (e.g., negative self-talk like "I'm worthless unless I'm buff"), which can be treated through cognitive restructuring and thought- stopping techniques; Interpersonal (e.g., putting off social interactions for fear of eating too much or in favor of exercising), which can be treated through the paradoxical intention technique (i.e., "Okay, then for the next week avoid your friends at all costs, you don't need to see them"; this strategy should help the client develop a new respect for friends) or social skills training if such skills are lacking; and Drugs (e.g., continuous use of body-enhancing drugs), which can be treated by exposure to different role models (e.g., men who keep fit but do not use drugs), as well as bibliotherapy related to problems with repeated use of these types of drugs.

Other recommended techniques include mindfulness meditation, self-monitoring and journaling, mirror exposure (Stewart, 2004), distraction or "the purposeful act of shifting attention away from distressing symptoms toward more pleasant or neutral thoughts or activities" (Wade et al., 2009, p. 846), motivational interviewing techniques, and pharmacotherapy (Grieve et al., 2009). Harvey and Robinson (2003) identified anxiety as an issue; thus, anxiety reduction techniques, such as biofeedback or rapid eye movement, may be helpful. The feminist counseling techniques of empowerment, gender-role intervention, and reframing may help minority populations of men who are "member[s] of multiple social categories and . . . racial group identifications" (Oney et al., 2011, p. 629). Additionally, exposure to more appropriate male role models, reinforcement of other non-physical activities, mentoring programs, life skills training (especially focused on problem solving, critical thinking skills, and an internal locus of control), media literacy training (Choate, 2007), and paradoxical intention (Frankl, 1984) can address excessive exercising and BID.

A variety of treatment strategies/techniques have been recommended for male clients having BID; other applicable techniques originated in the treatment of women with similar disorders. Our goal in this article was to provide an overview of techniques that can be useful in the treatment of BID issues so that counselors can select the most appropriate techniques to use with men exhibiting BID symptoms. Although care should be taken when utilizing techniques or instruments that have not been researched with male populations, these approaches can provide a good starting point for working with male clients experiencing BID. Detailed descriptions of the noted interventions are beyond the scope of this discussion, but citations are provided for additional information on the recommended approaches.

Conclusion

Many men and male adolescents feel pressure to conform to an ideal body image, particularly through exercise and fitness (McCabe & McGreevy, 2010). Like women, men and male adolescents experience BID and related disorders. However, men's

experiences and behaviors related to BID can differ from those of women. Additionally, counselors and other professionals may not identify BID in their male clients because many symptoms are at the subclinical level and do not meet diagnostic criteria, or professionals may hold a stereotype that such symptoms are more readily identified in women than in men (Greenhill, 2003; Harvey & Robinson, 2003). Male clients also may not seek counseling for BID simply because they do not view their beliefs or behaviors as unusual or problematic. Thus, counselors and other professionals must be knowledgeable about the risk factors associated with BID in men, the subclinical symptoms of BID, and possible diagnoses or disorders comorbid with BID. However, more research is needed to assess the extent of the problem and empirically identify valid treatment strategies (Davey & Bishop, 2006; Green & Pritchard, 2003; Grieve et al., 2009).

References

Agliata, D., & Tantleff-Dunn, S. (2004). The impact of media exposure on males' body image. *Journal of Social and Clinical Psychology, 23,* 7–22.

American Psychiatric Association. (2000). *Diagnostic and statistical manual of mental disorders* (4th ed., text rev.). Washington, DC: Author.

Baum, A. (2006). Eating disorders in the male athlete. *Sports Medicine, 36,* 1–6.

Becker, C. B., Smith, L. M., & Ciao, A. C. (2006). Peer-facilitated eating disorder prevention: A randomized effectiveness trial of cognitive dissonance and media advocacy. *Journal of Counseling Psychology, 53,* 550–555.

Boisvert, J. A., & Harrell, W. (2009). Homosexuality as a risk factor for eating disorder symptomatology in men. *Journal of Men's Studies, 17,* 210–225. doi:10.3149/jms.1703.210

Brennan, M. A., Lalonde, C. E., & Bain, J. L. (2010). Body image perceptions: Do gender differences exist? *Psi Chi Journal of Undergraduate Research, 15,* 130–138.

Buber, M. (1970). *I and thou* (W. Kaufmann, Trans.). New York, NY: Scribner.

Carlat, D. J., Camargo, C. A., Jr., & Herzog, D. B. (1997). Eating disorders in males: A report on 135 patients. *The American Journal of Psychiatry, 154,* 1127–1132.

Cash, T. F., & Szymanski, M. L. (1995). The development and validation of the Body-Image Ideals Questionnaire. *Journal of Personality Assessment, 64,* 466–477.

Chaney, M. P. (2008). Muscle dysmorphia, self-esteem, and loneliness among gay and bisexual men. *International Journal of Men's Health, 7,* 157–170. doi: 10.3149/jmh .0702.157

Choate, L. H. (2007). Counseling adolescent girls for body image resilience: Strategies for school counselors. *Professional School Counseling, 10,* 317–326.

Crocker, J. (2002). The costs of seeking self-esteem. *Journal of Social Evaluations, 58,* 597–615.

Davey, C. M., & Bishop, J. B. (2006). Muscle dysmorphia among college men: An emerging gender-related counseling concern. *Journal of College Counseling, 9,* 171–182.

Draycott, S., & Dabbs, A. (1998). Cognitive dissonance 1 : An overview of the literature and its integration into theory and practice in clinical psychology. *British Journal of Clinical Psychology, 37,* 341–353. doi:10.1111/j.2044-8260.1998.tb01390.x

Duggan, S. J., & McCreary, D. R. (2004). Body image, eating disorders, and the drive for muscularity in gay and heterosexual men. *Journal of Homosexuality, 47,* 45–58.

Esnaola, I., Rodriguez, A., & Goni, A. (2010). Body dissatisfaction and perceived socio-cultural pressures: Gender and age differences. *Salud Mental, 33,* 21–29.

Filiault, S. M. (2007). Measuring up in the bedroom: Muscle, thinness, and men's sex lives. *International Journal of Men's Health, 6,* 127–142.

Frankl, V. E. (1984). *Man's search for meaning* (Rev.). New York, NY: Washington Square Press.

Galli, N., Reel, J., Petrie, T, Greenleaf, C., & Carter, J. (2011). Preliminary development of the Weight Pressures in Sport Scale for male athletes. *Journal of Sport Behavior, 34,* 47–68.

Green, S. P., & Pritchard, M. E. (2003). Predictors of body image dissatisfaction in adult men and women. *Social Behavior and Personality, 31,* 215–222.

Greenhill, W. D. (2003). Loving Adonis: Could your man suffer from disordered eating? *American Fitness, 21,* 29–31.

Grieve, F. G. (2007). A conceptual model of factors contributing to the development of muscle dysmorphia. *Eating Disorders, 15,* 63–80.

Grieve, F. G., Truba, N., & Bowersox, S. (2009). Etiology, assessment, and treatment of muscle dysmorphia. *Journal of Cognitive Psychotherapy: An International Quarterly, 23,* 306–314.

Halkitis, P. N., Green, K. A., & Wilton, L. (2004). Masculinity, body image, and sexual behavior in HIV-seropositive gay men: A two-phase formative behavioral investigation using the Internet. *International Journal of Men's Health, 3,* 27–42.

Harvey, J. A., & Robinson, J. D. (2003). Eating disorders in men: Current considerations. *Journal of Clinical Psychology in Medical Settings, 10,* 297–306.

Kimmel, S. B., & Mahalik, J. R. (2004). Measuring masculine body ideal distress: Development of a measure. *International Journal of Men's Health, 3,* 1–10.

Koran, L. M., Abujaoude, E., Large, M. D., & Serpe, R. T. (2008). The prevalence of body dysmorphic disorder in the United States adult population. *CNS Spectrums, 13,* 316–322.

Lazarus, A. A. (2008). Multimodal therapy. In R. J. Corsini & D. Wedding (Eds.), *Current psychotherapies* (8th ed., pp. 368–401). Belmont, CA: Brooks/Cole.

Lobera, J., Cid, S. T., Fernandez, M. J. S., & Rios, E B. (2011). Body shape model, physical activity and eating. *Nutricion Hospitalaria, 26,* 201–207.

Maida, D. M., & Armstrong, S. L. (2005). The classification of muscle dysmorphia. *International Journal of Men's Health, 4,* 73–91.

Mahalik, J. R., Talmadge, W T., Locke, B. D., & Scott, R. P. J. (2005). Using the Conformity to Masculine Norm Inventory to work with men in a clinical setting. *Journal of Clinical Psychology, 61,* 661–874.

McCabe, M. P, & McGreevy, S. (2010). The role of partners in shaping the body image and body change strategies of adult men. *Health, 2,* 1002–1009.

McCreary, D. R., Hildebrandt, T. B., Heinberg, L. J., Boroughs, M., & Thompson, J. K. (2007). A review of body image influences on men's fitness goals and supplement use. *American Journal of Men's Health, 1,* 307–316.

Naylor, A. H., Gardner, D., & Zaichkowsky, L. (2001). Drug use patterns among high school athletes and nonathletes. *Adolescence, 36,* 627–639.

O'Dea, J. A., & Abraham, S. (2002). Eating and exercise disorders in young college men. *Journal of American College Health, 50,* 273–278.

Olivardia, R. (2002). Body image obsession in men. *Healthy Weight Journal, 16,* 59.

Oney, C. N., Cole, E. R., & Sellers, R. M. (2011). Racial identity and gender as moderators of the relationship between body image and self-esteem for African Americans. *Sex Roles, 65,* 619–631.

Phillips, K. A., Coles, M. E., Menard, W., Yen, S., Fay, C., & Weisberg, R. B. (2005). Suicide ideation and suicide attempts in body dysmorphic disorder. *Journal of Clinical Psychiatry, 66,* 717–725.

Phillips, N., & deMan, A. F. (2010). Weight status and body image satisfaction in adult men and women. *North American Journal of Psychology, 12,* 171–183.

Pope, H. G., Jr., & Katz, D. L. (1994). Psychiatric and medical effects of anabolic-androgenic steroids: A controlled study of 160 athletes. *Archives of General Psychiatry, 51,* 375–382.

Raevuori, A., Keski-Rahkonen, A., Hoek, H. W., Sihvola, E., Rissanen, A., & Kaprio, J. (2008). Lifetime anorexia nervosa in young men in the community: Five cases and their co-twins. *International Journal of Eating Disorders, 41,* 458–463.

Ricciardelli, L. A., McCabe, M. P., Williams, R. J., & Thompson, J. K. (2007). The role of ethnicity and culture in body image and disordered eating among males. *Clinical Psychology Review, 27,* 582–606.

Rogers, C. R. (1961). *On becoming a person: A therapist's view of psychotherapy.* Oxford, England: Houghton Mifflin.

Schneider, V., Cockcroft, K., & Hook, D. (2008). The fallible phallus: A discourse analysis of male sexuality in a South African men's interest magazine. *South African Journal of Psychology, 38,* 136–151.

Siconolfi, D., Halkitis, P N., Allomong, T. W., & Burton, C. L. (2009). Body dissatisfaction and eating disorders in a sample of gay and bisexual men. *International Journal of Men's Health, 8,* 254–264.

Silva, M. (2006, April). Body image dissatisfaction: A growing concern among men. *Newsletter for Mental Health.* Retrieved from http://www.msoe.edu/life_at_msoe /current_student_resources/student_resources/counseling _services/newsletters_for_mental_health/body_image _dissatisfaction.shtml

Slevin, K. (2008). Disciplining bodies: The aging experiences of older heterosexual and gay men. *Generations, 32,* 36–42.

Stewart, T. M. (2004). Light on body image treatment: Acceptance through mindfulness. *Behavior Modification, 28,* 783–811.

Swanson, S. A., Crow, S. J., LeGrange, D., Swendsen, J., & Merikangas, K. R. (2011). Prevalence and correlates of eating disorders in adolescents: Results from the National Comorbidity Survey Replication Adolescent Supplement. *Archives of General Psychiatry, 68,* 714–723.

Tiggemann, M., & Kuring, J. K. (2004). The role of body objectification in disordered eating and depressed mood. *British Journal of Clinical Psychology, 43,* 299–311.

Veale, D., Boocock, A., Gournay, K., Dryden, W., Shah, F., Willson, R., & Walburn, J. (1996). Body dysmorphic disorder: A survey of fifty cases. *British Journal of Clinical Psychology, 169,* 196–201.

Wade, T., George, S. M., & Atkinson, M. (2009). A randomized controlled trial of brief interventions for body dissatisfaction. *Journal of Consulting and Clinical Psychology, 77,* 845–854.

Yalom, L. D. (2003). *The gift of therapy: An open letter to a new generation of therapists and their patients.* New York, NY: HarperCollins.

Zimmerman, M, & Mattia, J. I. (1998). Body dysmorphic disorder in psychiatric outpatients: Recognition, prevalence, comorbidity, demographic, and clinical correlates. *Comprehensive Psychiatry, 39,* 265–270. doi: 10.1016 /S0010-440X(98)90034-7

At the time the article was published both **Larry D. Burlew** and **W. Matthew Shurts** worked in the Department of Counseling and Educational Leadership at Montclair State University in New Jersey. Dr. Burlew has expertise in the area of developmental issues, especially in relation to male issues. Dr. Shurts works in the area of counseling and has expertise in the areas of romantic relationship development, counselor education pedagogy, and premarital and pre-union counseling.

EXPLORING THE ISSUE

Is the Pressure to have a Muscular Physique Recognized Equally between Male and Female Adolescents?

Critical Thinking and Reflection

1. The NO selection discusses the male body ideal and the differences related to this ideal as compared to female body ideal. Given the information found within this study, what steps do you feel are important in being able to recognize possible body image dissatisfaction in male adolescents? What steps can society take to help intervene with this crisis?
2. The YES selection brings to light the use of muscle-enhancing strategies by both genders. What does this study tell us about the risk-taking behaviors of adolescents, especially as it portrays to an adolescent's perceived body image? How would you go about explaining the differences in which strategies are utilized across gender? What helps account for these differences?
3. Males and females both report feeling pressure from parents, friends, and society to be muscular. Consider your own experiences with muscularity discourses. Was being muscular or toned a topic of conversation among your peer group in high school? What sorts of messages did you hear about the importance of muscularity in "beautiful" bodies?

Is There Common Ground?

This issue examines the body ideal for both adolescent males and females and suggests that there has been a gradual merger of the ideal body image to one of being fit/toned or muscular. While the NO selection emphasizes that the muscular physique is the focus of male adolescents, it does acknowledge the impact of achieving a body ideal image on the adolescent's development. Furthermore, the YES selection provides evidence of the impact on the adolescent's development, especially in light of engaging in muscle-enhancing strategies, across both genders. This message seems to be impacting the development of both genders. The NO selection discusses an increase in various body image issues, leading to increases in criteria being met for various body image dissatisfaction disorders, while the YES selection discusses how they found that all students reported engaging in at least one muscle-enhancing behavior and how it is important to monitor what behaviors they choose so as to reduce the potential impact of any unhealthy behaviors.

Future research should examine the role that media play in shaping people's views of muscularity in relation to the ideal male and female physique. How do teen and women's magazines, with their tips on how to "lose belly fat" or get "toned arms" impact this shift in muscularity concerns for young women? Do media play a role in the pressure young girls experience from parents and friends to become more muscular?

Additional Resource

Mulgrew, K. E., Volcevski-kostas, D., & Rendell, P. G. (2014). The effect of music video clips on adolescent boys' body image, mood, and schema activation. *Journal of Youth and*

Adolescence, 43(1), 92–103. doi:http://dx.doi.org/10.1007/s10964-013-9932-6

References

Bearman, S. K., & Stice, E. (2008). Testing a gender additive model: The role of body image in adolescent depression. *Journal of Abnormal Child Psychology, 36*(8), 1251–1263. doi:http://dx.doi.org/10.1007/s10802-008-9248-2

Cafri, G., Thompson, J. K., Ricciardelli, L., McCabe, M., Smolak, L., & Yesalis, C. (2005). Pursuit of the muscular ideal: Physical and psychological consequences and putative risk factors. *Clinical Psychology Review, 25*(2), 215–239.

Markey, C. N. (2010). Invited commentary: Why body image is important to adolescent development. *Journal of Youth and Adolescence, 39*(12), 1387–1391.

Riccardelli, L. A., & McCabe, M. P. (2003). Sociocultural and individual influences on muscle gain and weight loss strategies among adolescent boys and girls. *Psychology in the Schools, 40*, 209–224.

Rodgers, R. F., Faure, K., & Chabrol, H. (2009). Gender differences in parental influences on adolescent body dissatisfaction and disordered eating. *Sex Roles, 61*, 837–849. doi:http://dx.doi.org/10.1007/s11199-009-9690-9

Internet References . . .

Body Image and Self-Esteem

kidshealth.org/en/teens/body-image.html

Is Social Media Giving Your Teen a Negative Body Image?

https://www.commonsensemedia.org/blog/is-social
-media-giving-your-teen-a-negative-body-image#

Life & Body Image Issues for Teens

www.pamf.org/teen/life/bodyimage

National Eating Disorder Association

www.nationaleatingdisorders.org

Unit 3

UNIT

Peer and Family Relationships

*S*ocial relationships are critical in the growth, development, and behavior of adolescents. There are many different types of relationships that are important for teens, including family ties, friendships, and romantic relationships. The issues in this unit address some aspect of the social relations of youth and the impact that these relationships have on adolescent development.

Selected, Edited, and with Issue Framing Material by:
Scott R. Brandhorst, *Southeast Missouri State University*

ISSUE

Does Having Same-Sex Parents Negatively Impact Children?

YES: Michelle Cretella, from "Homosexual Parenting: Is It Time for Change?," *American College of Pediatricians* (2012)

NO: Simon R. Crouch et al., from "Parent-Reported Measures of Child Health and Wellbeing in Same-Sex Parent Families: A Cross-Sectional Survey," *BMC Public Health* (2014)

Learning Outcomes
After reading this issue, you will be able to:
• List the areas of contention about same-sex parenting impacts on children.
• Form an opinion on same-sex parenting.
• Consider your opinion and understand how the same research pieces can be used to support diametrically opposite viewpoints.
• Understand the impact of the stigma associated with having same-sex parents on children

ISSUE SUMMARY

YES: Michelle Cretella, a physician writing a position statement for The American College of Pediatricians, argues that having biological, heterosexual parents is the best situation for the development of children. She criticizes the same-sex parenting outcome literature as being fraught with design flaws and she argues that homosexual lifestyles pose dangers to children.

NO: Dr. Crouch and colleagues examined the physical, mental, and social well-being of children with same-sex attracted parents. They conducted a cross-sectional survey that included 315 parents and 500 children, which included both female and male index parents. The researchers found children with same-sex attracted parents are faring well on most measures of child health and well-being, and demonstrate higher levels of family cohesion than population samples. However, the researchers found a negative impact on the child's development due to the "stigma" associated with being raised by a same-sex attracted parent. So any negative impact is not a result of the sexual orientation of the parent, but due to the social stigma associated with the parent's sexual orientation.

The issue of same-sex couples, marriage, and relationship rights seems to be integrally linked with same-sex parenting. Often, arguments for marriage move into arguments about same-sex parenting and vice versa. Same-sex couples' marriage rights set the stage for same-sex parenting. In 2015, The United States Supreme Court ruled that same-sex marriage was legal in the United States. United States became the 21st country to legalize same-sex marriage. As of March 2016 it became legal for same-sex couples to adopt children in all 50 states as a federal judge ruled Mississippi's ban on same-sex adoption unconstitutional. However, there are still many roadblocks to same-sex parents being able to adopt children (e.g., denying services based on conflict with religious beliefs).

A set of beliefs exists that are used as the rationale for assessing same-sex couples as less acceptable than traditional couples. These beliefs can be loosely grouped into the following: (1) a negative impact on the children including personal psychosexual (e.g., inappropriate gender role, gender identity, homosexual or bisexual orientation), interpersonal (e.g., teasing, rejection from peers), and family relations' difficulties (e.g., lack of attachment to parents) and (2) objections about parenting abilities (e.g., parenting skills, adult relationship quality). People often admit that same-sex adoption is better than a child being without any parents but that heterosexual couples would be preferable (Dent, 2011). Biological ties are also cited as a factor leading to superiority of heterosexual parents. The preference of one type of parent over another without scientific rationale would be considered an –ism (like sexism or racism); the preference of heterosexual couples over homosexual couples might be best termed heterosexism rather than homophobia or homonegativity, per se (Szymanski & Moffitt, 2012). This preference for heterosexual over homosexual couples as adoptive parents is evident in adoptive research (e.g., Rye & Meaney, 2010).

As you read the YES and NO selections, consider the perspectives and the backgrounds of the authors and their underlying position on the issue of sexual orientation. Dr. Crouch, who is openly gay, and who is the father to twin year-old boys, stated his decision to conduct the study was prompted by politicians on both sides of the equal marriage and adoption debate asserting that children did better when raised by a straight couple (McCormick, 2013). Crouch has written about the topic of child well-being and non-traditional families (e.g., Crouch, McNair, Waters, & Power, 2015). He clearly has pro-gay leanings.

Michelle Cretella is a pediatrician who is a member of the American College of Pediatricians; she has held executive positions in this organization, including president, vice president, and the chair of the sexuality committee. Cretella has written critically about the topic of gay marriage and homosexuality (e.g., Goldberg & Cretella, 2009). The American College of Pediatricians is a national organization that expects "societal forces to support the two-parent, father-mother family unit and provide for children role models of ethical character and responsible behavior" (American College of Pediatricians, n.d.). It would be fair to characterize Cretella and the American College of Pediatricians as having anti-gay leanings.

The perspectives of the two authors influence how they interpret studies of same-sex parenting and how the arguments presented in their writing are supported.

YES

Michelle Cretella

Homosexual Parenting: Is It Time for Change?

Biology Matters

Over thirty years of research confirms that children fare best when reared by their two biological parents in a loving low conflict marriage. Children navigate developmental stages more easily, are more solid in their gender identity, perform better academically, have fewer emotional disorders, and become better functioning adults when reared within their natural family.[1,2,3,4,5,6,7] This is, in part, because biology contributes to parent-child bonding.[9]

While single parenthood, adoption, and remarriage are each loving responses to failure of the natural family, children reared in these settings face unique challenges.[8,9] Single parents face greater financial challenges and time constraints. Consequently, children of single mothers often spend significantly less time with both biological parents. Children within stepfamilies can experience difficulties forging a relationship with the stepparent, and be faced with a sense of divided loyalties. Every adopted child must come to terms with a sense of rejection from her biologic parents and a longing to know her roots. While not insurmountable, these challenges can have a negative impact on a child's development. Clearly, apart from rare situations, depriving a child of one or both biologic parents, as same-sex parenting requires in every case, is unhealthy.

Children Need a Mother and a Father

There are significant innate differences between male and female that are mediated by genes and hormones and go well beyond basic anatomy. These biochemical differences are evident in the development of male and female brain anatomy, psyche, and even learning styles.[10] Consequently, mothers and fathers parent differently and make unique contributions to the overall development of the child.[10,11,12] Psychological theory of child development has always recognized the critical role that mothers play in the healthy development of children. More recent research reveals that when fathers are absent, children suffer as well. Girls without fathers perform more poorly in school, are more likely to be sexually active and become pregnant as teenagers. Boys without fathers have higher rates of delinquency, violence, and aggression.[11,12]

Gender-linked differences in child rearing styles between parents are complementary and protective for children. Erik Erikson was among the first to note that mother-love and father-love are qualitatively different. Mothers are nurturing, expressive, and more unconditional in their love for their children. Father-love, by contrast, often comes with certain expectations of achievement.[12] Subsequent research has consistently revealed that parenting is most effective when it is both highly expressive and highly demanding. This approach to parenting "provides children with a kind of communion characterized by inclusiveness and connectedness, as well as the drive for independence and individuality [which is] virtually impossible for a man or woman alone to combine effectively."[12]

Gender differences are also reflected in the way mothers and fathers use touch with their children. Mothers frequently soothe, calm, and comfort with touch. Fathers are more likely to use touch to stimulate or excite their children during play. Mothers tend to engage with children on their level providing opportunities for children to take charge and proceed at their own pace. As fathers engage in rough and tumble play, they take on a teaching role like that of a coach. Roughhousing between fathers and sons is associated with the development of greater self-control in adolescent boys.[12]

Gender-linked diversity is also observed in parental approaches to discipline. "The disciplinary approaches of fathers tend toward firmness, relying on rules and principles. The approach of mothers tends toward more responsiveness, involving more bargaining, more adjustment toward the child's mood and context, and is more often based on an intuitive understanding of the child's needs and emotions of the moment."[12] Consequently, being reared by a mother and a father helps sons and daughters moderate their own gender-linked inclinations. Boys generally embrace reason over emotion, rules over relationships, risk-taking over caution, and standards over compassion. Girls generally place greater emphasis on emotional ties, relationships, caution, and compassion. Over time opposite-sexed parents demonstrate to their children the value of opposing tendencies.

Research on Same-Sex Parenting

Studies that appear to indicate neutral to favorable child outcomes from same-sex parenting have critical design flaws. These include non-longitudinal design, inadequate sample size, biased sample selection, lack of proper controls, failure to account for confounding variables, and perhaps most problematic—all claim to affirm the null hypothesis.[13,14,15] Therefore, it is impossible for these studies to provide any support for the alleged safety or potential benefits to children from same-sex parenting.

Data on the long-term outcomes of children placed in same-sex households is sparse and gives reason for concern.[16] This research has revealed that children reared in same-sex households are more likely to experience sexual confusion, engage in risky sexual experimentation, and later adopt a same-sex identity.[17,18,19,20,21,22] This is concerning since adolescents and young adults who adopt the homosexual lifestyle are at increased risk for mental health problems, including major depression, anxiety disorders, conduct disorders, substance dependence, and especially suicidal ideation and suicide attempts.[23]

Risks of the Homosexual Lifestyle to Children

Finally, research has demonstrated considerable risks to children exposed to the homosexual lifestyle. Violence between same-sex partners is two to three times more common than among married heterosexual couples.[24,25,26,27,28] Same-sex partnerships are significantly more prone to dissolution than heterosexual marriages with the average same-sex relationship lasting only two to three years.[29,30,31,32] Homosexual men and women are reported to be promiscuous, with serial sex partners, even within what are loosely-termed "committed relationships."[33,34,35,36,37] Individuals who practice a homosexual lifestyle are more likely than heterosexuals to experience mental illness,[38,39,40] substance abuse,[41] suicidal tendencies[42,43] and shortened life spans.[44] Although some would claim that these dysfunctions are a result of societal pressures in America, the same dysfunctions exist at inordinately high levels among homosexuals in cultures where the practice is more widely accepted.[45]

Conclusion

In summary, tradition and science agree that biological ties and dual gender parenting are protective for children. The family environment in which children are reared plays a critical role in forming a secure gender identity, positive emotional well-being, and optimal academic achievement. Decades of social science research documents that children develop optimally when reared by their two biological parents in a low conflict marriage. The limited research advocating childrearing by same-sex parents has severe methodological limitations. There is significant risk of harm inherent in exposing a child to the homosexual lifestyle. Given the current body of evidence, the American College of Pediatricians believes it is inappropriate, potentially hazardous to children, and dangerously irresponsible to change the age-old

prohibition on same-sex parenting, whether by adoption, foster care, or reproductive manipulation. This position is rooted in the best available science.

References

1. Heuveline, Patrick, et al., Shifting Childrearing to Single Mothers: Results from 17 Western Countries, *Population and Development Review 29,* no. 1 (March 2003) p. 48.

2. Kristen Andersen Moore, et al., *Marriage from a Child's Perspective: How Does Family Structure Affect Children and What Can We Do About It?* (Washington, D.C.: Child Trends, Research Brief, June 2002) pp. 1–2.

3. Sara McLanahan and Gary Sandfeur, *Growing Up with a Single Parent: What Hurts, What Helps* (Cambridge: Harvard University Press, 1994), p. 45.

4. Sotirios Sarantakos, Children in Three Contexts: Family, Education, and Social Development, *Children Australia,* vol. 21 (1996): 23–31.

5. Jeanne M. Hilton and Esther L. Devall, Comparison of Parenting and Children's Behavior in Single-Mother, Single-Father, and Intact Families, *Journal of Divorce and Remarriage* 29 (1998): 23–54.

6. Elizabeth Thomson et al., Family Structure and Child Well-Being: Economic Resources vs. Parental Behaviors, *Social Forces* 73 (1994): 221–42.

7. David Popenoe, *Life Without Father* (Cambridge: Harvard University Press, 1996), pp. 144, 146.

8. Glenn Stanton, *Why Marriage Matters* (Colorado Springs: Pinon Press, 1997) p. 97–153.

9. Schneider B., Atteberry A., Owens A, *Family Matters: Family Structure and Child Outcomes.* Birmingham, AL: Alabama Policy Institute; 2005: 1–42. Available at www .alabamapolicyinstitute.org/PDFs/currentfamilystructure .pdf.

10. Sax, Leonard, *Why Gender Matters: What Parents and Teachers Need to Know About the Emerging Science of Sex Differences* (New York: Doubleday, 2005).

11. Blankenhorn, David, *Fatherless America.* (New York: Basic Books, 1995).

12. Byrd, Dean, Gender Complementarity and Child-Rearing: Where Tradition and Science Agree, *Journal of Law & Family Studies,* University of Utah, Vol. 6 no. 2, 2005. http://narth.com/docs/gendercomplementarity.html

13. Robert Lerner, Ph.D., Althea Nagai, Ph.D., *No Basis: What the Studies Don't Tell Us About Same Sex Parenting,* Washington DC; Marriage Law Project/Ethics and Public Policy Center, 2001.

14. P. Morgan, *Children as Trophies? Examining the Evidence on Same-Sex Parenting,* Newcastle upon Tyne, UK; Christian Institute, 2002.

15. J. Paul Guiliani and Dwight G. Duncan, *Brief of Amici Curiae Massachusetts Family Institute and National Association for the Research and Therapy of Homosexuality,* Appeal to the Supreme Court of Vermont, Docket No. S1009–97CnC.

16. Perrin, E. C., Technical report: Co parent or Second-Parent Adoption by Same-Sex Parents, *Pediatrics.* 109 (2002): 343. The Academy acknowledges that the "small, non-representative samples . . . and the relatively young age of the children suggest some reserve."

17. F. Tasker and S. Golombok, Adults Raised as Children in Lesbian Families, *American Journal of Orthopsychiatric Association*, 65 (1995): 213.

18. J. Michael Bailey et al., Sexual Orientation of Adult Sons of Gay Fathers, *Developmental Psychology* 31 (1995): 124–129.

19. Ibid., pp. 127, 128.

20. F. Tasker and S. Golombok, Do Parents Influence the Sexual Orientation of Their Children? *Developmental Psychology* 32 (1996): 7.

21. Judith Stacey and Timothy J. Biblarz, (How) Does the Sexual Orientation of Parents Matter, *American Sociological Review* 66 (2001): 174, 179.

22. Nanette K. Gartrell, Henny M. W. Bos, and Naomi G. Goldberg, Adolescents of the U.S. National Longitudinal Lesbian Family Study: Sexual Orientation, Sexual Behavior, and Sexual Risk Exposure, *Archive of Sexual Behavior,* 40 (2011): 1199–1209, p. 1205.

23. Judith Stacey and Timothy J. Biblarz, (How) Does the Sexual Orientation of Parents Matter, *American Sociological Review* 66 (2001): 174, 179.

24. Gwat Yong Lie and Sabrina Gentlewarrier, Intimate Violence in Lesbian Relationships: Discussion of Survey Findings and Practice Implications, *Journal of Social Service Research* 15 (1991): 41–59.

25. D. Island and P. Letellier, *Men Who Beat the Men Who Love Them: Battered Gay Men and Domestic Violence* (New York: Haworth Press, 1991), p. 14.

26. Lettie L. Lockhart et al., *Letting Out the Secret: Violence in Lesbian Relationships, Journal of Interpersonal Violence* 9 (1994): 469–492.

27. *Violence Between Intimates,* Bureau of Justice Statistics Selected Findings, November 1994, p. 2.

28. *Health Implications Associated With Homosexuality* (Austin: The Medical Institute for Sexual Health, 1999), p. 79.

29. David P. McWhirter and Andrew M. Mattison, *The Male Couple: How Relationships Develop* (Englewood Cliffs: Prentice-Hall, 1984), pp. 252–253.

30. M. Saghir and E. Robins, Male and Female Homosexuality (Baltimore: Williams & Wilkins, 1973), p. 225; L.A. Peplau and H. Amaro, Understanding Lesbian Relationships, in *Homosexuality: Social, Psychological, and Biological Issues,* ed. J. Weinrich and W. Paul (Beverly Hills: Sage, 1982).

31. Schumm, Walter R.(2010), Comparative Relationship Stability of Lesbian Mother and Heterosexual Mother Families: A Review of Evidence, *Marriage & Family Review,* 46: 8, 499–509.

32. M. Pollak, Male Homosexuality, in *Western Sexuality: Practice and Precept in Past and Present Times,* ed. P. Aries and A. Bejin, translated by Anthony Forster (New York, NY: B. Blackwell, 1985), pp. 40–61, cited by Joseph Nicolosi in *Reparative Therapy of Male Homosexuality* (Northvale, New Jersey: Jason Aronson Inc., 1991), pp. 124, 125.

33. A. P. Bell and M. S. Weinberg, *Homosexualities: A Study of Diversity Among Men and Women* (New York: Simon and Schuster, 1978), pp. 308, 309; See also A. P. Bell, M. S. Weinberg, and S. K. Hammersmith, *Sexual Preference* (Bloomington: Indiana University Press, 1981).

34. Paul Van de Ven et al., A Comparative Demographic and Sexual Profile of Older Homosexually Active Men, *Journal of Sex Research* 34 (1997): 354.

35. A. A. Deenen, Intimacy and Sexuality in Gay Male Couples, *Archives of Sexual Behavior,* 23 (1994): 421–431.

36. Sex Survey Results, *Genre* (October 1996), quoted in "Survey Finds 40 percent of Gay Men Have Had More Than 40 Sex Partners," *Lambda Report,* January 1998, p. 20.

37. Marie Xiridoui, et al., The Contribution of Steady and Casual Partnerships to the Incidence of HIV infection among Homosexual Men in Amsterdam, *AIDS* 17 (2003): 1029–1038. [Note: one of the findings of this recent study is that those classified as being in "steady relationships" reported an average of 8 casual partners a year in addition to their partner (p. 1032)]

38. J. Bradford et al., National Lesbian Health Care Survey: Implications for Mental Health Care, *Journal of Consulting and Clinical Psychology* 62 (1994): 239, cited in Health Implications Associated with Homosexuality, p. 81.

39. Theo G. M. Sandfort, et al., Same-sex Sexual Behavior and Psychiatric Disorders, *Archives of General Psychiatry* 58 (January 2001): 85–91.

40. Bailey, J. M. Commentary: Homosexuality and mental illness. *Archives of General Psychiatry* 56 (1999): 876–880. Author states, These studies contain arguably the best published data on the association between homosexuality and psychopathology, and both converge on the same unhappy conclusion: homosexual people are at substantially higher risk for some form of emotional problems; including suicidality, major depression, and anxiety disorder, conduct disorder, and nicotine dependence . . .

41. Joanne Hall, Lesbians Recovering from Alcoholic Problems: An Ethnographic Study of Health Care Expectations, *Nursing Research* 43 (1994): 238–244.

42. R. Herrell et al., Sexual Orientation and Suicidality, Co-twin Study in Adult Men, *Archives of General Psychiatry* 56 (1999): 867–874.

43. Vickie M. Mays, et al., Risk of Psychiatric Disorders among Individuals Reporting Same-sex Sexual Partners in the National Comorbidity Survey, *American Journal of Public Health*, vol. 91 (June 2001): 933–939.

44. Robert S. Hogg et al., Modeling the Impact of HIV Disease on Mortality in Gay and Bisexual Men, *International Journal of Epidemiology* 26 (1997): 657.

45. Sandfort, T.G.M.; de Graaf, R.; Bijl, R.V.; Schnabel. Same-sex sexual behavior and psychiatric disorders. *Archives of General Psychiatry* 58 (2001): 85–91.1

Simon R. Crouch et al.

 **NO**

Parent-Reported Measures of Child Health and Wellbeing in Same-Sex Parent Families: A Cross-Sectional Survey

Background

It is estimated that in 2011 there were 6,120 children under the age of 25 years living with two same-sex parents in Australia [1], with the number of same-sex couple households increasing from around 19,000 to more than 33,000 over the preceding ten years [1, 2]. These figures are a conservative estimate as they do not capture children living with same-sex attracted single parents, or parents who are reluctant to self-identify as same-sex attracted due to fear of stigma and discrimination. Ongoing reforms in Australia around same-sex adoption, surrogacy and fertility treatments will only see this number rise, with a recent national survey on the health and wellbeing of gay, lesbian, bisexual and transgender Australians identifying that 22.1% of respondents have children or step children [3].

Two decades of research from Northern Europe and the United States suggests that the health and wellbeing of children with same-sex attracted parents is no different when compared to children from other family backgrounds, particularly in relation to social and emotional development and educational outcomes [4–6]. Stacey and Biblarz (2001) argue however that a more detailed consideration of the literature identifies a number of areas that do not necessarily follow this commonly acknowledged 'no difference' consensus [7]. This includes a focus on sexual orientation, although it is now generally accepted that child sexual orientation is not a measure of quality parenting [7]. In fact, a number of authors agree that simply asking a question that compares the sexual orientation of children with same-sex parents to children with heterosexual parents reinforces a heterosexist viewpoint that stigmatises same-sex families [8].

What the research is beginning to show however is the importance of such stigmatisation, as it is a key factor that impacts on the health and wellbeing of children with same-sex attracted parents [4, 9, 10, 11, 12, 13, 14, 15]. Numerous studies have found that when there is perceived stigma, experienced rejection or homophobic bullying, children with same-sex attracted parents are more likely to display problems in their psychosocial development [16, 17, 18, 19,20, 21, 22]. These experiences and their impacts differ globally with children from the US experiencing more homophobia, and associated higher levels of problem behaviour, when compared to children from the Netherlands [17]. The only Australian study to date to consider these issues identified high levels of bullying toward children with same-sex attracted parents but did not consider health outcomes [21].

Previous research has taken a narrow perspective when considering broader aspects of health, limiting data to a few common childhood ailments [23]. Prevention, early intervention, continuity of care and integration of healthcare services are particularly important for child health during early years [24] and it has been suggested that lesbian parents perceive barriers when dealing with the healthcare system in Australia [25]. As such it is important to determine whether potential barriers, such as perceived stigma, have an impact on the physical wellbeing of children with same-sex attracted parents.

When considering child health in same-sex parent families, research on the role of parent gender is conflicted. While some studies suggest that mothers are more emotionally invested in raising children than fathers are in general [26, 27, 28], further work suggests that absent fathers may be detrimental to self-rated cognitive and physical competence [29]. Regardless of gender however it is becoming clear that same-sex attracted parents construct their parenting roles more equitably than heterosexual parents and this may be of benefit to family functioning [30]. With this in mind it should be noted that there is a lack of research looking at male same-sex parented families [31], and too often authors extrapolate results from research on lesbian parenting to the whole range of same-sex families [32]. When studies have looked at gay male parents it is usually in the context of a kinship arrangement where the father acts as a sperm donor [33].

Studies to date have often relied on small samples. Such sample sizes limit statistical analysis and the wider application of findings to the broader community. Convenience samples are also commonly used and are often fraught with problems. As participants are self-selecting such studies are open to accusations of bias that might skew results in favour of same-sex parent families and capture only specific subsets of the gay and lesbian community [34]. It is not clear whether such bias is at play in previous samples however, but by employing recruitment strategies that actively seek to reach a broad range of families a more representative sample can be achieved [35]. In some contexts researchers have aimed to overcome limitations of convenience sampling by extrapolating same-sex attracted parents from population surveys [36]. In such cases many assumptions are made as same-sex attraction is presumed based on other demographic characteristics (such as children indicating two parents of the same gender). This limits data to same-sex couple families and does not allow for a broader representation of the community, such as single same-sex attracted parents and co-parenting arrangements to name but two [37]. In Australia current political and cultural discourse does not allow the capturing of sexual orientation in national population surveys. Although household surveys may be of benefit, cost constraints and likely small sample sizes make them impractical and as such the only methodology available to capture child health in the context of same-sex parent families is through convenience sampling. By utilising strategic and broad ranging recruitment techniques however, the best available study population can be achieved under difficult research constraints.

The overall aim of this study was to understand the multidimensional experiences of physical, mental and social wellbeing of children in same-sex parent family contexts, in addition to providing a contemporary policy relevant profile of the diversity and complexity of families and their social and physical environments [38]. The objectives were: to describe the characteristics of a convenience sample of families with at least one same-sex attracted parent; to measure the physical, mental and social wellbeing of children living in this context; and to determine the relationship between perceived stigma and child health and wellbeing.

Methods

The full methodology for the Australian Study of Child Health in Same-Sex Families is described in the study protocol [38], while the methods relating to the results presented here are summarised below.

Study Participants and Data Collection

The study, named the Australian Study of Child Health in Same-Sex Families (ACHESS), was conducted throughout Australia using a confidential cross-sectional survey to collect data between May and December 2012. Strategies were employed to contact same-sex attracted parents who both identified with the gay and lesbian community, and those who were less engaged [35]. The survey was available to complete online and in paper form. Data was collected from index parents who self-identified as being same-sex attracted, were residing in Australia, and were over the age of 18 years. Parents reported information for all children under the age of 18 years. The convenience sample was recruited using online and traditional recruitment techniques, accessing same-sex attracted parents through news media, community events and community groups. Three hundred and ninety eligible parents contacted the researchers in the first instance with two reminders for non-completion. Population normative data was available for two of the survey instruments, the Child Health Questionnaire (from the Health of Young Victorians Survey, HOYVS) [39] and the Strengths and Difficulties Questionnaire (from the Victorian Child Health and Wellbeing Survey, VCHWS) [40].

Survey Instrument

Survey preparation comprised a scoping review of the literature [38], consultations with same-sex attracted parents and adult children with same-sex attracted parents. The survey was constructed around embedded, established, psychometrically validated and reliable measures of child health which included the Child Health Questionnaire (CHQ), the Infant Toddler Quality of Life survey (ITQOL), and the Strengths and Difficulties Questionnaire [38]. Standard demographic characteristics from population surveys and previous work with same-sex parent families were included [41, 42]. The survey aimed to identify a contemporary picture of same-sex parent family socioeconomic contexts and family structures. Child health and wellbeing and perceived stigma were the two main outcome measures.

Family Structure and Socioeconomic Context

Parents were asked to report on their sexual orientation, current socioeconomic context, methods of family formation, and family structure as listed in Table 1.

Table 1

Child Demographic Characteristics

Child Demographic Characteristics	All Children (n = 500)[a]	Number of Children (%) With Male Parent/s (n = 91)	With Female Parent/s (n = 400)
Gender			
Male	264 (53)	49 (54)	214 (54)
Female	230 (46)	40 (44)	182 (46)
Mean age, years	5.12	3.86	5.43
Median age, years	4	2	4
Age range, years	0–17	0–16	0–17
Geographical location			
Inner metropolitan	261 (52)	64 (70)	195 (49)
Outer metropolitan	123 (25)	10 (11)	106 (27)
Regional center	69 (14)	3 (3)	66 (17)
Rural	35 (7)	8 (9)	27 (7)
Remote	1 (<1)	0 (0)	1 (<1)
Other	8 (2)	3 (3)	5 (1)
State			
Victoria	244 (48)	41 (45)	196 (49)
New South Wales	89 (18)	26 (29)	63 (16)
Queensland	74 (15)	3 (3)	71 (18)
Western Australia	30 (6)	6 (7)	24 (6)
South Australia	26 (5)	6 (7)	18 (5)
Australian Capital Territory	23 (5)	6 (7)	17 (4)
Tasmania	14 (3)	3 (3)	11 (3)
Country of birth			
Australia	427 (85)	31 (34)	387 (97)
India	36 (7)	36 (40)	0 (0)
USA	21 (4)	20 (22)	1 (<1)
UK	6 (1)	0 (0)	6 (2)
New Zealand	2 (<1)	1 (1)	1 (<1)
Thailand	1 (<1)	1 (1)	0 (0)
Other	7 (1)	2 (2)	5 (1)
Language			
English only	444 (89)	65 (71)	374 (93)
Language other than English	56 (11)	26 (29)	26 (7)
Index parent's highest level of education			
4 years high school	8 (2)	0 (0)	8 (2)
Year 12	28 (6)	7 (8)	21 (5)
Diploma or certificate	77 (15)	11 (12)	61 (15)
Undergraduate degree	133 (27)	33 (36)	98 (25)
Postgraduate degree	232 (46)	36 (40)	194 (49)
Other	19 (4)	4 (4)	15 (4)
Household income (AUD)			
$10,000–$19,000	13 (3)	0 (0)	13 (3)
$20,000–$29,999	25 (5)	4 (4)	16 (4)
$30,000–$59,999	56 (11)	4 (4)	50 (13)
$60,000–$99,999	112 (22)	11 (12)	101 (25)
$100,000–$149,999	129 (26)	23 (25)	106 (27)

(Continued)

Table 1–Continued

Child Demographic Characteristics

Child Demographic Characteristics	All Children (n = 500)[a]	Number of Children (%) With Male Parent/s (n = 91)	With Female Parent/s (n = 400)
$150,000–$249,999	95 (19)	22 (24)	71 (18)
$250,000 or more	70 (14)	27 (30)	43 (10)
Index parent's sexual orientation			
Lesbian	344 (69)	—	337 (84)
Gay	92 (18)	85 (93)	7 (2)
Bisexual	41 (8)	1 (1)	40 (10)
Queer	11 (2)	2 (2)	9 (2)
Heterosexual	3 (1)	0 (0)	3 (1)
Other	9 (2)	3 (3)	4 (1)
Transgender parent	6 (1)	2 (2)	1 (<1)
Child relationship to index parent[b]			
Biological child	310 (62)	46 (51)	256 (64)
Non-biological child	123 (24)	18 (20)	104 (26)
Partner's biological child	98 (20)	17 (19)	80 (20)
Fostered	13 (3)	8 (9)	5 (1)
Adopted	2 (<1)	2 (2)	0 (0)
Parent relationship status at time of conception, fostering or adoption			
Current relationship	347 (69)	66 (73)	279 (70)
Index parent's previous heterosexual relationship	50 (10)	10 (11)	40 (10)
Index parent's previous same-sex relationship	37 (7)	2 (2)	35 (9)
While index parent single	33 (7)	8 (9)	23 (6)
Partner's previous heterosexual relationship	19 (4)	0 (0)	19 (5)
While partner single	2 (<1)	2 (2)	0 (0)
Other	5 (1)	0 (0)	2 (1)
Where child lives			
With index parent full time	411 (82)	70 (77)	335 (84)
With index parent part time	50 (10)	16 (18)	24 (6)
With another parent full time	12 (2)	3 (3)	9 (2)
Lives independently	1 (<1)	0 (0)	1 (<1)
Other	24 (5)	2 (2)	19 (5)
Index parent currently in a relationship	464 (93)	83 (91)	374 (94)
Method of conception[b]			
Heterosexual intercourse	102 (20)	18 (20)	79 (20)
Home insemination—known or own gametes	137 (27)	7 (8)	127 (32)
ART[c]—unknown donor	148 (30)	3 (3)	145 (36)
ART—known donor or own gametes	51 (10)	2 (2)	48 (12)
Surrogacy—own gametes	44 (9)	42 (46)	1 (<1)
Surrogacy—unknown donor	23 (5)	23 (25)	0 (0)
Surrogacy—known donor	10 (2)	10 (11)	0 (0)

[a]Includes data from 5 children with other gendered parents and 4 children where parent gender was not identified.
[b]Multiple responses possible.
[c]Assisted Reproductive Technology.

Child Health and Wellbeing

Common childhood conditions were recorded, as well as breastfeeding data and current immunisation status. Child health was measured using three scales. The Child Health Questionnaire (CHQ), for children aged 5–17 years, and the complementary Infant Toddler Quality of Life survey (ITQOL), for children aged 0–4 years, were used to measure multidimensional aspects of functioning and health-related quality of life [43, 44]. These instruments produce scores from 0–100 for child health across a number of scales, with higher scores representing better health and/or wellbeing.

The Strengths and Difficulties Questionnaire (SDQ) is a brief behavioural screening questionnaire with five scales for children aged 3–17 years [45]. Individual scale scores range from 0–10, with a total difficulties score ranging from 0–40 (excluding the prosocial scale). A lower score indicates better social and emotional wellbeing, with the exception of the prosocial scale where a higher score indicates better social and emotional wellbeing.

Perceived Stigma

Measures of perceived stigma were based on the stigmatisation scale for lesbian-parent families developed by Bos et al, the Bos Stigmatisation Scale (BSS) [18]. This was adapted to represent all same-sex attracted parents. Parents were asked to indicate how often in the past year their family had experienced stigma related to the their same-sex attraction (eg have people gossiped about you and your family, have people excluded you and your family?). Each of the seven items is scored from 1 (never) to 3 (regularly) with the final score being the mean of all items. A higher score represents more frequent experiences of perceived stigma. Internal consistency of the adapted scale was good and compared favourably to the internal consistency in its original setting (Cronbach's $\alpha = 0.76$ vs Cronbach's $\alpha = 0.72$) [18].

Data Management and Analysis

Online surveys were automatically recorded into a database during survey completion and then exported into Microsoft Excel for Mac, version 14.0.2. Paper surveys were double entered into the spreadsheet for cleaning and scoring. Initially, descriptive statistics were used to describe health and wellbeing. For the CHQ and SDQ complete

normative datasets were available for comparison from the Health of Young Victorians Survey (HOYVS) and the Victorian Child Health and Wellbeing survey (VCHWS) respectively [39, 40].

The Health of Young Victorians Survey (HOYVS)

The HOYVS was a school-based epidemiological study of the health and wellbeing of children aged 5–18 years conducted to provide Australian normative data for the CHQ and establish its reliability and validity in the Australian context [39]. A two stage stratified design selected 24 primary and 24 secondary schools across Victoria, Australia, within each educational sector followed by the random sampling of an entire class at each year level in each school. Parents completed a paper version of the Authorised Australian Adaptation of the CHQ between July and November 1997 for a total of 5414 children (response 72%).

The Victorian Child Health and Wellbeing Survey (VCHWS)

The VCHWS collected data on 5025 randomly selected Victorian children aged under 13 years by parent interview between February and May 2009 (response 75%) [40]. Participants were recruited using random digit dialing and were stratified by geographical distribution. Data were collected via a computerised assisted telephone interview with only one child per household included in the survey. The Strengths and Difficulties Questionnaire formed one component of the survey.

Each of the scale scores for child health from the CHQ and SDQ were used as dependent variables in mixed effects linear regression models to compare the independent variable 'sample' (ACHESS data or HOYVS/VCHWS normal population datasets), adjusting for socio-demographic characteristics as fixed effects predictors, while family clustering was included as a random effects predictor (see Table 2). The categorical binary variable 'sample' was included in the model with the ACHESS data allocated as 1 and either the HOYVS or VCHWS data allocated as 2 for each of the CHQ and SDQ. The output from the model, β, represents the difference between the ACHESS scale scores and either the HOYVS or VCHWS scale scores.

Table 2

Summary of Scale Score Comparisons Between the ACHESS and Population Data from the HOYVS (CHQ) and VCHWS (SDQ) Using Mixed Effects Multiple Linear Regression Models

Scale		β (%95 CI)	P value
CHQ [a]	Physical functioning	0.78 (−1.79, 3.35)	.55
	Role-emotional/behavioral	−1.22 (−4.02, 1.57)	.39
	Role-physical	−0.89 (−3.60, 1.81)	.52
	Bodily pain	−1.70 (−4.60, 1.20)	.25

(Continued)

Table 2–Continued

Summary of Scale Score Comparisons Between the ACHESS and Population Data from the HOYVS (CHQ) and VCHWS (SDQ) Using Mixed Effects Multiple Linear Regression Models

Scale		β (%95 CI)	P value
	General behavior	2.93 (0.35, 5.52)	.03
	Mental health	−0.85 (−3.05, 1.35)	.45
	Self esteem	1.13 (−1.56, 3.82)	.41
	General health	5.60 (2.69, 8.52)	<.001
	Parental impact-emotional	0.16 (−2.92, 3.24)	.92
	Parental impact-time	−1.45 (−3.96, 1.05)	.23
	Family activities	0.38 (−3.22, 2.46)	.79
	Family cohesion	6.01 (2.84, 9.17)	<.001
SDQ [b]	Emotional symptoms	−0.02 (−0.23, 0.28)	.91
	Conduct problems	−0.05 (−0.29, 0.18,	.65
	Hyperactivity/inattention	−0.10 (−0.49, 0.29)	.61
	Peer problems	−0.01 (−0.27, 0.25)	.93
	Prosocial	−0.03 (−0.30, 0.24)	.83
	Total difficulties	−0.20 (−1.05, 0.65)	.65

[a]Children aged 5–18 years; adjusted for fixed effects predictors of child's gender, child's age, biological child, parent's age, parent's gender, parent's country of birth, in a relationship, parent's education, and parent's employment status, and the random effects predictor of family.
[b]Children aged 4–12 years; adjusted for fixed effects predictors of child's gender, child's age, biological child, parent's age, in a relationship, parent's education, and household income, and the random effects predictor of family.

To determine whether there was an association between stigma and child health each of the scale scores from the CHQ, SDQ and ITQOL were used as dependent variables in mixed effects linear regression models with the BSS scale score as an independent continuous variable, again adjusting for socio-demographic characteristics as fixed effects predictors, with family clustering as a random effects predictor (see Table 3). The output from the model, β, represents the change in each of the scale scores for every one point increase on the BSS scale.

Table 3

Summary of the Relationship Between BSS Score and Child Health Scale Scores from the ACHESS Using Mixed Effects Multiple Linear Regression Models[a]

Scale	β (%95 CI)	P value
ITQOL (0–4 years)		
Physical activity	−3.03 (−5.86, −0.21)	.04
Growth and development	−0.08 (−3.24, 3.08)	.96
Bodily pain	−7.32 (−15.07, 0.42)	.06
Temperament and mood	−2.21 (−7.40, 2.98)	.41
General behavior	−8.33 (−17.85, 1.19)	.09
Global behavior	−8.00 (−17.45, 1.43)	.10
Behavior	−5.07 (−10.72, 0.58)	.08
Combined behavior	−6.35 (−12.75, 0.06)	.05
General health	−4.76 (−11.38, 1.87)	.16
Parental impact-emotional	−3.38 (−8.46, 1.71)	.19
Parental impact-time	−1.25 (−6.32, 3.81)	.63
Family cohesion	−4.87 (−12.27, 2.52)	.20
CHQ (5–17 years)		
Physical functioning	−5.57 (−14.07, 2.93)	.20
Role-emotional/behavioral	−7.15 (−15.56, 1.262)	.10

Summary of the Relationship Between BSS Score and Child Health Scale Scores from the ACHESS Using Mixed Effects Multiple Linear Regression Models[a]

Scale	β (%95 CI)	P value
Role-physical	−1.34 (−8.90, 6.21)	.73
Bodily pain	−2.60 (−12.69, 7.50)	.61
General behavior	−4.87 (−14.16, 4.42)	.30
Mental health	−10.45 (−18.48, −2.42)	.01
Self esteem	−4.04 (−15.93, 7.85)	.51
General health	2.54 (−7.72, 12.80)	.63
Parental impact-emotional	−4.50 (−13.88, 4.87)	.35
Parental impact-time	−0.20 (−9.55, 9.15)	.97
Family activities	−7.98 (−18.06, 2.10)	.12
Family cohesion	−9.82 (−17.86, −1.78)	.02
SDQ (3–17 years)		
Emotional symptoms	0.94 (0.08, 1.81)	.03
Conduct problems	0.39 (−0.41, 1.19)	.34
Hyperactivity-inattention	0.69 (−0.46, 1.83)	.24
Peer problems	−0.20 (−1.02, 0.62)	.63
Prosocial behavior	0.76 (−0.19, 1.72)	.12
Total difficulties	1.84 (−0.74, 4.42)	.16

[a]Data adjusted for fixed effects predictors of: parent in a relationship, parent gender, biological child, family formation (heterosexual sex, home insemination, ART, surrogacy, unknown donor), relationship at conception, parent education, household income, parent age, and region, and the random effects predictor of family.

Where appropriate, socio-demographic characteristics were dichotomised. Missing values were omitted and a significance level of 2-sided P < .05 was used. Model assumptions of normality and equality of variance were supported by appropriate residual plots. All statistical analyses were performed using STATA version 12.0.

Ethics

All procedures were approved by the University of Melbourne Health Sciences Human Ethics Subcommittee, ethics ID number 1136875.1. All participants gave informed consent before taking part.

Results

Three hundred and ninety eligible parents made contact with the research team and 315 completed the survey (81%), only two of which used a paper survey. These parents provided data on 500 children.

Family Structure and Socioeconomic Context

The socio-demographic characteristics and family structures are summarised in Table 1. Ninety-one children (18%) had a male index parent, 400 (80%) had a female index parent and 5 (1%) had an other-gendered index parent. The majority of children were living in an inner metropolitan area (261, 52%). Most children were born in Australia (427, 85%), followed by India (36, 7%) and

the USA (21, 4%). Fifty-six children (11%) spoke a language other than English at home. Overall, parents had completed high levels of education with almost three quarters of children having parents who had completed a tertiary education (365, 73%). Data from the Longitudinal Study of Australian Children suggests that 28.5% of mothers with 4–8 year old children have a tertiary education [46]. Seventy-two children (79%) with a male index parent lived in households with a high combined income (over AUD $100,000), with around half of children with a female index parent living in such households (220, 55%). Median household income in Australia in 2011 was $64,168 [47].

Most children were the biological child of the index parent or of the index parent's partner (408, 82%), with few children being fostered or adopted (15, 3%). More than two thirds of the children were born in the context of the current same-sex relationship (347, 69%), although a notable number of children were born in the context of a previous heterosexual relationship or when the parent was single (69, 14% and 33, 7% respectively). Four hundred and sixty-four (93%) children had parents who were currently in a relationship.

A comparison of key characteristics from the ACHESS with characteristics from the HOYVS and VCHWS normative datasets can be seen in Table 4. The most striking difference is in parent education level where a much higher proportion of parents from the ACHESS have a tertiary education. Both the HOYVS and

Table 4

Comparison of Key Sociodemographic Characteristics for the ACHESS and CHQ/SDQ Normative Datasets

	CHQ (n)		SDQ (n)	
	ACHESS (219)	**HOYVS (5355)**	**ACHESS (213)**	**SDQ (3404)**
Mean child age, years (SD)	9.41 (3.75)	11.08 (3.53)	6.88 (2.43)	8.15 (2.64)
Boys, n (%)	126 (58.06)	2727 (50.37)	114 (54.03)	1795 (52.73)
Mean parent age, years (SD)	42.43 (6.54)	39.82 (5.96)	41.07 (5.92)	40.13 (6.38)
Parents with tertiary education, n (%)	149 (68.04)	1230 (22.97)	147 (69.34)	1,195 (35.18)
Household income[1] > $100,000, n (%)	N/A	N/A	170 (79.81)	1911 (61.57)
Single parent family, n (%)	18 (8.18)	709 (13.16)	11 (5.16)	585 (17.19)

[1]Household income not collected in the HOYVS.

VCHWS data were collected from children in Victoria. Although the ACHESS sample provides information from children across Australia, almost half (48%) live in Victoria.

Child Health and Wellbeing

Asthma was the most commonly reported medical condition for all children (63, 13%). For children aged 0–14 years old the prevalence was slightly lower at 11.6%. This compares with 10% of children in this age group across Australia (2007–2008) [48]. The prevalence of medical conditions for children in the ACHESS is summarised in Table 5.

Table 5

Prevalence of Common Childhood Medical Conditions in the ACHESS Sample

Condition	Number	Prevalence
Asthma	63	12.7
Dental	34	6.9
Anxiety	30	6.1
Allergies	29	5.9
Attention	28	5.7
Behavior	26	5.3
Vision	20	4.1
Learning	18	3.6
Sleep	16	3.2
Speech	15	3.1
Development	11	2.2
Orthopedic/joint	9	1.8
Depression	8	1.6
Chronic respiratory	6	1.2
Hearing	5	1.0
Diabetes	0	0
Epilepsy	0	0

The proportion of children from the ACHESS who were fully immunised at ages 1, 2 and 5 remained constant at 93%. This compared with 92%, 93% and 89% respectively for all children in Australia (2011) [48]. Eighty percent of children under the age of five years from the ACHESS were breastfed at some point. For children with a female index parent this figure was 96% and for children with a male index parent it was 22%. This compares to 90% of all Australian children who were initiated with breastfeeding (2010) [48]. The proportion of children under five years from the ACHESS who were still breastfeeding at four months was 33% (5% for children with a male index parent and 40% for children with a female index parent). This compares to 39% of children in the general population who were exclusively breastfeeding at 4 months [48].

The overall child health and wellbeing scores from the ITQOL, CHQ and SDQ for boys and girls from the ACHESS are presented in Table 6. After adjusting for socio-demographic characteristics there were no differences in SDQ scale scores for children aged 4–12 years when compared to population data (Table 2).

On the CHQ, after adjusting for socio-demographic characteristics, the overall mean score for general behaviour, general health and family cohesion was 3%, 6% and 6% higher respectively for children from the ACHESS compared to population data ($\beta = 2.93$, 95% CI $= 0.35$ to 5.52, P $= .03$; $\beta = 5.60$, 95% CI $= 2.69$ to 8.52, P $= <.001$; and $\beta = 6.01$, 95% CI $= 2.84$ to 9.17, P $= <.001$ respectively). There were no significant differences identified for other CHQ scales (Table 2).

Perceived Stigma

For two thirds of children (333, 67%) parents reported perceived stigma on at least one item of the BSS. The mean score on the BSS for all children from the ACHESS was 1.25 (SD 0.28). Perceived stigma was associated with a worse score on the physical activity scale of the ITQOL (P $= .04$), the mental health and family cohesion scales on the CHQ (P $= .01$ and P $= .02$), and the emotional

Table 6

Summary of the ACHESS Scale Scores (CHQ, ITQOL and SDQ) for Boys and Girls

Scale	Mean scale score (SD)	
	Boys	Girls
ITQOL (0–4 years)	*N = 112–138*	*N = 104–138*
Physical activity	98.26 (7.06)	97.90 (5.60)
Growth and development	96.99 (7.95)	98.22 (5.53)
Bodily pain	77.63 (17.05)	79.62 (16.06)
Temperament and mood	80.83 (12.05)	83.06 (10.37)
General behavior	77.08 (18.06)	74.98 (18.39)
Global behavior	86.74 (18.39)	85.82 (18.24)
Behavior	80.45 (11.13)	82.19 (9.67)
Combined behavior	79.81 (12.72)	79.93 (11.55)
General health	82.56 (15.11)	85.01 (12.61)
Parental impact-emotional	88.74 (10.06)	90.56 (10.60)
Parental impact-time	92.85 (12.15)	94.38 (9.98)
Family cohesion	87.68 (17.22)	86.05 (17.62)
CHQ (5–17 years)	*N = 125–126*	*N = 91–92*
Physical functioning	96.34 (13.43)	94.26 (16.51)
Role-emotional/behavioral	91.27 (17.98)	96.01 (11.94)
Role-physical	95.24 (14.43)	95.65 (14.17)
Bodily pain	84.32 (17.34)	79.35 (18.62)
General behavior	71.61 (17.79)	78.08 (15.11)
Mental health	82.08 (15.95)	82.43 (14.00)
Self esteem	80.09 (23.76)	86.68 (17.52)
General health	83.36 (18.26)	85.82 (16.72)
Parental impact-emotional	80.20 (17.97)	82.47 (15.73)
Parental impact-time	90.00 (15.55)	90.22 (15.26)
Family activities	83.90 (20.44)	87.50 (14.23)
Family cohesion	81.56 (19.39)	85.27 (14.85)
SDQ (3–17 years)	*N = 161*	*N = 138*
Emotional symptoms	1.66 (2.00)	1.56 (1.77)
Conduct problems	1.60 (1.64)	1.26 (1.52)
Hyperactivity-inattention	3.38 (2.51)	2.57 (2.30)
Peer problems	1.61 (1.89)	1.20 (1.38)
Prosocial behavior	7.81 (2.07)	8.27 (1.86)
Total difficulties	8.25 (5.98)	6.59 (4.72)

symptoms scale on the SDQ (P = .03). The combined behavior scale on the ITQOL also approached significance (P = .052) (Table 3).

Discussion

This is the first study of child health in same-sex parented families in Australia and the largest study of its kind internationally, to date. As such it can be used to understand a broad range of families where at least one parent is same-sex attracted. The findings suggest that there is no evidence to support a difference in parent-reported child health for most measures in these families when compared to children from population samples, which was also found with the previous smaller studies and those of lesbian families [4, 18, 49]. The ACHESS makes a significant contribution to the literature as it succeeded in representing children being raised by same-sex attracted parents from a broader range of family contexts than studies previously. The recruitment of 91 children with male same-sex attracted parents allows for the first time a sample size large enough to enable analysis of child health and wellbeing that includes children growing up with at least one gay male parent. Eleven per cent of children in same-sex couple households had male parents when the Australian census measured in 2011 [1], and as this number grows it is necessary to better understand child health and wellbeing in this context.

Socio-demographically, the parent sample has a high level of education and income, relative to population median income [47], and normative samples. While there is evidence to suggest that maternal education in particular is related to improved child health [50] it is not clear how this translates to same-sex families where the relationship between gender roles and parenting is less clear [30]. This difference in education and income must be considered however when viewing these results, even having adjusted for disparities in statistical analyses. Higher relative income in same-sex families is not surprising however, given that there is often a need to engage in costly and complex medical procedures in order to create a family where the parents are same-sex attracted. Children with male index parents are more commonly born through surrogacy arrangements. However, with commercial surrogacy illegal throughout Australia, and altruistic surrogacy poorly established, these arrangements often take place overseas, and thus parents with lower incomes may be less likely to avail this method. This situation also explains the number of children with a male index parent who were born in the US and India, two of the more commonly accessed territories for this process. Further, despite the fact that Australia is yet to have legislated to ensure marriage equality it appears that family transitions in our sample of same-sex parent families are similar to the general population. For our sample over two thirds of children were born in the context of their parents' current relationship compared with 65–81% of children, depending on the age of the youngest child, for all families in Australia (2006–7) [51].

Key child health promotion and illness prevention strategies appear to resonate well with our sample of same-sex parent families as seen by the rates of immunisation and breastfeeding. Despite the lack of an easy supply, a number of our male parents strove to ensure that their children receive some breast milk in early life, with a significant proportion of these children born via surrogacy (64%). This is usually achieved via surrogate milk donation and is an indication that same-sex male parents make efforts to support this health strategy for their children.

In comparing CHQ and SDQ scale scores from the ACHESS to population normative data it is possible to understand the multidimensional aspects of child health and wellbeing in a broader context. The three areas where statistically significant differences were seen are general behavior, general health and family cohesion. Population and clinical studies have demonstrated that there are socially and clinically meaningful differences of 5 points on the scales within the CHQ. The small difference seen between the ACHESS sample and the general population on the general behaviour domain was not observed with the behavioural components of the SDQ, which may be related to the origin and development of the two measures, where the CHQ is more related to functioning and the SDQ used as a screening tool. This is an important area for further exploration. The general health scale is a broad concept measured by a single item within the CHQ, however the size of difference is notable. Qualitative interviews accompanying this study might raise themes and issues to enable greater understanding of what could be influencing this finding, possibly related to improved communication via family cohesion. The results for family cohesion are significant. Previous research has suggested that same-sex attracted parents are much more likely to share household duties equally when compared to their heterosexual counterparts, and they make decisions about work/family balance based more on circumstance than preconceived gender-based ideals [30]. Individual suitability rather than societal convention is more likely therefore to inform parenting roles. This has the potential to engender greater family harmony in the long-term.

Whilst children with same-sex attracted parents from our sample demonstrate comparable health to other children across the population, it is clear that they, and their families, are experiencing stigma. Previous work has suggested that stigma and homophobia are related to problem behavior and conduct problems in children with same-sex attracted parents [17, 33,18]. Our findings support and strengthen the idea that stigma related to parental sexual orientation is associated with a negative impact on child mental and emotional wellbeing. Other family contexts have seen similar associations between stigma and child mental health including race-based stigma in Aboriginal and Torres Strait Islander families, and social stigma in single-parent families [52, 53]. Stigma can be experienced in numerous social contexts, educational settings and healthcare environments. Lesbian parents in Australia have previously described the barriers they perceive when accessing healthcare services and often times have to choose a disclosure strategy to adopt when dealing with practitioners [25]. Instead of feeling accepted when seeking healthcare for their children this perceived stigma can lead to a sense of vulnerability where in fact healthcare services should "be a safe place for lesbians [and gay men] to authentically talk about their relationships with lovers, friends and family [54]".

If the negative impact of perceived stigma on child mental and emotional wellbeing is compounded in a healthcare environment, where parents do not feel free to discuss their family in its entirety, then the health ramifications for children will only be amplified.

Limitations

Whilst the ACHESS is the largest study of its kind to date, the use of a convenience sample to access the highest number of participants needed to be worked through carefully as there are no current options to access data through regular population surveys or administrative datasets. Every effort was made to recruit a representative sample [35], and from the limited data available about same-sex parent families it appears that the ACHESS sample does reflect the general context of these families in contemporary Australia [37]. The self-selection of our convenience sample has the potential to introduce bias that could distort results. It is clear that the families from the ACHESS are earning more and are better educated than the general population. This has in part been allowed for in the statistical analysis by incorporating numerous control variables that are recognised to have an impact on child health outcomes but the results should be read with these differences in mind. If systematic bias was at play however, it would be anticipated that all outcome variables would demonstrate higher scores across the sample. As it is, only three key variables on the CHQ demonstrated significant difference, and none of the scale scores from the SDQ. Whether there are real differences between the ACHESS sample and the normative population or not, it is clear that there are aspects at play in our sample of same-sex families that allow improved outcomes in general behavior, general health, and in particular family cohesion.

Parent-report of child health also has its limitations. While parents are not able to fully understand the lived experience of their children's health in all aspects of life it is possible to draw inferences from the data that they represent. In particular comparisons with population normative data are valid given that parent-report was used in both contexts. There is no evidence to suggest that any group of parents would systematically respond in a particular way on any given scale, however this cannot be discounted entirely. Future research will report on child-reported measures of health, as well as a contextual analysis of qualitative data drawn from family interviews, in order to draw out any bias that parental reporting might have.

Conclusions

This study demonstrates that children with same-sex attracted parents in Australia are being raised in a diverse range of family types. These children are faring well on most measures of child health and wellbeing, and demonstrate higher levels of family cohesion than population samples. Perceived stigma is experienced by children with same-sex attracted parents, which is an issue that requires attention in all settings. In particular this is of importance to healthcare services, where parents seek assistance for their own physical and mental health, as well as that of their children. As perceived stigma already has a negative impact on mental and emotional wellbeing, negative experiences in healthcare settings will serve to exacerbate any problems that these children, and their families, might face. Future work should further explore the ways in which stigma affects the mental health of children with same-sex attracted parents and in particular ways in which these children can be protected from experiences of discrimination. Same-sex families are becoming increasingly visible globally. These results from Australia provide important epidemiological data across health, wellbeing, morbidity and perceived stigma of children with same-sex attracted parents, and an essential contemporary contribution to the current policy-research interface.

Abbreviations

ACHESS: The Australian Study of Child Health in Same-Sex Families CHQ: Child Health Questionnaire ITQOL: Infant Toddler Quality of Life Survey SDQ: Strengths and Difficulties Questionnaire BSS: Bos Stigmatization Scale HOYVS: Health of Young Victorians Survey VCHWS: Victorian Child Health and Wellbeing Survey.

Competing Interests

The authors declare that they have no competing interests.

Authors' Contributions

SRC initiated the project, designed the survey instrument, implemented the survey, monitored data collection for the survey, developed the statistical analysis plan, cleaned and analysed the data, and drafted and revised the paper. He is guarantor. EW designed the survey instrument, monitored data collection for the survey, revised the paper, and supervised SRC. RM designed the survey instrument, monitored data collection for the survey, revised the paper, and supervised SRC. JP designed the survey instrument, and revised the paper. ED designed the survey, analysed the data, and revised the paper. All authors, external and internal, had full access to all the data (including statistical reports and tables) in the study and take responsibility for the integrity of the data and the accuracy of the data analysis. All authors read and approved the final manuscript.

Acknowledgements

We are grateful to Sandy Clarke PhD AStat of the Statistical Consulting Centre, the University of Melbourne, for her statistical guidance. We thank Rodney Chiang-Cruise of Gay Dads Australia for his guidance on community engagement. This work could not have been conducted without the support of Vanessa Ho from the Department of General Practice, the University of Melbourne who provided technical support for the online survey.

This work was funded by an Australian Government National Health and Medical Research Council Postgraduate Scholarship.

References

1. **Same-sex couple families**.http://www.abs.gov.au/ausstats/abs@.nsf/Lookup/2071.0main+features852012–2013.

2. Trewin D: *2005 Year Book Australia*. Canberra: Australian Bureau of Statistics; 2005.

3. Leonard W, Pitts M, Mitchell A, Lyons A, Smith A, Patel S, Couch M, Barrett A: *Private Lives 2: the Second National Survey of the Health and Wellbeing of Gay, Lesbian, Bisexual and Transgender (GLBT) Australians*. Melbourne: The Australian Research Centre in Sex, Health & Society, La Trobe University; 2012.

4. Bos HMW, Van Balen F, Van Den Boom DC: **Lesbian families and family functioning: an overview.** *Patient Educ Couns* 2005, **59:**263–275.

5. Perrin EC, Hagan JF Jr, Coleman WL, Foy JM, Goldson E, Howard BJ, Navarro A, Tanner JL, Tolmas HC: **Technical report: coparent or second-parent adoption by same-sex parents.** *Pediatr* 2002, **109:**341–344.

6. Tasker F: **Children in lesbian-led families: a review.** *Clin Child Psychol Psychiatry* 1999, **4:**153–166.

7. Stacey J, Biblarz T: **(How) does the sexual orientation of parents matter?** *Am Soc Rev* 2001, **66:**159–183.

8. Kuvalanka KA, Teper B, Morrison OA: **COLAGE: providing community, education, leadership, and advocacy by and for children of GLBT parents.** *J GLBT Fam Stud* 2006, **2:**71–92.

9. Anderssen N, Amlie C, Ytter EA: **Outcomes for children with lesbian or gay parents. A review of studies from 1978 to 2000.** *Scand J Psychol* 2002, **43:**335–351.

10. Clarke V, Kitzinger C, Potter J: **'Kids are just cruel anyway': lesbian and gay parents' talk about homophobic bullying.** *Brit J Soc Psychol* 2004, **43:**531–550.

11. Fairtlough A: **Growing up with a lesbian or gay parent: young people's perspectives.** *Health Soc Care Community* 2008, **16:**521–528.

12. Fitzgerald B: **Children of lesbian and gay parents: a review of the literature.** *Marriage Fam Rev* 1999, **29:**57–75.

13. Heineman TV: **A boy and two mothers: new variations on an old theme or a new story of triangulation? Beginning thoughts on the psychosexual development of**

children in nontraditional families. *Psychoanal Psychol* 2004, **21**:99–115.

14. Pawelski JG, Perrin EC, Foy JM, Allen CE, Crawford JE, Del Monte M, Kaufman M, Klein JD, Smithi K, Springer S, Tanner JL, Vickers DL: **The effects of marriage, civil union, and domestic partnership laws on the health and well-being of children.** *Pediatr* 2006, **118**:349–364.

15. Rimalower L, Caty C: **The mamas and the papas: the invisible diversity of families with same-sex parents in the United States.** *Sex Educ* 2009, **9**:17–32.

16. Bos H, Gartrell N: **Adolescents of the USA national longitudinal lesbian family study: can family characteristics counteract the negative effects of stigmatization?** *Fam Process* 2010, **49**:559–572.

17. Bos HMW, Gartrell NK, van Balen F, Peyser H, Sandfort TGM: **Children in planned lesbian families: a cross-cultural comparison between the United States and the Netherlands.** *Am J Orthopsychiatry* 2008, **78**:211–219.

18. Bos HMW, van Balen F, van den Boom DC, Sandfort TGM: **Minority stress, experience of parenthood and child adjustment in lesbian families.** *J Reprod Infant Psychol* 2004, **22**:291–304.

19. Gershon TD, Tschann JM, Jemerin JM: **Stigmatization, self-esteem, and coping among the adolescent children of lesbian mothers.** *J Adolesc Health* 1999, **24**:437–445.

20. Javaid GA: **The children of homosexual and heterosexual single mothers.** *Child Psychiatry Hum Dev* 1993, **23**:235–248.

21. Va Ray RG: **School experiences of the children of lesbian and gay parents.** *Fam Matters* 2001, **59**:7.

22. Tasker F, Golombok S: **Adults raised as children in lesbian families.** *Am J Orthopsychiatry* 1995, **65**:203–215.

23. Gartrell N, Rodas C, Deck A, Peyser H, Banks A: **The national Lesbian family study: 4. Interviews with the 10-year-old children.** *Am J Orthopsychiatry* 2005, **75**:518–524.

24. Schmied V, Donovan J, Kruske S, Kemp L, Homer C, Fowler C: **Commonalities and challenges: a review of Australian state and territory maternity and child health policies.** *Contemp Nurse* 2011, **40**:106–117.

25. McNair R, Brown R, Perlesz A, Lindsay J, De Vaus D, Pitts M: **Lesbian parents negotiating the health care system in Australia.** *Health Care Women Int* 2008, **29**:91–114.

26. Brewaeys A, Van Hall EV: **Lesbian motherhood: the impact on child development and family functioning.** *J Psychosom Obstet Gynaecol* 1997, **18**:1–16.

27. Chan RW, Brooks RC, Raboy B, Patterson CJ: **Division of labor among lesbian and heterosexual parents:** associations with children's adjustment. *J Fam Psychol* 1998, **12**:402–419.

28. Flaks DK, Ficher I, Masterpasqua F, Joseph G: **Lesbians choosing motherhood: a comparative study of lesbian and heterosexual parents and their children.** *Dev Psychol* 1995, **31**:105–114.

29. Golombok S, Tasker F, Murray C: **Children raised in fatherless families from infancy: family relationships and the socioemotional development of children of lesbian and single heterosexual mothers.** *J Child Psychol Psychiatry* 1997, **38**:783–791.

30. Perlesz A, Power J, Brown R, McNair R, Schofield M, Pitts M, Barrett A, Bickerdike A: **Organising work and home in same-sex parented families: findings from the work love play study.** *Aust N Z J Fam Therapy* 2010, **31**:374–391.

31. Biblarz TJ, Stacey J: **How does the gender of parents matter?** *J Marriage Fam* 2010, **72**:3–22.

32. Cameron P: **Gay fathers' effects on children: a review.** *Psychol Rep.* 2009, **104**:649–659.

33. Bos HHMW: **Planned gay father families in kinship arrangements.** *Aust N Z J Fam Therapy* 2010, **31**:356–371.

34. Dempsey D: *Same-Sex Parented Families in Australia.*; 2013

35. Crouch S, Waters EB, McNair R, Power J, Davis E, van Mourik L: **Triumphs and challenges in recruiting same-sex parent families.** *Aust N Z J Public Health* 2014, **38**:37–38.

36. Wainright JL, Russell ST, Patterson CJ: **Psychosocial adjustment, school outcomes, and romantic relationships of adolescents with same-sex parents.** *Child Dev* 2004, **75**:1886–1898.

37. Crouch S, McNair R, Waters EB, Power J: **What makes a same-sex parented family?** *Med J Aust* 2013, **199**:94–96.

38. Crouch SR, Waters E, McNair R, Power J, Davis E: **ACHESS–the Australian study of child health in same-sex families: background research, design and methodology.** *BMC Public Health* 2012, **12**:646.

39. Waters E, Salmon L, Wake M: **The parent-form child health questionnaire in Australia: comparison of reliability, validity, structure, and norms.** *J Pediatr Psychol* 2000, 25:381–391.

40. Data Outcomes and Evaluation Division: *Preliminary Findings: 2009 Victorian Child Health and Wellbeing Survey.* Melbourne: Department of Education and Early Childhood Development; 2009.

41. Davis E, Waters E, Wake M, Goldfeld S, Williams J, Mehmet-Radji O, Oberklaid F: **Population health and**

wellbeing: identifying priority areas for Victorian children. *Aust New Zealand Health Policy* 2005, **2**:16.

42. Power JJ, Perlesz A, Schofield MJ, Pitts MK, Brown R, McNair R, Barrett A, Bickerdike A: **Understanding resilience in same-sex parented families: the work, love, play study.** *BMC Public Health* 2010, **10**:115.

43. Landgraf JM, Abetz L, Ware JA: *The CHQ User's Manual.* Firstth edition. Boston, MA: The Health Institute, New England Medical Center; 1996.

44. Raat H, Landgraf JM, Oostenbrink R, Moll HA, Essink-Bot ML: **Reliability and validity of the infant and toddler quality of life questionnaire (ITQOL) in a general population and respiratory disease sample.** *Qual Life Res* 2007, **16**:445–460.

45. Hawes DJ, Dadds MR: **Australian data and psychometric properties of the strengths and difficulties questionnaire.** *Aust N Z J Psychiatry* 2004, **38**:644–651.

46. Taylor CL, Christensen D, Lawrence D, Mitrou F, Zubrick SR: **Risk factors for children's receptive vocabulary development from four to eight years in the longitudinal study of Australian children.** *PLoS One* 2013, **8**:e73046.

47. **2011 census QuickStats.** http://www.censusdata.abs.gov.au/census_services/getproduct/census/2011/quickstat/0.

48. Australian Institute of Health and Welfare: *A picture of Australia's Children 2012.* Canberra: AIHW; 2012.

49. Golombok S, Perry B, Burston A, Murray C, Mooney-Somers J, Stevens M, Golding J: **Children with lesbian parents: a community study.** *Dev Psychol* 2003, **39**:20–33.

50. Desai S, Alva S: **Maternal education and child health: is there a strong causal relationship?** *Demogr* 1998, **35**:71–81.

51. **Family characteristics and transitions, Australia, 2006–07.** http://www.abs.gov.au/ausstats/abs@.nsf/mf/4442.0.

52. Barrett AE, Turner RJ: **Family structure and mental health: the mediating effects of socioeconomic status, family process, and social stress.** *J Health Soc Behav* 2005, **46**:156–169.

53. Priest N, Paradies Y, Stewart P, Luke J: **Racism and health among urban aboriginal young people.** *BMC Public Health* 2011, **11**:568.

54. McDonald C, Anderson B: **The view from somewhere: locating lesbian experience in women's health.** *Health Care Women Int* 2003, **24**:697–711.

SIMON R. CROUCH, ELIZABETH WATERS, and ELISE DAVIS are affiliated with the Jack Brockhoff Child Health and Wellbeing Program in the Melbourne School of Population and Global Health at the University of Melbourne in Australia. Ruth McNair is affiliated with the Department of General Practice at the University of Melbourne in Australia. Jennifer Power is affiliated with the Bouveire Centre at La Trobe University in Australia.

EXPLORING THE ISSUE

Does Having Same-Sex Parents Negatively Impact Children?

Critical Thinking and Reflection

1. What constitutes being "a good parent"? What would make a person an unsuitable parent versus a suitable parent? Should there be a hierarchy of desirability in terms of parent constellations (e.g., no 1 heterosexual, racially and religiously the same; no. 2 heterosexual, bi-religious, and racially the same; no. 3 heterosexual, bi-religious, and bi-racial; no. 4 homosexual, racially, and religiously the same; no. 5 single parent; etc.)?
2. Does biology really matter in terms of family impact? To answer this question, read the academic literature on the impact of adoption on children. Are adult outcomes different for children who were adopted compared to children who were raised in comparable homes by biological families?
3. Is parental gender critical in childrearing? Do children need a father and a mother as parents in order to develop psychosexually "normally"? Do children learn gender roles and rules from sources other than parents (e.g., teachers, extended family)? To address these questions, access the empirical literature on psychosexual development (e.g., gender role development).
4. One argument against same-sex parenting is that same-sex relationships are more turbulent and transient than other-sex relationships. To address this issue, search the psychological and sociological work on relationship quality of same-sex and other-sex relationships. Is this underlying claim valid? Are same-sex relationships quantitatively poorer than other-sex relationships?

Is There Common Ground?

Both sets of authors would agree that what is paramount is what is in the best interest of the children. The issue is that the two would disagree on what is "in the best interest." Both would agree that parents and family are critical components in children's health, well-being, and overall development. However, the two differ on their opinions about the form the parents and family are to take. Clearly, Crouch et al. would argue that same-sex parents are equivalent in parenting practices and the children of same-sex parents have equivalent outcomes (e.g., adjustment) to children of other-sex couples.

The American Academy of Pediatrics support the position of Crouch et al. On the other side, Cretella, outlining the position of her organization, takes a stance against same-sex parenting. In another position paper regarding adoption, the American College of Pediatricians state definitively and succinctly that "scientific studies consistently demonstrate that lifetime outcomes are best for children in a married mother-father household" (Wilson, 2013). Crouch et al. take the debate a step further and contend the stigma associated with having same-sex parents has more of a negative impact on the child than the actual sexual orientation of the parents.

References

American College of Pediatricians: About us. (n.d.). Retrieved from https://www.acpeds.org/about-us

Crouch, S. R., McNair, R., Waters, E., & Power. J. (2015). The health perspective of Australian adolescents from same-sex parent families: A mixed methods study. *Child: Care, Health, and Development, 41*(3), 356–364.

Dent Jr., G. W. (2011). No difference: An analysis of same-sex parenting. *Ave Maria L. Rev.*, 10, 53.

Goldberg, A. E., & Cretella, M. (2009, June 25). Gay marriage: Bad science, bad politics. Retrieved from http://anglicanmainstream.org/gay-marriage-bad-science-bad-politics/

McCormick, J. P. (2013, July 20). Study finds that children of gay parents are generally happier than those with straight parents. Retrieved from http://www.pinknews.co.uk/2013/07/20/study-finds-that-children-of-gay-parents-are-generally-happier/

Rye, B. J., & Meaney, G. J. (2010). Self-defense, sexism, and etiological beliefs: Predictors of attitudes toward gay and lesbian adoption. *Journal of GLBT Family Studies*, 6, 1–24.

Szymanski, D. M., & Moffitt, L. B. (2012). Sexism and hetero-sexism. In D. M. Szymanski & L. B. Moffitt (Eds.), *APA handbook of counseling psychology: Practice, interventions, and applications* (Vol. 2, pp. 361–390). Washington DC: American Psychological Association.

Wilson, L. (2013, April). Statement on adoption. Retrieved from https://www.acpeds.org/the-college-speaks/position-statements/parenting-issues/statement-on-adoption

Internet References . . .

American Foundation for Equal Rights

www.afer.org

Human Rights Campaign Foundation

www.hrc.org

RaiseAChild.US

www.raiseachild.us

Selected, Edited, and with Issue Framing Material by:
Scott R. Brandhorst, *Southeast Missouri State University*

ISSUE

Does Dating in Early Adolescence Impede Developmental Adjustment?

YES: Diann M. Ackard, Marla E. Eisenberg, and Dianne Neumark-Sztainer, from "Associations Between Dating Violence and High-Risk Sexual Behaviors Among Male and Female Older Adolescents," *Journal of Child & Adolescent Trauma* (2012)

NO: K. Paige Harden and Jane Mendle, from "Adolescent Sexual Activity and the Development of Delinquent Behavior: The Role of Relationship Context," *Journal of Youth and Adolescence* (2011)

Learning Outcomes

After reading this issue, you will be able to:

- Understand the relationship between dating, violence/delinquency, and sexual activity within the developmental period of adolescence.
- Identify the various types of dating relationships in which adolescents may engage.
- Describe the role of genes in adolescent sexual and delinquent behavior.
- Critically analyze the roles that biology and environment play in developmental adjustment for adolescents who date.

ISSUE SUMMARY

YES: Diann M. Ackard, Marla E. Eisenberg, and Dianne Neumark-Sztainer examine dating relationships among adolescent males and females and the possible correlations between dating violence and high-risk sexual behaviors. The researchers note a strong positive correlation between dating violence and high-risk sexual behaviors. They discuss the potential impact on development and health of the adolescent and the need to provide resources and opportunities to talk to adolescents who are dating.

NO: K. Paige Harden and Jane Mendle, assistant professors of psychology at the University of Texas and the University of Oregon, respectively, examined the associations between adolescent dating, sexual activity, and delinquency, after controlling for genetic influences. They found evidence for genetic influences on sexual behavior and for a link between these genetic predispositions and an increased likelihood to engage in delinquent behavior. They argue that early dating and/or early sexual activity do not cause delinquent behavior; in fact, this study suggests that sex in romantic relationships is related to lower levels of delinquency in both adolescence and later life.

W hen should teens be allowed to date? Are early romantic relationships just inconsequential "puppy love"? Are these relationships good, bad, or even dangerous for adolescents? Does early dating invite early sexual activity? Should adults attempt to dissuade teens from dating? These are just a few questions that capture the debate about adolescent romantic relationships.

Dating is an important developmental process for adolescents. Much of teens' time is spent thinking about dating, talking about dating, attempting to date, actually dating, and recovering from dating relationships. Thus, teen romantic relationships seem like a normal part of adolescent development. Early development theorists in the 1950s, such as Harry Stack Sullivan and Erik Erikson, argued that dating in early and middle adolescence prepares the teen for developing mature, functional adult interpersonal relationships. However, little research has addressed the impact of romantic relationships on adolescent development. Rather, most research in the area of close adolescent relationships has focused on relationships with peers or parents.

Much of the research that does exist seems to focus on adolescent romantic relationships as a negative outcome; that is, romantic relationships are often viewed as part of a constellation of problem behavior such as early initiations of intercourse and other sexual activities, alcohol and substance use, parental defiance, and delinquency. Other research focuses on abuse and violence in teen dating relationships. Indeed, romantic relationships have been linked to stressful experiences for adolescents. For example, research suggests that teens sometimes enter into romantic relationships for undesirable motivations such as to elevate their social status, to prove their "maturity," or to help them separate from their family. Teen romance can increase stress levels by interfering with friendships and parental relationships, as well as distracting the adolescent from his/her focus on academic achievement. These romantic relationships have also been investigated as contributing to negative emotions that may lead to depression. Breaking up, in particular, can have a variety of negative effects on youth, including negatively impacting self-image and self-worth, and contributing to feeling undesirable, betrayed, and sad.

Less attention has been placed on the many benefits of teen romantic relationships. For example, romantic partners are a significant source of social support for the adolescent, relationships are a source of strong positive emotions, and dating helps the adolescent to become more autonomous. Romantic relationships can also be a means of developing better interpersonal skills and competencies, gaining status and popularity, and helping to solidify various social identities. Intrapersonally, teens may develop a positive sense of self through dating (i.e., feel desirable, wanted, intimate) and positive self-regard. Research seems to suggest that affiliation, companionship, and friendship are critical components of romantic relationships for adolescent development and that experiencing romantic relationships in adolescence also helps to prepare youth for adult relationships.

Adolescence is a long developmental period marked by increases in physical, emotional, and social maturity, and a developing sense of self or identity. Early and late adolescents significantly differ developmentally across these domains; therefore, the dating debate needs to be considered in terms of varying levels of social-emotional maturity. Is it reasonable to assume that the process of dating (and its outcomes) is different for youth in early and late adolescence? The focus of this issue is does dating in early adolescence impact youth negatively? Are early adolescents "just too young" to date?

The YES and NO selections investigate dating and sexual activity in adolescence. Ackard and colleagues found a relationship between violence within the dating relationship and increased high-risk sexual behavior, for both male and female adolescents. They go to discuss the research that suggests there is an association between dating violence and serious health concerns in adolescence. Harden and Mendle took a different approach and examined delinquency and sexual behavior and controlled for genetic influences within their study. They found evidence for genetic influences on sexual behavior and the likelihood to engage in delinquent behavior for younger adolescents. The influence of environment, rather than genetics, was stronger for older adolescents in this sample. For early adolescents, sexual activity within the context of romantic or non-romantic relationships was not related to future delinquency. In fact, this study found that after controlling for genetic influences, sex in romantic relationships was related to lower levels of delinquency in both adolescence and later life.

YES ⤶

**Diann M. Ackard, Marla E. Eisenberg,
and Dianne Neumark-Sztainer**

Associations Between Dating Violence and High-Risk Sexual Behaviors Among Male and Female Older Adolescents

In the United States, 2% to 10% of male (Ackard & Neumark-Sztainer, 2002; Ackard, Neumark-Sztainer, & Hannan, 2003; Coker et al., 2000; Howard & Wang, 2003; Howard, Wang, & Yan, 2008; Kreiter et al., 1999) and 4% to 20% of female (Ackard & Neumark- Sztainer, 2002; Ackard et al., 2003; Coker et al., 2000; Howard & Wang, 2003; Kreiter et al., 1999; Silverman, Raj, Mucci, & Hathaway, 2001; Thompson, Wonderlich, Crosby, & Mitchell, 2001) adolescents have reported physical or sexual abuse by the person he or she is dating. Dating violence (physical and/or sexual violence perpetrated by a dating partner) has been shown to be associated with a broad range of compromised health, including depression (Ackard, Eisenberg, & Neumark-Sztainer, 2007; Ackard & Neumark-Sztainer, 2002; Howard, Wang, & Yan, 2007; Howard et al., 2008; Wolitzky-Taylor et al., 2008), posttraumatic stress disorder (Wolitzky-Taylor et al., 2008), alcohol and substance use (Ackard et al., 2007; Eaton, Davis, Barrios, Brener, & Noonan, 2007; Silverman et al., 2001), disordered eating behaviors (Ackard et al., 2007; Ackard & Neumark-Sztainer, 2002; Silverman et al., 2001), and suicidal behaviors (Ackard et al., 2007; Ackard & Neumark-Sztainer, 2002; Howard & Wang, 2003; Howard et al., 2007; Silverman et al., 2001).

Other health risk behaviors associated with dating violence among youth include high-risk sexual health behaviors. Among female adolescents in large, demographically diverse cross-sectional studies of youth, research findings have indicated an association between dating violence and high-risk sexual behaviors such as early intercourse before 13 years of age (Eaton et al., 2007) or before 15 years of age (Silverman et al., 2001), unprotected sexual intercourse (Howard et al., 2007, 2008), diagnosis of a sexually transmitted infection (Decker, Silverman, & Raj, 2005), multiple lifetime sexual partners (Eaton et al., 2007), and/or pregnancy among females (Silverman, Raj, & Clements, 2004). However, only a few studies have investigated the associations between dating violence and high-risk sexual behaviors among males, all of which have focused on physical dating violence only (Eaton et al., 2007; Howard & Wang, 2003; Howard et al., 2008).

In one study that examined associations between physical dating violence only (e.g., hitting, slapping, other forms of physical hurting) among both male and female adolescents (Eaton et al., 2007), males and females who reported having been physically abused by a dating partner were more likely to report being sexually active than those who did not report physical abuse. Physical dating violence was also associated with a greater number of lifetime sex partners among both genders, even when potential confounding variables such as race, age, grades in school, and lifetime alcohol and drug use were controlled. These findings are concerning in that physical violence by a date may increase sexual risk behaviors such as being sexually active and having a greater number of partners, both of which can place youth at greater risk for harm, transmission of infections, and unintended pregnancy. However, because many studies focus on females only and on dating violence only of a sexual nature, an area that remains under investigated among both male and female adolescents is the association between physical and sexual dating violence and high-risk sexual behaviors.

The current research makes a significant contribution to the extant literature by including both male and female youth who could report physical and/or sexual dating violence and engagement in high-risk sexual behaviors. The study examined associations between type of dating violence (none, physical only, sexual only, both physical and sexual) and a broad range of high-risk sexual behaviors with the hypothesis that dating violence would be associated with greater high-risk sexual behaviors. Specifically, it examined relationship status of most recent sexual partner (casual versus not casual or not sexually active), number of sexual partners, birth control use, and condom use across dating violence categories. Associations were examined separately for male and female youth. Study findings have implications toward the understanding of factors associated with dating violence and may inform interventions for both prevention and treatment.

Method

Design, Setting, and Participants

The 1,651 participants in the current study were drawn from Project EAT (Eating Among Teens), an epidemiologic study with two waves of data collection five years apart. Project EAT participants were originally drawn from 31 public middle and high schools in urban and suburban school districts in the greater St. Paul/ Minneapolis, Minnesota area; the study sample was representa-

Ackard, Diann M.; Eisenberg, Marla E.; Neumark-Sztainer, Dianne "Associations between Dating Violence and High-Risk Sexual Behaviors among Male and Female Older Adolescents" *Journal of Child & Adolescent Trauma* 5(4) October 2012. Reproduced by permssion of Taylor & Francis LLC, http://www.tandfonline.com

tive of the area where the data were collected. In Wave 1 (1999), participants completed Project EAT surveys and anthropometric measures of height and weight. After receiving a description of the study, written informed consent was obtained. Full descriptions of study procedures have been provided elsewhere (Neumark-Sztainer, Croll et al., 2002a; Neumark-Sztainer, Story, Hannan, & Croll, 2002; Neumark-Sztainer, Wall, Eisenberg, Story & Hannan, 2006a; Neumark-Sztaine et al., 2006b). Approval for the study was granted by the University of Minnesota's Institutional Review Board Human Subjects Committee and by the research boards of the participating school districts.

Although the Project EAT survey focused primarily on eating and weight-issues in adolescents, items of relevance to other areas of adolescent health also were included. The Project EAT Wave 1 survey was revised for use in Wave 2 and several new items were added to the Wave 2 survey to explore issues of relevance among older adolescents, including violence by a dating partner. Several items were added in order to make the demographic measures relevant for young adults (e.g., housing, employment status). A draft of the survey was pilot tested with 20 young adults, after which minor changes were made based on feedback. Wave 2 surveys were sent by mail to the address provided by the participant during Wave 1. Data collection ran from April 2003 to June 2004.

Only those participants who had been in high school during Project EAT (wave 1) were included in the current analysis, as only these individuals were asked about sexual behaviors. Of the original Wave 1 cohort of high school students, 561 (18.2%) were lost to follow-up for various reasons, primarily missing contact information at Wave 1 and no address found at follow-up. Of the remaining 2,513 participants contacted, 1,710 completed surveys, representing 55.6% of the original cohort and 68.0% of participants who were contacted for Wave 2. The final Wave 2 sample consisted of 764 males (44.7%) and 946 females (55.3%).

For the current study, participants included 1,651 older adolescents (aged 18–23 years, mean age 20.4 (SD = 0.82); 44.9% males; 55.1% females) who completed the Project EAT survey (young adult version) at Wave 2 and who completed questions on dating violence. They averaged 20.4 years of age at Wave 2. The sample was reasonably distributed by socioeconomic status; 13.4% in the lower quintile, 16.4% lower-middle, 23.7% middle, 30.6% upper middle, and 15.8% upper quintile. Participants described themselves as White (68.8 %), Asian (15.6%), Black (8.6%), Hispanic (3.7%), or other (3.4%) ethnicity.

Measures

Dating violence was assessed with two questions: one for physical violence ("Have you ever been hit, shoved, held down, or had some other physical force used against you by someone you were dating?") and another for sexual violence ("In a dating relationship, have you ever been forced to touch your date sexually or have they forced some type of sexual behavior on you?"); both questions were adapted from the Conflict Tactics Scale (Straus, 1979) and the Sexual Experiences Scale (Koss & Gidycz, 1985). Response options included: no; yes, in the past year; or yes, more than a year ago. Analyses were run comparing "no" responses to "yes" responses, regardless of time period.

Most recent sexual partner was identified by participants using the following categories: not applicable (I am not sexually active); a stranger; a casual acquaintance; a close but not exclusive partner; an exclusive dating partner; or fiancé, spouse, or spousal equivalent; or other (Eisenberg, Neumark-Sztainer, & Lust, 2005). Participants were grouped into categories: casual (stranger, casual acquaintance or a close but not exclusive partner) or committed/ not sexually active (exclusive dating partner or fiancé, spouse, or spousal equivalent, or not sexually active).

The *number of sexual partners* within the past 12 months, asked separately for male and female partners, was queried for all respondents (Eisenberg et al., 2005). Responses were none, 1, 2, 3, and 4 or more. Those with two or more male or female sexual partners in the past year were defined as having "multiple partners" and compared to those reporting 0 or 1 partner.

Contraceptive use was assessed with one item, modified from the Youth Risk Behavior Survey (Grunbaum et al., 2004) to include sexually transmitted infections, which asked about the "method you or your partner used to prevent pregnancy and/or sexually transmitted infections" at last intercourse. All those who reported using birth control pills, injectable birth control, condoms or "some other method" with a reliable form of contraception written in (e.g., ring, patch, diaphragm) were considered contraceptive users at last intercourse; those who left the "other" line blank or filled it in with an unreliable form of contraception were categorized as "missing." Those who reported using withdrawal, no method or "not sure" were considered to have used no birth control at last intercourse. Those respondents who were not sexually active were considered to be using safe practices.

Unprotected intercourse was assessed by inspecting answers to the item, "method you or your partner used to prevent pregnancy and/or sexually transmitted infections" at last intercourse; this item was modified from the Youth Risk Behavior Survey (Grunbaum et al., 2004) to include sexually transmitted infections in the question. Respondents who indicated that they used condoms at last intercourse were compared to those who did not. Those respondents who were not sexually active were categorized in the current analyses as not having unprotected intercourse.

A *high risk sex behavior* variable was developed for use in the current study to capture individuals reporting any one or more of the four previously analyzed behaviors considered high risk: casual sexual partner; multiple sexual partners; sexually active yet no contraceptive use of any type and/or unprotected intercourse. *Data Analysis.* Chi-square tests of association were used to compare the prevalence of categorical sex behavior risks for older adolescents reporting dating violence and those with no dating violence history. All analyses were stratified by gender, and conducted using SAS version 8.2 (SAS Institute, Cary, NC).

Results

Overall, 9.6% ($n = 71$) of males and 20.8% ($n = 189$) of females reported physical and/or sexual dating violence. Among males, 6.9% ($n = 51$) reported physical abuse only, 1.6% ($n = 12$) reported sexual abuse only, and 1.1% ($n = 8$) reported both physical and sexual abuse by a dating partner. Among females, 12.4% ($n = 113$) reported physical abuse only, 2.6% ($n = 24$) reported sexual abuse only, and 5.7% ($n = 52$) reported both physical and sexual abuse by a dating partner.

Among males, those with both physical and sexual dating violence reported the highest rates of having a casual sexual partner, having multiple sexual partners, and not using any contraception than those with either physical or sexual dating violence or those with no dating violence history (see Table 1). Compared to males reporting physical only (76.6%), sexual only (81.8%), or no dating violence (53.7%), all males (100.0%) with both physical and sexual dating violence reported engaging in at least one of the high-risk sexual behaviors studied. Among females, those with a history of sexual dating violence only (and no physical dating violence) reported the highest rates of having a casual sexual partner and having multiple sexual partners, whereas those with no, physical only, or both physical and sexual dating violence reported lower rates. Compared to females with sexual only or no dating violence, females with histories of physical dating violence only and both physical and sexual dating violence were most likely to report no contraceptive use and engaging in any of the high-risk sexual behaviors studied. Over half of females reporting physical only, both physical and sexual, or no dating violence also reported unprotected intercourse at most recent intercourse.

Discussion

The current study sought to investigate the associations between physical and sexual victimization by a dating partner and high-risk sexual behaviors among a large, population-based sample of both male and female older adolescents. This study is unique in that it studies both males and females who have been victims of dating violence (including both physical and sexual offenses by a dating partner). Investigating the associations between dating violence and high-risk sexual behaviors has implications for both physical and psychological health complications among this vulnerable population. In the current study, physical and sexual dating violence among males was associated with having a casual sexual partner, multiple sexual partners, and not using any contraception during last intercourse; the highest rates of high-risk sexual behavior were noted by males who reported *both* physical and sexual dating violence. Female youth who reported dating violence of a sexual nature were most likely to report a casual sexual partner, to report multiple sexual partners and to report unprotected intercourse during last intercourse, whereas those reporting dating violence of a physical nature only were most likely not to use contraception during last intercourse and to be at greatest risk for any high-risk sexual behavior.

Our findings stress dating violence of both a physical and sexual nature is associated with a myriad of high-risk sexual behaviors. Our findings are in line with previous studies showing associations between dating violence and an array of serious health concerns in adolescents (Ackard et al., 2007; Ackard & Neumark-Sztainer, 2002; Ackard et al., 2003; Coker et al., 2000; Howard & Wang, 2003; Silverman et al., 2004; Silverman et al., 2001;

Table 1

Percents and Numbers of Male and Female Older Adolescents Engaging in Different High-Risk Sexual Behaviors by Physical and Sexual Dating Violence (DV) Victimization

	Casual sexual partner	Multiple sexual partners	Sexually active; no contraceptive use	Unprotected intercourse	Any high-risk behavior
Male older adolescents	(N = 185)	(N = 220)	(N = 77)	(N = 360)	(N = 401)
No DV (N = 671)	25.4%	29.4%	9.4%	50.7%	53.7%
Physical DV only (N = 51)	17.7	27.5	23.4	59.6	76.6
Sexual DV only (N = 12)	36.4	41.7	25.0	33.3	81.8
Physical and sexual DV (N = 8)	62.5	75.0	37.5	37.5	100.0
	$X^2 = 8.12$	$X^2 = 8.79$	$X^2 = 17.45$	$X^2 = 3.48$	$X^2 = 18.75$
	$p = .044$	$p = .032$	$p < .001$	$p = .323$	$p < .001$
Female older adolescents	(N = 100)	(N = 211)	(N = 100)	(N = 529)	(N = 474)
No DV (N = 720)	10.0%	19.7%	10.0%	62.4%	50.2%
Physical DV only (N = 113)	16.4	37.2	20.4	54.4	75.2
Sexual DV only (N = 24)	26.1	54.2	8.3	29.2	58.3
Physical and sexual DV (N = 52)	10.2	28.9	18.4	65.3	70.0
	$X^2 = 9.07$	$X^2 = 30.94$	$X^2 = 11.77$	$X^2 = 13.04$	$X^2 = 28.93$
	$p = .028$	$p < .001$	$p = .008$	$p = .005$	$p < .001$

Thompson et al., 2001; Wolitzky-Taylor, et al., 2008). However, the vast majority of research investigating the associations between dating violence and sexual risk behaviors has included only female youth (Silverman et al., 2004); male youth have virtually been uninvestigated (Eaton et al., 2007; Wolitzky-Taylor et al., 2008). In the current study, which included both male and female youth reporting dating violence of a physical and/or sexual nature, findings indicate there are serious sexual health risks associated with dating violence. Our findings are similar to that of Eaton and colleagues (2007) in that male and female youth who report being the victim of physical dating violence also report sexual behaviors that are concerning from a psychological (multiple sexual partners) standpoint (Eaton et al., 2007). Yet, our findings expand this work by assessing sexual dating violence and additional sexual risk behaviors (specifically, casual versus not casual sexual partner, no use of contraceptives, and unprotected intercourse), and conclude that being the victim of sexual dating violence is of great concern among male and female youth in both psychological and physical (limited protection against sexually transmitted diseases and pregnancy) ways.

Findings from the current study and others suggest individuals in caring roles (e.g., parents, healthcare providers, school personnel) need to screen for detrimental dating situations, optimizing for the highest level of disclosure while ensuring safety, security, and confidentiality (Hamberger & Ambuel, 1998). Only 32% of adolescent males and 44% of adolescent females who report dating violence seek help (Ashley & Foshee, 2005). There are significant opportunities to discuss sensitive matters such as dating violence with youth. Providing resources and opportunities to talk (e.g., internet chat rooms, small-group discussions, pamphlets in guidance and doctors' offices) may help to reduce the deleterious effects of dating violence as one study found that talking about an abusive experience was associated with lower rates of disordered eating behaviors (Ackard, Neumark-Sztainer, Hannan, French, & Story, 2001). Because dating violence has been found to be a nonspecific risk factor (Ackard et al., 2007), changes in *any* physical or psychological health behavior may signal the need to ask about the possibility of an abusive experience.

Strengths and Limitations

There are several noteworthy strengths to the current study. Primarily, this nonclinical sample of older adolescents which included both genders provides generalizability of the study findings to demographically similar populations of both male and female youth. The use of this population offers the opportunity to understand more fully the dating violence experiences and sexual behaviors of females as well as males who often are not assessed. Furthermore, surveying both physical and sexual dating violence experiences allows for a greater understanding of the sequelae to violence within dating relationships. Study limitations also need to be considered in interpreting the findings. First, the study is cross sectional in nature and thus causal inferences cannot be drawn. Just as dating violence may lead to the emergence or worsening of high-risk sexual behaviors, it is also possible adolescents who engage in high-risk sexual practices may choose sexual partners who are more likely to be physically or sexually violent within the relationship. Future longitudinal studies are needed to address the direction of these associations.

Second, given the comprehensive nature of the study, some of the questions were single items, which cannot fully capture the complexity of some of the primary outcome constructs. In addition, the survey did not collect information on dating violence perpetration, which may be relevant to high-risk sexual behavior and could provide further elucidation on why dating violence victimization is associated with high-risk sexual behavior. Furthermore, even with a relatively large initial sample, some cells of interest were very small (e.g., ethnicities, physical only vs. sexual only vs. both physical and sexual dating violence) for robust analyses. This precluded a more robust analysis, as adjustment for possible covariates would result in unstable estimates. Consequently, conclusions should be drawn conservatively, as some associations may not be statistically significant, however, nonsignificant findings may mark the emergence of a general pattern of high-risk sexual behavior despite not being significant.

Conclusion

Findings from the current study indicate both physical and sexual dating violence is associated with high-risk sexual behaviors among older adolescents. Additional research is indicated for understanding the long-term impact of dating violence on the health and well-being of adolescents and adults. Given the health and psychological implications of both dating violence and high-risk sexual behaviors, concerned adults, health programs, and care professionals should target violence prevention and contraception education for all youth, and early intervention to reduce sexual risk behaviors for youth reporting dating violence. Early intervention is necessary to address dating violence and possible sequelae to violence. Today's older adolescents may be less inclined to establish a romantic relationship with a single partner, and more likely to engage in brief sexual interludes or to incorporate occasional sexual activity into an otherwise platonic friendship. Concerned adults should initiate and encourage discussions about guidelines for appropriate social interactions as well as strategies for handling high-risk dating dilemmas. Interventions may be helpful with higher-risk populations (Wekerle & Wolfe, 1999; Wolfe et al., 2003), including those who engage in violence perpetration as well as those who are victims of sexual violence (Foshee et al., 2005).

Acknowledgments

This study was supported by Grant R40 MC 00319-02 (Neumark-Sztainer, principal investigator) from the Maternal and Child Health Bureau (Title V, Social Security Act), Health Resources and Services Administration, Department of Health and Human Services.

References

Ackard, D. M., Eisenberg, M., & Neumark-Sztainer, D. (2007). Long-term impact of adolescent dating violence on the behavioral and psychological health of male and female youth. *Journal of Pediatrics, 151,* 476–481.

Ackard, D. M., & Neumark-Sztainer, D. (2002). Date violence and date rape among adolescents: Associations with disordered eating behaviors and psychological health. *Child Abuse and Neglect, 26,* 455–473.

Ackard, D. M., Neumark-Sztainer, D., & Hannan, P. (2003). Dating violence among a nationally- representative sample of adolescent girls and boys: Associations with behavioral and mental health. *Journal of Gender-Specific Medicine, 6*(3), 39–48.

Ackard, D. M., Neumark-Sztainer, D., Hannan, P. J., French, S., & Story, M. (2001). Binge and purge behavior among adolescents: Associations with sexual and physical abuse in a nationally representative sample: The Commonwealth Fund survey. *Child Abuse and Neglect, 25,* 771–785.

Ashley, O. S., & Foshee, V. A. (2005). Adolescent help-seeking for dating violence: Prevalence, sociodemographic correlates, and sources of help. *Journal of Adolescent Health, 36,* 25–31.

Coker, A., McKeown, R., Sanderson, M., Davis, K., Valois, R., & Huebner, E. (2000). Severe dating violence and quality of life among South Carolina high school students. *American Journal of Preventive Medicine, 19,* 220–227.

Decker, M. R., Silverman, J. G., & Raj, A. (2005). Dating violence and sexually transmitted disease/HIV testing and diagnosis among adolescent females. *Pediatrics, 116*(2), e272–e276.

Eaton, D. K., Davis, K. S., Barrios, L., Brener, N. D., & Noonan, R. K. (2007). Associations of dating violence victimization with lifetime participation co-occurrence, and early initiation of risk behaviors among U.S. high school students. *Journal of Interpersonal Violence, 22*(5), 575–602.

Eisenberg, M., Neumark-Sztainer, D., & Lust, K. (2005). Weight-related issues and high-risk sexual behaviors among college students. *Journal of American College Health, 54,* 95–101.

Foshee, V. A., Bauman, K. E., Ennett, S. T., Suchindran, C., Benefield, T., & Linder, G. F. (2005). Assessing the effects of the dating violence prevention program "Safe Dates" using random coefficient regression modeling. *Prevention Science, 6,* 245–258.

Grunbaum, J. A., Kann, L., Kinchen, S., Ross, J., Hawkins, J., Lowry, R., . . . Collins, J. (2004). Youth risk behavior surveillance–United States, 2003. *Morbidity and Mortality Weekly Reports Surveillance Summary, 53*(2), 1–96.

Hamberger, L. K., & Ambuel, B. (1998). Dating violence. *Pediatric Clinics of North America, 45*(2), 381–390.

Howard, D. E., & Wang, M. Q. (2003). Psychosocial factors associated with adolescent boys' reports of dating violence. *Adolescence, 38,* 519–533.

Howard, D. E., Wang, M. Q., & Yan, F. (2007). Psychosocial factors associated with reports of physical dating violence among U.S. adolescent females. *Adolescence, 42*(166), 311–324.

Howard, D. E., Wang, M. Q., & Yan, F. (2008). Psychosocial factors associated with reports of physical dating violence victimization among U.S. adolescent males. *Adolescence, 43*(171), 449–460.

Koss, M., & Gidycz, C. (1985). Sexual experiences survey: Reliability and validity. *Journal of Consulting and Clinical Psychology, 53*(3), 422–423.

Kreiter, S. R., Krowchuk, D. P., Woods, C. R., Sinal, S. H., Lawless, M. R., & DuRant, R. H. (1999). Gender differences in risk behaviors among adolescents who experience date fighting. *Pediatrics, 104,* 1286–1292.

Neumark-Sztainer, D., Croll, J., Story, M., Hannan, P., French, S. A., & Perry, C. (2002a). Ethnic/racial differences in weight-related concerns and behaviors among adolescent girls and boys: Findings from Project EAT. *Journal of Psychosomatic Research, 53,* 963–974.

Neumark-Sztainer, D., Story, M., Hannan, P. J., & Croll, J. (2002b). Overweight status and eating patterns among adolescents: Where do youth stand in comparison to the Health People 2010 Objectives? *American Journal of Public Health, 92,* 844–851.

Neumark-Sztainer, D., Wall, M., Eisenberg, M., Story, M., & Hannan, P. (2006a). Overweight status and weight control behaviors in adolescents: Longitudinal and secular trends from 1999 to 2004. *Preventive Medicine, 43,* 52–59.

Neumark-Sztainer, D., Wall, M. M., Guo, J., Story, M., Haines, J. I., & Eisenberg, M. E. (2006b). Obesity, disordered eating and eating disorders in a longitudinal study of adolescents: How to dieters fare 5 years later? *Journal of the American Dietetic Association, 106,* 559–568.

Silverman, J. G., Raj, A., & Clements, K. (2004). Dating violence and associated sexual risk and pregnancy among adolescent girls in the United States. *Pediatrics, 114,* 220–225.

Silverman, J. G., Raj, A., Mucci, L., & Hathaway, J. (2001). Dating violence against adolescent girls and associated substance use, unhealthy weight control, sexual risk behavior, pregnancy, and suicidality. *Journal of the American Medical Association, 286,* 572–579.

Straus, M. (1979). Measuring intrafamily conflict and violence: The Conflict Tactics Scales. *Journal of Marriage and Family, 41,* 75–88.

Thompson, J. K., Wonderlich, S. A., Crosby, R. D., & Mitchell, J. E. (2001). Sexual violence and weight control techniques among adolescent girls. *International Journal of Eating Disorders, 29*(2), 166–176.

Wekerle, C., & Wolfe, D. A. (1999). Dating violence in mid-adolescence: Theory, significance, and emerging prevention initiatives. *Clinical Psychology Review, 19,* 435–456.

Wolfe, D. A., Wekerle, C., Scott, K., Straatman, A.-L., Grasley, C., & Reitzel-Jaffe, D. (2003). Dating violence prevention with at-risk youth: A controlled outcome evaluation. *Journal of Consulting and Clinical Psychology, 71,* 279–291.

Wolitzky-Taylor, K. B., Ruggiero, K. J., Danielson, C. K., Resnick, H. S., Hanson, R. F., Smith, D. W. et al. (2008). Prevalence and correlates of dating violence in a national sample of adolescents. *Journal of the American Academy of Child and Adolescent Psychiatry, 47*(7), 755–762

DIANN M. ACKARD was an Adjunct Assistant Professor in the Division of Epidemiology and Public Health at the University of Minnesota and currently works as a Research Scientist and a Licensed Psychologist and specializes in eating disorders, mood disorders, body dissatisfaction and traumatic events. Marla E. Eisenberg works in the Division of Adolescent Health and Medicine, Department of Pediatrics and Division of Epidemiology & Community Health, School of Public Health at the University of Minnesota, Minneapolis and has expertise in the area of adolescent development. Dianne Neumark-Sztainer works in the Division of Epidemiology & Community Health, School of Public Health at the University of Minnesota, Minneapolis and has expertise in the area of adolescent health.

K. Paige Harden and Jane Mendle

 **NO**

Adolescent Sexual Activity and the Development of Delinquent Behavior: The Role of Relationship Context

Introduction

As the number of sexually active American teenagers has increased over the past half-century (Kotchick et al. 2001), both researchers and policymakers have expressed concern about the sequelae of such behavior, particularly whether sexual activity during adolescence might precipitate adverse psychosocial consequences. . . . [A]wide body of research [demonstrates] that teenagers who are sexually active also report a breadth of psychosocial problems, including poor academic achievement, depression, and low self-esteem (Hallfors et al. 2005; Meier 2007; Spriggs and Halpern 2008). Historically, an earlier initiation of sexual activity has been seen as a marker of externalizing problems (Jessor and Jessor 1977). Sexually active adolescents are more likely to engage in delinquent activities (Armour and Haynie 2007; Leitenberg and Saltzman 2000), and adolescents with a history of childhood conduct disorder tend to have earlier ages at first intercourse and higher rates of teenage pregnancy (Emery et al. 1999; Woodward and Fergusson 1999).

While the correlation between adolescent sexual behavior and externalizing problems is well-documented, understanding how adolescent sexual experiences may impact the development of delinquency remains unclear. In the current article, we address two challenges to understanding the mechanisms by which sexual activity and delinquency are associated. First, we consider the diversity of relationship contexts in which adolescent sexual activity occurs. Second, we control for the role of common underlying genetic factors that impact both sexual activity and delinquency in adolescence. By simultaneously considering both the environmental contexts of adolescent sexual experience and the role of genetic predispositions, we hope to advance a more nuanced understanding of the developmental impact of adolescent sexual activity.

Romantic Versus Non-Romantic Relationship Contexts

One challenge in examining the psychosocial sequelae of adolescent sexual behavior is that teenagers are sexually active within different types of relationships, and these relationship contexts may moderate the developmental impact of sexual behaviors. In contrast to the perspective that adolescent sexual activity, in and of itself, is a manifestation of underlying adjustment difficulties, most adolescents first experience sexual intercourse in the course of a romantic relationship (Manning et al. 2000), and romantic relationships are a normative part of adolescent life. . . . Despite the obvious link between romantic relationships and sexual experiences—and the high subjective importance of romantic relationships for adolescents themselves—research on adolescent sexuality has paid little attention to the characteristics of relationships (Collins et al. 2009). In addition, although adolescents most commonly *initiate* sexual intercourse within the context of romantic relationships, they also have sex with people who are not established romantic partners and with whom there are no clear expectations of emotional intimacy, exclusivity, or commitment. . . . These non-romantic sexual experiences may have different developmental sequelae than sex that occurs exclusively within the context of a romantic relationship.

Colloquially, non-romantic sexual experiences are referred to as "hooking up" or "friends with benefits." The popular media broadly denigrates "hooking up" and its negative effects on adolescent well-being (e.g., Blow 2008; Denizet-Lewis 2004; Stepp 2007). However, few empirical studies have directly examined the developmental impact of sexual activity in non-romantic relationships. Of this limited body of research, results reported by McCarthy and Casey (2008) are most relevant for understanding the association between sex and delinquency. [They] found that sexual activity that occurred in the context of non-romantic relationships predicted a 20% increase in delinquency and a 31% increase in substance use, but that sexual activity occurring exclusively in a romantic relationship was not associated with either delinquency or substance use. Similar patterns have been reported for internalizing outcomes, including negative emotions (Donald et al. 1995) and depressive symptoms (Meier 2007). In contrast, other researchers have found negative effects for sex in non-romantic relationships only for girls (Grello et al. 2006; Shulman et al. 2009). Finally, still other studies have failed to find any effects of sex in non-romantic relationships, after controlling for preexisting differences in adolescents' psychosocial functioning

Harden, K. Paige and Mendle, Jane, "Adolescent sexual activity and the development of delinquent behavior: The role of relationship context" *Journal of Youth and Adolescence* 40(2) July 2011. Copyright © 2011 Springer Science + Business Media. With permission of Springer.

(Eisenberg et al. 2009; Grello et al. 2003; Monahan and Lee 2008). It therefore remains unclear whether non-romantic sex can precipitate delinquent behavior, or whether adolescents with pre-existing psychosocial problems are simply more likely to have sex in non-romantic relationship contexts.

The Role of Genes in the Link between Sexual Activity and Delinquency

An additional challenge when examining the psychosocial correlates of adolescent sexual activity is the importance of genetic factors and, specifically, that the association between sexual activity and adolescent delinquency may be partly due to a common set of genes influencing both traits. Developmental research has largely neglected the role of genes in adolescent sexual behavior, but it is certainly clear that adolescents actively shape and select their social environments—including their romantic and sexual experiences. This process is, in part, governed by their own genetically influenced traits and interests, including their personality traits and their levels of physical development. Thus, adolescent sexual activity can be seen as an example of *gene-environment correlation* (rGE), because the likelihood of an adolescent experiencing sexual intercourse within a particular type of relationship is related to his or her genetic propensities.

Three related lines of research support the importance of considering genes in the association between delinquency and adolescent sexual behavior. First, a number of twin studies have demonstrated that a variety of sexual behaviors—including whether a teenager is sexually active, when he or she first becomes sexually active, and his or her number of sexual partners—are all genetically influenced (Bricker et al. 2006; Dunne et al. 1997; Martin et al. 1977; Mustanski et al. 2007). Molecular genetic analyses suggest that genes related to the dopamine system, which is known to be important for sensation-seeking personality traits (Derringer et al. 2010), are also associated with earlier ages at first sex (Guo and Tong 2006; Miller et al. 1999), likelihood of having had sex (Eisenberg et al. 2007), and number of sexual partners (Guo et al. 2007, 2008; Halpern et al. 2007). In addition, genes influence a variety of other fertility-related phenotypes that are positively correlated with age at first sex (Udry and Cliquet 1982), such as age at menarche (Rowe 2002) and age at first birth (Kohler et al. 2002). Second, both twin and molecular genetic studies have shown that genes influence delinquency and antisocial behavior (e.g., Arsenault et al. 2003; D'Onofrio et al. 2007; Scourfield et al. 2004; Slutske et al. 1997; Young et al. 2002; for reviews see Miles and Carey 1997; Raine 2002; Rhee and Waldman 2002; Rowe 2001). Third, and most relevant for the current project, bivariate behavior genetic analyses suggest that the genes influencing sexual behavior overlap with those influencing antisocial behavior. For example, Verweij et al. (2009) found that the correlation between risky sexual behavior (e.g., sex without a

condom, multiple partners in 24-h period) and antisocial behavior in adults was primarily attributable to common genetic influences. Similar results have been obtained in a cross-generational analysis: The association between teenage childbearing and children's externalizing problems is due, in part, to the parent-to-child transmission of genes influencing both sexual behavior and externalizing symptomatology (Harden et al. 2007).

Analyses that control for the genetic influences common to adolescent sexual activity and delinquency can yield surprising results. In a previous article using twin data from the National Longitudinal Study of Adolescent Health (Add Health), we reported that earlier age at first sex was actually associated with *lower* involvement in delinquency in early adulthood after controlling genetic influences on both delinquency and age at first intercourse (Harden et al. 2008). This provocative finding suggests that adolescent sexual activity may represent a marker for underlying genetic predispositions for delinquent behavior, while also being a developmental transition that may confer some psychosocial benefits. Our previous study focused on a single dimension of sexual experience—age of first sexual intercourse. As we discussed above, however, sexual activity may occur in a variety of social contexts that may modify the relation between sex and delinquency.

Goals of the Current Article

In the current article, we extend previous behavior genetic analyses of the association between adolescent sexual activity and delinquency by examining differences between sexual activity that occurs in romantic relationships versus non-romantic relationships. . . . Specifically, we address two research questions. First, to what extent do common genetic factors account for the associations between delinquency and sexual activity in romantic and non-romantic relationship contexts? . . . Second, after controlling for these common genetic factors, does the association between sexual activity and the development of delinquent behavior differ between romantic and non-romantic contexts? . . .

Method

Participants: National Longitudinal Study of Adolescent Health

Data are drawn from the National Longitudinal Study of Adolescent Health (Add Health; Udry 2003), a nationally representative study designed to evaluate adolescent health behaviors. . . .

[A]dolescents were asked whether they currently lived with another adolescent in the same household. This information was used to deliberately oversample adolescent sibling pairs. . . . The focus of the current analyses is a subsample of 519 same-sex twin pairs divided into two age cohorts: *younger adolescents* were ages

13–15 at Wave I (*N* = 114 DZ pairs, 126 MZ pairs) and *older adolescents* were ages 16–18 at Wave I (*N* = 126 DZ pairs, 153 MZ pairs). Twin zygosity was determined primarily on the basis of self-report and responses to four questionnaire items concerning similarity of appearance and frequency of being confused for one's twin. . . . Analyses were restricted to same-sex twins, in order to prevent bias in estimates of genetic influence due to MZ twins necessarily being identical for sex. . . .

There have been three follow-up interviews with the Add Health participants: Wave II in 1996, Wave III in August 2001–2002, and Wave IV in 2007–2008. The current study examines the effects of sexual activity on desistance from delinquency from adolescence to early adulthood, thus we use data from the Wave I (adolescent) and Wave III (early adulthood; 6 year follow-up) interviews. At Wave III, the younger cohort was 19–21 years old, while the older cohort was 22–24 years old.

Measures

Delinquency

The current analyses use 6 items from the Wave I and Wave III interviews that measure engagement in the following delinquent activities: painting graffiti, deliberately damaging someone else's property, stealing something worth more than $50, stealing something worth less than $50, taking something from a house or store, and selling marijuana or drugs. . . . Participants rated how often they had engaged in each delinquent act in the past 12 months. . . . As expected, mean levels of delinquency were higher in adolescence . . . than in early adulthood. . . .

Sexual Activity

During the Wave I . . . interview, adolescents reported whether or not they had ever had sexual intercourse. Sexual intercourse was specifically defined as heterosexual vaginal penetration. Adolescents who reported a past history of sexual activity were classified as having had sex in romantic relationships and/or non-romantic relationships. First, adolescents reported whether they had a "special romantic relationship" with anyone in the last 18 months. If an adolescent denied being in a "special romantic relationship," but reported that he or she had told another person (who was not a family member) that he or she "loved or liked them," and had held hands and kissed this person, then the adolescent was classified as being in a "liked relationship." For each romantic or liked relationship in the last 18 months (up to 3 relationships), adolescents reported whether they had sexual intercourse in that relationship. If an adolescent reported intercourse in either a "special romantic" or a "liked" relationship in the last 18 months, then they were classified as Romantic Sex = 1. Adolescents also reported at Wave I whether they had ever had a "sexual relationship" with anyone, "not counting the people you described as romantic

relationships." Adolescents who reported sexual activity in the context of a non-romantic relationship were classified as Non-Romantic Sex = 1. Sex in romantic and non-romantic contexts were not mutually exclusive categories: Adolescents who reported both were scored as Romantic Sex = 1, Non-Romantic Sex = 1. . . . Finally, adolescents who reported that they were virgins were classified as not having sex in either romantic or non-romantic relationships [Romantic Sex = 0; Non-Romantic Sex = 0].

. . . As expected, a history of sexual intercourse was more common among older adolescents (approximately 42% of adolescents ages 16–18) than among younger adolescents (approximately 13% of adolescents ages 13–15). . . .

Results

Genetic and Environmental Influences on Sexual Activity in Romantic and Non-Romantic Relationships

. . . First, for both romantic and non-romantic sex in both older and younger adolescents, the MZ twin correlation substantially exceeded the DZ correlation, indicating the existence of genetic influences on adolescent sexual behavior generally. Second, the MZ correlations were higher for younger adolescents than for older adolescents, indicating that nonshared environmental influences were less important in younger adolescents. In fact, the correlation for non-romantic sex approached unity in younger adolescents: There were very few younger adolescent pairs discordant for reporting a history of non-romantic sex. Third, non-romantic sex in older adolescents was the only instance in which the MZ correlation did not exceed twice the value of the DZ correlation, suggesting that the role of shared environment was limited.

. . . Consistent with the observed twin correlations, sexual activity in younger adolescents was very strongly influenced by genetic factors . . . plus small non-shared environmental influences . . . [(shared environmental influences were negligible).]

Among 13–15 years olds, sexual activity, in both romantic and non-romantic contexts, is a relatively rare behavior that is almost entirely attributable to genetic factors.

. . . Among 16–18 year olds, . . ., the etiology of sexual activity differs by relationship context, with sex in romantic relationships more attributable to genes and sex in non-romantic relationships more attributable to environmental factors.

. . . For younger adolescents, the association between romantic and non-romantic sex was due entirely to a genetic path, whereas environmental differences between twins' sexual experiences in romantic relationships did not significantly predict non-romantic sex. Of the total variance in non-romantic sex in younger adolescents,

81% was due to genetic influences shared with romantic sex, 12% was due to genetic influences independent of romantic sex, and the final 7% was due to unique environmental influences.

In contrast, the association between romantic and non-romantic sex in older adolescents was due to both genetic *and* environmental pathways. Of the total variance in non-romantic sex in older adolescents, 29% was due to genetic influences shared with romantic sex, 24% was due to non-shared environmental influences shared with romantic sex, 16% was due to unique shared environmental influences, 30% was due to unique non-shared environmental influences. There were no genetic influences unique to non-romantic sex for older adolescents.

Environmental and Genetic Paths from Sexual Activity to Delinquency

Results from the longitudinal twin model for younger adolescents [indicate a] significant association between genetic influences on sex in romantic relationships and delinquency in adolescence; however, this association did not persist into early adulthood. Moreover, unique genetic influences on sex in non-romantic relationships that were independent of sex in romantic relationships did not predict delinquency at either time point. Finally, twins who differed in their sexual experiences did not show significantly different levels of delinquency in either adolescence or early adulthood. Overall, for younger adolescents (ages 13–15), associations between sexual activity and delinquency were limited to adolescence and were entirely driven by genetic factors.

. . . [F]or older adolescents . . ., [the] results are particularly notable. . . . First, genetic influences on romantic sex predicted higher levels of delinquency in adolescence, as well as increases in delinquency from adolescence to early adulthood. Second, after controlling for these genetic influences, twins who differed in whether they had sex in a romantic relationship showed significantly different levels of delinquency, such that the twin who had experienced sexual intercourse in a romantic relationship showed *lower* levels of delinquency. Moreover, this within-twin pair association persisted into early adulthood, with the twin who had experienced sex in a romantic relationship showing greater decreases in delinquent behavior. Third, there were also significant within-twin pair associations for sex in the context of a non-romantic relationship; however, the direction was reversed, such that the twin who had experienced non-romantic sex showed *higher* levels of delinquency cross-sectionally, and greater increases in delinquent behavior in early adulthood. . . .

Discussion

. . . The current article presents results from analyses of longitudinal, behavioral genetic data on sexual activity in romantic relationships and non-romantic relationships. We compared MZ and DZ twin pairs, in order to control for unmeasured genes that influence both sexual behavior and delinquent behavior. Overall,

our results are consistent with the hypothesis that the etiology and developmental impact of adolescent sexual activity depends on the relationship context and the developmental stage in which it occurs. For younger adolescents (ages 13–15), sexual activity was a relatively rare occurrence, and a common set of genetic factors was the predominant influence on sexual activity in both romantic and non-romantic relationship contexts. These genetic influences on sexual activity, in turn, were entirely responsible for the association between sexual activity and delinquency in early adolescents. That is, genetic propensities to engage in sex during early adolescence also increase propensity to engage in delinquent behavior. Notably, there was no evidence for an environmental path between sexual activity and delinquency among younger adolescents. That is, the few young adolescent twin pairs who were discordant for sexual activity did not demonstrate differing levels of involvement in delinquent behavior. Moreover, sexual activity at ages 13–15 was not significantly associated with future levels of delinquency in early adulthood beyond what could be predicted given initial levels of delinquency in adolescence.

A different pattern was evident for older adolescents (ages 16–18). Not only was sexual activity, regardless of context, more common, but it was also more influenced by environmental differences. Genetic influences on sexual activity were not context-specific; a common set of genetic factors influenced sexual ativity in both romantic and non-romantic contexts, but there was evidence of shared environmental influences specific to non-romantic sex. Genetic propensities to engage in sexual intercourse predicted higher involvement in delinquent behavior in adolescence, and predicted greater increases in delinquent behavior 6 years later in early adulthood. After controlling for these genetic influences, however, sex in romantic relationships was associated with *lower* levels of delinquency in adolescence and predicted future decreases in delinquency in early adulthood, whereas sex in non-romantic relationships was cross-sectionally associated with *higher* levels of delinquency in adolescence and predicted future increases in delinquency in early adulthood. Thus, the current article adds to a small but growing body of literature suggesting that the psychological correlates of adolescent sexual behavior are complex, and that—particularly for older adolescents—certain negative outcomes are only evident for sex outside the context of a romantic relationship (McCarthy and Casey 2008; Meier 2007). . . .

References

Armour, S., & Haynie, D. L. (2007). Adolescent sexual debut and later delinquency. *Journal of Youth and Adolescence, 36,* 141–152.

Arsenault, L., Moffitt, T. E., Caspi, A., Taylor, A., Rijsdijk, F. V., Jaffee, S. R., et al. (2003). Strong genetic effects on cross-situational antisocial behavior among 5-year old children according to mothers, teachers, examiner-observers, and twins' self-reports. *Journal of Child Psychology and Psychiatry, 44,* 832–848.

Blow, C. M. (2008, December 13). The demise of dating. *New York Times*. Retrieved from http://www.nytimes.com/2008/12/13/opinion/13blow.hfml.

Bricker, J. B., Stallings, M. C., Corley, R. P., Wadsworth, S. J., Bryan, A., Timberlake, D. S., et al. (2006). Genetic and environmental influences on age at sexual initiation in the Colorado Adoption Project. *Behavior Genetics, 36,* 820–832.

Collins, W. C., Welsh, D. P., & Furman, W. (2009). Adolescent romantic relationships. *Annual Review of Psychology, 60,* 631–652.

Denizet-Lewis, B. Friends, Friends With Benefits and the Benefits of the Local Mall. New York Times. May 30, 2004.

Donald, M., Lucke, J., Dunne, M., & Raphael, B. (1995). Gender differences associated with young people's emotional reactions to sexual intercourse. *Journal of Youth and Adolescence, 24,* 453–464.

Dunne, M. P., Martin, N. G., Statham, D. J., Slutske, W. S., Dunwiddie, S. H., Bucholz, K. K., et al. (1997). Genetic and environmental contributions to variance in age at first sexual intercourse. *Psychological Science, 8,* 211–216.

Eisenberg, M. E., Ackard, D. M., Resnick, M. D., & Neumark-Sztainer, D. (2009). Casual sex and psychological health among young adults: Is having "friends with benefits" emotionally damaging? *Perspectives on Sexual and Reproductive Health, 41,* 231–237.

Emery, R. E., Waldron, M., Kitzmann, K. M., & Aaron, J. (1999). Delinquent behavior, future divorce or nonmarital childbearing, and externalizing behavior among offspring: A 14-year prospective study. *Journal of Family Psychology, 13,* 568–579.

Grello, C. M., Welsh, D. P., & Harper, M. S. (2006). No strings attached: The nature of casual sex in college students. *Journal of Sex Research*, *43,* 255–267.

Grello, C. M., Welsh, D. P., Harper, M. S., & Dickson, J. W. (2003). Dating and sexual relationship trajectories and adolescent functioning. *Adolescent and Family Health, 3,* 103–112.

Hallfors, D. D., Waller, M. W., Bauer, D., Ford, C. A., & Halpern, C. T. (2005). Which comes first in adolescence—sex and drugs or depression? *American Journal of Preventive Medicine, 29*(3), 163–170.

Jessor, R., & Jessor, S. L. (1977). *Problem behavior and psychosocial development: A longitudinal study of youth.* New York: Academic Press.

Kotchick, B. A., Schaffer, A., Miller, K. S., & Forehand, R. (2001). Adolescent sexual risk behavior: A multi-system perspective. *Clinical Psychology Review, 21,* 493–519.

Leitenberg, H., & Saltzman, H. (2000). A statewide survey of age at first intercourse for adolescent females and age of their male partners: Relation to other risk behaviors and statutory rape implications. *Archives of Sexual Behavior, 29,* 203–215.

Manning, W. D., Longmore, M. A., & Giordano, P. C. (2000). The relationship context of contraceptive use at first intercourse, *Family Planning Perspectives, 32,* 104–110.

Martin, N. G., Eaves, L. J., & Eysenck, H. J. (1977). Genetical, environmental, and personality factors influencing the age of first sexual intercourse in twins, *Journal of Biosocial Science, 9,* 91–97.

McCarthy, B., & Casey, T. (2008). Love, sex and crime: Adolescent romantic relationships and offending. *American Sociological Review, 73,* 944–969.

Meier, A. M. (2007). Adolescent first sex and subsequent mental health. *American Journal of Sociology, 11,* 1811–1847.

Meier, A. M. Adolescent First Sex and Subsequent Mental Health. *American Journal of Sociology,* Vol 112, No. 6 (May 2007).

Monahan, K. C., & Lee, J. M. (2008). Adolescent sexual activity: Links between relational context and depressive symptoms. *Journal of Youth and Adolescence, 37,* 917–927.

Mustanski, B., Viken, R. J., Kaprio, J., Winter, T., & Rose, R. J. (2007). Sexual behavior in young adulthood: A population-based twin study. *Health Psychology, 26,* 610–617.

Shulman, S., Walsh, S. D., Weisman, O., & Schelyer, M. (2009). Romantic contexts, sexual behavior, and depressive symptoms in adolescent males and females. *Sex Roles, 61,* 850–863.

Spitz, E., Moutier, R., Reed, T., Busnel, M. C., Marchaland, C., Roubertoux, P. L., et al. (1996). Comparative diagnoses of twin zygosity by SSLP variant analysis, questionnaire, and dermatoglyphic analysis. *Behavior Genetics, 26,* 55–63.

Spriggs, A. L., & Halpern, C. T. (2008). Timing of sexual debut and initiation of postsecondary education by early adulthood. *Perspectives on Sexual and Reproductive Health, 40,* 152–161.

Stepp, L. S. (2007). *Unhooked: How young women pursue sex, delay love and lose at both.* New York: Riverhead Books.

Stepp, L.S. Unhooked: How Young Women Pursue Sex, Delay Love, and Lose at Both. Penguin Group (New York, 2007).

Udry, J. R., & Cliquet, R. L. (1982). A cross-cultural examination of the relationship between ages at menarche, marriage, and first birth. *Demography, 19,* 53–63.

Woodward, L., & Fergusson, D. (1999). Early conduct problems and later risk of teenage pregnancy in girls. *Development and Psychopathology, 11,* 127–141.

EXPLORING THE ISSUE

Does Dating in Early Adolescence Impede Developmental Adjustment?

Critical Thinking and Reflection

1. All dating relationships involve some form of sexual activity (from holding hands and kissing to sexual intercourse); however, the range of sexual activities in which adolescents engage varies across age and other variables. Is dating in early adolescence less harmful when sexual activity is minimal? Does sex complicate the relationship and set youths up for negative outcomes?
2. According to Harden and Mendle, sexual behavior is genetically programmed—genetics plays a larger role than environment in determining when youth become sexually active. What are the implications of this research for parents of young adolescents? How should they approach sexuality and dating with their teenagers?
3. Ackard and colleagues examine the impact of both physical and sexual violence within the dating relationships of male and female adolescents and suggests that this violence leads to increased high-risk behaviors (i.e., casual sexual partners; multiple sexual partners; unprotected intercourse). What are the implications of this research for parents of young adolescents? How should they approach sexuality and dating with their teenagers?

Is There Common Ground?

Ackard and colleagues argue relationships between adolescents that are marked by physical and sexual violence are more likely to lead to an increase in high-risk sexual behaviors by the victims of this violence. This would lead to a possible environmental explanation for increased sexual behavior by adolescents. Other researchers have suggested that adolescents, especially early adolescents, are not psychosocially equipped to handle the demands of dating relationships and they do not have the resources to manage age-appropriate relationships. Harden and Mendle examine the biological rather than the psychosocial influences on development in adolescence and find evidence that suggest that genetic influences play a greater role in sexual and delinquent behavior than environment, at least in early adolescence. According to this study, the timing of dating and involvement in sexual relationships is not a major determinant of adjustment for adolescents.

What do we make of these results? Are positive and negative outcomes with respect to dating and sexual behavior more a product of environmental influences or genetics? Is there a "nature versus nurture" debate on this issue? Or is it more opaque, with nature and nurture working together in some way? Future research should examine various cognitive developmental concepts (i.e., adolescent decision-making) on the influence and outcome of sexual behavior in dating relationships. Also, future research should examine the environmental/genetic influences more closely and look at how might environmental variables navigate the direction

of biological influences with respect to early dating and developmental adjustment.

Additional Resources

East, P. L., & Hokoda, A. (2015). Risk and protective factors for sexual and dating violence victimization: A longitudinal, prospective study of Latino and African American adolescents. *Journal of Youth and Adolescence, 44*(6), 1288–1300.

Furman, W., & Collibee, C. (2014). A matter of timing: Developmental theories of romantic involvement and psychosocial adjustment. *Development and Psychopathology, 26*(4), 1149–1160.

Herbert, K. R., Fales, J., Nangle, D. W., Papadakis, A. A., & Grover, R. L. (2013). Linking social anxiety and adolescent romantic relationship functioning: Indirect effects and the importance of peers. *Journal of Youth and Adolescence, 42*(11), 1708–20.

Houser, J. J., Mayeux, L., & Cross, C. (2015). Peer status and aggression as predictors of dating popularity in adolescence. *Journal of Youth and Adolescence, 44*(3), 683–695.

Rauer, A. J., Pettit, G. S., Samek, D. R., Lansford, J. E., Dodge, K. A., & Bates, J. E. (2016). Romantic relationships and alcohol use: A long-term, developmental perspective. *Development and Psychopathology, 28*(3), 773–789.

Internet References . . .

Advocates for Youth

www.advocatesforyouth.org

Center for Research on Adolescent Health & Development

crahd.phi.org

Establishing Dating Guidelines for Your Teen

http://www.familylife.com/articles/topics/parenting
/ages-and-stages/teens/establishing-dating-guidelines
-for-your-teen

Romantic Relationships in Adolescence

http://www.actforyouth.net/sexual_health/sexual
_development/romantic.cfm

When to Let Your Teenager Start Dating

https://www.healthychildren.org/English/ages-stages
/teen/dating-sex/Pages/When-To-Let-Your-Teenager
-Start-Dating.aspx

Selected, Edited, and with Issue Framing Material by:
Scott R. Brandhorst, *Southeast Missouri State University*

ISSUE

Should Parents Supervise Alcohol Use by or Provide Alcohol to Adolescents?

YES: Mark A. Bellis et al., from "Teenage Drinking, Alcohol Availability and Pricing: A Cross-Sectional Study of Risk and Protective Factors for Alcohol-Related Harms in School Children," *BMC Public Health* (2009)

NO: Barbara J. McMorris et al., from "Influence of Family Factors and Supervised Alcohol Use on Adolescent Alcohol Use and Harms: Similarities Between Youth in Different Alcohol Policy Contexts," *Journal of Studies on Alcohol and Drugs* (2011)

Learning Outcomes

After reading this issue, you will be able to:

- Understand the harm-reduction arguments underlying the rationale for parental supervision of teen alcohol consumption.
- Articulate a position on zero-tolerance alcohol policies for youth.
- Understand how adult-supervised alcohol use might be a risk factor for or a protective factor against harms for youth.
- Form an informed opinion about supervised teen alcohol consumption.

ISSUE SUMMARY

YES: Mark A. Bellis, a professor at Liverpool John Moores University in the UK, and colleagues suggest that potential harms to youth can be reduced by having them drink in the safety of their own home where they can be supervised by their parents.

NO: Barbara J. McMorris, a senior research associate in the Healthy Youth Development Prevention Research Center within the medical school at the University of Minnesota, and colleagues argue that early alcohol use coupled with adult supervision of alcohol consumption leads to increased alcohol-related problems.

Alcohol-use prevention may not seem like a controversial issue, and parental supervision of teen alcohol use may seem even less controversial—after all, alcohol use is strictly regulated and illegal for adolescents. Substance abuse can create a host of social, health, and legal problems; therefore, adolescent prohibition is easily justified, and adult supervision of underage drinking can lead to charges against the adult. Organizations such as MADD (Mothers Against Drunk Driving) and AA (Alcoholics Anonymous) attest to the potential harm of alcohol use; this harm is thought to be even more detrimental for adolescents relative to adults. So, what makes the provision of alcohol to minors by parents even a question, let alone a controversial issue? The majority of youth try alcohol at some point

during their adolescence. Among youth, the prevalence of current alcohol use increases with age; a national survey found that from 14 percent of 8th graders to 29 percent of 10th graders to 41 percent of 12th graders admitted to drinking alcohol in the last month (Johnston et al., 2011). Further, adolescents often engage in "binge drinking"—heavy, excessive drinking at one time—which is a particularly dangerous drinking behavior. Between 7 percent (grade 8) and 23 percent (grade 12) of youth reported having engaged in binge drinking in the last two weeks (in 2010—Table 8, Johnston et al., 2011). Those who drink at younger ages are also at more risk to develop alcohol dependence relative to those who drink at later ages (Hingson et al., 2006). Some evidence suggests that adolescent use of alcohol is a root cause of later harms (e.g., criminal behavior, sexually transmitted infection, unexpected pregnancy; Odgers et al., 2008). These findings suggest that youth drinking patterns may have a significant negative impact on later life.

Most countries have regulations governing the use and sale of alcohol—called alcohol control measures. One common control measure is an "age of majority." This differs from place to place; for example, in Wisconsin, the age of majority for drinking is 21 years, while in Quebec, it is 18 years. In some European countries (e.g., Belgium, Germany), 16-year-olds can drink wine and beer but not liquor. Interestingly, most of the age-of-majority regulations speak to public consumption and purchase; very little mention of consumption in the home typically occurs within these policies (ICAP, 2012). Regardless of the legislation around age of majority, states tend to have one of two orientations toward alcohol consumption by youth: zero tolerance or harm reduction.

Zero tolerance is an abstinence-only policy. Under this philosophy, policies exist that prohibit the purchase, possession, and consumption of alcohol by youth. Alcohol control laws and ordinances target retailers and bars (i.e., commercial hosts) as well as private adult social sources who may provide adolescents with alcohol (e.g., social-host-liability laws; Coppock, 2009). The effectiveness of these types of laws is somewhat mixed, but these laws generally seem to lead to the reduction of alcohol-related harms (Wagoner, 2010).

The harm-reduction orientation views youth as inevitably going to experiment with alcohol. Youth drinking is considered a normal, if undesirable, part of adolescence. The goals of policies guided by a harm-reduction philosophy are to minimize the harm that can occur from underage drinking and to teach the youth to become responsible adult drinkers. One way to reach these goals would be to have adults—typically parents—supervise the drinking context of the adolescents or have parents provide alcohol to the youth (i.e., limiting the amount and type of alcohol). Parents who provide alcohol to their teens or who supervise underage drinking parties are usually subscribing to a harm-reduction paradigm (Graham et al., 2006). They feel that by providing alcohol or watching their children while they drink, short-term harms (such as impaired driving or binge drinking) will be reduced.

There are cultural or regional differences in relation to the philosophies adopted and the ensuing legislation and policy enacted. The United States and Canada have zero-tolerance policies. Other countries, such as Australia and the Netherlands, have been more supportive of harm-reduction policies when it comes to youth and alcohol consumption. The cultural and policy contexts surrounding drinking may contribute to youth alcohol consumption and parental influence on teen drinking behavior.

In the YES and NO selections, Bellis et al. present findings that suggest that adolescents who drink experience different harm outcomes based on who provides them with alcohol. In particular, having parents provide alcohol acted as a protective factor for youth—as long as they were not binge drinking. In contrast, McMorris et al. conducted a study with youth in both the United States and Australia and found that parental provision of alcohol was related to alcohol-related harms (such as regretted sex and violence). As you read the two selections, consider how these two conflicting results could be reconciled.

YES ↵

Mark A. Bellis et al.

Teenage Drinking, Alcohol Availability and Pricing: A Cross-Sectional Study of Risk and Protective Factors for Alcohol-Related Harms in School Children

Background

In recent decades alcohol has emerged as one of the major international threats to public health,[1] and is now the third largest risk factor for disability and death in Europe[2]. . . . Despite much of the chronic burden of alcohol-related disease falling on adults,[3] the foundations of such damage are often established in childhood. Early alcohol initiation (e.g. before age 15)[4,5] and drinking in larger quantities in childhood and adolescence[6,7] are associated with a wide range of negative outcomes. . . .

Misuse of alcohol by children is an international problem. . . . [I]ncreases in alcohol-related ill health in children are not restricted to the UK (e.g. Germany,[10] Australia[11]).

Despite considerable acute and chronic health and social consequences relating to child alcohol consumption, evidence based guidance on whether children should drink alcohol at all, and how to moderate potential harm, is still being sought.[12] In particular, the effects of moderate or occasional consumption are unclear. Thus, while drinking at early ages (under 15 years) is linked to experiencing a range of health and social problems, the effects of alcohol use at age 15 can depend on amounts consumed, frequency of consumption, types of alcohol consumed and the context in which consumption takes place.[13,14] Alcohol illicitly obtained by children is associated with misuse.[15] However, alcohol provided by parents has been associated with reduced involvement in binge drinking and drinking in public places[15,16] compared with other means of access, and strict alcohol-specific parenting rules have been associated with reduced consumption.[17,19] However, in those aged 12, easy access to alcohol from parents is associated with increased alcohol abuse[20] and parental provision for parties has been linked to increased drinking.[16] With no clear understanding of the relationships between drinking behaviours, environments where alcohol is accessed and consumed, and resultant harms, more research is urgently needed to examine how such factors interact and to inform appropriate interventions.

In this paper we examine the drinking behaviours of alcohol-consuming 15–16 year olds and their relationships with a range of adverse alcohol-related outcomes. Thus, based on previous associations between alcohol consumption and violence[21] we examine experience of violence when drunk and how it relates to current drinking behaviours. With greater alcohol consumption at early ages also being associated with sexual risk-taking,[22,23] we explore relationships between drinking behaviours and having experienced regretted sex following alcohol consumption. As a proxy measure of potential damage to mental health we analyse associations between drinking patterns and reported tendency to forget things after drinking.[24] Finally, to measure effects on others through public nuisance and potentially anti-social behaviour, we examine which drinking patterns are associated with consumption in public places (here; outside in streets, around shops and in parks). Together, analyses are also used to examine potential thresholds for safer drinking and explore factors that may moderate relationships between consumption and immediate harms. . . .

Methods

. . . [A]n anonymous school based survey was undertaken . . . to examine drinking behaviours. . . . [T]he questionnaire consisted of closed, self-completed questions including: demographics (age, sex and postcode of residence); usual frequency of alcohol consumption and bingeing (here, drinking five or more drinks in one session[8]); and how individuals accessed alcohol and types of alcohol products consumed in a typical week (e.g. cans of beer, bottles of wine). . . . Individuals were . . . asked to identify if they drank alcohol in public places and these were described to respondents as outside in streets, parks or shops. The questionnaire asked respondents to identify (by tick box) if they had ever been violent or in a fight whilst drunk; whether they had regretted having had sex with someone after drinking; and whether they tended to forget things when they had been drinking alcohol. . . . For access to alcohol, variables measured were: personal purchase from on- and off-licence settings; access through parents, friends and family; and proxy purchasing through other adults. Access through parents distinguished between deliberate provision of alcohol by parents and alcohol covertly taken by youths.

. . . [T]he sample was . . . restricted to those aged 15 or 16 (n = 9,833). . . . To study drinking behaviour the sample was further limited only to those who identified that they drank alcohol (n = 8,263; 84%). . . .

Results

Regretted sex after drinking (12.5%), having been involved in violence when drunk (28.8%), consuming alcohol in public places (e.g. streets, parks and shops; 35.8%) and forgetting things after drinking (45.3%) had all been experienced by relatively large proportions of respondents. Violence when drunk and alcohol-related regretted sex both increased with age. While violence when drunk and drinking in public places were more common amongst boys, alcohol-related regretted sex and forgetting things after drinking were more commonly reported by girls. . . . Importantly, accessing alcohol through parents was associated with significantly lower levels of having experienced all (negative outcomes (Table 1). . . .

Table [2] presents the relationship between three reported drinking measures (units per week, frequency of drinking, and of bingeing) and proportions reporting each negative outcome overall and separately for those who do and do not have alcohol provided by parents. Overall, all negative outcomes increased in frequency significantly as drinking frequency, bingeing frequency and units of alcohol consumed per week increased. However, provision of alcohol by parents was associated with lower levels of harm at the same drinking and bingeing frequency, and at the same weekly quantities of consumption. Thus, while 19.9% of individuals

whose parents provide alcohol and who drink once a week had been involved in violence when drunk, this rises to 35.9% in those whose parents do not provide alcohol (Table [2]). Similarly for those without parental provision of alcohol, 15.2% of those who drink up to five units of alcohol per week reported some alcohol-related regretted sex, while for those with parental provision rates are only 11.7% even at >10–20 units per week (Table [2]). However, such protective effects were not sustained across all adverse outcomes at higher levels of consumption (especially at high levels of binge drinking). . . .

Discussion

Consistent with studies in the USA,[7,21] our results show that substantial proportions of even those that drink at relatively low frequencies (e.g. weekly) or never binge have experienced adverse effects. Thus, 10.6% of individuals who drink less than once a month have still experienced violence when drunk and nearly a third report forgetting things after drinking (Table [2]). However, amongst children whose parents provide alcohol, violence when drunk and forgetfulness drop to 6.1% and 25.5% in such lower frequency drinkers. Previous studies suggest that both parental attitudes towards, and their supervision of youth drinking can affect young people's drinking behaviours.[15,20] However, results here suggest that similar drinking patterns are more likely to be related to adverse outcomes when alcohol is accessed outside of parental environments. Thus, as well as drinking frequency, parental provision also appears to have a mediating effect on risks associated with binge drinking and units consumed per week (Table [2]). However, any protective effects are limited. Thus, 35.4% of those bingeing once a week, even with parental provision,

Table 1

Relationships Between Sources of Alcohol and Percentage of Children Aged 15 to 16 Years Having Experienced Negative Alcohol-Related Outcomes

			n	Drink in public places (streets, parks, shops)	Violence when drunk	Alcohol-related regretted sex	Tend to forget things after drinking
Source	Buy my own	No	5923	32.15	22.41	8.86	42.61
		Yes	2340	45.00	44.82	21.39	51.98
		P		<0.001	<0.001	<0.001	<0.001
	Parents provide	No	4182	47.0	37.1	15.3	51.4
		Yes	4081	24.3	20.3	9.6	39.1
		P		<0.001	<0.001	<0.001	<0.001
	Get adults outside shop to buy it	No	7060	27.9	24.7	11.1	42.8
		Yes	1203	82.2	52.4	20.8	59.7
		P		<0.001	<0.001	<0.001	<0.001

Table 2

Percentage of 15–16 Year Olds Having Experienced Negative Alcohol-Related Outcomes, by Drinking Behaviour and Parental Alcohol Provision.

Percentage Reporting Negative Outcomes Related to Alcohol

		Sample Characteristics			Drink in public places (streets, parks, shops)				Violence when drunk				Alcohol-related regretted sex				Tend to forget things after drinking			
			Parents Provide			Parents Provide				Parents Provide				Parents Provide				Parents Provide	
		n	No	Yes	All	No	Yes	p§	All	No	Yes	p§	All	No	Yes	p§	All	No	Yes	p§
Binge Frequency	Never	1007	36.4	63.6	11.2	24.0	3.9	***	7.1	13.0	3.7	***	3.8	6.9	2.0	***	21.6	32.4	15.6	***
	<1/month	2302	43.1	56.9	21.4	33.1	12.5	***	13.6	21.0	8.1	***	6.1	8.0	4.7	**	36.6	43.7	31.2	***
	1–3/month	1894	48.9	51.1	34.2	43.5	25.3	***	24.6	30.9	18.6	***	8.6	9.8	7.4	ns	47.4	51.5	43.7	***
	1/week	1533	60.9	39.1	48.9	55.0	39.5	***	40.0	42.9	35.4	**	15.4	16.6	13.5	ns	54.9	55.6	53.8	ns
	2/week	1173	62.4	37.6	64.5	69.3	56.7	***	59.8	63.6	53.6	***	28.4	29.0	27.4	ns	61.9	62.4	60.9	ns
	3+/week	254	65.0	35.0	63.4	61.8	66.3	ns	72.4	75.5	66.7	ns	39.1	39.5	38.3	ns	63.6	66.7	58.1	ns
	P		***		***	***	***		***	***	***		***	***	***		***	***	***	
Drinking Frequency	<1/month	1750	44.2	55.8	14.9	24.3	7.5	***	10.6	16.5	6.1	***	4.7	5.4	4.2	ns	31.6	39.6	25.5	***
	1–3/month	2097	46.8	53.2	27.2	37.8	17.9	***	17.9	24.3	12.3	***	7.1	8.5	5.9	*	40.8	46.1	36.3	***
	1/week	2041	53.7	46.4	40.7	52.1	27.5	***	28.4	35.9	19.9	***	11.0	13.5	8.2	***	47.5	52.1	42.2	***
	2/week	1791	56.9	43.1	54.3	63.5	42.2	***	48.4	55.8	38.8	***	21.7	24.3	18.3	**	57.5	61.0	53.0	***
	3+/week	575	53.0	47.0	55.8	62.3	48.2	***	61.7	69.9	52.1	***	30.2	36.3	23.0	***	56.1	63.1	48.5	***
	P		***		***	***	***		***	***	***		***	***	***		***	***	***	
Units per week§	<= 5	469	39.9	60.1	27.1	51.3	11.0	***	18.2	33.7	8.4	***	9.4	15.2	5.8	**	36.5	47.2	29.5	***
	>5–10	700	41.7	58.3	29.7	41.1	21.6	***	20.4	29.5	13.9	***	8.8	13.6	5.4	***	42.7	52.1	35.9	***
	>10–20	1106	51.9	48.1	45.6	54.9	35.5	***	35.1	40.9	28.8	***	13.2	14.5	11.7	ns	56.1	57.2	55.0	ns
	>20–30	604	59.8	40.2	60.1	67.3	49.4	***	55.3	57.8	51.5	ns	21.4	19.8	23.8	ns	57.7	58.0	57.2	ns
	>30	700	60.4	39.6	68.1	72.1	62.1	**	64.9	69.0	58.8	**	32.7	36.3	27.4	*	59.5	60.8	57.5	ns
	P		***		***	***	***		***	***	***		***	***	***		***	*	***	

p§compares those whose parents provide and do not provide any alcohol for proportions having experienced each negative risk behaviour within categories of units per week, drinking and binge drinking frequency. * P < 0.05, ** P < 0.01, *** P < 0.001. §Units per week consumed could only be calculated for those reporting a drinking frequency of once per week or greater and for those individuals providing details of types of alcohol products consumed and quantities of each product consumed in a typical week.

have been involved in violence when drunk (Table [2]) and amongst respondents reporting the highest frequency of binge drinking, protective effects of parental provision disappear (Table [2]). However, as we were unable to differentiate types of parental provision (e.g. for unsupervised parties or consumption at family meals), here we cannot identify specifically how context relates to risks . . .

With our results showing cheaper alcohol products linked most strongly to adverse drinking outcomes and other work identifying underage alcohol consumption being sensitive to price,[25] governments should establish a minimum price for alcohol (per unit). Drinking bottles and cans of beer was also linked to violence, regretted sex and public drinking while alcopops and wine appeared protective against alcohol-related violence and public drinking respectively. Although it is possible to speculate that such effects may relate to the image of each product (e.g. beer may be considered a drink for tougher youths than alcopops) or the location in which such drinks are consumed (e.g. wine may be more likely to be consumed in moderating environments such as at home with parents) understanding such factors requires further investigation.[26]

As with any questionnaire based cross-sectional study this survey has a number of limitations. Both drinking behaviours and negative outcomes were self-reported and relied on the honesty and recollection of respondents.[27] Whilst guaranteed anonymity can encourage the former, . . . recollection of behaviours relating to alcohol consumption may be incomplete because of forgetting things after drinking, especially amongst those who binge. Calculations of units of alcohol consumed per week could only be broad approximations as a wide variety of products are available. . . . [W]hile the survey specifically examined alcohol-related outcomes (e.g. violence when drunk), it did not provide information on the amount individuals had consumed precisely when such outcomes occurred but only measured their current typical drinking patterns. Consequently, we cannot rule out that some adverse drinking behaviours may have developed as a coping mechanism after, for instance, being a victim of alcohol-related violence or regretted sex[28,29]. . . . Adverse effects of alcohol were limited to four measures and did not include correlates with prevalence of injury (e.g. hospital attendance) or other potential consequences (e.g. effects on education, relationship problems).[8,30] However, chosen outcomes did include adverse measures previously associated with males (violence),[21] an adverse sexual outcome linked to alcohol (regretted sex),[22,23] a measure of potential damage to mental health and development (forgetting things after drinking)[24] and a proxy for involvement in public nuisance (drinking in public places). . . .

Conclusion

Our results support those of others that suggest even low levels of consumption can not be considered safe for children.[19] While studies suggest that levels of youth alcohol consumption may be high in England, and especially in the North West region,[31] the reality in many countries is that by the ages of 15 and 16 a higher proportion

of children drink alcohol than abstain.[8,9] Any efforts to move more children towards or into abstinence through parental rules and controls may be effective for some individuals,[18,19] but may also result in alcohol consumption moving out of the family environment into parks, streets or other public spaces. Our results suggest that such a move, even if overall consumption did not increase, could exacerbate negative outcomes from alcohol consumption amongst teenagers. More studies and meta-analyses are needed to refine public information on alcohol consumption by children. Our results, nevertheless, do suggest that those parents who allow children aged 15–16 years to drink may limit harms by restricting consumption to lower frequencies (e.g. no more than once a week) and under no circumstances permitting binge drinking. However, parental efforts should be matched by genuine legislative and enforcement activity to reduce independent access to alcohol by children, and examination of costs per unit and bottle sizes to discourage large bottle purchases. While these measures are unlikely to eradicate the negative effects of alcohol on children, they may reduce them substantially while allowing children to prepare themselves for life in an adult environment dominated by this drug. . . .

References

1. World Health Organization: *WHO Expert Committee on Problems Related to Alcohol Consumption. Second report WHO technical report series 944* Geneva: World Health Organization; 2007.

2. Ezzati M, Lopez AD, Rodgers A, Murray CJ, eds: *Comparative quantification of health risks. Global and regional burden of disease attributable to selected major risk factors* Geneva: World Health Organization; 2004.

3. Alcohol-related deaths in the United Kingdom 1991–2006 [http://www.statistics.gov.uk/statbase/Product.asp?ylnk=14496]

4. Gruber E, DiClemente RJ, Anderson MM, Lodico M: Early drinking onset and its association with alcohol use and problem behavior in late adolescence. *Prev Med* 1996, 25:293–300.

5. Swahn M, Bossart R: Gender, early alcohol use and suicide ideation and attempts: finding from the 2005 Youth Risk Factor Behaviour Survey. *J Adolesc Health* 2007, 41:175–181.

6. Best D, Manning V, Gossop M, Gross S, Strang J: Excessive drinking and other problem behaviours among 14–16 year old children. *Addict Behav* 2006, 31:1424–1435.

7. Miller JW, Naimi TS, Brewer RD, Everett Jones S: Binge drinking and associated health risk behaviors among high school students. *Pediatrics* 2007, 119:76–85.

8. Hibell B, Guttormsson U, Ahlström S, Balakireva O, Bjarnason T, Kokkevi A, Kraus L: *The 2007 ESPAD*

Report: substance use among students in 35 European countries Stockholm: Swedish Council for Information on Alcohol and Other Drugs; 2009.

9. Fuller E. ed: *Smoking, drinking, and drug use among young people in England in 2008* London: National Centre for Social Research and National Foundation for Educational Research; 2009.

10. Meyer S, Steiner M, Mueller H, Nunold H, Gottschling S, Gortner L: Recent trends in the burden of alcohol intoxication on pediatric in-patient services in Germany. *Klin Padiatr* 2008, 220:6–9.

11. Livingston M: Recent trends in risky alcohol consumption and related harm among young people in Victoria, Australia. *Aust N Z J Public Health* 2008, 32:266–271.

12. HM Government; *Safe Sensible Social. The next steps in the National Alcohol Strategy* London: HM Government; 2007.

13. Andersen A, Due P, Holstein BE, Iversen L: Tracking drinking behaviour from age 15–19 years. *Addiction* 2003, 98:1505–1511.

14. Kuntsche E, Knibbe R, Gmel G, Engels R: 'I drink spirits to get drunk and block out my problems . . .' Beverage preference, drinking motives and alcohol use in adolescence. *Alcohol Alcohol* 2006, 41:566–573.

15. Bellis MA, Hughes K, Morleo M, Tocque K, Hughes S, Allen T, Harrison D, Fe-Rodriguez E: Predictors of risky alcohol consumption in schoolchildren and their implications for preventing alcohol-related harm. *Subst Abuse Treat Prev Policy* 2007, 2:15.

16. Foley KL, Altman D, Durant RH, Wolfson M: Adults approval and adolescent alcohol use. *J Adolesc Health* 2004, 34:345e17–26.

17. O'Donnell L, Stueve A, Duran R, Myint-U A, Agronick G, San Doval A, Wilson-Simmons R: Parenting practices, parents' underestimation of daughters' risks, and alcohol and sexual behaviors of urban girls. *J Adolesc Health* 2008, 42:496–502.

18. Vorst H Van der, Engels RCME, Meeus W, Dekovic M, Van Leeuwe J: The role of alcohol-specific socialization in adolescents' drinking behaviour. *Addiction* 2005, 100:1464–1476.

19. Van Zundert RM, Vorst H Van Der, Vermulst AA, Engels RC; Pathways to alcohol use among Dutch students in regular education and education for adolescents with behavioral problems: the role of parental alcohol use, general parenting practices, and alcohol-specific parenting practices, *J Fam Psychol* 2006, 20:456–467.

20. Komro KA, Maldonado-Molina MM, Tobler AL, Bonds JR, Muller KE: Effects of home access and availability of alcohol on young adolescents alcohol use. *Addiction* 2007, 102:1597–1608.

21. French M, MacLean J: Underage alcohol use, delinquency, and criminal activity. *Health Econ* 2006, 15:1261–1281.

22. Bonomo Y, Coffey C, Wolfe R, Lynskey M, Bowes G, Patton G: Adverse outcomes of alcohol use in adolescents. *Addiction* 2001, 96(10): 1485–1496.

23. Wells JE, Horwood LJ, Fergusson DM: Drinking patterns in mid-adolescence and psychosocial outcomes in late adolescence and early adulthood. *Addiction* 2004, 99(12):1529–1541.

24. Zeigler DW, Wang CC, Yoast RA, Dickinson BD, McCaffree MA, Robinowitz CB, Sterling ML: The neurocognitive effects of alcohol on adolescents and college students. *Prev Med* 2005, 40:23–32.

25. Booth A, Meier P, Stockwell T, Sutton A, Wilkinson A, Wong K: *Independent review of the effects of alcohol pricing and promotion. Part A: systematic reviews* Sheffield; University of Sheffield; 2008.

26. Lintonen TP, Konu Al: Adolescent alcohol beverage type choices reflect their substance use patterns and attitudes. *J Youth Adolescence* 2003, 32:279–289.

27. Greenfield TK, Kerr WC: Alcohol measurement methodology in epidemiology: recent advances and opportunities. *Addiction* 2008, 103:1082–1099.

28. Bellis MA, Hughes K, Hughes S, eds: *World Health Organization. Interpersonal violence and alcohol: WHO Policy Briefing* Geneva: World Health Organization; 2006.

29. Young R, Sweeting H, West P: A longitudinal study of alcohol use and antisocial behaviour in young people. *Alcohol Alcohol* 2008, 43:204–214.

30. Lavikainen HM, Lintonen TP: Alcohol use in adolescence: identifying harms related to teenager's alcohol drinking. *Journal of Substance Use* 2009, 14:39–48.

31. North West Public Health Observatory: *Locol alcohol profiles for England* [http://www.nwph.net/alcohol/lape/].

Barbara J. McMorris et al.

Influence of Family Factors and Supervised Alcohol Use on Adolescent Alcohol Use and Harms: Similarities Between Youth in Different Alcohol Policy Contexts

Adolescent alcohol use is related to a variety of problem behaviors, including harmful alcohol use, drinking and driving, risky sex, and violence (Sise et al., 2009; World Health Organization, 2008). . . .

[T]he U.S. surgeon general issued a call to action promoting a zero-tolerance position toward youth alcohol use that was characterized by abstinence messages, severe consequences for use, and the illegality of underage drinking (U.S. Department of Health and Human Services, 2007). Despite this orientation, some parents still provide alcohol to their children, as illustrated by a 2005 American Medical Association study in which 25% of teens reported being at a party at which underage drinking was occurring in the presence of parents (American Medical Association, 2006). . . .

In Australia, surveys indicate that 30%–50% of adolescent drinkers obtain alcohol from their parents (Hayes et al., 2004), suggesting that it is more normative for parents to be involved in their children's alcohol use. . . . Harm-minimization advocates contend that exposure to supervised drinking contexts (i.e., drinking with parents or other adults present) may help youth learn responsible drinking (McBride et al., 2000, 2003) and, therefore, encourage responsible drinking in contexts where alcohol is available but adults are not present. . . .

The purpose of the current article is to examine and test hypotheses derived from zero-tolerance and harm-minimization policies regarding how family factors influence use in different policy contexts.

Research Objectives

This study investigates the impact of family factors on early adolescent use and harmful use among youth from Victoria, Australia, and Washington State, United States. Specifically, we explore whether adult-supervised alcohol use is a risk factor, as predicted by zero-tolerance policy, or a protective factor for harmful alcohol use, as predicted by harm-minimization policy, and whether the influence of other family risk factors on adolescent alcohol use and harmful use is mediated by adult-supervised alcohol use in different ways, cross-nationally. . . .

The current study has the following research objectives: (a) to examine cross-state variation in levels of seventh-grade family factors, opportunities to use alcohol in supervised settings in eighth grade, and alcohol use and harmful use in ninth grade; (b) to investigate the contribution of family factors to ninth-grade alcohol use and harmful use and whether these relationships are differentiated or moderated by states adopting zero-tolerance or harm minimization policies; and (c) to investigate whether adult supervision of alcohol use in eighth grade mediates the impact of seventh-grade family variables. . . .

Method

[S]ample

. . . The analysis sample ($n = 1,888$) comprised primarily 13-year-olds . . . (Victoria: $M = 13.0$, $SD = 0.4$; Washington: $M = 13.1$, $SD = 0.4$). . . .

Measures

. . . Frequency of alcohol use and number of harmful consequences as a result of alcohol use in the past year in Grade 9 were used as the two dependent variables. . . . Eight harmful consequences resulting from alcohol use were examined: . . . loss of control ("not able to stop drinking once you had started") and social conflict "arguments" violent [/], . . . "got injured or had an accident," "had sex with someone, which you later regretted," "got so drunk you were sick or passed out," and. . . .

[O]pportunities to use alcohol under adult supervision was measured on the Grade 8 survey by asking how many times in the past year the student had consumed alcohol: "at dinner, or on a special occasion or holiday, *with* adult supervision?" or "at parties *with* adult supervision?" . . .

[P]ositive family management . . . measu[red] the extent to which students perceive that their parents monitor their activities, that their families establish clear rules, and their likelihood of being caught by parents for drinking, carrying a weapon, or skipping school. . . . Second, parental attitudes favorable toward alcohol use was [measured by] asking how wrong would parents feel it would be for their child to drink beer or wine regularly and to drink distilled spirits regularly. . . . Third, substance use problems in the family was measured by . . . asking "Has anyone in your family ever had a severe alcohol or drug problem?". . .

Results

Differences in Prevalence of Alcohol Use

Predictably, the prevalence of alcohol use behavior in both states increased over time between seventh and ninth grades. Lifetime alcohol use by seventh grade among Victoria students was significantly higher than among Washington students (59% vs. 39%). By eighth grade, drinking in adult-supervised settings was reported by two thirds of students in Victoria and 35% of Washington youth. By ninth grade, rates of alcohol use had increased to 71% in Victoria and 45% in Washington. More than a third of Victoria students (36%) also reported having experienced any harmful consequences resulting from their alcohol use, compared with about a fifth of Washington students (21%). . . .

Path Models

. . . Hypothesized relationships between family risk and protective factors generally look similar across the two states, despite policy and cultural differences.

. . . For youth in both states, lifetime alcohol use (Grade 7), family alcohol/drug problems (Grade 7), and adult-supervised alcohol use (Grade 8) were positively related and positive family management practices (Grade 7) were negatively related to later alcohol use and alcohol harms in Grade 9. . . .

Favorable parental attitudes indirectly influenced alcohol use and alcohol harm through the impact of adult-supervised alcohol use at eighth grade for youth in both Washington State and Victoria. . . . [Thus,] adult-supervised alcohol use served as a mediator of the association between parental attitudes and alcohol use and harm for youth in both states.

Lifetime alcohol use in seventh grade was . . . partially mediated by adult-supervised alcohol use at eight-grade . . . on ninth-grade alcohol use and harms. . . .

[F]indings indicated that the overall . . . relationships . . . [are] similar for students in Washington and Victoria.

. . . [U]sing single measures of supervised alcohol use, one at a time, results indicated that supervised alcohol use in either context—"at parties" or "at dinner or a special occasion"—increased the risk of alcohol use and harms for students in both states. . . .

Discussion

The national policy contexts concerning adolescent drinking were strikingly different in Washington and Victoria at the time of this study, reflecting different perspectives on underage drinking. Despite policy differences, results from the multiple-group path analysis demonstrate that relationships between family context variables and alcohol use and harms are remarkably similar between youth in both states; thus, there was no evidence for a moderating effect of state context on these relationships. . . .

Higher levels of early alcohol use seem to set the stage for increased use during middle adolescence regardless of country; however, the impact of frequency of ever using alcohol by seventh grade on adult supervision of alcohol use in eighth grade is 1.5 times larger in Victoria, contributing to increases in alcohol use and harms in ninth grade. Supervised drinking is a response that parents make to adolescent alcohol use in both states but more strongly in Victoria. It appears likely that, in the Australia harm-minimization context, a greater number of parents find themselves in the position of having to manage adolescent drinking. Our findings suggest that higher rates of early-age alcohol use and higher levels of adult-supervised use contribute to higher rates of alcohol-related problems in Australia. This clearly contradicts the position that supervised alcohol use or early experience with alcohol will have a reduced impact on the development of adolescent alcohol problems in the harm-minimization setting. Thus, our results run counter to harm-minimization hypotheses, which contend that youth will learn how to use alcohol safely in controlled, supervised settings and apply that knowledge to future opportunities to drink. . . .

In summary, although harm-minimization perspectives contend that youth drinking in adult-supervised settings is protective against future harmful use, we found that adult-supervised drinking in both states resulted in higher levels of harmful alcohol use. This finding has implications for many national contexts that encourage parents to supervise their children's drinking. In addition to Australia, many European countries favor this approach to prevention of alcohol-related harm (Bellis et al., 2007; Pavis et al., 1997; van der Vorst et al., 2010). However, evidence from the current study and previous studies (van der Vorst et al., 2010) provides little support for parental supervision of alcohol use as a protective factor for adolescent drinking.

Providing opportunities for drinking in supervised contexts did not inhibit alcohol use or harmful use in either state. These results, coupled with recent evidence from van der Vorst and colleagues (2010), lead us to suggest that policies should not encourage parents to drink with their children nor provide opportunities to supervise their use. Even after adolescents begin to drink, adult supervision of alcohol use appears to exacerbate

Figure 1

Standardized Coefficients from the Unconstrained Path Models for Washington State and Victoria Students. Analysis Sample Sizes: Washington State: *n* = 918; Victoria: *n* = 908. All Estimates Are Standardized. Coefficients for Victoria Are in Parentheses. The Significant Between-State Difference Is Indicated by the Bold Line. G7 = Grade 7; G8 = Grade 8; G9 = Grade 9.

$*p < .05$ or better.

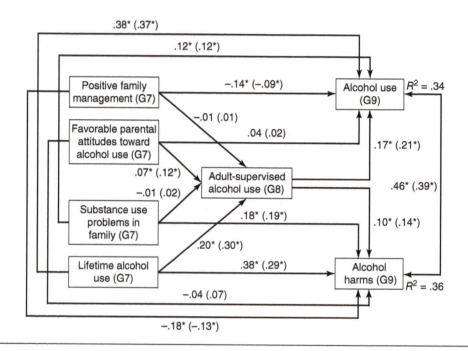

continued drinking and harms associated with drinking. Kypri and colleagues (2007) suggest parental supervision of children's drinking at a young age might set in motion a developmental process by which progression to unsupervised drinking is made more rapidly than it otherwise would be. Similar findings were noted in differing policy contexts by van der Vorst and colleagues (2010) and Warner and White (2003), who found that alcohol use in a supervised setting and subsequent alcohol use outside a supervised setting both influenced the likelihood of progression to misuse in adulthood. Results from the current study provide consistent support for parents adopting a "no-use" standard if they want to reduce harmful alcohol use among their adolescents.

References

American Medical Association. (2006). *Teenage drinking: Key findings of the Teenage Research Unlimited (TRU) survey of teenagers and Harris Interactive survey of parents.* Chicago. IL; Office of Alcohol and Other Drug Abuse.

Bellis, M. A., Hughes, K., Morleo, M., Tocque, K., Hughes, S., Allen, T., . . . Fe-Rodriguez, E. (2007). Predictors of risky alcohol consumption in schoolchildren and their implications for preventing alcohol-related harm. *Substance Abuse Treatment, Prevention, and Policy, 2,* 15. Retrieved from http://www .substanceabusepolicy.com/content/2/1/15

Hayes, L., Smart, D., Toumbourou, J. W., & Sanson, A. (2004). *Parenting influences on adolescent alcohol use* (Research report No. 10). Melbourne, Australia: Australian Institute of Family Studies. Retrieved from http://www.aifs.gov .au/institute/pubs/resreport10/main.html

Kypri, K., Dean, J. I., & Stojanovski, E. (2007). Parent attitudes on the supply of alcohol to minors. *Drug and Alcohol Review. 26,* 41–47.

McBride, N., Farringdon, F., Midford, R., Meuleners, L., & Phillips, M. (2003). Early unsupervised drinking—reducing the risks: The School Health and

Alcohol Harm Reduction Project. *Drug and Alcohol Review, 22,* 263–276.

McBride, N., Midford, R., Farringdon, F., & Phillips, M. (2000). Early results from a school alcohol harm minimization study: The School Health and Alcohol Harm Reduction Project. *Addiction, 95,* 1021–1042.

Pavis, S., Cunningham-Burley, S., & Amos, A. (1997). Alcohol consumption and young people: exploring meaning and social context. *Health Education Research. 12,* 311–322.

Sise, C. B., Sack, D. I., Sise, M. J., Riccoboni, S. T., Osler, T. M., Swanson, S. M., & Martinez, M. D. (2009). Alcohol and high-risk behavior among young first-time offenders. *The Journal of Trauma: Injury, Infection, and Critical Care, 67,* 498–502.

U.S. Department of Health and Human Services. (2007). *The Surgeon General's call to action to prevent and reduce underage drinking.* Rockville, MD: Office of the Surgeon General.

van der Vorst, H., Engels, R. C. M. E., & Burk, W. J. (2010). Do parents and best friends influence the normative increase in adolescents' alcohol use at home and outside the home? *Journal of Studies on Alcohol and Drugs, 71,* 105–114.

Warner, L. A., & White, H. R. (2003). Longitudinal effects of age at onset and first drinking situations on problem drinking. *Substance Use & Misuse, 38,* 1983–2016.

World Health Organization. (2008). *Strategies to reduce the harmful use of alcohol.* Retrieved from http://apps.who .int/gb/ebwha/pdf_files/A61/A61_13-en.pdf

EXPLORING THE ISSUE

Should Parents Supervise Alcohol Use by or Provide Alcohol to Adolescents?

Critical Thinking and Reflection

1. How does harm reduction work as a philosophy in relation to adolescent drinking? Are there other harm-reduction strategies that would work to facilitate safer adolescent drinking aside from parental provision/supervision of alcohol consumption? Does the culture or locale have any implication for harm-reduction strategies?
2. How does zero-tolerance work as a philosophy in relation to adolescent drinking? How does zero-tolerance for alcohol consumption by youth compare to other zero-tolerance strategies for other areas of contention (such as substance use or teenage sexuality)? What is the impact of zero-tolerance policies within different cultural milieu?
3. What role does binge drinking play in policy development, implementation, and enforcement? What is the role of moderate drinking? What might the role of differing types of alcohol (e.g., spirits versus wine versus beer) be in adolescent drinking?
4. Consider your local environment; which policy (i.e., zero-tolerance or harm reduction) would likely be most effective and why?
5. If a parent were to ask you, "What should I do in relation to my child's drinking?" what would your recommendation be based on your reading of the empirical literature?

Is There Common Ground?

The authors of the YES and NO selections seem to be in direct conflict with each other. Bellis et al. state that parental provision of alcohol is a protective factor—provides protection against harms such as regretted sex, violence, and blacking out. In contrast, McMorris et al. state explicitly that adult supervision and provision of alcohol to teens resulted in increased risk of alcohol use and associated harms. One major difference between the two studies was the age of the youth involved. Bellis et al. were studying 15–16-year-olds whereas McMorris et al. were studying 13–15-year-olds. Both authors would likely agree that drinking at younger ages (i.e., before 15 years) is associated with a greater risk of alcohol-related harms for the youth.

Both authors would likely agree that binge drinking (i.e., usually defined as drinking five or more alcoholic beverages on one drinking occasion) is a particularly risky behavior. In the literature, binge drinking has been found to be a particularly noxious drinking behavior; it is a very common drinking behavior in youth (64 percent of those who reported drinking in the past month), and it is associated with a large variety of harms to these youth (academic problems, involvement with drinking and driving, being sexually active, smoking, dating violence, suicide attempts, and illicit drug use; Miller et al., 2007). Bellis et al. found that the protective effects of parental supervision tended to disappear for those youth who had high levels of binge drinking.

Both sets of authors would agree that family (i.e., parents) is really important in relation to adolescent drinking; just what role family takes in reducing teen alcohol use or how family acts as a protective or risk factor is not entirely clear. Part of the problem for both of these studies is that the context in which parental alcohol provision/supervision occurred was not well defined. For example, neither study compared alcohol provision for "parties" versus family functions. The results of these types of supervision/provision may be very different. Further, the role that parental supervision/provision plays in teen harms may not be a simple one. This may interact with or be mediated through some other variable (e.g., the parents own drinking behavior or drinking attitudes).

In sum, there is research to support both perspectives. A person who says that it is bad for parents to provide alcohol to their drinking teens is correct (McMorris et al. support this). A person who says that it is good for parents to provide alcohol to their drinking teens is correct (Bellis et al. support this). Regardless of which approach we take, programs aimed at reducing alcohol consumption should be part of a broader societal response. Youth attitudes about alcohol likely reflect the modeling of adult attitudes and behavior.

Additional Resources

Bellis, M., Hughes, K., Morleo, M., Tocque, K., Hughes, S., Allen, T., et al. (2007). Predictors of risky alcohol consumption in schoolchildren and their implications for preventing alcohol-related harm. *Substance Abuse Treatment, Prevention, and Policy* 2007, *2*(15) [page numbers unknown]. Retrieved from doi:10.1186/1747-597X-2-15

An additional study by the Bellis lab that also argues that parental provision of alcohol to youth may be warranted.

Foley, K. L., Altman, D., Durant, R. H., & Wolfson, M. (2004). Adults' approval and adolescents' alcohol use. *Journal of Adolescent Health, 35*(4), 345 e17–e26.

This classic citation has caused much controversy. "Parents who provided alcohol to their adolescent children or drank with them were more likely to have children who neither regularly used nor abused alcohol" (p. e25) caused many to conclude that parental provision of alcohol to youth might be a protective factor for teens.

Kliewer, W. (2010). Family processes in drug use etiology. In L. M. Scheier (Ed.), *Handbook of drug use etiology: Theory, methods, and empirical findings* (pp. 365–381). Washington, DC: American Psychological Association.

This chapter presents an overarching socialization model of adolescent substance use behavior—the majority of which involves familial influences. Three family influence areas are parental coaching (messages relayed from parents to their adolescent children), parental modeling (parental use of substances), and family context (all areas of family climate such as family structure, parent–child relations, and parenting). These are thought to influence coping processes, which, in turn, is thought to impact adolescent substance abuse.

Komro, K. A., Maldonado-Molina, M. M., Tobler, A. L., Bonds, J. R., & Muller, K. E. (2007). Effects of home access and availability of alcohol on young adolescents' alcohol use. *Addiction, 102*, 1597–1608.

A longitudinal study of the impact of provision of alcohol by parents at age 12 on alcohol-related outcomes at age 14. Parental provision of alcohol was associated with greater use of alcohol and greater intentions to use alcohol in the future by the youth. The authors concluded that it is risky for parents to provide alcohol to their children.

Logan, D. E., & Marlatt, G. A. (2010). Harm reduction therapy: A practice-friendly review of the research. *Journal of Clinical Psychology: In Session, 66*(2), 201–214.

A review paper of harm-reduction theory and clinical research applied to cigarettes and substance use in addition to alcohol. Aimed at practitioners and therapists, this paper focuses on research involving the individual as opposed to more general policies.

Maloney, E., Hutchinson, D., Vogl, L., Essau, C., & Mattick, R. (2010). Adolescent drinking: The social influence of the family. In K. T. Everly & E. M., Cosell (Eds.), *Social drinking: Uses, abuses, and psychological factors* (pp. 141–175). New York: Nova Science Publishers.

This chapter is an excellent review of the family characteristics that are associated with adolescent alcohol use and abuse. Three key areas reviewed include parental provi-sion of alcohol, parental alcohol attitudes, and modeling. Recommendations for parents based on the academic literature are made.

Nakaya, A. C. (2008). *Alcohol.* Farmington Hills, MI: Greenhaven Press.

This book addresses a number of alcohol-related issues from an "opposing sides" perspective—which is much like the current *Taking Sides* series. In particular, Chapter 2 of this book has two pieces that address the seriousness of underage drinking. Chapter 4 of this book has two pieces that speak to parental supervision of teenage drinking (one being "benefi-cial" and the other being "encourages dangerous behavior"). These latter two pieces are excerpts from news sources.

Nelson, D. E. (2011). *Teen drug abuse.* Farmington Hills, MI: Greenhaven Press.

This book addresses a number of drug-related issues from an "opposing sides" perspective—which is much like the current *Taking Sides* series. In particular, Chapter 2 of this book addresses the threat that alcohol may pose to teens. Two pieces, in particular, speak to parental supervision of teenage drinking; one is titled "It is healthy for teens to drink moderately in the home," while the other is called "The dangers of allowing children to drink in the home." The first piece is an excerpt from a newspaper, while the second is an excerpt from a self-help book aimed at parents.

Toomey, T. L, Lenk, K. M. & Wagenaar, A. C. (2007). Environmental policies to reduce college drinking: An update of research findings. *Journal of Studies on Alcohol and Drugs, 68*(2), 208–219.

This paper reviews the published literature on the effects of campus policies on drinking by university students. The authors conclude that policies can make a difference in drinking behavior but a multi-strategy policy (i.e., combining different policies such as required server intervention training plus increasing roadside checks) would probably be the most effective. However, the authors caution that more research is needed regarding the impact of policies.

References

Coppock, L. A. (2009). Social host immunity: A new paradigm to foster responsibility. *Capital University Law Review, 38*(1), 19–40.

This article reviews the history of social host respon-sibility (e.g., people who host a party where alcohol is present or bars where alcohol is served) for the actions of people who are drunk and describes the current state of social host laws in the United States. Finally, the author presents arguments for and against holding social liability. The author concludes in favor of social host liability laws. Retrieved February 2012 from http://law .capital.edu/Inside_Capital_Law/Current_Students /Law_Review/Articles/Volume_38_Issue_1/Volume_38 _Issue_1_—_Back_Issues.aspx

Graham, M. L., Ward, B., Munro, G., Snow, P., & Ellis, J. (2006). Rural parents, teenagers, and alcohol: What are parents thinking? *Rural and Remote Health*, 6(383). Retrieved from http://www.rrh.org.au/publishedarticles /article_print_383.pdf

This was a qualitative focus-group study where the investigators interviewed parents in an attempt to understand why parents would provide alcohol to their adolescent children. The interviews indicated that parents were using a number of harm-reduction strategies to ward off short-term harms (e.g., youth drinking and driving, aspiration of vomit) and were not as concerned about longer-term risks. However, parents felt ill-prepared to apply harm-reduction strategies and struggled with how to deal with youth alcohol consumption.

Hingson R. W., Heeren T, & Winter M. R. (2006). Age at drinking onset and alcohol dependence: age at onset, duration, and severity. *Archives of Pediatric Medicine, 160*, 739–746.

A large, cross-sectional sample of adults were surveyed about their current and adolescent drinking. Results suggested that clinical alcohol dependence was associated with age; those who drank at younger ages were more likely to have some experience with alcohol dependence in their lifetime.

International Center for Alcohol Policies (ICAP). (2012). *Young people's drinking: Key facts and issues.* Washington, DC. Retrieved from www.icap.org/PolicyIssues /YoungPeoplesDrinking/KeyFactsandIssues/tabid/119 /Default.aspx

The International Center for Alcohol Policies (ICAP) is a not-for-profit organization, *supported* by major producers of alcoholic beverages with the stated mission to understand alcohol's role in the U.S. society and reduce the abuse of alcohol. The organization publishes scholarly books and many other papers are available on the ICAP Web page. The Web site is well sourced. This fact sheet is from the Policy section of the ICAP Web site dedicated to "Young People's Drinking."

Johnston, L. D., O'Malley, P. M., Bachman, J. G., & Schulenberg, J. E. (2011). *Monitoring the Future national results on adolescent drug use: Overview of key findings, 2010.* Ann Arbor, MI: Institute for Social Research, The University of Michigan.

This document is one of many overviews of a long-running study of youth. Each year, a large, representative sample of grade-12 students (and, since 1991, grades 8 and 10 students) are surveyed about their drug use—this includes alcohol. This type of long-term investigation, with reliable and valid data, allows researchers, educators, and politicians to monitor the trends in adolescent alcohol and other substance use.

Miller, J. W., Naimi, T. S., Brewer, R. D., & Jones, S. E. (2007). Binge drinking and associated health risk behaviors among high school students. *Pediatrics, 119*, 76–85.

A population-based study of binge drinking by U.S. adolescents; a variety of harms had a much greater likelihood (called odds ratio) for binge drinkers compared to drinkers who did not report binge drinking or compared to non-drinkers.

Odgers, C. L., Caspi, A., Nagin, D. S., Piquero, A. R., Slutske, W. S., Milne, B. J., et al. (2008). Is it important to prevent early exposure to drugs and alcohol among adolescents? *Psychological Science, 19*(10), 1037–1044.

This is a research article describing a 30-year longitudinal study that investigated the impact of early alcohol exposure on adult outcomes. The findings suggested two key things: (1) early exposure to alcohol (before 15 years of age) resulted in negative adult outcomes and (2) children who were "normal" (i.e., no pre-existing conduct problems) demonstrated negative adult outcomes of early alcohol exposure. This last finding is particularly poignant because, prior to these findings, people argued it was youth who had "problems" that led them to drink and this led to adult problems. This well-designed study speaks to that idea—and disconfirms it. Age when drinking begins is the key, not who the child is.

Wagoner, K. G. (2010). *An Examination of Social Host Policies: Relationship with Social Drinking Context and Alcohol Use among Adolescents.* Dissertation, The University of North Carolina at Greensboro (UNCG). Retrieved from http://libres.uncg.edu/ir/uncg/f/Wagoner _uncg_0154D_10351.pdf

This is a dissertation where the author investigated the impact of social host laws, specifically aimed at private adults who serve alcohol to adolescents or allow alcohol to be consumed by adolescents at their home. Her findings suggest that these policies are not immediately effective at achieving the ultimate goal of reducing youth drinking.

Internet References . . .

CDC: Fact Sheets—Underage Drinking

http://www.cdc.gov/alcohol/fact-sheets/underage
-drinking.htm

National Council on Alcoholism and Drug Dependence, INC.: Self Test for Teenagers

https://www.ncadd.org/get-help/take-the-test/self-test
-for-teenagers

ProCon.org: 45 States That Allow Underage (Under 21) Alcohol Consumption

http://drinkingage.procon.org/view.resource
.php?resourceID=002591

Substance Abuse and Mental Health Services Administration

http://www.samhsa.gov/underage-drinking

The Cool Spot

www.thecoolspot.gov

Selected, Edited, and with Issue Framing Material by:
Scott R. Brandhorst, *Southeast Missouri State University*

ISSUE

Should Parental Consent Be Required for Adolescents Seeking Abortion?

YES: Teresa Stanton Collett, from Testimony Before the United States House of Representatives Committee on the Judiciary, Subcommittee on the Constitution. H.R. 2299 the "Child Interstate Abortion Notification Act" (2012)

NO: Advocates for Youth "Abortion and Parental Involvement Laws: A Threat to Young Women's Health and Safety," *Advocates for Youth*

Learning Outcomes

After reading this issue, you will be able to:

- Understand some of the reasons for and against the existence of parental involvement laws and policies.
- Define the role of *judicial bypass* in adolescent abortion—from a legal standpoint and a *Loco Parentis*—"in place of parents or instead of a parent"—perspective.
- Examine the concept of "maturity" in abortion decisions from psychological, legal, and moral perspectives.

ISSUE SUMMARY

YES: Teresa Stanton Collett, law professor at the University of St. Thomas School of Law in Minnesota, testified about the "Child Interstate Abortion Notification Act" before a U.S. House of Representatives subcommittee that minors would benefit greatly from parental involvement in youth abortion decisions. She argues a federal law is needed to protect girls from exploitation and improve medical care.

NO: *Advocates for Youth* reviews the differences between parental consent and parental notification and provides data in relation to what different states require in relation to these concepts. The authors put forth the position that parental involvement laws do more harm than good in relation to the well-being of adolescent females.

In 1973, the U.S. Supreme Court decision *Roe v. Wade* guaranteed a woman's right to access to abortion without restriction during the first trimester. The decision did not mention, however, the age of the woman seeking the abortion. One of the most contentious controversies surrounding adolescent abortion involves consultation: A majority of individual states have introduced requirements that a girl under the age of 18 have one or both parents' or legal guardians' consent in order to obtain an abortion. Alternatively, states may require that parents/guardians be notified prior to their daughter's abortion.

Since two key legal decisions in 1969 and 1988, abortion has been legal in Canada and it is treated like any other medical procedure. Canada has no age restrictions, and nothing similar to the U.S. state parental notifications/consent laws is required when adolescents

seek abortions. However, some Canadian provinces have general consent-to-treatment law age limits, which would apply to abortion, and some hospitals have policies requiring youth to obtain parental consent for abortions, specifically (Downie & Nassar, 2007). Because the Canadian legal situation is quite different than that of the United States, parental notification/consent is not as contentious issue.

Discussions about abortion rights are rooted in the fundamental support or opposition to abortion itself. It can be quite challenging, then, to separate out one's opinion about abortion, per se, from a minor's ability to make an informed decision about abortion. People who hold opinions that abortion is morally wrong would argue that, at minimum, parental notification/consent from a minor's abortion is mandatory. Even some adults who are pro-choice would advocate for parental notification/consent requirements. And still others believe that any girl or woman, regardless of age, is able and has the right to make this personal decision for herself. Ultimately, the question of consultation with parents implies that some people think that adolescents are competent, while others think those adolescents are not competent to make this decision.

Scholars in favor of parental involvement legislation and policies argue that parental involvement laws reduce abortion rates through various mechanisms: For example, parents will intervene and prevent a teen from having an abortion, such laws will deter teens from becoming pregnant (e.g., encourage greater/more consistent contraceptive use or encourage less sexual activity), and abortion providers may be more cautious about performing abortions on teens. As well, those in favor of parental notification/consent requirements also argue that parental involvement is a protective factor for their children: The parents know the unique medical history of their child (of which, she herself may be unaware), sexual abuse or coercion may have resulted in the pregnancy and the parents may take action, and family communication may be enhanced.

Scholars who are opposed to parental involvement legislation and policies argue that family communication is not enhanced, that when girls do not communicate with their parents about their pregnancies, it is because they fear family discord, harm to the parent-child relationship, or physical reactions from parents. Medical associations support the involvement of parents in adolescent abortion decisions but do not support such involvement when it compromises the girl's medical privacy/confidentiality (Webster et al., 2010). Opponents also argue that these laws result in greater travel for out-of-state abortions (which may account for the decrease in abortion rates/ratios), delays in obtaining abortion (later abortions being a greater health hazard), and potentially creates a high-risk living environment for the resultant child of the unexpected pregnancy (e.g., Sen et al., 2012). Opponents are unconvinced that evidence exists that the parental consent/information laws result in greater practice of birth control or reductions in teen pregnancy (Dennis et al., 2009).

In the United States, girls who want an abortion, who do not want, or who are unable to obtain parental consent can access a process called "judicial bypass." A judge can decide if a youth is mature enough to make her own decision regarding abortion or, even if she is not mature enough, an abortion would be in her best interest. The existence of judicial bypass allows states to have parental consent laws and not be in violation of the constitutional rights of the pregnant teen (Bonny, 2007). Thirty-eight states have some form of judicial bypass available as of January 2015 (Advocates for Youth, n.d.). Based on the writings around judicial bypass of parental involvement (e.g., Bonny, 2007; Rebouche, 2011), it is clear that adolescent maturity and competence is the key question and purpose underlying parental consent/notification laws and policies.

The *Advocates for Youth* argues that parental involvement provides more of a threat to the well-being of adolescent females because it leaves many of them alone and at risk and has many more negative outcomes than positive ones (i.e., no clear impact on birth rates or abortion rates). Furthermore, the authors provide obstacles to judicial bypass and provide the position of medical experts within the field. Stanton Collett argues that parental involvement benefits teens because parents are more capable of obtaining information and better equipped to deal with the medical aspects of abortion relative to a panicky teen. She also argues that parents should be involved in abortion decisions in order to reduce coercion—either leading to the pregnancy or leading to the abortion decision.

YES ⤶

Teresa Stanton Collett

Testimony Before the United States House of Representatives Committee on the Judiciary, Subcommittee on the Constitution. H.R. 2299 the "Child Interstate Abortion Notification Act"

... [T]he "Child Interstate Abortion Notification Act" ("CIANA") . . . bill is the culmination of a decade of Congressional effort to insure that young girls are not coerced or deceived into crossing state lines to obtain secret abortions. . . . [It is] premised on what Justice O'Connor has called "the quite reasonable assumption that [pregnant] minors will benefit from consultation with their parents and that children will often not realize that their parents have their best interests at heart."

Sizable bipartisan majorities of both Congressional houses voted to enact this common sense legislation during the last legislative session, only to have those votes nullified by opponents' last-minute procedural maneuvering. House leadership refused to even allow a hearing on CIANA during the 2008 legislative session. This outcome is particularly troubling in light of the public's strong support for parental involvement.[1]

My testimony today is based on my scholarly study of parental involvement laws, and my practical experience in assisting state legislators across the country evaluate parental involvement laws during the legislative process. It also represents my experience in assisting the attorneys general of Florida, New Hampshire, and Oklahoma in defending their parental involvement laws. [Recently] I testified as an expert witness in an Alaska District Court regarding judicial bypass of parental notification laws.

. . . I . . . discuss [how] minors benefit from parental involvement when deciding whether to continue or terminate a pregnancy. . . .

Minors Benefit from Parental Involvement

There is widespread agreement that as a general rule, parents should be involved in their minor daughter's decision to terminate an unplanned pregnancy. The national consensus in favor of this position is illustrated by the fact that there are parental involvement laws on the books in forty-five of the fifty states although

only thirty-seven are in force due primarily to judicial actions Only five states in the nation have not attempted to legislatively insure some level of parental involvement in a minor's decision to obtain an abortion.[2]

This agreement even extends to young people, ages 18 to 29.[3] To my knowledge, no organizations or individuals, whether abortion rights activists or pro-life advocates, dispute this point. On an issue as contentious and divisive as abortion, it is both remarkable and instructive that there is such firm and long-standing support for laws requiring parental involvement.

Various reasons underlie this broad and consistent support. As Justices O'Connor, Kennedy, and Souter observed in *Planned Parenthood v. Casey* [1992], parental consent and notification laws related to abortions "are based on the quite reasonable assumption that minors will benefit from consultation with their parents and that children will often not realize that their parents have their best interests at heart." Writing for a unanimous court in 2005, Justice O'Connor noted "States unquestionably have the right to require parental involvement when a minor considers terminating her pregnancy, because of their 'strong and legitimate interest in the welfare of [their] young citizens, whose immaturity, inexperience, and lack of judgment may sometimes impair their ability to exercise their rights wisely'."[4]

. . . I will limit my remarks to examining two of the benefits that are achieved by parental involvement statutes: improved medical care for young girls seeking abortions and increased protection against sexual exploitation by adult men.

Improved Medical Care of Minor Girls

Medical care for minors seeking abortions is improved by parental involvement in three ways. First, parental involvement laws allow parents to assist their daughter in the selection of the abortion provider.

As with all medical procedures, one of the most important guarantees of patient safety is the professional competence of those who perform the medical procedure. In *Bellotti v. Baird,* the United States Supreme Court acknowledged the superior ability of parents to evaluate and select appropriate healthcare providers [1979].

> In this case, however, we are concerned only with minors who according to the record range in age from children of twelve years to 17-year-old teenagers. Even the latter are less likely than adults to know or be able to recognize ethical, qualified physicians, or to have the means to engage such professionals. Many minors who bypass their parents probably will resort to an abortion clinic, without being able to distinguish the competent and ethical from those that are incompetent or unethical.

Historically, the National Abortion Federation has recommended that patients seeking an abortion confirm that the abortion will be performed by a licensed physician in good standing with the state Board of Medical Examiners and that the doctor have admitting privileges at a local hospital not more than twenty minutes away from the location where the abortion is to occur in order to insure adequate care should complications arise.[5] These recommendations were deleted after they were introduced into evidence in malpractice cases against abortion providers. Notwithstanding this change in the NAF recommendations, a well-informed parent seeking to guide her child is more likely to inquire regarding these matters than a panicky teen who just wants to no longer be pregnant.

Second, parental involvement laws insure that parents have the opportunity to provide additional medical history and information to abortion providers prior to performance of the abortion.

In *Edison v. Reproductive Health Services,* 863 S.W.2d 621 (Mo. App. E.D. 1993), the court confronted the question of whether an abortion provider could be held liable for the suicide of Sandra, a fourteen-year-old girl, due to depression following an abortion. Learning of the abortion only after her daughter's death, the girl's mother sued the abortion provider, alleging that her daughter's death was due to the failure to obtain a psychiatric history or monitor Sandra's mental health. *Id.* at 624. An eyewitness to Sandra's death "testified that he saw Sandra holding on to a fence on a bridge over Arsenal Street and then jumped in front of a car traveling below on Arsenal. She appeared to have been rocking back and forth while holding onto the fence, then deliberately let go and jumped far out to the driver's side of the car that struck her. A second car hit her while she was on the ground. Sandra was taken to a hospital and died the next day of multiple injuries." *Id.* at 622.

The court ultimately determined that Sandra was not insane at the time she committed suicide. Therefore her actions broke the chain of causation required for recovery. Yet evidence was presented that the daughter had a history of psychological illness, and that her behavior was noticeably different after the abortion. *Id.* at 628. If Sandra's mother had known that her daughter had obtained an abortion, it is possible that this tragedy would have been avoided.

The medical, emotional, and psychological consequences of an abortion are serious and can be lasting; this is particularly so when the patient is immature. An adequate medical and psychological case history is important to the physician. Parents can provide medical and psychological data, refer the physician to other sources of medical history, such as family physicians, and authorize family physicians to give relevant data.[6]

Abortion providers, in turn, have the opportunity to disclose the medical risks of the procedure to the adult who can advise the girl in giving her informed consent to the surgical procedure. Parental notification insures that the abortion providers inform a mature adult of the risks and benefits of the proposed treatment, after having received a more complete and thus more accurate medical history of the patient.

The third way in which parental notification will improve medical treatment of pregnant minors is by insuring that parents have adequate knowledge to recognize and respond to any post-abortion complication that may develop. While it is often claimed that abortion is one of the safest surgical procedures performed today, the actual rate of many complications is simply unknown because there is no coordinated national effort to collect and maintain this information. . . .

Many minors may ignore or deny the seriousness of post-abortion symptoms or may lack the financial resources to respond to those symptoms. This is because some of the most serious complications are delayed and only detected during the follow-up visit; yet, only about one-third of all abortion patients actually keep their appointments for post-operative checkups. Absent parental notification, hemorrhaging may be mistaken for a heavy period and severe depression as typical teenage angst.

Effectiveness of Judicial Bypass

In those few cases where it is not in the girl's best interest to disclose her pregnancy to her parents, state laws generally provide the pregnant minor the option of seeking a court determination that either involvement of the girl's parent is not in her best interest, or that she is sufficiently mature to make decisions regarding the continuation of her pregnancy. This is a requirement for parental consent laws under existing United States Supreme Court cases, and courts have been quick to overturn laws omitting adequate bypass.

In the past, opponents to the predecessor of this Act, the Child Custody Protection Act, have argued that passage of federal legislation in this area would endanger teens since parents may be abusive and many teens would seek illegal abortions. This is a phantom fear. Parental involvement laws are on the books in over two-thirds of the states, some for over thirty years, and there is no case where it has been established that these laws led to parental abuse or to self-inflicted injury.[7] Similarly, there is no evidence that these laws have led to an increase in illegal abortions or attempted self-induced abortions.

It often asserted that parental involvement laws do not increase the number of parents notified of their daughters' intentions to obtain abortions, since minors will commonly seek judicial bypass of the parental involvement requirement. Assessing the accuracy of this claim is difficult since parental notification or consent laws rarely impose reporting requirements regarding the use of judicial bypass. Alabama, Idaho, South Dakota and Wisconsin are four of the few states that report the number of minors who obtain judicial bypass orders related to abortion. Data regarding the number of bypasses granted in those states from 2005 to 2010 reveals that the judicial bypass is relatively rare and its use varies significantly among states. . . .

CIANA Addresses a Real Problem

It is beyond dispute that young girls are being taken to out-of-state clinics in order to procure secret abortions. In 2005, the House Subcommittee on the Constitution heard the testimony of Marsha Carroll, the mother of a fourteen year-old-girl, who was secretly taken out-of-state by her boyfriend's parents to obtain an abortion. Upon arriving at the abortion clinic, Mrs. Carroll's daughter began to cry and tried to refuse the abortion. The boy's parents told her they would leave her in New Jersey if she resisted. She gave in to their pressure, had the abortion, and now suffers from depression and guilt.[8]

A recent study of the literature documenting the impact of parental involvement laws concluded, "Some minors travel to other states with no, or at least less restrictive, parental involvement laws in order to obtain an abortion. To travel out of state, a minor must have access to transportation and must be within a reasonable distance of a state with less restrictive laws. The degree to which minors exercise this option varies by age, socioeconomic status and access to public transportation." "In general, the impact of these laws on minors' travel appears to vary widely, depending on the specifics of the requirements, the abortion regulations of surrounding states and the state's geography."[9]

Statutory Rape

Some teens who obtain abortions are pregnant as the result of statutory rape. National studies reveal "[a]lmost two thirds of adolescent mothers have partners older than 20 years of age."[10] "Younger teenagers are especially vulnerable to coercive and nonconsensual sex. Involuntary sexual activity has been reported by 74% of sexually active girls younger than 14 years and 60% of those younger than 15 years."[11] In a study of over 46,000 pregnancies by school-age girls in California, researchers found that "71%, or over 33,000, were fathered by adult post-high-school men whose mean age was

22.6 years, an average of 5 years older than the mothers. . . . Even among junior high school mothers aged 15 or younger, most births are fathered by adult men 6–7 years their senior. *Men aged 25 or older father more births among California school-age girls than do boys under age 18.*"[12] Other studies have found that most teenage pregnancies are the result of predatory practices by men who are substantially older.[13]

Failure to Report by Abortion Providers

Abortion providers are reluctant to report information indicating a minor is the victim of statutory rape.[14] The clearest example of this reluctance is the arguments presented in the lawsuit filed by a Kansas abortion provider to prohibit enforcement of that state's reporting requirement related to sexual abuse of minors. Claiming that children under the age of sixteen were sufficiently mature to engage in non-abusive sexual intercourse, Aid for Women, a Kansas City abortion provider, sued to enjoin the state's mandatory reporting law on the basis that it violated minors' constitutional right to informational privacy. The district court, adopting the arguments of the abortion provider, ruled that minors between the ages of twelve and fifteen had a constitutional right to engage in non-coercive sexual activity, including but not limited to "penile-vaginal intercourse, oral sex, anal sex, and touching of another's genitalia by either sex." On appeal from a preliminary injunction in the case, the Court . . . rejected such a constitutional right, but the district continued to assert the unconstitutionality of the reporting law at the conclusion of trial. Unfortunately the appeal to the Tenth Circuit was rendered moot by unrelated legislative changes in the law.[15]

Failure to report the sexual abuse of minor may result in the minor returning to an abusive relationship. In Ohio, a thirteen-year-old girl was impregnated by her twenty-one-year old soccer coach, John Haller. In order to conceal the illegal relationship, Mr. Haller arranged for the girl to obtain an abortion by first impersonating her father during a telephone call with the clinic, and then pretending to be her brother while accompanying the girl to the clinic to obtain an abortion. The sexual abuse was only discovered after another teacher overheard the girl arguing with Haller about their relationship, and reported the conversation to law enforcement. Subsequently the girl and her parents sued the abortion provider, Planned Parenthood of Southwest Ohio Region, for failure to comply with the Ohio sexual abuse reporting statute. "Planned Parenthood did not deny that it had not filed an abuse report."[16]

In 2001 an Arizona Planned Parenthood affiliate was found civilly liable for failing to report the fact that the clinic had performed an abortion on a twelve-year-old girl who had been impregnated by her foster brother. The abortion provider did not report the crime as required by law and the girl returned to the foster home where she was raped and impregnated a second time.[17] In 2003 two

Connecticut doctors were prosecuted for failing to report to public officials that an eleven-year old girl had been impregnated by a seventy-five year old man.[18]

By failing to report, abortion providers reduce the chances that rapes will be discovered, and by failing to preserve fetal tissue, they may make it impossible to effective prosecute those rapes that are discovered. . . .

Conclusion

In balancing the minor's right to privacy and her need for parental involvement, the majority of states have determined that parents should know before abortions are performed on minors. This is a reasonable conclusion and well within the states' police powers. However, the political authority of each state stops at its geographic boundaries. States need the assistance of the federal government to insure that the protection they wish to afford their children is not easily circumvented by strangers taking minors across state lines.

By passage of the Act before this Committee, Congress will protect the ability of the parents to be involved in the decisions of their minor daughters facing an unplanned pregnancy.

Experience in states having parental involvement laws has shown that, when notified, parents and their daughters unite in a desire to resolve issues surrounding an unplanned pregnancy. If the minor chooses to terminate the pregnancy, parents can assist their daughters in selecting competent abortion providers, and abortion providers may receive more comprehensive medical histories of their patients. In these cases, the minors will more likely be encouraged to obtain post-operative check-ups, and parents will be prepared to respond to any complications that arise.

If the minor chooses to continue her pregnancy, involvement of her parents serves many of the same goals. Parents can provide or help obtain the necessary resources for early and comprehensive prenatal care. They can assist their daughters in evaluating the options of single parenthood, adoption, or early marriage. Perhaps most importantly, they can provide the love and support that is found in the many healthy families of the United States.

Regardless of whether the girl chooses to continue or terminate her pregnancy, parental involvement laws have proven desirable because they afford greater protection for the many girls who are pregnant due to sexual assault. By insuring that parents know of the pregnancy, it becomes much more likely that they will intervene to insure the protection of their daughters from future assaults.

In balancing the minor's right to privacy and her need for parental involvement, the majority of states have determined that parents should know before abortions are performed on minors. This is a reasonable conclusion and well within the states' police powers. However, the political authority of each state stops at its geographic boundaries. States need the assistance of the federal government to insure that the protection they wish to afford their children is not easily circumvented by strangers taking minors across state lines.

The Child Interstate Parental Notification Act has the unique virtue of building upon two of the few points of agreement in the national debate over abortion: the desirability of parental involvement in a minor's decisions about an unplanned pregnancy, and the need to protect the physical health and safety of the pregnant girl. . . .

Notes

[1]. "Even among those who say abortion should be legal in most or all cases, 71% favor requiring parental consent." Pew Research Center for The People and The Press, *Support for Abortion Slips* at 9 (conducted August, 2009).

[2]. Hawaii etc.

[3]. A 2011 Poll by the Public Religion Research Institute found that 71% of millennial youth (18–29) supported parental consent laws. *Committed to Availability, Conflicted about Morality* at 17 available at http://publicreligion.org/site/wp-content/uploads/2011/06/Millenials-Abortion-and-Religion-Survey-Report.pdf (conduct May 2011).

[4]. *Ayotte v. Planned Parenthood,* 546 U.S. 320, 326 (2006).

[5]. National Abortion Federation, *Having an Abortion? Your Guide to Good Care* (2000) which was available at <http://www.prochoice.org/pregnant/goodcare.htm> (visited Jan. 1, 2000).

[6]. *H.L. v. Matheson,* 450 U.S. 398 at 411 (1981). Accord *Ohio v. Akron Ctr. for Reproductive Health,* 497 U.S. 502, 518–19 (1990).

[7]. A 1989 memo prepared by the Minnesota Attorney General regarding Minnesota's experience with its parental involvement law states that "after some five years of the statute's operation, the evidence does not disclose a single instance of abuse or forceful obstruction of abortion for any Minnesota minor." Testimony before the Texas House of Representatives on the Massachusetts' experience with its parental consent law revealed a similar absence of unintended, but harmful, consequences. Ms. Jamie Sabino, chair of the Massachusetts Judicial Consent for Minors Lawyer Referral Panel, could identify no case of a Massachusetts' minor being abused or abandoned as a result of the law. *See Hearing on Tex. H.B. 1073 Before the House State Affairs Comm.,* 76th Leg., R.S. 21 (Apr. 19, 1999) (statement by Jamie Sabino, JD).

[8]. *Child Interstate Abortion Notification Act: Hearing on HR 748 before the Subcomm. on the Constitution, H. Comm. on the Judiciary,* 109th Cong. (2005) (testimony of Marsha Carroll in support of HR 748).

In 1998, Joyce Farley testified before the House Subcommittee on the Constitution about the complications her daughter, Crystal, suffered as a result of a secret abortion. Crystal became pregnant at the age of twelve when Michael Kilmer, an eighteen-year-old neighbor, got her drunk and then raped her. Mr. Kilmer's mother, Rosa Hartford, took the young girl to a New York abortion clinic to avoid Pennsylvania's parental consent law. Crystal's mother, a registered nurse, learned of her daughter's abortion when Crystal began experiencing severe pain and hemorrhaging at home following the abortion. The abortion was incomplete, and additional surgery was required. Ms. Hartford was convicted for interfering with the custody of the child's parent. *Commonwealth v. Hartford,* No. 95–98 (Ct. Com. Pl. Sullivan County, Pa. Dec. 5, 1996). Ms. Hartford's conviction was reversed for failure to provide proper jury instructions on the elements of interference with custody. *Commonwealth v. Hartford,* No. 00088PHL97 (Pa. Super. Ct. Oct. 28, 1997).

[9]. Dennis A *et al., The Impact of Laws Requiring Parental Involvement for Abortion: A Literature Review* at 4, New York: Guttmacher Institute, 2009.

[10]. American Academy of Pediatrics Committee on Adolescence, *Adolescent Pregnancy—Current Trends and Issues: 1998,* 103 Pediatrics 516, 519 (1999).

[11]. American Academy of Pediatrics Committee on Adolescence, *Adolescent Pregnancy—Current Trends and Issues,* 116 Pediatrics 281, 281 (2005).

[12]. Mike A. Males, *Adult Involvement in Teenage Childbearing and STD,* Lancet 64 (July 8, 1995) (emphasis added).

[13]. *Id.* citing [others].

[14]. *See* Chinué Turner Richardson and Cynthia Dailard, *Politicizing Statutory Rape Reporting Requirements: A Mounting Campaign?,* The Guttmacher Report on Public Policy 1 (Aug. 2005) and Patricia Donovan, *Caught Between Teens and the Law: Family Planning Programs and Statutory Rape Reporting,* 3 Fam. Plan. Perspectives 5 (1998).

[15]. *Aid to Women v. Foulston,* [2004–2007].

[16]. *Roe v. Planned Parenthood Southwest Ohio Region,* [2007–2009].

[17]. See *Glendale Teen Files Lawsuit Against Planned Parenthood,* THE ARIZONA REPUBLIC, Sept. 2, 2001 and *Judge Rules Against Planned Parenthood* at www.12news.com/headline/PlannedParenthood122602.html

[18]. *See* Charlotte Allen, *Planned Parenthood's Unseemly Empire,* 13 Weekly Standard (2007).

Advocates for Youth    **NO**

Abortion and Parental Involvement Laws

A Threat to Young Women's Health and Safety

The majority of states—thirty-nine as of December 2013—currently enforce laws that require a young woman to notify or obtain consent from one or both parents before she can receive abortion care. Yet research has shown that these laws often delay young women's access, endangering young women's health and safety, and leaving too many alone and afraid. Ideally, any woman, including a young woman, who is faced with an unintended pregnancy can seek the advice of those who care for her. But for those who can't, those afraid to anger or disappoint, or who face the threat of violence in their homes—it is best for them to seek the advice of a trained medical professional than to face the situation alone and afraid.

Most States Require Parental Involvement in Minors' Abortions

Parental involvement laws fall into two categories: those that require parental notification and those that require parental consent before a young person seeks abortion services. Parental notification laws require written notification to parents by a medical provider before a young person can receive abortion services. Parental consent laws require that a young person obtain consent by one or both parents before an abortion can be performed. The Supreme Court has ruled that states may not give parents absolute veto over their daughter's decision to have an abortion. Most state parental involvement requirements include a judicial bypass procedure that requires a minor to receive court approval for an abortion without her parents' knowledge or consent.

- Twenty-one states require parental consent for a minor's abortion. Three of these require both parents to consent. Eight states require that the consent document be notarized.[1]
- Thirteen states require parental notification only. Five states require both consent and notification.[1]
- Twenty-three states require parental involvement even if the minor is a victim of incest.[1]

- The only way for minors to access abortion without involving their parents in these states is via judicial bypass, where they must petition the courts for permission.[1]

Requiring Parental Involvement Leaves Many Young Women Alone and at Risk

- Most young women do consult their parents before seeking abortion care.[4] Nonetheless, many teens live in dysfunctional family environments, and parental involvement laws cannot transform these families into stable homes nor facilitate communications. Forcing teens to involve parents in these circumstances puts them at risk.
- Fifty percent of pregnant teens have experienced violence[5]; thirty percent of teens who do not tell their parents about their abortions feared violence or being forced to leave home.[6]
- Just 16 of the 39 states with parental involvement laws provide exceptions for minors who are victims of sexual and physical assault, incest or neglect.[1]
- Parental involvement laws also disproportionately affect young women of color, who are more likely to experience unintended pregnancy as minors and are disproportionately living in states where parental involvement laws are in effect.[7]

Many Negative Outcomes, Few Positive Ones

- Parental involvement laws often delay young women's abortion care, leading to riskier, later-term abortion procedures.[2]
- Parental notification laws do not guarantee that a minor will talk to her parents before she has an abortion. Research shows parental notification laws have almost no effect on a young woman's decision to talk with her parent or guardian about her decision prior to an abortion. The chief factor determining whether a teen consulted her parent was, not legislation, but the quality of the teen's relationship with her parent.[8]

- Parental involvement laws have no clear impact on birth rates or abortion rates.[4]

Judicial Bypass Is Not a Reasonable Alternative

While judicial bypass is technically available in states which mandate parental involvement, there are powerful obstacles to young people attaining it. Many minors do not know judicial bypass is available or do not know how to get it; do not have access to transportation to travel to the necessary courts; or simply are denied bypass by resistant or biased judges.[2] For instance, in 2013 the Nebraska Supreme Court denied an abortion to a young woman of 16, ruling that she was not "mature" enough to have an abortion. The young woman already had to navigate the court system, retain an attorney, and face delay while the courts decided her fate – and she still was told she must go through with the pregnancy.[3]

Medical Experts Oppose Parental Consent and Notification Laws

- Parental involvement laws place access to abortion care in a special category. In many states, minors may independently consent to a range of sensitive health care services, including access to contraceptives, prenatal care, and STI care. Minors can consent to most other pregnancy-related medical procedures, including prenatal care, labor and delivery procedures, and can even choose adoption without parental consent or notification.[4]
- The federal government requires confidentiality for minors' contraception and STI services at federally funded Title X clinics. These regulations are based on research that young people are less likely to seek reproductive and sexual health care if they fear their privacy will be violated.[4] Confidentiality in medical treatment, especially related to sexual and reproductive health, is a protected constitutional right to privacy for young women.[9]
- The American Medical Association, the Society for Adolescent Medicine, the American Public Health Association, the American College of Obstetricians and Gynecologists, the American Academy of Pediatrics, and other health professional organizations stand in agreement against mandatory parental involvement in abortion decision making.[10]

Conclusion

Young people deserve the right to access the full range of reproductive and sexual health services they need, which includes abortion care. And right now, young people are at the forefront of the reproductive rights, health and justice movements. Activists must stand with them against the harmful parental involvement restrictions

that can put their health and well being at risk. Yet few are fighting to abolish parental involvement laws; and even when pro-active abortion rights legislation is introduced, it rarely, if ever, addresses minors' needs. Legislation which seeks to protect women's access to abortion must include younger women and protect their access to safe, legal, and affordable abortion care.

For more information on parental consent and notification laws, please contact Jeryl Hayes, Domestic Policy Analyst, jeryl@ advocatesforyouth.org.

References

1. Guttmacher Institute. "State Policies in Brief: Minors' Access to Contraceptive Services." Accessed from http:// www.guttmacher.org/statecenter/spibs/spib_MACS.pdf on November 20, 2013.

2. Dennis A et al., The Impact of Laws Requiring Parental Involvement for Abortion: A Literature Review, New York: Guttmacher Institute, 2009.

3. Nebraska Supreme Court. In Re Petition of Anonymous 5, a Minor. Accessed from http://supremecourt .ne.gov/sites/supremecourt.ne.gov/files/sc/opinions/s13 -510009.pdf on November 8, 2013.

4. Dailard C and Richardson CT. "Teenagers' Access to Confidential Reproductive Health Care Services." The Guttmacher Report on Public Policy, 2005: 8(4).

5. American Psychological Association, Parental Consent Laws for Adolescent Reproductive Health Care: What Does the Psychological Research Say? (Feb. 2000), citing A.B. Berenson, et al., Prevalence of Physical and Sexual Assault in Pregnant Adolescents, 13 J. of Adolescent Health 466-69 (1992).

6. Martin Donohoe, Parental Notification and Consent Laws for Teen Abortions: Overview and 2006 Ballot Measures MEDSCAPE Ob/Gyn & Women's Health, February 9, 2007.

7. Kost K, et al. U.S. Teenage Pregnancies, Births and Abortions, 2008: National Trends by Age, Race and Ethnicity. Guttmacher Institute, 2013. Available from: http://www .guttmacher.org/pubs/USTPtrends08.pdf.

8. Davis AR, Beasley AD. Abortion in adolescents: epidemiology, confidentiality, and methods. Curr Opin Obstet Gynecol. 2009;21(5):390–3.

9. Carey v. Population Services International, 431 U.S. 678 (1977).

10. American Medical Association. "Opinion 5.055 – Confidential Care for Minors." Accessed from http:// www.ama-assn.org/ama/pub/physician-resources

/medical-ethics/code-medical-ethics/opinion5055.page on November 22, 2013. American Public Health Association. "Ensuring Minors' Access to Confidential Abortion Services." Accessed from http://www.apha.org/advocacy /policy/policysearch/default.htm?id=1415 on November 8, 2013. American Academy of Pediatrics. "Achieving Quality Health Services for Adolescents." Accessed from http://pediatrics.aappublications.org/content/121/6/1263 .full?sid=7322b383-0e96-4d24-a3ba-2914a99307bb on November 8, 2013. Center for Adolescent Medicine. Policy Compendium on Confidential Health Care Services for Adolescents, 2nd Edition. Accessed from http://www .cahl.org/PDFs/PolicyCompendium/PolicyCompendium .pdf on November 8, 2013.

Advocates for Youth partners with youth leaders, adult allies, and youth-serving organizations to advocate for policies and champion programs that recognize young people's rights to honest sexual health information; accessible, confidential, and affordable sexual health services; and the resources and opportunities necessary to create sexual health equity for all youth.

EXPLORING THE ISSUE

Should Parental Consent Be Required for Adolescents Seeking Abortion?

Critical Thinking and Reflection

1. What constitutes "mature" enough to make a decision about having an abortion? Who should decide a person's level of maturity? Is maturity a psychological concept—is it about decision-making abilities or is it about morality, executive functions (i.e., supervisory cognitive skills), logical reasoning, or psychosocial capacities (e.g., ability to delay gratification, not be impulsive, etc.)? Or, is maturity a legal term?
2. While *judicial bypass* is meant to provide an alternative to parental consent/notification, it is not an ideal process (see Bonny, 2007; Rebouche, 2011). Given the problems identified with judicial bypass (e.g., its inaccessibility, delay in decision due to the court petition process, potential judicial bias), are these laws fair to girls?
3. Given the fact that many young pregnant women discuss their decision to have an abortion with their parents or a trusted adult before they seek an abortion (Webster et al., 2010), are these laws and policies necessary? Are we simply legislating common practice? Do these parental consent and parental notification laws violate the constitutional right of girls to have authority over their own body?
4. Consider the differences in laws between Canada and the United States with regard to parental involvement in teen abortion. What differences exist in abortion trends between the two countries? Do similarities exist? Could a cross-country examination help inform the issue?

Is There Common Ground?

Both of the selections for this issue take different perspectives in relation to the issue. Stanton Collett argues that parental involvement provides improved medical care and discusses the effectiveness of judicial bypass, whereas the *Advocates for Youth* comes from the other end of the spectrum and states there are many obstacles to judicial bypass and parental involvement does not lead to improved medical care, but in fact provide the potential for harm to the well-being of the adolescent. Another factor that is not considered per se by either author, involved in the issue of parental involvement and abortions, is the cognitive maturity of the adolescent and her decision-making capabilities. Ultimately, the issue of parental involvement laws must consider many different factors and various moral perspectives.

Additional Resources

Finken, L. L. (2005). The role of consultants in adolescents' decision making: A focus on abortion decisions. In J. E. Jacobs & P. A. Klaczynski (Eds.), *The development of judgment and decision making in children and adolescents* (pp. 255–278). Mahwah, NJ: Erlbaum.

Haugen, D., Musser, S., & Lovelace, K. (2010). *Abortion.* Farmington Hills, MI: Greenhaven Press.

Holder, A. R. (2010). From chattel to consenter: Adolescents and informed consent. 2009 Grover Powers Lecture. *Yale Journal of Biology and Medicine, 83*(1), 35–41. Retrieved from www.ncbi.nih.gov/pmc/articles/PMC2844691

Judicial Bypass Procedures. (n.d.). www.advocatesforyouth.org

New, M. (2011). Analyzing the effect of anti-abortion U.S. state legislation in the post-*Casey* era. *State Politics & Policy Quarterly, 11*(1), 28–47.

Watkins, C. (2009). *Teens at risk.* Farmington Hills, MI: Greenhaven Press.

Webster, R. D., Neustadt, A. N., Whitaker, A. K., & Gilliam, M. L. (2010). Parental involvement laws and parent-daughter communication: Policy without proof. *Contraception, 10*, 310–313.

References

Bonny, A. C. (2007). Parental consent and notification laws in the abortion context: Rejecting the "maturity" standard in judicial bypass proceedings. *UC Davis Journal of Juvenile Law & Policy, 11*(2), 311–333.

Dennis, A., Henshaw, S. K., Joyce, T. J., Finer, L. B., & Blanchard, K. (2009). *The impact of laws requiring parental involvement for abortion: A literature review.* New York: Guttmacher Institute.

Downie, J. & Nassar, C. (2007). Barriers to access to abortion through a legal lens. *Health Law Journal, 15,* 143–174.

Rebouche, R. (2011). Parental involvement laws and new governance. *Harvard Journal of Law & Gender, 34,* 175–223.

Sen, B., Wingate, M. S., & Kirby, R. (2012). The relationship between state abortion-restrictions and homicide deaths among children under 5 years of age: A longitudinal study. *Social Science & Medicine,* 1–9 [uncorrected proofs]. doi:10.1016/j.socscimed.2012.01.037

Internet References . . .

Facts and Statistics About Teenage Abortion

http://www.choicespregnancy.org/facts-and-statistics
-about-teenage-abortion

Laws Restricting Teenagers' Access to Abortion

https://www.aclu.org/laws-restricting-teenagers-access
-abortion

Teen Abortion: Requiring Parental Consent Makes No Sense

http://www.rit.org/essays/teenabortion.php

Teen Abortion Resources

http://www.bandbacktogether.com/teen-abortion
-resources/

What Are Teen Abortion Laws in the United States

http://thelawdictionary.org/article/teen-abortion-laws
-in-the-united-states/

Unit 4

UNIT

Technology, Mass Media, and Criminal Justice

*T*here are many areas where adolescent behavior can cause problems for the developing teen. This area of study is sometimes called abnormal adolescent psychology or the sociology of juvenile delinquency. By studying these behaviors, we can attempt to prevent problems before they occur and intervene when problems do occur. What is defined as a "problem" or an antisocial behavior can change depending on the social, political, and economic climate of the time. The following unit deals with some of the contemporary problem issues, most of them specifically connected to the technological climate in which our contemporary youths reside.

Selected, Edited, and with Issue Framing Material by:
Scott R. Brandhorst, *Southeast Missouri State University*

ISSUE

Does Playing Violent Video Games Harm Adolescents?

YES: Benedict Carey, from "Shooting in the Dark," *The New York Times* (2013)

NO: Christopher J. Ferguson and Cheryl K. Olson, from "Video Game Violence Use Among "Vulnerable" Populations: The Impact of Violent Games on Delinquency and Bullying Among Children with Clinically Elevated Depression or Attention Deficit Symptoms," *Journal of Youth and Adolescence* (2014)

Learning Outcomes

After reading this issue, you will be able to:

- Compare and contrast the relationship between violent video games and violent/aggressive behavior.
- Explain the methodological problems with violent video games' research.
- Explain the theoretical problems with violent video games' research.
- Critically evaluate the relationship between violent video games and the impact on vulnerable populations.

ISSUE SUMMARY

YES: Benedict Carey provides an article examining the relationship between violent video games and violent behavior. In reviewing the relevant research, he states that there is evidence of short-term increases in hostile urges and mildly aggressive behavior. However, upon reviewing the long-term effects, the results are more mixed, and he notes that it is hard to control for all possible variables within the studies that examine this relationship. Some research looks at the socialization effect video games have on adolescents over the long-term, leading to imitation of behaviors seen within the video games and questions the kinds of values and social skills the child is learning.

NO: Christopher J. Ferguson and Cheryl K. Olson examine the impact of violent video games on children with clinically elevated depression or attention deficit symptoms. They state that there is a need to examine the impact of video games on vulnerable populations. The researchers found no evidence for increased bullying or delinquent behaviors among youth with clinically elevated mental health symptoms who also played violent video games.

Understanding adolescent behavior (both prosocial and antisocial) requires an understanding of the way adolescents think. Not surprising, research on adolescent cognition and behavior focuses on the many variables in their lives that could have an impact on their developing brains. A variable that has received much attention is the media. It has been documented in many studies how the media influence adolescent thinking and hence behavior. A recent focus in the research is on the form and impact of the deleterious effects of violent video games on adolescents, such as the potential for increased antisocial behavior—for example, aggression—as well as examining whether or not positive effects of violent video game exposure exist.

Video games were first introduced in 1958 with Tennis for Two and have taken various forms over the years, changing with the advances of technology. There are many different genres available (i.e., action; adventure; simulation; role play; strategy) and many different platforms available to play these games (i.e., Xbox One; Wii; PlayStation 3; PCs; Smartphones). The advancements in technology and game sophistication have led to more realistic and immersive games. This contributes to a more capturing and addictive form of entertainment, with an increasing number of people playing video games. It, therefore, comes as no surprise that research on the effects of playing video games has increased substantially in the past few decades.

Most research has focused on the negative effects that video games have on social and emotional development, such as the relationship between violent video game play (e.g., Call of Duty, Grand Theft Auto series) and aggressive and violent behaviors. For example, Willoughby, Adachi, & Good (2012) have linked violent video games to an increase in aggression. However, there have also been many studies that have not found a link between violent video games and aggression. For example, Ferguson, Trigani, Pilato, Miller, Foley, & Barr (2016) found that the impact of violent video on teen hostility was minimal. These mixed findings have led to the current debate regarding the effects of violent video games on all aspects of adolescent development (i.e., social, emotional, cognitive).

In the YES and NO selections, the authors of the respective articles review the relevant research and make valid arguments for their positions. Carey cites the relevant research that shows a relationship between violent video games and aggression, while also discussing some of the variables that lead to the mixed results of the studies. Carey concludes that at the very least researchers believe parents should be aware of the types of video games their kids are playing and what kind of values and social skills the kids are learning from these games. Ferguson and Olson also review the relevant research and discuss some of the variables leading to the mixed results found within the literature. They examined the potential relationship between violent video games on criminal delinquency and bullying behaviors in a sample of children with mental health symptoms and found no relationship between these variables.

YES ↵

Benedict Carey

Shooting in the Dark

The young men who opened fire at Columbine High School, at the movie theater in Aurora, Colo., and in other massacres had this in common: they were video gamers who seemed to be acting out some dark digital fantasy. It was as if all that exposure to computerized violence gave them the idea to go on a rampage—or at least fueled their urges.

But did it really?

Social scientists have been studying and debating the effects of media violence on behavior since the 1950s, and video games in particular since the 1980s. The issue is especially relevant today, because the games are more realistic and bloodier than ever, and because most American boys play them at some point. Girls play at lower rates and are significantly less likely to play violent games.

A burst of new research has begun to clarify what can and cannot be said about the effects of violent gaming. Playing the games can and does stir hostile urges and mildly aggressive behavior in the short term. Moreover, youngsters who develop a gaming habit can become slightly more aggressive—as measured by clashes with peers, for instance—at least over a period of a year or two.

Yet it is not at all clear whether, over longer periods, such a habit increases the likelihood that a person will commit a violent crime, like murder, rape, or assault, much less a Newtown-like massacre. (Such calculated rampages are too rare to study in any rigorous way, researchers agree.)

"I don't know that a psychological study can ever answer that question definitively," said Michael R. Ward, an economist at the University of Texas, Arlington. "We are left to glean what we can from the data and research on video game use that we have."

The research falls into three categories: short-term laboratory experiments; longer-term studies, often based in schools; and correlation studies—between playing time and aggression, for instance, or between video game sales and trends in violent crimes.

Lab experiments confirm what any gamer knows in his gut: playing games like, "Killzone 3" or "Battlefield 3" stirs the blood. In one recent study, Christophe, a psychologist at Iowa State University, led a research team that had 47 undergraduates play "Mortal Kombat: Deadly Alliance" for 15 minutes. Afterward, the team took various measures of arousal, both physical and psychological. It also tested whether the students would behave more aggressively, by having them dole out hot sauce to a fellow student who, they were told, did not like spicy food but had to swallow the sauce.

Sure enough, compared with a group who had played a nonviolent video game, those who had been engaged in "Mortal Kombat" were more aggressive across the board. They gave their fellow students significantly bigger portions of the hot sauce.

Many similar studies have found the same thing: A dose of violent gaming makes people act a little more rudely than they would otherwise, at least for a few minutes after playing.

It is far harder to determine whether cumulative exposure leads to real-world hostility over the long term. Some studies in schools have found that over time digital warriors get into increasing numbers of scrapes with peers—fights in the schoolyard, for example. In a report published last summer, psychologists at Brock University in Ontario found that longer periods of violent video game playing among high school students predicted a slightly higher number of such incidents over time.

"None of these extreme acts, like a school shooting, occurs because of only one risk factor; there are many factors, including feeling socially isolated, being bullied, and so on," said Craig A. Anderson, a psychologist at Iowa State University. "But if you look at the literature, I think it's clear that violent media is one factor; it's not the largest factor, but it's also not the smallest."

Most researchers in the field agree with Dr. Anderson, but not all of them. Some studies done in schools or elsewhere have found that it is aggressive children who are the most likely to be drawn to violent video games in the first place; they are self-selected to be in more schoolyard conflicts. And some studies are not able to control for outside factors, like family situation or mood problems.

"This is a pool of research that, so far, has not been very well done," said Christopher J. Ferguson, associate professor of psychology and criminal justice at Texas A &M International University and a critic of the field whose own research has found no link. "I look at it and I can't say what it means."

Neither Dr. Ferguson, nor others interviewed in this article, receive money from the gaming industry.

Many psychologists argue that violent video games "socialize" children over time, prompting them to imitate the behavior of the game's characters, the cartoonish machismo, the hair-trigger rage, the dismissive brutality. Children also imitate flesh and blood people in their lives, of course—parents, friends, teachers, siblings—and one question that researchers have not yet answered is when, exactly, a habit is so consuming that its influence trumps the socializing effects of other major figures in a child's life.

That is, what constitutes a bad habit? In surveys about 80 percent of high school-age boys say they play video games, most of which are thought to be violent, and perhaps a third to a half of those players have had a habit of 10 hours a week or more.

The proliferation of violent video games has not coincided with spikes in youth violent crime. The number of violent youth offenders fell by more than half between 1994 and 2010, to 224 per 100,000 population, according to government statistics, while video game sales have more than doubled since 1996.

In a working paper now available online, Dr. Ward and two colleagues examined week-by-week sales data for violent video games, across a wide range of communities. Violence rates are seasonal, generally higher in summer than in winter; so are video game sales, which peak during the holidays. The researchers controlled for those trends and analyzed crime rates in the month or so after surges in sales, in communities with a high concentrations of young people, like college towns.

"We found that higher rates of violent video game sales related to a decrease in crimes, and especially violent crimes," said Dr. Ward, whose co-authors were A. Scott Cunningham of Baylor University and Benjamin Engelstätter of the Center for European Economic Research in Mannheim, Germany.

No one knows for sure what these findings mean. It may be that playing video games for hours every day keeps people off the streets who would otherwise be getting into trouble. It could be that the games provide "an outlet" that satisfies violent urges in some players—a theory that many psychologists dismiss but that many players believe.

Or the two trends may be entirely unrelated.

"At the very least, parents should be aware of what's in the games their kids are playing," Dr. Anderson said, "and think of it from a socialization point of view: what kind of values, behavioral skills, and social scripts is the child learning?"

BENEDICT J. CAREY is a science reporter for *The New York Times* and focuses on brain and behavior topics.

Christopher J. Ferguson and Cheryl K. Olson

 **NO**

Video Game Violence Use Among "Vulnerable" Populations: The Impact of Violent Games on Delinquency and Bullying Among Children with Clinically Elevated Depression or Attention Deficit Symptoms

Introduction

Whether violent video games do or do not contribute to behavioral aggression and societal violence among youth has been debated, at the time of this writing, for three decades. By societal violence, we refer to a range of behaviors, from bullying and physical fighting to criminal assault and even homicide, which are of concern to lawmakers and parents. We contrast societal violence with the measures of relatively mild aggression (or perhaps competition) often used in laboratory studies of college students, which arguably do not tap well into the issue of societal violence (Kutner and Olson 2008). Caution is required in generalization of laboratory aggression measures to societal violence as the potential for misinformation is considerable (Ferguson et al. 2011). To date, no consensus has been reached on the matter of whether violent games and societal violence are linked: some scholars argue that violent games contribute to behavioral aggression (Fraser et al. 2012) or even societal violence (Strasburger 2007), while others suggest that video games have a negligible influence on aggression (Puri and Pugliese 2012) or may even reduce aggression (Colwell and Kato 2003).

Existing societal concerns about video games have intensified after the 1999 Columbine High School massacre (Ferguson 2013) and other well-publicized school shootings. The tragic 2012 Sandy Hook Elementary School murders in Newtown, Connecticut resurrected these debates amid reports that the 20-year-old shooter was an avid gamer (e.g., Henderson 2012). The Newtown shooting also brought renewed attention to wide discrepancies in opinion regarding whether violent video games influence criminal behavior. The Brown v EMA (2011) Supreme Court decision, in which the Court ruled that a California law restricting the sale or rental of violent games to minors was an unconstitutional violation of the First Amendment, highlighted the limitations of existing studies of violent video games and the difficulty of applying this pool of research to policy-relevant questions. A series of appellate court rulings made similar points (see Brown v EMA 2011, p. 12). Given these court rulings, and the recurring media focus on video games, researchers need to do more to answer the questions of greatest public concern regarding video games and any potential harm to youth. The recurrence of these concerns with each school shooting or court ruling points to the need for studies that can meaningfully inform policy and legal debates.

Video Game Violence Research: What Is the Evidence?

Much speculation focuses on the issue of whether violence in video games or other entertainment media, such as television, can contribute to real-life violence. Evidence to date is scant. For instance, in a recent meta-analysis that focused on criminal aggression, Savage and Yancey (2008) found that exposure to media violence shared only trivial amounts of variance with criminal aggression. Similarly, in a large sample of youth aged 10–15, Ybarra et al. (2008) found that violent media exposure did not predict violence once other confounding variables were controlled. It is also noteworthy that the explosion in popularity and availability of video games has coincided with a precipitous decline in youth violence, not a rise (see Ferguson 2013 for discussion).

C. J. Ferguson (&)
Department of Psychology, Stetson University,
DeLand, FL 32729, USA
e-mail: CJFerguson1111@Aol.com

C. K. Olson
Reston, VA, USA

Ferguson, Christopher J.; Olson, Cheryl K., "Video Game Violence Use Among ''Vulnerable' Populations: The Impact of Violent Games on Delinquency and Bullying Among Children with Clinically Elevated Depression or Attention Deficit Symptoms" *Journal of Youth and Adolescence,* 43(1) January 2014. 127–136. With permission of Springer.

There exists a large pool of studies examining video game violence effects in college students using laboratory methods and measures of relatively mild aggression. The validity of these measures has been debated within the research community (e.g., Giancola and Zeichner 1995; Ritter and Eslea 2005). One point of contention is the lack of clear correspondence between these measures and the types of aggressive behaviors of interest to policy makers and parents. For instance, such studies have examined outcomes such as filling in the missing letters of words, where "kill" rather than "kiss" is considered more aggressive (Farrar et al. 2013); self-ratings of hostile feelings (Williams 2011); or administering non-painful bursts of annoying noise to consenting opponents in a reaction-time test (Anderson and Dill 2000). Taken at face value, such studies may be generalizable to competitiveness rather than aggression, or perhaps to mild aggressive acts (the equivalent of children sticking tongues out at each other), but cannot be generalized to societal violence. Even these studies produce mixed results, however, and have been criticized for methodological issues such as failing to match violent and non-violent video game play conditions carefully (Adachi and Willoughby 2011), using unstandardized outcome measures that may allow researchers to pick and choose outcomes fitting their hypotheses (Ferguson 2013), and high potential for demand characteristics.

By contrast, studies of video game effects on violent behaviors among children, conducted outside laboratory settings, remain relatively few in number. Such studies differ in quality and standardized approach to measurement. One study (Anderson et al. 2008) found weak links between video game violence and aggression in US and Japanese children, although interpretation of results is complicated by the use of non-standard measures of aggression and inadequate control for other variables. A later German study tying media violence, including video game play, to aggression in children (Krahé et al. 2012) also did not use standardized assessments. That study may have been compromised by the introduction of a media education program into the schools mid-way through the longitudinal period (e.g., Möller et al. 2012) introducing demand characteristics (i.e., advertising the study hypotheses to prime respondents to answer surveys in a particular way, not representative of how they actually behave). Another recent study that links violent games with aggression, by Willoughby et al. (2012), carefully controlled for important "third" variables. With other variables controlled, exposure to violent video games correlated with later aggression with an effect size equivalent to $r = .07$, indicating that violent game use was associated with approximately half a percent increase in aggressive behavior. The authors noted, however, that it may be competitive qualities of the games, not violent content, which led to this increase (see Adachi and Willoughby 2011). In a follow-up longitudinal study (Adachi and Willoughby 2013), the authors confirmed that competition predicts later aggression, irrespective of violent game exposure history.

Few other studies of children and video games have made a solid case for a connection to aggression or violent outcomes.

Several have suggested that use of violent video games might reduce aggression (Colwell and Kato 2003; Shibuya et al. 2008[1]). Others indicate that, with other factors controlled, effects are null (Ferguson 2011; von Salisch et al. 2011; Wallenius and Punamäki 2008; Ybarra et al. 2008) or that effects may be idiosyncratic among children (Unsworth et al. 2007). Meta-analyses (e.g., Sherry 2007) have found weaker effects in studies of children than for college students, the opposite of what might be expected developmentally. Thus, overall, it is difficult to make clear conclusions about links between video game violence and childhood aggression or violence.

Post-Sandy Hook, a view emerged, typified by the report of the US House of Representatives Gun Violence Prevention Task Force (2013), that current research probably did not support concerns that the average child was harmed by video game violence. Rather, attention should be focused on prevention and early intervention with "at-risk youth," with particular emphasis on mental health. This is a reasonable hypothesis, but one that has not been studied extensively. Several studies of college students by Patrick Markey found that violent video games may interact with preexisting anger symptoms in some young adults to increase hostility, although he has been cautious about extending these findings to violence in children (Giumetti and Markey 2007; Markey and Markey 2010; Markey and Scherer 2009). These warnings are consistent with those of criminologists who warn against generalizing laboratory aggression measures to criminal violence (Savage 2008). One recent analysis with children (Ferguson 2011) was unable to confirm the hypothesis that children with preexisting antisocial traits were adversely influenced by violent video games. However, more research would certainly be welcome.

The Current Study

The current study is intended to address gaps in the existing literature by considering the impact of exposure to violence in video games on criminal delinquency and bullying behaviors in a sample of children with clinically elevated mental health symptoms. It is important to note at the outset that the vast majority of children with mental health symptoms do not engage in violent behavior. Although some symptoms of mental health problems such as depression (Ferguson 2011) and attention deficit disorder (Wymbs et al. 2012) have been identified as risk factors for aggressive or violent behavior, this occurs only in combination with other significant risk factors, not as a direct result of the mental health symptoms. Thus, scholars must exercise caution not to further stigmatize mental illness by insinuating links with violence.

Rather, our analyses are intended to address the hypothesis that children with clinically elevated mental health symptoms consistitute a "vulnerable" population of individuals who may be susceptible to video game violence effects even if clinically "normal" children are not. We thus test two main hypotheses. First, it was hypothesized that children with clinically elevated symptoms of depression will demonstrate a correlation between violent video game exposure and criminal delinquency and bullying behavior-related outcomes. Second, it was hypothesized that children with clinically elevated attention deficit symptoms will demonstrate a correlation between violent video game exposure and criminal delinquency and bullying behavior related outcomes.

Methods

Participants

The current study includes a subset of participants from a large federally funded project examining video game violence effects on youth. Details related to the initial development and recruitment for this project can be found at Kutner and Olson (2008). Only children who scored in the clinically significant range on clinically validated scales related to depressive or attention deficit symptoms (scales discussed below) were included in the current analyses. These included 377 children: 182 with clinically elevated attention deficit symptoms, and 284 with clinically elevated depressive symptoms. Clinically elevated symptoms were comorbid for 89 (23.6%) children. There were 234 females in the sample and 140 males (3 chose not to report their gender). The mean age of the children was 12.93 (SD = .76). Children were recruited from both an urban and suburban school. The ethnic makeup of students in the urban school was 50% white, 43% black, 2% Asian, 5% Hispanic and \ 1% other. The ethnic makeup of students in the suburban school was 90% white, 4% black, 4% Asian, 1% Hispanic and 1% other (individual students were not asked to report their ethnic background).

Measures

Depression/Attention Symptoms

Symptoms of depression and attention-deficit/hyperactivity problems were assessed using the relevant subscales of the youth self-report version of the Pediatric Symptom Checklist—17 (PSC; Gardner et al. 1999). This instrument is a validated, brief screening device for mental health problems in children, and provides clinical cut-offs to identify children whose symptoms merit further evaluation. Participants were asked to rate whether they experienced particular mental health symptoms "never," "sometimes" or "often." With the current sample, coefficient alpha for the ADHD subscale was .75 and for the depression subscale .80. The sample reported mean was 5.41 and standard deviation was 2.28.

Trait Aggression

The Attitudes Toward Conflict scale (ATC; Dahlberg et al. 1998) consists of eight Likert items related to potential aggressive responses to various hypothetical situations. Sample items include, "It's OK for me to hit someone to get them to do what I want" and

"I try to talk out a problem instead of fighting." Due to the stability in trait aggression it is commonly regarded as an important control variable and we include it here for this reason. Trait aggression correlated with video game exposure at r = .24 for youth with elevated attention deficit symptoms and .23 for youth with elevated depressive symptoms. However, predictive relationships between exposure to video game violence and trait aggression became non-significant in regression equations with gender, parental involvement, stress and family/peer support controlled. Thus, we are confident that our use of trait aggression as a control variable does not miss relationships between video game violence and trait aggression with other factors controlled. Coefficient alpha for the current sample for the ATC was .76. The sample reported mean was 16.48 and standard deviation was 4.60.

Parental Involvement

To measure parents' involvement with their children's media use, sharing media consumption with children and making media consumption decisions for them, a nine-item Likert-scale was created for this study. Examples of questions included in this scale are "My parents play electronic games with me," and "My parents tell me I can't play a particular electronic game." Coefficient alpha for the current sample was .68. The sample reported mean was 18.48 and standard deviation was 4.12.

Support from Others

We compiled a sixteen item Likert-scale measure of perceived support from peers and family. This measure was based on two existing measures (Lerner et al. 2005; Phillips and Springer 1992) of peer support and family support. Overall coefficient alpha for the resultant scale was .87. The sample reported mean was 44.35 and standard deviation was 10.22.

Stress

The Stressful Urban Life Events scale (SULE; Attar et al. 1994), a 19 item yes/no scale, was used to measure total stress that children in the current sample had experienced during the past year. The SULE addressed stressors such as getting suspended from school, getting poor grades on one's report card, or experiencing the death of a family member. Coefficient alpha for the total stress scale was .67 for the current sample. The sample reported mean was 4.82 and standard deviation was 2.96.

Exposure to Video Game Violence

In the current study, we used Entertainment Software Ratings Board (ESRB) video game ratings as an estimate of exposure to violence in video games. Respondents were asked to write the names of five video games that they had "played a lot" in the past

6 months. ESRB ratings were then obtained for each game, and ordinally coded (a maximal score of 5 for "Mature," 4 for "Teen," etc.). The sample reported mean was 29.97 and standard deviation was 30.09.

Many factors go into an ESRB rating, including language, sexual content, and use of (or reference to) drugs or gambling. However, among those factors that determine the age-based rating, violence appears to take priority. Descriptors of listed games were reviewed to ensure that high ratings had not been obtained primarily for sexual content; this was not the case for any of the games. Common violence-containing games named by participants included those in the Halo, Grand Theft Auto, and Mortal Kombat series. The ratings were summed across the 5 games listed, then multiplied by the number of hours per week that the child reported playing video games. As with all attempts to assess game content exposure, this is only an estimate; however, it removes some of the subjectivity inherent in previous methods. This approach has been found to be reliable and valid in previous research (Ferguson 2011; Lenhart et al. 2008).

Delinquency

A six-item Likert scale of general delinquency was compiled from several existing delinquency scales (Brener et al. 2002; Elliot et al. 1985; Leffert et al. 1998). Questions addressed physical aggression (been in a physical fight; hit or beat up someone) as well as more general delinquency (stole something from a store; got into trouble with the police; damaged property just for fun, such as breaking windows, scratching a car, or putting paint on walls; skipped classes or school without an excuse). Participants were asked to report how often these behaviors occurred within the previous twelve months. Coefficient alpha for the resultant scale was .75 for the current sample. The sample reported mean was 3.00 and standard deviation was 3.95.

Bullying

The Revised Olweus Bully/Victim Questionnaire (Olweus 1996) was used to assess bullying behaviors. The bullying perpetration scale consisted of 9 items in which participants were asked to rate how often they had engaged in bullying behaviors over the past couple of months. Items inquire about physical aggression, verbal aggression, threats and social exclusion. A coefficient alpha of .86 was obtained for the current sample. The sample reported mean was 2.68 and standard deviation was 4.27.

Procedure

All procedures described within this study were approved by local IRB and designed to comport with APA standards for ethical human research. An "opt out" procedure was used for student involvement, with parents notified of the study through school newsletters and notices sent home to students. Youth assent for participation was obtained for all participants. Teachers were not present during data colection, which occurred during the school day.

Primary data analysis used for the testing of the study hypotheses were OLS multiple regressions. Gender, parental involvement, trait aggression, stress, family/peer support and exposure to video game violence, as well as the interaction between exposure to violent video game and trait aggression, were entered simultaneously in the regression equation. In keeping with the recommendations of Simmons et al. (2011), we certify that this analysis approach was selected in advance and was not altered to produce particular results. An interaction between trait aggression and exposure to video game violence was tested by first centering the variables to avoid multicollinearity. Collinearity diagnostics for all regressions revealed absence of any concerns with all VIFs below 2.0. Youth with depressive or attention deficit symptoms will be considered separately.

Results

Video Game Exposure

Children in our sample were generally very familiar with electronic games. Of our sample, 84.4% reported playing video games on a computer, 81.2% on a console and 50.4% on a handheld device in the previous 6 months. Only 6.1% reported playing no games at all during that time. Similarly, only 11.4% of our sample had no exposure to violent video games. Boys had considerably more exposure to violent video games than did girls [$t(189.24) = 9.07$, $p \backslash .001$, $r = .46$, 95% CI = .38, .54]. Kurtosis and skew were acceptable, suggesting a normal distribution of scores.

Video Game Influences

With the sample of children with clinically elevated depressive symptoms and regarding delinquent criminality as an outcome, only stress ($b = .30$) and trait aggression ($b = .42$) were predictive of delinquent criminality. Neither exposure to video game violence nor the interaction between trait aggression and exposure to video game violence was predictive of delinquent outcomes. The adjusted R^2 for this regression equation was .36. These results are presented in Table 1.

With the same sample of children with clinically elevated depressive symptoms but considering bullying behaviors as an outcome, once again only stress ($b = .23$) and trait aggression ($b = .28$) were predictive of bullying behaviors. Neither exposure to video game violence nor the interaction between exposure to video game violence and trait aggression was predictive of bullying related outcomes. The adjusted R^2 for this regression equation was .22. These results are presented in Table 2.

With the sample of children with clinically elevated attention deficit symptoms and regarding delinquent criminality, as with the

Table 1

Delinquency Regression: Beta Weights and Significance of Entered Variables for Adolescents with Clinical Elevated Depressive Symptoms

Variable	b	95% Confidence Interval	t test	Significance
Gender	.06		0.92	.36
Parental involvement	−.01		−0.05	.96
Stress	.30	(.19, .40)	4.73	.001*
Family/peer support	−.07		−0.96	.34
Trait aggression	.42	(.32, .51)	6.08	.001*
VGV	.04		0.55	.59
VGV 9 trait aggression	.04		0.64	.53

VGV exposure to video game violence

Table 2

Bullying Regression: Beta Weights and Significance of Entered Variables for Adolescents with Clinical Elevated Depressive Symptoms

Variable	b	95% Confidence Interval	t test	Significance
Gender	−.11		−1.74	.14
Parental involvement	−.01		−0.09	.92
Stress	.23	(.12, .34)	3.24	.001*
Family/peer support	−.05		−0.67	.50
Trait aggression	.28	(.17, .38)	3.74	.001*
VGV	−.07		−0.95	.34
VGV 9 trait aggression	−.02		−0.23	.82

VGV exposure to video game violence

sample of children with clinically elevated depressive symptoms, only stress (b = .32) and trait aggression (b = .38) were predictive of delinquent criminality. Neither exposure to video game violence nor the interaction between trait aggression and exposure to video game violence was predictive of delinquent outcomes. The adjusted R^2 for this regression equation was .37. These results are presented in Table 3.

Finally, with the sample once again of children with clinically elevated attention deficit symptoms and with regards to bullying behavior only trait aggression (b = .41) was predictive of bullying behaviors along with the interaction between trait aggression and exposure to violent games (b = −.22) suggesting that highly trait aggressive children who also played violent video games were less likely to engage in bullying behaviors. Exposure to Video game

Table 3

Delinquency Regression: Beta Weights and Significance of Entered Variables for Adolescents with Clinical Elevated Attention Deficit Symptoms

Variable	b	95% Confidence Interval	t test	Significance
Gender	.06		0.71	.48
Parental involvement	.06		0.70	.49
Stress	.32	(.18, .44)	4.21	.001*
Family/peer support	−.15		−1.69	.10
Trait aggression	.38	(.25, .50)	4.23	.001*
VGV	.04		0.45	.65
VGV 9 trait aggression	.03		0.39	.70

VGV exposure to video game violence

violence was not a significant predictor of bullying behaviors. The adjusted R^2 for this regression equation was .19. These results are presented in Table 4.

Discussion

The 2011 Supreme Court (Brown v EMA 2011) case seemed to have briefly cooled speculation about video game violence effects on children. The tragic 2012 shooting of young children in Newtown, Connecticut by a 20-year-old male reportedly fond of playing violent video games put the issue back on the front burner (Gun Violence Prevention Task Force 2013). The consensus from the

Table 4

Bullying Regression: Beta Weights and Significance of Entered Variables for Adolescents with Clinical Elevated Attention Deficit Symptoms

Variable	b	95% Confidence Interval	t test	Significance
Gender	−.06		−0.61	.54
Parental involvement	−.06		0.65	.52
Stress	.12		1.38	.17
Family/peer support	−.01		0.02	.99
Trait aggression	.41	(.28, .52)	4.17	.001*
VGV	−.06		0.60	.55
VGV 9 trait aggression	−.22	(-.08, -.35)	−2.27	.03*

VGV exposure to video game violence

government (e.g., Gun Violence Prevention Task Force 2013) seems to have been that current research does not consistently link exposure to video game violence with aggression or societal violence, but more research is necessary to assess effects on potentially vulnerable subgroups of children. The current study is an attempt to fill that gap by considering correlational violent video game effects in a sample of youth with clinically elevated mental health symptoms. Our results did not provide support for the hypotheses that exposure to violent video games would be associated with increased delinquency or bullying behaviors in children with elevated mental health symptoms.

Our results indicated that violent video games were associated with neither delinquent criminality nor bullying behaviors in children with either clinically elevated depressive or attention deficit symptoms. Nor did we find support for the belief that trait aggression would interact with video game violence within this sample of youth. That is a particularly interesting finding given that a combination of mental health symptoms and long-term aggressive traits are common elements to attackers who carried out school shootings (US Secret Service and US Department of Education 2002). Our results cannot, of course, be generalized to mass homicides. We do note that our findings with more general forms of youth violence are similar to those of the Secret Service report, in that trait aggressiveness and stress were risk factors for negative outcomes where exposure to video game violence was not. The only exception was our finding that, for children with elevated attention deficit symptoms, trait aggression and video game violence interacted in such a way as to predict reduced bullying. This could be considered some small correlational evidence for a cathartic type effect, although we note it was for only one of four outcomes and small in effect size. Thus we caution against overinterpretation of this result.

None of the hypotheses related to video game violence effects on vulnerable youth were supported. Although this is only one piece of evidence, this early result does not support the belief that certain at-risk populations of youth, at least related to clinically elevated depression and attention deficit symptoms and trait aggression, demonstrate negative associations between violent video games and aggression related outcomes. It may be that the influence of media is simply too distal to impact children, even those with mental health symptoms. We do note that our results do not rule out motivational models of media use, wherein effects are driven by user motivations rather than automatic modeling of content. However, we found little evidence to support beliefs in reliable probabilistic models of automatic media modeling of violence in children with elevated depressive or attention deficit symptoms.

We note that our results differ from those of Patrick Markey (Giumetti and Markey 2007; Markey and Markey 2010; Markey and Scherer 2009). There are several possible explanations for the differing results. For example, Markey's work considered hostile feelings in the short term as outcome. It may be that such feelings do not persist or do not extend to actual violent behavior. Markey's

work also examined college students, whereas ours look at youth. Differences between laboratory-based work and correlational work also may help explain the differences in findings.

Developmental and Theoretical Perspectives

Across youth and across outcomes, the current levels of stress and trait aggression were the most consistent predictors of negative outcomes in youth. These results are consistent with a model of aggression known as the Catalyst Model, which is basically a diathesis stress model of violence (Ferguson et al. 2008). Although we did not specifically set out to test the Catalyst Model, our results are a good fit for this theory's predictions that violence is the product of crystallized personality traits coupled with stressful triggers from the environment.

From a developmental perspective, the Catalyst Model suggests that such personality traits results from a combination of genetic propensity coupled with harsh upbringing, although these were variables beyond our current dataset. However, the Catalyst Model generally assumes that exposure to media violence is a normative rather than deviant experience (see also Olson 2010). This may differ from the perspective of many commentators concerned about harmful media influences. For instance, much attention has focused on whether Adam Lanza (the Newtown, Connecticut shooter) had significant exposure to violent video games (e.g., Henderson 2012). It is worth noting that, statistically speaking, it would be more unusual if he did not play violent video games, given that the majority of youth and young men play such games at least occasionally (Lenhart et al. 2008; Olson et al. 2007). Thus, it may be a mistake to take the perspective that exposure to violent video games or other media is a developmentally abnormal experience. Our results support that generally accepted thinking, even for children with elevated mental health systems, may need to be changed.

The Catalyst Model has the advantage of acknowledging that not all learning opportunities are equal. That is to say, proximal influences, such as family environment, are considered to have a greater impact than distal influences, such as electronic media. We believe that this is superior to traditional social cognitive models of aggression that equate all learning opportunities and thus lack nuance and an acknowledgement of developmental trends in which children are known to process different sources of information differently (Woolley and Van Reet 2006). The Catalyst Model also relies less on the assumption that aggressive cognitions and behaviors are based primarily on cognitive aggressive scripts, which does not appear to be an effective approach to understanding serious aggression. The Catalyst Model fits best with our observations of stress and trait aggression as the primary predictors of delinquency and bullying in youth, although as a correlational study our findings can not address the causal assumptions of the Catalyst Model.

In addition to looking at violence from more of a diathesis-stress approach, there may be value in viewing media use from more of a motivational perspective, such as the uses and gratifications approach (Sherry et al. 2006) or Self-Determination Theory (Przybylski et al. 2010; Ryan et al. 2006). These theoretical approaches have in common the value of taking the user experience as a primary driving factor of the relationship between the user and media, rather than presuming that content drives the relationship. In the typical "hypodermic needle model" of media effects, effects are traditionally conceptualized as Stimulus/Response, or perhaps Stimulus/Organism/Response if the individual is considered as a moderating variable (see Ferguson and Dyck 2012 for discussion). There may be greater value in considering the relationship from more of an Organism/Stimulus/Response arrangement, with the organism rather than the stimulus as the primary driving force of the relationship between media and behavior. That is to say, individuals may select certain kinds of media in order meet needs they have or reach desired emotional states. Even specific forms of media may have idiosyncratic effects on users dependent upon how they consume and process media.

Limitations and Conclusions

As with all studies, ours has limitations that are important to consider. First, our sample includes children with mental health symptoms above clinical cut-off points on a validated screening tool, but screening results do not constitute official diagnoses of mental health disorders. Further, although we considered mental health and trait aggression, it is possible that other issues may place some children in vulnerable populations that we did not identify. Our study involves concurrent correlational data; thus, it is not possible to make causal inferences or to test the directionality of observed relationships. Reliabilities of the stress and parental involvement scales were also lower than ideal. These two scales appear to tap into a broad array of issues, which may explain this result; future researchers may wish to consider more narrowly constructed scales. Lastly, although our delinquency scale was compiled from existing well-validated scales, it would be valuable to see our results replicated using clinical outcomes such as the Child Behavior Checklist or criminological outcomes such as the Negative Life Events scale (Paternoster and Mazerolle 1994).

Our results suggest that the association between violent video games and aggression related outcomes in children, even those with clinically elevated mental health symptoms, may be minimal. Our research contributes to the field of youth and media by providing evidence that a timely, policy-relevant, and seemingly reasonable hypothesis— that mentally vulnerable children may be particularly influenced by violent video games—does not appear to be well supported. However, more research on this population, and on others likely to be at increased risk (such as children exposed to violence in their homes or neighborhoods), is needed to guide parents, health professionals and policymakers. It may be valuable for future researchers to consider alternate models of youth's media use,

particularly those that focus on motivational models in which users, rather than content, drive experiences. Content-based theoretical models do not appear to be sufficient for a sophisticated understanding of media use and effects.

A Word of Caution

Scholarship produced in the emotional and politicized environment that follows a national tragedy (see Ferguson 2013) can give the appearance of a "wag the dog" effect, with research commissioned based upon, and then used to support, an a priori political agenda. As Hall et al. (2011) noted in their article on the Supreme Court and video games, a rush to judgment grounded in legislators' interpretations of "unsettled science" may damage the credibility of the scientific process. Scholars would be wise to proceed carefully, with close attention to sound methodology and discussion of limitations, as they design and conduct the next wave of studies. Studies which move beyond traditional social cognitive automatic processes to consider how youth select, interpret and involve media in their identity development as active consumers of media would be of particularly high value.

Author contributions CJF conducted the main analyses for the paper and wrote the initial draft. CO collected the data an contributed to revising drafts of this paper. Both authors participated equally in conceiving and designing the analyses. Both authors read and approved of the final manuscript.

References

Adachi, P. C., & Willoughby, T. (2011). The effect of video game competition and violence on aggressive behavior: Which characteristic has the greatest influence? Psychology of Violence, 1(4), 259–274.

Adachi, P. C., & Willoughby, T. (2013). Demolishing the competition: The longitudinal link between competitive video games, competitive gambling, and aggression. Journal of Youth and Adolescence,. doi:10.1007/s10964-013-9952-2.

American Psychological Association. (2005). Resolution on violence in video games and interactive media. Retrieved July 3, 2011 from http://www.apa.org/about/governance/council/policy/inter active-media.pdf.

Anderson, C. A., Gentile, D. A., & Dill, K. E. (2012). Prosocial, antisocial, and other effects of recreational video games. In D. G. Singer & J. L. Singer (Eds.), Handbook of children and the media (2nd ed., pp. 249–272). Thousand Oaks, CA: Sage.

Anderson, C., Sakamoto, A., Gentile, D., Ihori, N., Shibuya, A., Yukawa, S., et al. (2008). Longitudinal effects of violent video games on aggression in Japan and the United States. Pediatrics, 122(5), e1067–e1072.

Attar, B., Guerra, N., & Tolan, P. (1994). Neighborhood disadvantage, stressful life events, and adjustment in urban elementary-school children. Special issue: Impact of poverty on children, youth, and families. Journal of Clinical Child Psychology, 23(4), 391–400.

Australian Government, Attorney General's Department. (2010). Literature review on the impact of playing violent video games on aggression. Commonwealth of Australia.

Bavelier, D., Green, C., Han, D., Renshaw, P. F., Merzenich, M. M., & Gentile, D. A. (2011). Brains on video games. Nature Reviews Neuroscience, 12(12), 763–768.

Brener, N., Kann, L., McManus, T., Kinchen, S., Sundberg, E., & Ross, J. (2002). Reliability of the 1999 Youth Risk Survey Questionnaire. Journal of Adolescent Health, 34, 336–342.

Brown v EMA. (2011). Retrieved July 1, 2011 from http://www.supremecourt.gov/opinions/10pdf/08-1448.pdf.

Cohen, J. (1992). A power primer. Psychological Bulletin, 112, 155–159.

Colwell, J., & Kato, M. (2003). Investigation of the relationship between social isolation, self-esteem, aggression and computer game play in Japanese adolescents. Asian Journal of Social Psychology, 6(2), 149–158.

Dahlberg, C., Toal, S., & Behrens, C. (Eds.). (1998). Measuring violence-related attitudes, beliefs, and behaviors among youths: A compendium of assessment tools. Atlanta, GA: Center of Disease Control and Prevention, National Center for Injury Prevention and Control.

Elliot, D., Huizinga, D., & Ageton, S. (1985). Explaining delinquency and drug use. Beverly Hills, CA: Sage.

Ferguson, C. J. (2011). Video games and youth violence: A prospective analysis in adolescents. Journal of Youth and Adolescence, 40(4), 377–391.

Ferguson, C. J. (2013). Violent video games and the Supreme Court: Lessons for the scientific community in the wake of Brown v EMA. American Psychologist, 68(2), 57–74.

Ferguson, C. J., Coulson, M., & Barnett, J. (2011). Psychological profiles of school shooters: Positive directions and one big wrong turn. Journal of Police Crisis Negotiations, 11(2), 141–158.

Ferguson, C. J., & Dyck, D. (2012). Paradigm change in aggression research: The time has come to retire the General Aggression Model. Aggression and Violent Behavior, 17(3), 220–228. doi:10.1016/j.avb.2012.02.007.

Ferguson, C. J., Rueda, S., Cruz, A., Ferguson, D., Fritz, S., & Smith, S. (2008). Violent video games and aggression: Causal relationship or byproduct of family violence and intrinsic violence motivation? Criminal Justice and Behavior, 35, 311–332.

Fraser, A. M., Padilla-Walker, L. M., Coyne, S. M., Nelson, L. J., & Stockdale, L. A. (2012). Associations between violent video gaming, empathic concern, and prosocial behavior toward strangers, friends, and family members. Journal of Youth and Adolescence, 41(5), 636–649.

Gardner, W., Murphy, M., Childs, G., Kelleher, K., Pagano, M., Jellinek, M., et al. (1999). The PSC-17: A brief pediatric symptoms checklist with psychosocial problem subscales. A report of PROS and ASPN. Ambulatory Child Health, 5, 225–236.

Giancola, P. R., & Zeichner, A. (1995). Construct validity of a competitive reaction-time aggression paradigm. Aggressive Behavior, 21, 199–204.

Giumetti, G. W., & Markey, P. M. (2007). Violent video games and anger as predictors of aggression. Journal of Research in Personality, 41(6), 1234–1243.

Gun Violence Prevention Task Force. (2013). It's time to act: A comprehensive plan that reduces gun violence and respects the 2nd amendment rights of law-abiding Americans. Washington, DC: US House of Representatives.

Hall, R., Day, T., & Hall, R. (2011). A plea for caution: Violent video games, the Supreme Court, and the role of science. Mayo Clinic Proceedings, 86(4), 315–321.

Henderson, B. (2012). Connecticut school massacre: Adam Lanza 'spent hours playing Call of Duty.' The Telegraph. Retrieved April 18, 2013 from http://www.telegraph.co.uk/news/worldnews/northamerica/usa/9752141/Connecticut-school-massacre-Adam-Lanza-spent-hours-playing-Call-Of-Duty.html.

Krahé, B., Busching, R., & Möller, I. (2012). Media violence use and aggression among German adolescents: Associations and trajectories of change in a three-wave longitudinal study. Psychology of Popular Media Culture, 1(3), 152–166.

Kutner, L., & Olson, C. (2008). Grand theft childhood: The surprising truth about violent video games and what parents can do. New York: Simon & Schuster.

Leffert, N., Benson, L., Scales, P., Sharma, A., Drake, D., & Blyth, D. (1998). Developmental assets: Measurement and prediction of risk behaviors among adolescents. Applied Developmental Science, 2, 209–230.

Lenhart, A., Kahne, J., Middaugh, E., MacGill, A., Evans, C., & Mitak, J. (2008). Teens, video games and civics: Teens' gaming experiences are diverse and include significant social interaction and civic engagement. Pew Internet & American Life Project. Retrieved December 29, 2010 from http://www.pewinternet.org/PPF/r/263/report_display.asp.

Lerner, R., Lerner, J., Almerigi, J., Theokas, C., Phelps, E., Gestsdottir, S., et al. (2005). Positive youth development, participation in community youth development programs, and community contributions of fifth-grade adolescents: Findings from the first wave of the 4-H study of positive youth development. Journal of Early Adolescence, 25, 17–71.

Lewis, T. (2013). Report links violent media, mental health and guns to mass shootings. Consumer Affairs. Retrieved February 21, 2013 from http://www.consumeraffairs.com/news/report-links-violent-media-mental-health-and-guns-to-mass-shootings-021413. html.

Markey, P. M., & Markey, C. N. (2010). Vulnerability to violent video games: A review and integration of personality research. Review of General Psychology, 14(2), 82–91.

Markey, P. M., & Scherer, K. (2009). An examination of psychoticism and motion capture controls as moderators of the effects of violent video games. Computers in Human Behavior, 25(2), 407–411.

Möller, I., Krahé, B., Busching, R., & Krause, C. (2012). Efficacy of an intervention to reduce the use of media violence and aggression: An experimental evaluation with adolescents in Germany. Journal of Youth and Adolescence, 41(2), 105–120.

Olson, C. K. (2010). Children's motivations for video game play in the context of normal development. Review of General Psychology, 14(2), 180–187.

Olson, C., Kutner, L., Warner, D., Almerigi, J., Baer, L., Nicholi, A., et al. (2007). Factors correlated with violent video game use by adolescent boys and girls. Journal of Adolescent Health, 41, 77–83.

Olweus, D. (1996). The Revised Olweus Bully/Victim Questionnaire. Mimeo. Bergen: Research Center for Health Promotion (HEMIL Center), University of Bergen.

Paternoster, R., & Mazerolle, P. (1994). General strain theory and delinquency: A replication and extension. Journal of Research in Crime and Delinquency, 31(3), 235–263.

Phillips, J., & Springer, F. (1992). Extended National Youth Sports Program 1991-1992 evaluation highlights, part two: Individual Protective Factors Index (IPFI) and risk assessment study. Report prepared for the National Collegiate Athletic Association. Sacramento, CA: EMT Associates.

Przybylski, A. K., Rigby, C., & Ryan, R. M. (2010). A motivational model of video game engagement. Review of General Psychol- ogy, 14(2), 154–166. doi:10.1037/a0019440.

Puri, K., & Pugliese, R. (2012). Sex, lies, and video games: Moral panics or uses and gratifications. Bulletin of Science, Technology & Society, 32(5), 345–352.

Reinecke, L. (2009). Games and recovery: The use of video and computer games to recuperate from stress and strain. Journal of Media Psychology: Theories, Methods, And Applications, 21(3), 126–142.

Ritter, D., & Eslea, M. (2005). Hot sauce, toy guns and graffiti: A critical account of current laboratory aggression paradigms. Aggressive Behavior, 31, 407–419.

Ruggiero, T. E. (2000). Uses and gratifications theory in the 21st century. Mass Communication & Society, 3(1), 3–37.

Russoniello, C. V., O'Brien, K., & Parks, J. M. (2009). The effectiveness of casual video games in improving mood and decreasing stress. Journal of Cybertherapy and Rehabilitation, 2(1), 53–66.

Ryan, R. M., Rigby, C., & Przybylski, A. (2006). The motivational pull of video games: A self-determination theory approach. Motivation and Emotion, 30(4), 347–363.

Savage, J. (2008). The role of exposure to media violence in the etiology of violent behavior: A criminologist weighs in. American Behavioral Scientist, 51, 1123–1136.

Savage, J., & Yancey, C. (2008). The effects of media violence exposure on criminal aggression: A meta-analysis. Criminal Justice and Behavior, 35, 1123–1136.

Sherry, J. (2007). Violent video games and aggression: Why can't we find links? In R. Preiss, B. Gayle, N. Burrell, M. Allen, & J. Bryant (Eds.), Mass media effects research: Advances through meta-analysis (pp. 231–248). Mahwah, NJ: L. Erlbaum.

Sherry, J. L., Lucas, K., Greenberg, B. S., & Lachlan, K. (2006). Video game uses and gratifications as predictors of use and game preference. In P. Vorderer & J. Bryant (Eds.), Playing video games: Motives, responses, and consequences (pp. 213–224). Mahwah, NJ: Lawrence Erlbaum Associates.

Shibuya, A., Sakamoto, A., Ihori, N., & Yukawa, S. (2008). The effects of the presence and context of video game violence on children: A longitudinal study in Japan. Simulation and Gaming, 39(4), 528–539.

Simmons, J. P., Nelson, L. D., & Simonsohn, U. (2011). False-positive psychology: Undisclosed flexibility in data collection and analysis allows presenting anything as significant. Psychological Science, 22(11), 1359–1366. doi:10.1177/09567976114 17632.

Strasburger, V. (2007). Go ahead punk, make my day: It's time for pediatricians to take action against media violence. Pediatrics, 119, e1398–e1399.

Swedish Media Council. (2011). Våldsamma datorspel och aggression—en översikt av forskningen 2000–2011. Retrieved January 14, 2011 from http://www.statensmedierad.se /Publikationer/Produkter/Valdsamma-datorspel-och -aggression/.

United States Secret Service and United States Department of Education. (2002). The final report and findings of the Safe School Initiative: Implications for the prevention of school attacks in the United States. Retrieved July 2, 2011 from http:// www.secretservice.gov/ntac/ssi_final_report.pdf.

Unsworth, G., Devilly, G., & Ward, T. (2007). The effect of playing violent videogames on adolescents: Should parents be quaking in their boots? Psychology, Crime and Law, 13, 383–394.

Von Salisch, M., Oppl, C., & Kristen, A. (2006). What attracts children? In P. Vorderer, J. Bryant, P. Vorderer, & J. Bryant (Eds.), Playing video games: Motives, responses, and consequences (pp. 147–163). Mahwah, NJ: Lawrence Erlbaum Associates Publishers.

von Salisch, M., Vogelgesang, J., Kristen, A., & Oppl, C. (2011). Preference for violent electronic games and aggressive behavior among children: The beginning of the downward spiral? Media Psychology, 14(3), 233–258.

Wallenius, M., & Punamäki, R. (2008). Digital game violence and direct aggression in adolescence: A longitudinal study of the roles of sex, age, and parent–child communication. Journal of Applied Developmental Psychology, 29(4), 286–294.

Willoughby, T., Adachi, P. C., & Good, M. (2012). A longitudinal study of the association between violent video game play and aggression among adolescents. Developmental Psychology, 48(4), 1044–1057.

Woolley, J., & Van Reet, J. (2006). Effects of context on judgments concerning the reality status of novel entities. Child Development, 77, 1778–1793.

Wymbs, B., Molina, B., Pelham, W., Cheong, J., Gnagy, E., Belendiuk, K., et al. (2012). Risk of intimate partner violence among young adult males with childhood ADHD. Journal of Attention Disorders, 16(5), 373–383.

Ybarra, M., Diener-West, M., Markow, D., Leaf, P., Hamburger, M., & Boxer, P. (2008). Linkages between internet and other media violence with seriously violent behavior by youth. Pediatrics, 122(5), 929–937.

Note

1. We note the issue that some research reports insinuate links between violent games and aggression, where their data fail to support such insinuations. We note that in Shibuya et al. 2008, in their Table 2, the video game exposure by violence presence variable is associated with a reduction in aggression in boys, but not girls. For Ybarra et al. (2008) the null effect for violent video games is noted in their Figure 2, although they largely ignore their own results to imply links between violent games and youth aggression. These papers highlight the need to closely examine research results when understanding the true implications of a research study. The rhetoric employed by scholars in their abstracts and discussion sections does not always match their data.

CHRISTOPHER J. FERGUSON is associate professor and department chair at Stetson University. His research interests focus on media effects on children and adolescents, particularly violent media, and thin images on body dissatisfaction.

CHERYL K. OLSON currently works as a consultant and her research interests focus on public health and policy related to media issues.

EXPLORING THE ISSUE

Does Playing Violent Video Games Harm Adolescents?

Critical Thinking and Reflection

1. An area of research receiving increasing attention is the relationship between playing video games and cognitive development—attention span, executive functioning, and performance at school and work. Do you think playing video games can make you smarter or do you think they turn our youth into inattentive zombies?
2. Given some of the reported positive effects of playing video games, do you see a place for some (or all) of them in the classroom?
3. Do you think there is a difference between the effects of TV and film violence versus video games' violence?
4. We have heard in the media that many school and other mass shootings are linked to violent video game playing. We also know that there are thousands of well-adjusted adolescents who play these games and never exhibit any form of antisocial behavior. Do you think there are other variables involved in the relationship that has been reported between violent video games and both bullying and aggression?
5. If you were to design the "perfect" study examining the effects of violent video games, what would it look like? What variables would you measure? What variables would you control for?

Is There Common Ground?

There is much debate about the impacts of violent video games on an adolescent's development. Some researchers argue video game playing leads to a negative impact while others believe that video games can benefit children. The research shows mixed results and oftentimes researchers point out that methodological error is one of the main factors in the mixed results. The YES and NO selections are excellent examples of this. Although Carey argues there is a relationship between aggression and violent video games, he fully acknowledges the limitations within the research. He also points out more recent research that examines socialization and habits as possible variables within this relationship and as such suggests this is an area for future research. Ferguson and Olson found no significant relationship between the variables within their study, but do acknowledge that future research needs to examine levels of exposure in the home and if there is any relationship between personality traits, video games, and aggressive behaviors.

Additional Resources

Ferguson, C. J., Garza, A., Jerabeck, J., Ramos, R., & Galindo, M. (2013). Not worth the fuss after all? Cross-sectional and prospective data on violent video game influences on aggression, visuospatial cognition and mathematics ability in a sample of youth. *Journal of Youth and Adolescence, 42*(1), 109–122.

Gauthier, J. M., Zuromski, K. L., Gitter, S. A., Witte, T. K., Cero, I. J., Gordon, K. H., . . . Joiner, T. (2014). The interpersonal-psychological theory of suicide and exposure to video game violence. *Journal of Social and Clinical Psychology, 33*(6), 512–535.

Griffiths, M. (1999). Violent video games and aggression: A review of the literature. *Aggression and Violent Behavior, 4*(2), 202–212.

References

Ferguson, C. J., Trigani, B., Pilato, S., Miller, S., Foley, K., & Barr, H. (2016). Violent video games don't increase hostility in teens, but they do stress girls out. *Psychiatric Quarterly, 87*(1), 49–56.

Willoughby, T., Adachi, P. C., & Good, M. (2012). A longitudinal study of the association between violent video game play and aggression among adolescents. *Developmental Psychology, 48*(4), 1044–1057.

Internet References . . .

Do Violent Video Games Contribute to Youth Violence?

http://videogames.procon.org

The Effect of Video Games on Kids' Behavior and Achievement

https://www.washingtonpost.com/national/health
-science/the-effect-of-video-games-on-kids-behavior
-achievement/2015/04/06/0781f084-d96f-11e4
-8103-fa84725dbf9d_story.html

The Impact of Video Games

http://www.pamf.org/parenting-teens/general
/media-web/videogames.html

Video Games and Children: Playing with Violence

http://www.aacap.org/AACAP/Families_and_Youth
/Facts_for_Families/FFF-Guide/Children-and-Video
-Games-Playing-with-Violence-091.aspx

Video Games Are Key Elements in Friendships for Many Boys

http://www.pewinternet.org/2015/08/06/chapter-3
-video-games-are-key-elements-in-friendships-for
-many-boys/

Selected, Edited, and with Issue Framing Material by:
Scott R. Brandhorst, *Southeast Missouri State University*

ISSUE

Should Juvenile Offenders Be Tried and Convicted as Adults?

YES: Charles D. Stimson and Andrew M. Grossman, from "Adult Time for Adult Crime. Life Without Parole for Juvenile Killers and Violent Teens," *The Heritage Foundation* (2009)*

NO: Laurence Steinberg, from "Adolescent Development and Juvenile Justice," *Annual Review of Clinical Psychology* (2009)

Learning Outcomes

After reading this issue, you will be able to:

- Outline the history of the juvenile justice system in Canada and the United States.
- Describe the current juvenile justice system in Canada and the United States.
- Explain why adolescents do not "think" and "behave" in the same way as mature adults.
- Justify why adolescents may not be as culpable as adults.
- Explain why some crimes committed by adolescents may warrant a "get tough" approach.

ISSUE SUMMARY

YES: Charles D. Stimson, senior legal fellow and Andrew M. Grossman, past senior legal policy analyst, Center for Legal and Justice Studies, The Heritage Foundation, argue that for serious offenses, trying juveniles in adult court and imposing adult sentences—such as life without parole—is effective and appropriate because youth who commit adult crimes should be treated as adults.

NO: Laurence Steinberg, Distinguished University Professor, Department of Psychology at Temple University, argues that adolescents often lack the cognitive, social, and emotional maturity to make mature judgments and therefore should not be sanctioned in the same way as adults. He supports a separate juvenile justice system where adolescents should be judged, tried, and sanctioned in ways that do not adversely affect development.

Not much more than a century ago, little distinction was made between how children and adults were tried and convicted. This changed, however, when child development researchers recognized the time between childhood and adulthood as a distinct period of development. As such, child advocacy groups argued that children and adolescents should be removed from adult courts and prisons. This led to the first juvenile court in the United States in 1899 and the Juvenile Delinquent's Act of 1908 in Canada. These changes to the justice system were based on arguments of providing care and custody to vulnerable children with a focus on rehabilitation and reintegration.

For over 50 years, both systems ran smoothly. It was not until the 1960s when the recognition and protection of children's legal rights were questioned. Child welfare groups argued that juveniles within the system were not being rehabilitated and were being given long cruel sentences. By the 1970s, following several class-action lawsuits alleging cruel and unusual punishment, governments reexamined the way youth were tried, convicted, and rehabilitated, resulting in the United States's 1974 Juvenile Justice and Delinquency Prevention Act (JJDPA) and Canada's 1984 Young Offenders Act (YOA). Both acts, focusing on children's rights, rehabilitation and reintegration, mandated that juveniles be protected and cared for and not be placed in adult jails. The

JJDPA is still in effect in the United States, while the YOA was replaced in 2003 with the Youth Criminal Justice Act (YCJA). The change in Canada was made to address the escalating incarceration rates that had been higher than other western countries. Custody in Canada now is reserved for violent offenders and serious repeat offenders.

Although the JJDPA and YCJA addressed the rehabilitation of youth, problems continue to exist. As youth violence and crime rates rose through the 1980s and 1990s, there was public demand for a "get tougher" approach to juvenile crime. Public perception was that the JJDPA and YCJA protected youth too much, resulting in higher crime rates and compromised social order. In the United States this "get tougher" approach resulted in government taking action and the majority of states having laws making it easier to try young juveniles in adult criminal court. For example, the youngest in American history was Michigan's Nathaniel Abraham. He was 11 years old when, in 1999, he was charged and prosecuted as an adult for murder (Tuell, 2002). Interestingly, youth crime rates have dropped since the mid-1990s.

If adolescents can be tried and convicted as adults, can they also be executed like adults? In the United States, the answer is yes. Every nation in the world prohibits the execution of juvenile offenders, except for the United States where only 13 U.S. jurisdictions prohibit the execution of juveniles (Tuell, 2002). Between 1973 and 2003, 2.6 percent (22 of 859) of the total executions in the United States were juvenile offenders. How are these decisions made? Who essentially decides which juveniles to transfer to adult court, and what factors do they consider in the decision? In the United States and in Canada, judicial waiver (i.e., one method of transfer to adult court) is initiated by the prosecutor, decided by the judge, and usually based on age, criminal history, seriousness of offense, likelihood to rehabilitate, and threat to the public. Is this the right way to deal with young offenders? Should adolescents who commit serious offenses be tried and convicted as adults? Should the decision be based on public opinion, threat to society, seriousness of the crime, or age and maturity of the defendant? How do we balance the individuals' rights against those of society? These questions will be addressed in the selections that follow.

Charles D. Stimson and Andrew M. Grossman argue that adult sentences for juveniles who commit serious offenses do not violate U.S. law or the Constitution, negating the argument that adult sentences are inhuman, cruel, or a violation of human rights. Reference is also made to the *Roper* case, which prohibits the death penalty in relation to juveniles, and Stimson and Grossman base their arguments on the continued existence of *Roper's* reliance on life without parole. They argue that while most juvenile offenders should not and do not receive adult sentences in an adult criminal justice system, some juvenile crimes evince enough cruelty, wantonness, and disregard of human life that these juveniles have characteristics that put them beyond the discipline abilities of a juvenile court.

Laurence Steinberg, on the other hand, argues that cognitive development is still in process through adolescence and into adulthood, and that the social and emotional capacities of adolescents will continue to develop beyond late adolescence. As a result, adolescents are more impulsive, more susceptible to peer pressure, and less cognizant of potential future consequences. Adolescents are not as able as fully developed adults and thus should be less blameworthy. Steinberg also argues that adult sentencing of juveniles may have a significant negative effect on their future development, putting them at higher risk of repeat offenses and increasing antisocial behavior.

*(Note: these selections have been heavily edited due to space restrictions. We recommend the readers access and read the full documents to gain a better understanding of this debate.)

YES

**Charles D. Stimson and
Andrew M. Grossman**

Adult Time for Adult Crime. Life Without Parole for Juvenile Killers and Violent Teens

Introduction

The United States leads the Western world in juvenile crime and has done so for decades. Juveniles commit murder, rape, robbery, aggravated assault, and other serious crimes—particularly violent crimes—in numbers that dwarf those of America's international peers.

The plain statistics are shocking. Between 1980 and 2005, 43,621 juveniles were arrested for murder in the United States. The picture is just as bleak with respect to arrests for rape (109,563), robbery (818,278), and aggravated assault (1,240,199).

In response to this flood of juvenile offenders,[1] state legislatures have enacted commonsense measures to protect their citizens and hold these dangerous criminals accountable. The states spend billions of dollars each year on their juvenile justice systems, which handle the vast majority of juvenile offenders. Most states have also enacted laws that allow particularly violent and mature juveniles to be tried as adults. And for the very worst juvenile offenders, 43 state legislatures and the federal government have set the maximum punishment at life without the possibility of parole.[2]

This represents an overwhelming national consensus that life without parole (LWOP) is, for certain types of juvenile offenders, an effective, appropriate, and lawful punishment. Moreover, no state court that has addressed the constitutionality of sentencing juvenile offenders to life without parole has struck the sentence down as unconstitutional. Federal courts have consistently reached the same conclusion.[3]

Nonetheless, the right of the people, acting through their representatives, to impose this punishment is under attack. . . .

A Small but Coordinated Movement

Opponents of tough sentences for serious juvenile offenders have been working for years to abolish the sentence of life without the possibility of parole. . . . Emboldened by the Supreme Court's decision in *Roper*, which relied on the "cruel and unusual punishments" language of the Eighth Amendment to the Constitution to prohibit capital sentences for juveniles, they have set about to extend the result of *Roper* to life without parole.

These groups wrap their reports and other products in the language of *Roper* and employ sympathetic terms like "child" and "children" and *Roper*-like language such as "death sentence" instead of the actual sentence of life without parole. Their reports are adorned with pictures of children, most of whom appear to be five to eight years old, despite the fact that the youngest person serving life without parole in the United States is 14 years old and most are 17 or 18 years old.

A careful reading of these groups' reports, articles, and press releases reveals that their messages and themes have been tightly coordinated. There is a very unsubtle similarity in terminology among organizations in characterizing the sentence of life without parole for juvenile offenders. For example, they consistently decline to label teenage offenders "juveniles" despite the fact that the term is used by the states, lawyers, prosecutors, state statutes, judges, parole officers, and everyone else in the juvenile justice system. Instead, they use "child."

There is nothing wrong, of course, with advocacy groups coordinating their language and message. The problem is that this important public policy debate has been shaped by a carefully crafted campaign of misinformation.

The issue of juvenile offenders and the proper sentence they are due is much too important to be driven by manufactured statistics, a misreading of a Supreme Court case, and fallacious assertions that the United States is in violation of international law. Instead, the debate should be based on real facts and statistics, a proper reading of precedent, an intelligent understanding of federal and state sovereignty, and a proper understanding of our actual international obligations.

The Public Is Disserved by a One-Sided Debate

Regrettably, that has not been the case, as opponents of life without parole for juvenile offenders have monopolized the debate. As a result, legislatures, courts, the media, and the public have been misled on crucial points.

One prominent example is a frequently cited statistic on the number of juvenile offenders currently serving life-without-parole sentences. Nearly all reports published on the subject and dozens of newscasts and articles based on those reports state that there are at least 2,225 juveniles sentenced to life without parole. That number first appeared in a 2005 report by Amnesty International and Human Rights Watch, *The Rest of Their Lives: Life Without Parole for Child Offenders in the United States.*[4]

But a careful look at the data and consultation with primary sources—that is, state criminal-justice officials—reveals that this statistic is seriously flawed. [O]fficials in some states reject as incorrect the figures assigned to their states. Others admit that they have no way of knowing how many juvenile offenders in their states have been sentenced to life without parole—and that, by extension, neither could activist groups.

Nonetheless, this statistic has gone unchallenged even as it has been cited in appellate briefs[5] and oral arguments[6] before state supreme courts and even in a petition to the United States Supreme Court. All of these courts have been asked to make public policy based on factual representations that even cursory research would demonstrate are questionable.

Another example is the unrealistic portrait of the juvenile offenders who are sentenced to life without parole that activist groups have painted. Nearly every report contains sympathetic summaries of juvenile offenders' cases that gloss over the real facts of the crimes, deploying lawyerly language and euphemism to disguise brutality and violence.

For example, consider the case of Ashley Jones [(see case study 6 after the end notes)]. The Equal Justice Initiative's 2007 report describes Ms. Jones's offense as follows: "At 14, Ashley tried to escape the violence and abuse by running away with an older boyfriend who shot and killed her grandfather and aunt. Her grandmother and sister, who were injured during the offense, want Ashley to come home."[7]

The judge's account of the facts, however, presents a somewhat different picture. An excerpt:

When Ashley realized her aunt was still breathing, she hit her in the head with a heater, stabbed her in the chest and attempted to set her room on fire. . . .

As ten-year old Mary Jones [Ashley's sister] attempted to run, Ashley grabbed her and began hitting her. [Ashley's boyfriend] put the gun in young Mary's face and told her that that was how she would die. Ashley intervened and said, "No, let me do it," and proceeded to stab her little sister fourteen times.[8]

In a similar vein, many of the studies feature pictures of children who are far younger than any person actually serving life

without parole in the United States.[9] When these reports do include an actual picture of a juvenile offender, the picture is often one taken years before the crime was committed.[10] The public could be forgiven for believing incorrectly that children under 14 are regularly sentenced to life behind bars without the possibility of release.

A final example is the legality of life-without-parole sentences for juvenile offenders. Opponents make the claim, among many others, that these sentences violate the United States' obligations under international law. Yet they usually fail to mention that no court has endorsed this view, and rarely do they explain the implications of the fact that the United States has not ratified the treaty that they most often cite, the Convention on the Rights of the Child, and has carved out legal exceptions (called "reservations") to others.

Further, they often abuse judicial precedent by improperly extending the death penalty–specific logic and language of *Roper* into the non–death penalty arena,[11] an approach that the Supreme Court has repeatedly rejected.[12] Again, the public could be forgiven for believing incorrectly that the Supreme Court, particularly in *Roper*, has all but declared the imposition of life sentences without parole for juvenile offenders to be unconstitutional. A more honest reading of the precedent, however, compels the opposite conclusion: that the sentence is not constitutionally suspect.

The Whole Story

Public policy should be based on facts, not false statistics and misleading legal claims. For that reason, we undertook the research to identify those states that have authorized life without parole for juvenile offenders and wrote to every major district attorney's office across those 43 states. To understand how prosecutors are using life-without-parole sentences and the types of crimes and criminals for which such sentences are imposed, we asked each office for case digests of juvenile offenders who were prosecuted by their offices and received the specific sentence of life without parole.

The response from prosecutors around the country was overwhelming. Prosecutors from across the United States sent us case digests, including official court documents, police reports, judges' findings, photos of the defendants and victims, motions, newspaper articles, and more. From that collection of case digests, we selected typical cases, all concerning juvenile offenders, and assembled a complete record for each. In sharp contrast to the practices of other reports, these case studies recount all of the relevant facts of the crimes, as found by a jury or judge and recorded in official records, in neutral language. . . .

Based on this research, we conclude that the sentence of life without parole for juvenile offenders is reasonable, constitutional, and (appropriately) rare. Our survey of the cases shows that some juveniles commit horrific crimes with full knowledge of their actions and intent to bring about the results. In constitutional terms, the Supreme Court's own jurisprudence, including *Roper*, draws a clear line between the sentence of death and all others, including life without parole; further, to reach its result, *Roper* actually depends on the availability of life without parole for juvenile offenders. We also find that while most states allow life-without-parole sentences for juvenile offenders, judges generally have broad discretion in sentencing, and most juvenile offenders do not receive that sentence.

We conclude, then, that reports by activist groups on life without parole for juvenile offenders are at best misleading and in some instances simply wrong in their facts, analyses, conclusions, and recommendations. Regrettably, the claims made by these groups have been repeated so frequently that lawmakers, judges, the media, and the public risk losing sight of their significant bias.

To foster informed debate, more facts—particularly, good state-level statistics—are needed about the use of life-without-parole sentences for juvenile offenders. But even on the basis of current data, as insufficient as they are, legislators should take note of how these sentences are actually applied and reject any attempts to repeal life-without-parole sentences for juvenile offenders.

The U.S. Has a Juvenile Crime Problem

Underlying nearly every argument made by opponents of life without parole for juvenile offenders is the premise that, because many other countries have not authorized or have repealed the sentence, the United States should do the same so that it can be in conformance with the international "consensus" on the matter.

In fact, this premise is the cornerstone of the litigation strategy to extend the Eighth Amendment's prohibition on "cruel and unusual punishments" to reach life-without-parole sentences for juveniles. This application of foreign sources of law to determine domestic law, in addition to being legally problematic, too often overlooks the qualitative differences between the United States and other countries.

This has certainly been the case in the debate over life without parole for juvenile offenders. The leading reports on the issue do not grapple seriously with the facts concerning juvenile crime and how those facts differ between nations. Instead, they play a crude counting game, tallying up nations while ignoring the realities of their circumstances and juvenile justice systems.

The Facts on Worldwide Crime and Sentencing

The fact is that the United States faces higher rates of crimes, particularly violent crimes and homicides, than nearly any other country. Adults and juveniles commit crimes in huge numbers, from misdemeanor thefts to premeditated murders. The root causes of this epidemic have been debated, studied, tested, and analyzed for decades, but the fact of its existence is neither controversial nor in doubt.

After a decade of gains in deterring juvenile crime, the trend has turned the other way in recent years. According to the U.S. Department of Justice, there was "substantial growth in juvenile violent crime arrests. . . . in the late 1980s [which] peaked in

1994."[13] Between 1994 and 2004, the arrest rate for juveniles for violent crimes fell 49 percent, only to see a 2 percent uptick in 2005 and then a 4 percent gain in 2006.[14] In 2005 and 2006, arrests of juveniles for murder and robbery also increased.[15]

Despite the progress made through 2004, juvenile violent crime remains much higher in the United States than in other Western nations. Some statistics:

- In 1998 alone, 24,537,600 recorded crimes were committed in the United States.[16]
- Of the 72 countries that reported recorded crimes to the United Nations Seventh Survey of Crime Trends, the United States ranked first in total recorded crimes.[17]
- Worse still, the United States reported more crimes than the next six countries (Germany, England/Wales, rance, South Africa, Russia, and Canada) combined. Their total was 23,111,318.[18] . . .

In terms of violent crime rates, the U.S. ranks highly in every category, and the same is true in the realm of juvenile crime. For example:

- In 1998, teenagers in the United States were suspects in 1,609,303 crimes, and 1,000,279 juveniles were prosecuted.[19]
- That is as many juvenile prosecutions as the next seven highest countries combined.[20] Those countries are England/Wales, Thailand, Germany, China, Canada, Turkey, and South Korea.[21]
- According to 2002 World Health Organization statistics, the United States ranks third in murders committed by youths[22] and 14th in murders per capita committed by youths.[23] . . .

Given this domestic crime problem, it should come as no great surprise that the United States tops the lists of total prisoners and prisoners per capita.[24] . . .

These crucial statistics are not mentioned by those who urge abolition of life-without-parole sentences for juvenile offenders. The reason may be that it undercuts their arguments: If the juvenile crime problem in the United States is not comparable to the juvenile crime problems of other Western nations, then combating it may justifiably require different, and stronger, techniques. The fact that some other nations no longer sentence juvenile offenders to life without parole loses a significant degree of its relevance. In addition, the data on sentence length demonstrate that the use of life-without-parole sentences is not a function of excessive sentence lengths in the United States, but rather an anomaly in a criminal justice system that generally imposes shorter sentences than those of other developed nations.

Life Without Parole for Juvenile Offenders Is Constitutional

In 2005, the Supreme Court held in *Roper v. Simmons* that the Eighth and Fourteenth Amendments to the U.S. Constitution bar the application of the death penalty to offenders who were under the age of 18 when their crimes were committed.[25] Since then, the decision's reasoning has become the cornerstone of the efforts of those who oppose life without parole for juvenile offenders and has reinvigorated their legal crusade to put an end to the practice.

The text and history of the Eighth Amendment, however, provide little support for the idea that life without parole for juvenile offenders constitutes prohibited "cruel and unusual" punishment. Even departing from the text and employing a *Roper*-style analysis is unavailing; the factors that the Court considered in that case all mitigate in favor of life without parole's constitutionality, even as applied to juvenile offenders. [For information regarding the Eighth Amendment, please go to the original full document. . . .]

The U.S. Has No International Obligation to Ban Juvenile Life Without Parole

Many opponents of life without parole for juvenile offenders claim that the continued use of this sentence puts the United States in breach of its obligations under international law.[26] Specifically, they name three treaties as barring the administration of this sentence in the United States: the Convention on the Rights of the Child, the International Covenant on Civil and Political Rights, and the Convention Against Torture.

All of these assertions are false. . . .

A careful analysis of the treaties and, crucially, the United States' obligations under them refutes the claim that international law precludes U.S. states from sentencing juvenile offenders to life without parole.

The Constitution Is America's Fundamental Law

The Constitution is America's fundamental law, and it controls how treaties interact with its provisions and other domestic laws.[27] . . .

For the United States to become a party to a treaty, the President first must sign the treaty and send it to the Senate, at least two-thirds of which must give its advice and consent before the treaty can be ratified.[28] After the Senate has voted to give its consent to ratification, the President may then ratify it, if he so chooses, by signing the instrument of ratification.[29] Treaties that have not been approved in this way are generally not binding on the United States.[30] Even in the extremely rare circumstance that treaties or parts of treaties become a part of "customary" international law and thereby binding upon the United States even though unratified, they still cannot by themselves override domestic statutes.[31]

Many treaties, even if ratified, do not themselves preempt existing domestic laws, but must await subsequent legislation to implement their terms.[32] Only "self-executing" treaties—those that do not require implementing legislation—become the type of federal law that can preempt conflicting state and federal laws.[33]

Few modern treaties, however, are self-executing, and often a treaty will provide on its face that it is not self-executing. Whether express or implied, courts will not enforce treaties that are not self-executing until an act of Congress specifies how the rights or privileges are to be enforced. Thus, treaties that are not self-executing and that have not been implemented by Congress (which may include specifying available causes of action, remedies, court jurisdiction, etc.) do not themselves establish domestically binding legal remedies.

Further, the United States often does not agree to be bound by every term of an international convention, and it cannot do so if some terms conflict with the U.S. Constitution. As a matter of national sovereignty, the United States may adopt whatever portion of international conventions it deems appropriates. . . . When nations sign or ratify a treaty, they often enter "reservations" and "understandings" that govern the treaty's domestic and international implementation. . . .

Once a treaty has been properly executed and implementing legislation has been enacted, there is the question of how it interacts with other laws. In general, a federal statute and a properly executed treaty have equal status in law, with the latter in time taking precedence. This is true, though, only to the extent that a conflict actually exists between the two; to the extent possible, courts interpret statutes so as to avoid violation of international obligations.[34] Therefore, if Congress passes a law that clearly contradicts earlier treaty obligations, courts will enforce the law over the treaty.[35] The obligations of properly executed and implemented treaties, being a part of federal law, can be enforced against the states under the Supremacy Clause, but only if they do not violate the U.S. Constitution, including fundamental protections of state sovereignty. . . .

The result of these requirements is that those who would wield vague language in international treaties against state laws have a number of hurdles to clear before a court even considers the substance of their claims, and failure to clear even one of these hurdles will defeat the claim.

Conclusion: A Lawful and Appropriate Punishment

The United States has a juvenile crime problem that far exceeds the juvenile crime problems of other Western countries. Over the years, state legislatures have responded to this increase in the volume and severity of juvenile crime by providing for sentences that effectively punish offenders, incapacitate them, and deter serious offenses. They have determined by an overwhelming majority that fulfilling their duty to protect their citizens requires making available life-without-parole sentences for juvenile offenders.

The sentence stands up to constitutional scrutiny. All state supreme courts and federal courts that have considered the question have concluded that life without parole for juvenile offenders does not violate the Eighth Amendment's prohibition on cruel and unusual punishment. The Supreme Court's proportionality standard—the highest level of scrutiny it has applied to non-capital punishment—does not prohibit states from punishing murder and other serious offenses with lengthy prison terms; the Court has said that judges should second-guess state legislatures' determinations of criminal punishment only in the rarest cases where the punishment is wholly disproportionate to the harm of the offense.

Most juvenile offenders should not and do not have their cases adjudicated in the adult criminal justice system. Every state has a juvenile justice system, and those courts handle the majority of crimes committed by juveniles. But some crimes evince characteristics that push them beyond the leniency otherwise afforded to juveniles: cruelty, wantonness, a complete disregard for the lives of others. Some of these offenders are tried as adults, and a small proportion of those tried as adults are sentenced to life without parole—the strongest sentence available to express society's disapproval—to incapacitate the criminal and deter the most serious offenses. . . .

A fair look at the Constitution, whether from the perspective of original meaning or from the perspective of current interpretation, provides no basis for overruling the democratic processes of 43 states, the District of Columbia, and the U.S. Congress. Neither do international law, even under broad and sweeping interpretations of its terms, or the misleading and sometimes just wrong statistics and stories marshaled in activists' studies.

Used sparingly, as it is, life without parole is an effective and lawful sentence for the worst juvenile offenders. On the merits, it has a place in our laws.

Notes

1. Following the academic literature, this report uses the term "juvenile offender." *See, e.g.,* Joseph Sanborn, *Juveniles' Competency to Stand Trial: Wading Through the Rhetoric and the Evidence,* 99 J. Crim. L. & Criminology 135, 149 (2009). The term "juvenile killer" would be equally appropriate, because almost all juveniles sentenced to life without parole have committed homicides.

2. *See infra* app. III.

3. *See, e.g.,* United States v. Pete, 277 Fed. Appx. 730, 734 (9th Cir. 2008); United States v. Feemster, 483 F.3d 583, 588 (8th Cir. 2007), *vacated on other grounds,* 128 S. Ct. 880 (2008); United States v. Salahuddin, 509 F.3d 858 (7th Cir. 2007); Calderon v. Schribner, No. 2:06-CV-00770-TMB, 2009 WL 89279, *4–6 (E.D. Cal. Jan. 12, 2009); Price v. Cain, No. 07-937, 2008 U.S. Dist. LEXIS 23474, *17–23 (W.D. La. March 4, 2008); Pineda v. Leblanc, No. 07-3598, 2008 WL 294685, *3 (E.D. La. Jan. 31, 2008); Douma v. Workman, No. 06-CV-0462-CVE-FHM, 2007 WL 2331883, *3 (N.D. Okla. Aug 13, 2007).

4. AI/HRW Report, *supra* note, at 1, 25, 35, 52, 124.

5. *See* Appellant's Opening Brief at 8, Torres v. Delaware, No. 504 (Del. Supr. filed Nov. 14, 2008). Brian Stevenson, Executive Director of the Equal Justice Initiative, represented the appellant. *Id.* at cover. The appellant's brief cites the Equal Justice Initiative's report on juvenile life-without-parole sentences. *Id.* at 8 ("While at least 2,225 people in the United States are serving sentences of life without parole for crimes they committed under the age of 18, extensive research found that only 73 people in the United States are serving such sentences for crimes committed when they were fourteen or younger.").

6. Oral Argument, Torres v. Delaware, No. 504 (Del. Supr. held Feb. 4, 2009), *available at* http://courts.delaware.gov/Courts/Supreme%20Court/oral%20arguments/2009-02-04,_504,_2008_Torres_v_State.MP3. In this argument, counsel for Donald Torres cited misleading statistics regarding the number of states that had mandatory sentences of life without parole for juveniles and that had discretionary sentences for first-degree murderers. Deputy Attorney General Paul Wallace, who argued on behalf of the State of Delaware, took issue with the numbers asserted by Torres's counsel and provided the court with accurate statistics. He stated that 49 states permit a 14-year-old to be prosecuted as an adult for first-degree murder, 44 states permit juveniles to receive a life-without-parole sentence for first-degree murder, and only 29 states mandate a life-without-parole sentence for a juvenile who is tried as an adult and convicted of first-degree murder.

7. EJI Report, *supra* note 9, at 25.

8. Finding of Fact from Guilt Phase of Trial, Alabama v. Jones, No. CC-2000-0151 (Cir. Ct. Jefferson Cty. Ala. May 25, 2001).

9. For an example, see the cover of the University of San Francisco School of Law's report, which depicts a boy no older than eight years old. USF REPORT, *supra* note 9. *See also* EJI REPORT, *supra* note 9 (this report's unnumbered opening pages contain pictures of juveniles who appear to be from eight to 12 years old).

10. *See* AI/HRW REPORT, *supra* note 9, at 4, 19, 29, 43, 59, 68.

11. *See* AI/HRW REPORT, supra note 9, at 86, 115; EJI REPORT, *supra* note 9, at 11; USF REPORT, *supra* note 9, at 16.

12. Jeffrey Abramson, *Death-Is-Different Jurisprudence and the Role of the Capital Jury,* 2 OHIO ST. J. CRIM. L. 117, 117 n.l (2004); *Roper*, 543 U.S. at 568 ("Because the death penalty is the most severe punishment, the Eighth Amendment applies to it with special force.").

13. Howard Snyder, *Juvenile Arrests 2006*, JUVENILE JUSTICE BULLETIN, Nov. 2008, at 1, *available at* http://www.ncjrs.gov/pdffilesl/ojjdp/221338.pdf [hereinafter *Juvenile Arrests*].

14. *Id.*

15. *Id.*

16. DIVISION FOR POLICY ANALYSIS AND PUBLIC AFFAIRS, UNITED NATIONS OFFICE ON DRUGS AND CRIME, SEVENTH UNITED NATIONS SURVEY OF CRIME TRENDS AND OPERATIONS OF CRIMINAL JUSTICE SYSTEMS (1998–2000) 10–12 (2004), *available at* http://www.unodc.org/pdf/crime/seventh_survey/7pv.pdf [hereinafter SEVENTH SURVEY].

17. *Id.*

18. *Id.*

19. *Id.* at 154–155. The U.N. Report does not indicate whether that statistic includes all juveniles prosecuted in both adult and juvenile courts.

20. *Id.*

21. *Id.*

22. WORLD HEALTH ORGANIZATION, WORLD REPORT ON VIOLENCE AND HEALTH 28–29 (2002), *available at* http://whqlibdoc.who.int/hq/2002/9241545615.pdf.

23. *Id.*

24. ROY WALMSLEY, INTERNATIONAL CENTRE FOR PRISON STUDIES, KING'S COLLEGE LONDON, WORLD PRISON POPULATION LIST, EIGHTH EDITION (2009), *available at* http://www.kcl.ac.uk/depsta/law/research/icps/downloads/wppl-8th_41.pdf.

25. *Roper,* 543 U.S. at 551.

26. AI/HRW REPORT, *supra* note 9, at 94–109; USF REPORT, *supra* note 9, at 14–18; EJI REPORT, *supra* note 9, at 13.

27. Edwin Meese III, *The Meaning of the Constitution, in* THE HERITAGE GUIDE TO THE CONSTITUTION 5 (Edwin Meese III ed. 2005).

28. RESTATEMENT (THIRD) OF FOREIGN RELATIONS LAW OF THE UNITED STATES §§ 303(1), 303 cmt. a (1987).

29. *Id.* at § 305 cmt. d.

30. In some rare cases, treaties may become customary international law, though this is unlikely to bind those who are subject to U.S. law without the consent of the President and the Senate. *See infra* note 188. In other cases, Congress (that is, both the Senate and the House of Representatives) may authorize the President to enter into an international agreement. This arrangement, sometimes controversial, has not been used to accede to the kind of multilateral agreements discussed in this paper. *See generally* RESTATEMENT (THIRD) OF FOREIGN RELATIONS LAW OF THE UNITED STATES § 303 cmt. e (1987).

31. Even a concession by an American official that the U.S. is out of compliance with international practice cannot change binding domestic law. It certainly would not empower a court to do anything about the supposed non-compliance with international norms. *See infra* note 188.

32. Medellin v. Texas, 128 S.Ct. 1346, 1356–57 (2008).

33. Foster v. Nelson, 27 U.S. 253, 314–15 (1829) (explaining that, had the treaty at issue "acted directly on the subject" (i.e., been self-executing), it "would have repealed those acts of Congress which were repugnant to it"); Dennis Arrow, *Treaties,* in THE HERITAGE GUIDE TO THE CONSTITUTION 245 (Edwin Meese III ed., 2005).

34. RESTATEMENT (THIRD) OF FOREIGN RELATIONS LAW OF THE UNITED STATES § 114 (1987); Murray v. Schooner Charming Betsy, 6 U.S. 64, 118 (1804) (explaining that "an act of Congress ought never to be construed to violate the law of nations if any other possible construction remains").

35. RESTATEMENT (THIRD) OF FOREIGN RELATIONS LAW OF THE UNITED STATES § 114 (1987) (statutes should be construed so as not to conflict with international obligations only "where fairly possible" to do so) (quoting Ashwander v. Tennessee Valley Authority, 297 U.S. 288, 348 (1936)).

CASE STUDY 6

Defendant: Ashley Jones

Victims: Deroy Nalls (grandfather; murdered)

Millie Nalls (aunt; murdered)

Mary Elizabeth Nalls (grandmother; attempted murder)

Mary Elizabeth Jones (sister; attempted murder)

Crimes: Two counts, first degree capital murder

Two counts, attempted first degree murder

First degree robbery

Age: 14

Where: Birmingham, Alabama

Crime date: August 30, 1999

Summary

In a span of minutes, Ashley Jones and her boyfriend shot her grandfather twice in the face and then stabbed him until he died; shot her sleeping aunt three times; shot her grandmother in the shoulder and then stabbed her, poured lighter fluid on her, set her on fire, and watched her burn; and stabbed her 10-year old sister 14 times. Jones then took $300 from her grandfather's wallet and the keys to his Cadillac, which she drove away from the crime scene.

Facts

After Ashley Jones stabbed her father and pregnant mother in 1998, killing neither, she and her younger sister were sent to live with her grandparents and maternal aunt. Deroy Nalls, her 78-year-old grandfather, was a retired steelworker and deacon at his church. His wife, Mary Nalls, 73, was a homemaker.

By late August of 1999, the Nallses were growing tired of Jones's bad behavior and grounded her for staying out all night at a party. The Nallses did not approve of Jones's boyfriend, Geramie Hart, and told him not to visit their house. This angered Jones.

NO PHOTOS FOR THIS CASE STUDY AVAILABLE

Jones and Hart decided to kill everyone in the house, set it on fire, and take their money. To prepare, Jones stole two of her grandfather's guns and smuggled them out of the house to Hart. She mixed together rubbing alcohol, nail polish remover, and charcoal fire starter in anticipation of setting the house ablaze.

It took the couple two days to put their plan into action. On the evening of August 30,1999, Jones kept an eye on her relatives until they had settled in for the evening. Then she called Hart. He arrived around 11:15 p.m., and Jones led him into the house. He was carrying the .38 revolver taken from Jones's grandfather.

Jones and Hart sneaked into the den, where her grandfather was watching television. Hart shot him twice in the face; still alive, Deroy stumbled toward the kitchen. Next, they visited the bedroom of Millie Nalls, 30, Ashley's aunt, and shot her three times. Seeing that her aunt was still breathing, Jones hit her in the head with a portable heater, stabbed her in the chest, and attempted to set the room on fire.

The gunshots awakened Jones's grandmother, and she got out of bed. That was when Jones and Hart entered her bedroom and shot her once in the shoulder. It was their last bullet.

Jones and Hart returned to the den to discover that her grandfather was still alive. With knives from the kitchen, they stabbed him over and over again and left one knife embedded in his back. Jones poured charcoal lighter fluid on her grandfather, set him ablaze, and listened to him groan as he burned alive.

The noise attracted Jones's 10-year-old sister, Mary Elizabeth Jones, to the kitchen. From there, she could see her grandfather on the den floor, ablaze. Soon after, the wounded Mary Nalls entered the kitchen and called out to her dying husband. Jones stabbed her grandmother in the face with an ice pick. Jones then poured lighter fluid on her, set her on fire, and watched her burn.

Mary Elizabeth attempted to leave, but Jones grabbed her and began punching. Hart shoved the pistol in Mary's face and said that he was going to shoot her. Jones intervened: "'No, let me do it." She stabbed her sister 14 times and stopped only after Mary curled up in a ball on the floor and pretended to be dead. Jones and Hart piled sheets, towels, and paper on the floor and set the pile on fire.

Jones and Hart removed about $300 from her grandparents' mattress and took the keys to their Cadillac, which they drove to a local hotel. Jones spent the night partying at the hotel, with her grandfather's blood on her socks and grandmother's blood on her shirt.

Miraculously, Mary Elizabeth and her grandmother Mary had survived. Mary Elizabeth helped her grandmother out of the house and walked to a neighbor's home for help. They called the police, who quickly responded to the scene. Police officers found Deroy Nalls dead on the living room floor, Millie Nalls dead in her bed, and Mary Nalls heavily wounded. Firefighters were able to extinguish the fire lit by Jones and Hart.

Continued

The following morning, news outlets reported the murders, as well as the fact that Jones's sister had survived. The news angered her. "I thought I killed that bitch," she later explained.

Mary Elizabeth received stitches for her numerous stab wounds and was hospitalized with a collapsed lung. Mary was treated for gunshot and stab wounds and the burns that covered a third of her body. She spent a month in the burn unit of a local hospital, undergoing multiple skin grafts, before undergoing treatment at a rehabilitation facility to relearn how to use her arms after the burns.

Hart and Jones were arrested the next morning after police identified the Nallses' vehicle in the parking lot.

Speaking to police, Jones admitted that "we both" stabbed her grandfather. She explained further: "I mean we shot Millie second . . . me and Geramie just started shooting her. And then . . . and then I went back in there and she was still breathing, so . . . I hit her on the head with the heater and stabbed her in her heart. And she just started coughing up blood."

According to the prosecutor, Laura Poston, Ashley Jones displayed no emotion throughout the trial:

> Sociopaths can however be in the form of a 14, now 15 year old petite girl with a pretty face who can sit all week in a courtroom, look at pictures of her dead grandfather and aunt, listen to her sister cry as she recounts the horrors of that night, and not shed a tear. The first time Ashley showed any emotion about what happened that night was when the jury read the verdicts finding her guilty of two counts

of capital murder and two counts of attempted murder—she cried her first tears.

Judge Gloria Bahakel noted in her sentencing decision that Jones "did not express genuine remorse of her actions." The judge continued: "Although she apologized, at the prompting of the Court, her words were hollow and insincere. Furthermore, it was brought to the attention of the Court that while awaiting her sentencing, the defendant had threatened older female inmates in the Jefferson County Jail by telling them she would do the same thing to them that she had done to her family."

Sources

Letter from Laura Poston, Deputy District Attorney, Birmingham, AL, to Charles Stimson (Aug. 15, 2008) (on file with author); Letter from Laura Poston, Deputy District Attorney, Birmingham, AL, to Charles Stimson (Mar. 30, 2009) (on file with author); Carol Robinson, *Two Teens Accused of Bloody Rampage,* Birmingham News, Aug. 31,1999, at 1A; Steve Joynt, *Arrest of Teenager Revives Question of What Can Turn People into Killers,* Birmingham Post-Herald, Sept. 18, 1999, at E1; Carol Robinson, *Young Victim of Massacre Received 13 Stab Wounds,* Birmingham News, Sept. 1, 1999, at 1C; Carol Robinson, *Girl Accused in Family Attack Still in Detention,* Birmingham News, Sept. 2, 1999, at 4B; Carol Robinson, *Teen Guilty of Stabbing Family,* Birmingham News, Mar. 3, 2001, at 1A; Alabama v. Jones, No. CC-2000-0151 (Cir. Ct. of Jefferson County, AL. May 25) (finding of fact from guilt phase of trial)

Laurence Steinberg

 **NO**

Adolescent Development and Juvenile Justice

Juvenile Justice Issues Informed by Developmental Science

Criminal Culpability of Youth

The adult justice system presumes that defendants who are found guilty are responsible for their own actions, should be held accountable, and should be punished accordingly. Because of the relative immaturity of minors, however, it may not be justified to hold them as accountable as one might hold adults. If, for example, adolescents below a certain age cannot grasp the long-term consequences of their actions or cannot control their impulses, one cannot hold them fully accountable for their actions. In other words, we cannot claim that adolescents "ought to know better" if, in fact, the evidence indicates that they do not know better, or more accurately, cannot know better, because they lack the abilities needed to exercise mature judgment. It is important to note that culpability cannot really be researched directly. Because an individual's culpability is something that is judged by someone else, it is largely in the eye of the beholder. What can be studied, however, are the capabilities and characteristics of individuals that make them potentially blameworthy, such as their ability to behave intentionally or to know right from wrong.

I use the term "culpability" in this review as a shorthand for several interrelated phenomena, including responsibility, accountability, blame-worthiness, and punishability. These notions are relevant to the adjudication of an individual's guilt or innocence, because an individual who is not responsible for his or her actions by definition cannot be guilty, and to the determination of a disposition (in juvenile court) or sentence (in criminal court), in that individuals who are found guilty but less than completely blameworthy, owing to any number of mitigating circumstances, merit proportionately less punishment than do guilty individuals who are fully blameworthy.

The starting point in a discussion of criminal culpability is a principle known as penal proportionality. Simply put, penal proportionality holds that criminal punishment should be determined by two criteria: the harm a person causes and his blameworthiness in causing that harm. The law recognizes that different wrongful acts cause different levels of harm through a complex system of offense grading under which more serious crimes (rape, for example) are punished presumptively more severely than less serious crimes (shoplifting, for example). Beyond this, though, two people who engage in the same wrongful conduct may differ in their blameworthiness. A person may be less culpable than other criminals—or not culpable at all—because he inadvertently (rather than purposely) causes the harm, because he is subject to some endogenous deficiency or incapacity that impairs his decision making (such as mental illness), or because he acts in response to an extraordinary external pressure—a gun to the head is the classic example. Less-blameworthy offenders deserve less punishment, and some persons who cause criminal harm deserve no punishment at all (Scott & Steinberg 2008).

The concept of mitigation plays an important role in the law's calculation of blame and punishment, although it gets little attention in the debate about youth crime. Mitigation applies to persons engaging in harmful conduct who are blameworthy enough to meet the minimum threshold of criminal responsibility but who deserve less punishment than a typical offender would receive. Through mitigation, the criminal law calculates culpability and punishment along a continuum and is not limited to the options of full responsibility or complete excuse. Indeed, criminal law incorporates calibrated measures of culpability. For example, the law of homicide operates through a grading scheme under which punishment for killing another person varies dramatically depending on the actor's blameworthiness . . . Under standard homicide doctrine, mitigating circumstances and mental states are translated into lower-grade offenses that warrant less punishment.

Generally, a person who causes criminal harm is a fully responsible moral agent (and deserves full punishment) if, in choosing to engage in the wrongful conduct, he has the capacity to make a rational decision and a "fair opportunity" to choose not to engage in the harmful conduct. . . .

Under American criminal law, two very different kinds of persons can show that their criminal conduct was less culpable than that of the offender who deserves full punishment—those who are very different from ordinary persons due to impairments that contributed to their criminal choices and those who are ordinary persons whose offenses are responses to extraordinary circumstances or are otherwise aberrant conduct (Scott & Steinberg 2008).

Although it seems paradoxical, adolescents, in a real sense, belong to both groups. In the first group are individuals with endogenous traits or conditions that undermine their decision-making capacity, impairing their ability to understand the nature and consequences of their wrongful acts or to control their conduct. In modern times, this category has been reserved mostly for offenders who suffer from mental illness, mental disability, and other neurological impairments. . . .

Individuals in the second group are ordinary persons whose criminal conduct is less culpable because it is a response to extraordinary external circumstances: These cases arise when the actor faces a difficult choice, and his response of engaging in the criminal conduct is reasonable under the circumstances, as measured by the likely response of an ordinary law-abiding person in that situation. . . .

Although youths in mid-adolescence have cognitive capacities for reasoning and understanding that approximate those of adults, even at age 18 adolescents are immature in their psychosocial and emotional development, and this likely affects their decisions about involvement in crime in ways that distinguish them from adults. Teenagers are more susceptible to peer influence than are adults and tend to focus more on rewards and less on risks in making choices. They also tend to focus on short-term rather than long-term consequences and are less capable of anticipating future consequences, and they are more impulsive and volatile in their emotional responses. When we consider these developmental factors within the conventional criminal law framework for assessing blameworthiness, the unsurprising conclusion is that adolescent offenders are less culpable than are adults. The mitigating conditions generally recognized in the criminal law—diminished capacity and coercive circumstances—are relevant to criminal acts of adolescents and often characterize the actions of juvenile offenders. This does not excuse adolescents from criminal responsibility, but it renders them less blameworthy and less deserving of adult punishment.

Although in general lawmakers have paid minimal attention to the mitigating character of adolescents' diminished decision-making capacities, some legislatures and courts have recognized that immature judgment reduces culpability. . . . In *Roper v. Simmons,* the 2005 case that abolished the juvenile death penalty, the Court adopted the developmental argument for mitigation that follows from the research reviewed above. Justice Kennedy, writing for the majority, described three features of adolescence that distinguish young offenders from their adult counterparts in ways that mitigate culpability—features that are familiar to the reader at this point. The first is the diminished decision-making capacity of youths, which may contribute to a criminal choice that is "not as morally reprehensible as that of adults" because of its developmental nature. . . . Second, the Court pointed to the increased vulnerability

of youths to external coercion, including peer pressure. Finally, the Court emphasized that the unformed nature of adolescent identity made it "less supportable to conclude that even a heinous crime was evidence of irretrievably depraved character." Adolescents are less blameworthy than are adults, the Court suggested, because the traits that contribute to criminal conduct are transient, and because most adolescents will outgrow their tendency to get involved in crime as they mature. . . . Although most impulsive young risk takers mature into adults with different values, some adult criminals are impulsive, sensation-seeking risk takers who discount future consequences and focus on the here and now. Are these adolescent-like adults also less culpable than other adult offenders and deserving of reduced punishment? I think not. Unlike the typical adolescent, the predispositions, values, and preferences that motivate the adult offenders are not developmental but characterological, and they are unlikely to change merely with the passage of time. Adolescent traits that contribute to criminal conduct are normative of adolescence, but they are not typical in adulthood. In an adult, these traits are often part of the personal identity of an individual who does not respect the values of the criminal law and who deserves punishment when he or she violates its prohibitions (Scott & Steinberg 2008).

Competence of Adolescents to Stand Trial

Before discussing adolescents' competence to stand trial, it is worth underscoring the distinction between competence and culpability. . . . Competence to stand trial refers to the ability of an individual to function effectively as a defendant in a criminal or delinquency proceeding. In contrast, determinations of culpability focus on the defendant's blameworthiness in engaging in the criminal conduct and on whether and to what extent he will be held responsible. Although many of the same incapacities that excuse or mitigate criminal responsibility may also render a defendant incompetent, the two issues are analytically distinct and separate legal inquiries, and they focus on the defendant's mental state at two different points in time (the time of the crime and the time of the court proceeding).

The reason that competence is required of defendants in criminal proceedings is simple: When the state asserts its power against an individual with the goal of taking away his liberty, the accused must be capable of participating in a meaningful way in the proceeding against him. . . .

In 1960, the Supreme Court announced a legal standard for trial competence in *Dusky v. United States* that has since been adopted uniformly by American courts. . . . [T]here are two parts to the competence requirement: The defendant must be able to consult with her attorney about planning and making decisions in her defense, and she must understand the charges, the meaning, and purpose of the proceedings and the consequences of conviction (Scott & Grisso 2005). . . .

The competence requirement is functional at its core, speaking to questions about the impact of cognitive deficiencies on trial participation. Functionally it makes no difference if the defendant cannot understand the proceeding she faces or assist her attorney, whether due to mental illness or to immaturity (Scott & Grisso 2005). In either case, the fairness of the proceeding is undermined. In short, the same concerns that support the prohibition against trying criminal defendants who are incompetent due to mental impairment apply with equal force when immature youths are subject to criminal proceedings. . . .

Three broad types of abilities are implicated under the *Dusky* standard for competence to stand trial: (*a*) a factual understanding of the proceedings, (*b*) a rational understanding of the proceedings, and (*c*) the ability to assist counsel (Scott & Grisso 2005). . . .

Factual understanding focuses on the defendant's knowledge and awareness of the charges and his understanding of available pleas, possible penalties, the general steps in the adjudication process, the roles of various participants in the pretrial and trial process, and his rights as a defendant. Intellectual immaturity in juveniles may undermine factual understanding, especially given that youths generally have less experience and more limited ability to grasp concepts such as rights. . . .

The rational understanding requirement of *Dusky* has been interpreted to mean that defendants must comprehend the implications, relevance, or significance of what they understand factually regarding the trial process. . . . Intellectual, emotional, and psychosocial immaturity may undermine the ability of some adolescents to grasp accurately the meaning and significance of matters that they seem to understand factually.

Finally, the requirement that the defendant in a criminal proceeding must have the capacity to assist counsel encompasses three types of abilities. The first is the ability to receive and communicate information adequately to allow counsel to prepare a defense. This ability may be compromised by impairments in attention, memory, and concentration, deficits that might undermine the defendant's ability to respond to instructions or to provide important information to his attorney. . . . Second, the ability to assist counsel requires a rational perspective regarding the attorney and her role, free of notions or attitudes that could impair the collaborative relationship. . . . Third, defendants must have the capacity to make decisions about pleading and the waiver or assertion of other constitutional rights. These decisions involve not only adequate factual and rational understanding, but also the ability to consider alternatives. . . . Immature youths may lack capacities to process information and exercise reason adequately in making trial decisions. . . .

As juveniles' competence to stand trial began to emerge as an important issue in the mid-1990s, the need for a comprehensive study comparing the abilities of adolescents and adults in this realm became apparent. . . . In response to that need,

the MacArthur Foundation Research Network on Adolescent Development and Juvenile Justice sponsored a large-scale study of individuals between the ages of 11 and 24—half of whom were in the custody of the justice system and half of whom had never been detained—designed to examine . . . the relationship between developmental immaturity and the abilities of young defendants to participate in their trials (Grisso et al. 2003). The study also probed age differences in psychosocial influences on decision making in the criminal process.

Based on participants' responses to a structured interview . . . the researchers found that competence-related abilities improve significantly between the ages of 11 and 16 . . . There were no differences between the 16- and 17-year-olds and the young adults. . . . Nearly one-third of 11- to 13-year-olds and about one-fifth of 14- and 15-year-olds, but only 12 % of individuals 16 and older, evidenced impairment at a level comparable to mentally ill adults who had been found incompetent to stand trial with respect to either their ability to reason with facts or understand the trial process. Individual performance did not differ significantly by gender, ethnicity, or, in the detained groups, as a function of the extent of individuals' prior justice system experience. This last finding is important because it indicates that there are components of immaturity independent of a lack of relevant experience that may contribute to elevated rates of incompetence among juveniles.

A different structured interview was used to probe how psychosocial influences affect decision making by assessing participants' choices in three hypothetical legal situations involving a police interrogation, consultation with a defense attorney, and the evaluation of a proffered plea agreement. Significant age differences were found in responses to police interrogation and to the plea agreement. First, youths, including 16- to 17-year-olds, were much more likely to recommend waiving constitutional rights during an interrogation than were adults, with 55% of 11- to 13-year-olds, 40% of 14- to 15-year-olds, and 30% of 16- to 17-year-olds choosing to "talk and admit" involvement in an alleged offense (rather than "remaining silent"), but only 15% of the young adults making this choice. There were also significant age differences in response to the plea agreement. . . . [T]hese results suggest a much stronger tendency for adolescents than for young adults to make choices in compliance with the perceived desires of authority figures (Grisso et al. 2003). . . .

This research provides powerful and tangible evidence that some youths facing criminal charges may function less capably as criminal defendants than do their adult counterparts. This does not mean, of course, that all youths should be automatically deemed incompetent to stand trial any more than would a psychiatric diagnosis or low IQ score. It does mean, however, that the risk of incompetence is substantially elevated in early and mid-adolescence; it also means that policy makers and practitioners must address developmental incompetence as it affects the treatment of juveniles in court (Scott & Grisso 2005). . . .

Impact of Punitive Sanctions on Adolescent Development and Behavior

[T]he increasingly punitive orientation of the justice system toward juvenile offenders has resulted in an increase in the number of juveniles tried and sanctioned as adults and in the use of harsher sanctions in responding to the delinquent behavior of juveniles who have been retained in the juvenile justice system. Research on the impact of adult prosecution and punishment and on the use of punitive sanctions . . . suggests, . . . that these policies and practices may actually increase recidivism and jeopardize the development and mental health of juveniles (Fagan 2008). Consequently, there is a growing consensus among social scientists that policies and practices, such as setting the minimum age of criminal court jurisdiction below 18 (as about one-third of all states currently do), transferring juveniles to the adult system for a wide range of crimes, including nonviolent crimes, relying on incarceration as a primary means of crime control, and exposing juvenile offenders to punitive programs such as boot camps, likely do more harm than good, cost taxpayers much more than they need spend on crime prevention, and ultimately pose a threat to public safety (Greenwood 2006).

In order to understand why this is the case, it is important to begin with a distinction between adolescence-limited and life-course-persistent offenders (Moffitt 1993). Dozens of longitudinal studies have shown that the vast majority of adolescents who commit antisocial acts desist from such activity as they mature into adulthood and that only a small percentage—between five and ten percent, according to most studies—become chronic offenders. . . . This observation is borne out in inspection of what criminologists refer to as the age-crime curve, which shows that the incidence of criminal activity increases between preadolescence and late adolescence, peaks at about age 17 (slightly younger for nonviolent crimes and slightly older for violent ones), and declines thereafter. . . .

In view of the fact that most juvenile offenders mature out of crime . . . one must . . . ask how to best hold delinquent youth responsible for their actions and deter future crime . . . without adversely affecting their mental health, psychological development, and successful transition into adult roles. . . .

Within the juvenile system, of course, there is wide variation in the types and severity of sanctions to which offenders are exposed. Some youths are incarcerated in prison-like training schools, whereas others receive loosely supervised community probation—neither of which is effective at changing antisocial behavior. An important question therefore is, what can the juvenile system offer young offenders that will be effective at reducing recidivism? . . .

In general, successful programs are those that attend to the lessons of developmental psychology, seeking to provide young offenders with supportive social contexts and to assist them in acquiring the skills necessary to change problem behavior and to attain psychosocial maturity. In his comprehensive meta-analysis of 400 juvenile programs, Lipsey (1995) found that among the most effective programs in both community and institutional settings were those that focused on improving social development skills in the areas of interpersonal relations, self-control, academic performance, and job skills. Some effective programs focus directly on developing skills to avoid antisocial behavior, often through cognitive behavioral therapy. Other interventions that have been shown to have a positive effect on crime reduction focus on strengthening family support, including Multisystemic Therapy, Functional Family Therapy, and Multidimensional Treatment Foster Care, all of which are both effective and cost effective (Greenwood 2006). . . . Punishment-oriented approaches, such as "Scared Straight" or military-style boot camps, do not deter future crime and may even inadvertently promote reoffending. . . .

[A]dolescence is a formative period of development. In mid and late adolescence, individuals normally make substantial progress in acquiring and coordinating skills that are essential to filling the conventional roles of adulthood. First, they begin to develop basic educational and vocational skills to enable them to function in the workplace as productive members of society. Second, they also acquire the social skills necessary to establish stable intimate relationships and to cooperate in groups. Finally, they must begin to learn to behave responsibly without external supervision and to set meaningful personal goals for themselves. For most individuals, the process of completing these developmental tasks extends into early adulthood, but making substantial progress during the formative stage of adolescence is important. This process of development toward psychosocial maturity is one of reciprocal interaction between the individual and her social context. Several environmental conditions are particularly important, such as the presence of an authoritative parent or guardian, association with prosocial peers, and participation in educational, extracurricular, or employment activities that facilitate the development of autonomous decision making and critical thinking. For the youth in the justice system, the correctional setting becomes the environment for social development and may affect whether he acquires the skills necessary to function successfully in conventional adult roles (Steinberg et al. 2004).

Normative teenagers who get involved in crime do so, in part, because their choices are driven by developmental influences typical of adolescence. In theory, they should desist from criminal behavior and mature into reasonably responsible adults as they attain psychosocial maturity—and most do, especially as they enter into adult work and family responsibilities. Whether youths successfully make the transition to adulthood, however, depends in part on whether their social context provides opportunity structures for the completion of the developmental tasks described above. The correctional environment may influence the trajectories of normative adolescents in the justice system in important ways. Factors such as the availability (or lack) of good educational, skill building, and reha-bilitative programs; the attitudes and roles of adult supervisors; and the identity and behavior of other offenders shape the social context of youths in both the adult and the juvenile systems. These factors may affect the inclination of young offenders to desist or persist in their criminal activities and may facilitate or impede their develop-ment into adults who can function adequately in society. . . .

Summary

. . . Although justice system policy and practice cannot, and should not, be dictated solely by studies of adolescent development, the ways in which we respond to juvenile offending should at the very least be informed by the lessons of developmental science. Taken together, the lessons of developmental science offer strong support for the maintenance of a separate juvenile justice system in which adolescents are judged, tried, and sanctioned in developmen-tally appropriate ways. . . .

Reference

Lipsey M. 1995. What do we learn from 400 research studies on the effectiveness of treatment with juvenile delinquents? In *What Works? Reducing Reoffending,* ed. J McGuire, pp. 63–78. New York: Wiley

Moffitt T. 1993. Adolescence-limited and life-course per-sistent antisocial behavior: a developmental taxonomy. *Psychol. Rev.* 100:674–701

Roper v. Simmons, 541 U.S. 1040 2005

Scott E, Grisso T. 2005. Developmental incompetence, due process, and juvenile justice policy. *N. C. Law Rev.* 83:793–846

Scott E, Steinberg L. 2008. *Rethinking Juvenile Justice.* Cambridge, MA: Harvard Univ. Press.

Steinberg L, Chung H, Little M. 2004. Reentry of young offenders from the justice system: a developmental per-spective. *Youth Violence Juv. Just,* 1:21–38

EXPLORING THE ISSUE

Should Juvenile Offenders Be Tried and Convicted as Adults?

Critical Thinking and Reflection

1. Is there enough evidence in this issue to support a juvenile justice system separate from the adult system?
2. If adolescents are treated less harshly by the criminal justice system, will there be more incidents of crime in the future? Will there be more violent crime?
3. At present, most transfers to adult court are a function of age and seriousness of a crime (e.g., murder). Should the decision to transfer youth to adult court remain as it is? Should brain development be considered? How would "mature" be determined? Is there an upper age where examining brain development is not longer necessary?
4. Imagine you are the parent (or the sibling) of a 15-year-old who was brutally assaulted by a 16-year-old. What penalty would you want for the 16-year-old?
5. Imagine you are the parent (or the sibling) of a 16-year-old who brutally assaulted a 15-year-old. What penalty would you want for your son/daughter/brother/sister?
6. Should policies regarding juvenile justice reflect public sentiment? Are individual rights more important than collective rights or how can we balance the two?

Is There Common Ground?

Steinberg argues that the way we respond to juvenile offending should be somewhat guided by developmental science. He explains the factors that reduce culpability among adolescents, which he argues should reduce the grade of an offense and subsequently the punishment. Steinberg recommends a separate justice system for adolescents with a focus on rehabilitation, more lenient punishments, and laws prohibiting execution. Many brain researchers support Steinberg's argument stating that structurally, the brain is still growing and maturing during adolescence. For example, Jay Giedd (2004) of the National Institute of Mental Health (NIMH) considers 25 the age at which the brain has reached maturity. Because the adolescent brain is not fully developed, adolescents are more prone to erratic behavior driven by emotions and are not as morally culpable as adults.

Stimson and Grossman don't dispute brain development or a separate justice system for youth but they do argue that for *serious* offenses (e.g., murder), trying juveniles in adult court and imposing adult sentences do not violate human rights and do not violate the U.S. law. Their argument (based on their review) is that life without parole is both effective and appropriate because youth who commit adult crimes should be treated as adults. The U.S. law views adolescent decision making much the same as Stimson and Grossman. Essentially, past the age of 14 years, adolescents are competent decision makers under the informed-consent model as long as they are of average or above-average intelligence and can make a knowing, voluntary, intelligent decision (Ambuel & Rappaport, 1992). Steinberg, however, argues that the informed-consent model

is inadequate because it overemphasizes the cognitive components at the expense of the noncognitive components (e.g., social factors such as peer influence) that may influence mature judgment and sound decision making. Adolescents at 14 may or may not have the cognitive capacity necessary to make good choices and therefore deciding on an exact age for informed consent or transfer to adult court is impossible. According the Steinberg, the age is more likely to be over 16. He states that adolescents older than 16 are more likely to have adult-like capacities but those under 16 are not. Each case must be examined carefully.

Additional Resources

Beckman, M. (2004). Crime, culpability, and the adolescent brain. *Science, 305*, 596–599.

Grisso, T., Steinberg, L., Woolard, J., Cauffman, E., Scott, E., Graham, S., et al. (2003). Juveniles' competence to stand trial: A comparison of adolescents' and adults' capacities as trial defendants. *Law and Human Behavior, 27*, 333–363.

Loughran, T., Mulvey, E., Schubert, C., Chassin, L., Steinberg, L., Piquero, A., et al. (2010). Differential effects of adult court transfer on juvenile offender recidivism. *Law and Human Behavior, 34*, 476–488.

This research article examines the effect of transfer of adolescents to adult court on later crime. The sample consisted of serious juvenile offenders, 29 percent of whom were transferred. Results indicated no difference in re-arrest between those transferred to adult court and those retained in the juvenile system but there were differences based on offending histories. Transferred adolescents who committed "person" crimes showed lower rates of re-arrest.

Mears, D. P., Hay, C., Gertz, M., & Mancini, C. (2007). Public opinion and the foundation of the juvenile court. *Criminology, 45* (1), 223–257.

This study examines public views about abolishing juvenile justice and the upper age of original juvenile court jurisdiction. Results suggest, "support for the lingering appeal of juvenile justice among the public and the idea that youth can be 'saved' as well as arguments about the politicization and criminalization of juvenile justice" (p. 223).

Office of Juvenile Justice and Delinquency Prevention. (1999). *Juvenile justice: A century of change.* Washington, DC: Office of Juvenile Justice.

Shook, J. J. (2005). Contesting childhood in the US justice system: The transfer of juveniles to adult criminal court. *Childhood, 12,* 461–478.

Statistics Canada. (1997 through 2000). *Youth court statistics.* Ottawa: Canadian Centre for Justice Statistics.

Streib, V. L. (2003). The juvenile death penalty today: Death sentences and executions for juvenile crimes, January 1, 1973–June 30, 2003. Retrieved from www.law.onu.edu /faculty/streib

Tonry, M. (2007). Treating juveniles as adult criminals. *American Journal of Preventive Medicine, 32*(4S), S3-S4.

A report from the Task Force on Community Preventive Services examines whether transfers reduce or prevent violent crimes by youth under age 18. They conclude that youth transferred have higher rates of future violent crime compared to younger youth not transferred. The report also determines that there is insufficient evidence to reach conclusions regarding general deterrence.

References

Ambuel, B., & Rappaport, J. (1992). Developmental trends in adolescents' psychological and legal competence to consent to abortion. *Law and Human Behavior, 16,* 129–154.

The authors of this article argue that minors are not competent decision makers with respect to consenting to abortion.

Giedd, J. N. (2004). Structural magnetic resonance imaging of the adolescent brain. *Annals of the New York Academy of Science, 1021,* 77–85.

Tuell, J. A. (2002). *Juvenile offenders and the death penalty.* Washington, DC: Child Welfare League of America. National Center for Program Standards and Development.

Internet References . . .

Children in Prison

> http://www.eji.org/childrenprison

Juveniles Tried as Adults

> http://nyln.org/juveniles-tried-as-adults
> -pros-and-cons-list

KQED Education: Should Teens Who Commit Serious Crimes Be Sentenced as Adults?

> https://ww2.kqed.org/education/2016/03/25/should
> -teens-who-commit-serious-crimes-be
> -tried-and-sentenced-as-adults/

National Center for Youth Law

> http://youthlaw.org/issues/juvenile-justice
> /juveniles-tried-as-adults/

U.S. Department of Justice: Office of Juvenile Justice and Delinquency Prevention

> http://www.ojjdp.gov